Ivy Global

ISEE MATH

1ST EDITION

IVY GLOBAL, NEW YORK

This publication was written and edited by the team at Ivy Global.

Editor: Laurel Perkins
Layout Editor: Sacha Azor
Producers: Lloyd Min and Junho Suh

About Ivy Global
Ivy Global is a pioneering education company that provides a wide range of educational services.

E-mail: info@ivyglobal.com
Website: http://www.ivyglobal.com

CONTENTS

INTRODUCTION

CHAPTER 1

HOW TO USE THIS BOOK

SECTION 1

Welcome, students and parents! This book is intended for students preparing for the Quantitative Reasoning and Mathematics Achievement sections of the Lower, Middle, or Upper Level Independent School Entrance Exam (ISEE). For students applying to many top private and independent schools in North America, the ISEE is a crucial and sometimes daunting step in the admissions process. By leading you step-by-step through the fundamental content and most effective strategies for the ISEE, Ivy Global will help you build your confidence and maximize your score on this important exam.

This book is right for you if:

- you are applying to a private or independent school that requires the ISEE for admission
- you will be in grades 4-5 (Lower Level), 6-7 (Middle Level), or 8-11 (Upper Level) when you take the ISEE
- you would like to learn and practice the best strategies for the Quantitative Reasoning and Mathematics Achievement sections of the ISEE
- you are a parent, family member, or tutor looking for new ways to help your Lower, Middle, or Upper Level ISEE student

We know that no two students are exactly alike—each student brings a unique combination of personal strengths and weaknesses to his or her test preparation. For this reason, we've tailored our preparation materials to help students with a specific subject area or goal. Ivy Global's *ISEE Math* walks students through the best strategies for the ISEE Quantitative Reasoning and Mathematics Achievement sections, plus thorough review and practice for all of the math concepts tested at each level. This book includes:

- an up-to-date introduction to the ISEE's administration, format, and scoring practices
- targeted strategies for students new to standardized tests, including study schedules, pacing, and stress management
- a complete introduction to the ISEE Quantitative Reasoning and Mathematics Achievement sections, explaining in detail what concepts are tested and what types of questions are asked

- the most effective strategies to approach each type of question on these sections, including advanced strategies for Upper Level students
- a thorough review of all of the fundamental math concepts you will need to know for the ISEE, including arithmetic, algebra, geometry, and data interpretation
- online video tutorials for engaging supplementary explanations of each topic
- over 1,000 practice questions and drills, grouped into targeted practice sets for each concept and difficulty level

Work through the material that is appropriate to your level. If you are a Lower Level student, work through all of the material except any content marked "Middle Level" or "Upper Level." If you are a Middle Level student, work through all of the material except any content marked "Upper Level." If you are an Upper Level student, review all of the Lower Level and Middle Level material before you look at the Upper Level content. The three levels have the same basic format, so both younger and older students will benefit from learning the same fundamental strategies.

Finally, keep in mind that every student has a different learning style, and that there may be multiple ways to approach the same problem. If you come across a strategy or a concept that you find challenging, circle it and move on. You might find that some of the other strategies work better for you, and that is okay! Pick the strategies that are the best fit for your learning style and add them to your toolkit for taking the ISEE. You can always come back to more difficult material with the help of a trusted adult or tutor.

To get started, continue reading for an overview of the ISEE and some general test-taking advice. Good luck in this exciting new step in your education!

ABOUT THE ISEE

SECTION 2

The **ISEE (Independent School Entrance Exam)** is a standardized test administered to students in grades 1-11 to help determine placement into certain private and independent schools. Many secondary schools worldwide use the ISEE as an integral part of their admissions process. The ISEE is owned and published by the Educational Records Bureau.

You will register for one of four ISEE tests, depending on your grade level:

- The **Primary Level** exam is for students currently in grades 1-3.
- The **Lower Level** exam is for students currently in grades 4-5.
- The **Middle Level** exam is for students currently in grades 6-7.
- The **Upper Level** exam is for students currently in grades 8-11.

The Primary Level exam is administered only with the use of a computer, and includes auditory content. All other levels may be taken on a computer or in a paper-and-pencil format. Among levels, the exams differ in difficulty, length, and the types of questions which may appear. The Lower Level exam is shorter than the Middle and Upper Level exams.

WHEN IS THE TEST ADMINISTERED?

Administration dates for the ISEE vary between test locations. ISEE test sites and administration dates can be found online, at ERBlearn.org. In addition to taking the test at a school that administers large group tests, students applying to grades 5-12 can register to take the ISEE at a Prometric Testing Center, which administers computer-based exams.

HOW MANY TIMES CAN I TAKE THE TEST?

Students may only take the ISEE once within a six-month period. The version of the test doesn't matter: a student who has taken a paper-and-pencil test may not take another test on a computer, and a student who has taken a computer-based test may not take another test in a paper-and-pencil format.

HOW DO I REGISTER?

The easiest and fastest way to register is to complete the **online application**. Visit www.ERBlearn.org to register for an exam in your area. It is also possible to register over the phone by calling (800) 446-0320 or (919) 956-8524, or to register by mail. To register by mail, you must complete and submit the application form available only in the printed ISEE student guide. Visit www.ERBlearn.org to order a printed copy of the ISEE student guide.

WHAT IS THE FORMAT OF THE ISEE?

The Lower, Middle, and Upper Level ISEE exams consist of four scored sections (**Verbal Reasoning**, **Quantitative Reasoning**, **Reading Comprehension**, and **Mathematics Achievement**), plus an **Essay** that is used as a writing sample. The format of the test differs based on the level of the exam:

LOWER LEVEL			
Section	**Questions**	**Length**	**Topics Covered**
Verbal Reasoning	34	20 min	Synonyms, Sentence Completion
Quantitative Reasoning	38	35 min	Logical Reasoning, Pattern Recognition (Word Problems)
Reading Comprehension	25	25 min	Short Passages
Math Achievement	30	30 min	Arithmetic, Algebra, Geometry, Data Analysis
Essay	1	30 min	One age-appropriate essay prompt
Total testing time: 2 hours 20 minutes			

MIDDLE AND UPPER LEVEL			
Section	**Questions**	**Length**	**Topics Covered**
Verbal Reasoning	40	20 min	Synonyms, Sentence Completion
Quantitative Reasoning	37	35 min	Logical Reasoning, Pattern Recognition (Word Problems and Quantitative Comparison)
Reading Comprehension	36	35 min	Short Passages
Math Achievement	47	40 min	Arithmetic, Algebra, Geometry, Data Analysis
Essay	1	30 min	One age-appropriate essay prompt
Total testing time: 2 hours 40 minutes			

Except for the Essay, all questions are **multiple-choice** (A) to (D). You are not normally allowed to use calculators, rulers, dictionaries, or other aids during the exam. However, students with documented learning disabilities or physical challenges may apply to take the test with extra time, aids, or other necessary accommodations that they receive in school. For more information about taking the ISEE with a documented disability, visit the ISEE Website at ERBlearn.org.

HOW IS THE ISEE SCORED?

All of the multiple-choice questions on the ISEE are equal in value, and your **raw score** for these sections is the total number of questions answered correctly. There is no penalty for incorrect answers.

Within each section, there are also 5-6 **experimental questions** that do not count towards your raw score for the section. The ISEE uses these questions to measure exam accuracy and to test material for upcoming exams. You won't be told which questions are the experimental questions, however, so you have to do your best on the entire section.

Your raw score for each section is then converted into a **scaled score** that represents how well you did in comparison with other students taking the same exam. Scaled scores range from about 760-950 for each section, with total scaled scores ranging from about 2280-2850.

The **Essay** is not scored, but is sent to the schools you are applying to as a sample of your writing skills. Admissions officers may use your essay to evaluate your writing ability when they are making admissions decisions.

Scores are released to families, and to the schools that families have designated as recipients, within 7-10 business days after the test date. Scores will be mailed to the address you provided when registering for the ISEE, and to up to six schools and/or counselors. You may request expedited score reports, or send score reports to additional schools or counselors, for an additional fee.

WHAT ARE THE ISEE PERCENTILES AND STANINES?

The ISEE score report also provides **ISEE percentile** rankings for each category, comparing your performance to that of other students in the same grade who have taken the test in the past three years. If you score in the 60th percentile, this means you are scoring higher than 60% of other students in your grade taking the exam.

These percentile rankings provide a more accurate way of evaluating student performance at each grade level. However, the ISEE percentiles are a comparison against only other students who have taken the ISEE, and these tend to be very high-achieving students. Students should not be discouraged if their percentile rankings appear low.

The following chart shows the median (50th percentile) ISEE scores for students applying to grades 5-12.

MEDIAN SCORES (ISEE 50TH PERCENTILE) FOR 2012					
Level	**Grade Applying To**	**Verbal Reasoning**	**Quantitative Reasoning**	**Reading Comprehension**	**Mathematics Achievement**
Lower Level	5	840	843	834	848
	6	856	856	848	863
Middle Level	7	863	865	866	871
	8	869	871	871	876
Upper Level	9	879	878	880	882
	10	883	882	886	886
Level	**Grade Applying To**	**Verbal Reasoning**	**Quantitative Reasoning**	**Reading Comprehension**	**Mathematics Achievement**
Upper Level	11	886	885	889	890
	12	881	884	880	889

The ISEE score report also includes **stanine** rankings. A stanine is a number from 1-9 obtained by dividing the entire range of students' scores into 9 segments, as shown in the table below:

PERCENTILE RANK	STANINE
1 – 3	1
4 – 10	2
11 – 22	3
23 – 39	4
40 – 59	5
60 – 76	6

77 – 88	7
89 – 95	8
96 – 99	9

Stanine scores are provided because small differences in percentile rankings may not represent a significant difference in ability. Stanines represent a range of percentile rankings, and are intended to provide a better representation of student ability.

HOW DO SCHOOLS USE THE ISEE?

Schools use the ISEE as one way to assess potential applicants, but it is by no means the only tool that they are using. Schools also pay very close attention to the rest of a student's application—academic record, teacher recommendations, extracurricular activities, writing samples, and interviews—in order to determine which students might be the best fit for their program. The personal components of a student's application sometimes give schools a lot more information about the student's personality and potential contributions to a school's overall community. Different schools place a different amount of importance on ISEE and other test scores within this process, and admissions offices are good places to find out how much your schools of interest will weight the ISEE.

TEST-TAKING STRATEGIES

CHAPTER 2

APPROACHING THE ISEE

SECTION 1

Before you review the content covered on the ISEE, you need to focus on *how* you take the ISEE. If you approach the ISEE *thoughtfully* and *strategically*, you will avoid common traps and tricks planted in the ISEE by the test makers. Think of the ISEE as a timed maze—you need to make every turn cleverly and quickly so that you avoid getting stuck at a dead end with no time to spare.

In this section, you will learn about the ISEE's format and structure; this awareness will help you avoid any surprises or shocks on test day. The ISEE is a very predictable exam and will seem less challenging once you understand what it looks like and how it works. By learning and practicing the best test-taking strategies and techniques, you will discover how to work as efficiently as possible. Once you know what to expect, you can refine your knowledge of the actual material tested on the ISEE, such as the verbal and math skills that are based on your grade level in school.

This section on ISEE strategies will answer the following **major questions**:

1. How does the ISEE differ from a test you take in school?
2. What preparation strategies can you learn before you take the ISEE?
3. What strategies can you learn to use during the ISEE?
4. How can you manage stress before and during the ISEE?

In the process of answering your big questions, this section will also highlight key facts about smart test-taking:

- Your answer choice matters—your process does not. Enter your answer choices correctly and carefully to earn points. You have a set amount of time per section, so spend it wisely.
- The ISEE's format and directions do not change, so learn them now.
- All questions have the same value.
- Each level of the ISEE corresponds to a range of grades, and score expectations differ based on your grade level.
- Identify your areas of strength and weakness, and review any content that feels unfamiliar.

- Apply universal strategies—prediction-making, Process of Elimination, back-solving, and educated guessing—to the multiple-choice sections.
- Stay calm and be confident in your abilities as you prepare for and take the ISEE.

HOW DOES THE ISEE DIFFER FROM A TEST YOU TAKE IN SCHOOL?

The ISEE differs from tests you take in school in four major ways:

1. It is not concerned with the process behind your answers. Your answer is either right or wrong: there is no partial credit.
2. You have a set amount of time per section (and for the exam as a whole).
3. It is divided into four levels that correspond to four grade ranges of students.
4. It is extremely predictable given that its format, structure, and directions never vary.

NO PARTIAL CREDIT

At this point in your school career, you have probably heard your teacher remark, "Be sure to show your work on the test!" You are most likely familiar with almost every teacher's policy of "No work, no credit." However, the ISEE completely ignores this guideline. The machine that grades your exam does not care that you penciled brilliant logic in the margins of the test booklet—the machine only looks at your answer choice. Your answer choice is either right or wrong: **there is no partial credit**.

SET AMOUNT OF TIME

You have a **set amount of time per section**, so spend it wisely. The ISEE test proctors will never award you extra time after a test section has ended because you spent half of one section struggling valiantly on a single problem. Instead, you must learn to work within each section's time constraints.

You also must view the questions as equal because **each question is worth the same number of points** (one). Even though some questions are more challenging than others, they all carry the same weight. Rather than dwell on an overly challenging problem, you should skip it, work through the rest of the section, and come back to it if you have time.

FOUR LEVELS

There are four levels of the ISEE—Primary, Lower, Middle, and Upper—each of which is administered to a specific range of students. The Primary Level is given to students applying to grades 2, 3, and 4; The Lower Level is given to students applying to grades 5 and 6; the Middle Level is given to students applying to grades 7 and 8; and the Upper Level is given to students applying to grades 9, 10, 11, and 12. While you might be used to taking tests in school that are completely tailored to your grade, the ISEE is different: each test level covers content from a specific range of grade levels.

Score expectations differ based on your grade level. You are not expected to answer every question correctly on an Upper Level exam if you are only in eighth grade. Conversely, if you are in eleventh grade, you are expected to answer the most questions correctly on the Upper Level exam because you are one of the oldest students taking that exam.

STANDARD FORMAT

The ISEE is, by definition, a **standardized test**, which means that its format and directions are standard and predictable. While your teachers might change formats and directions for every assessment they administer, you can expect to see the same format and directions on every ISEE.

WHAT PREPARATION STRATEGIES CAN YOU LEARN BEFORE YOU TAKE THE ISEE?

Now that you are familiar with how the ISEE differs from the tests you take in school, you are ready to learn some test tips. You can prepare for the ISEE by following these three steps:

1. Learn the format and directions of the test.
2. Identify your areas of strength and weakness.
3. Create a study schedule to review and practice test content.

LEARN THE FORMAT AND DIRECTIONS

The structure of the ISEE is entirely predictable, so learn it now. Rather than wasting precious time reading the directions and understanding the format on test day, take the time now to familiarize yourself with the test's format and directions.

Refer to the tables on pages 6 and 7 for an overview of the ISEE's format. Continue reading for specific directions for the Quantitative Reasoning and Mathematics Achievement sections. Specific directions for the Verbal Reasoning, Critical Reading, and Essay sections can be found in Ivy Global's *ISEE English*.

IDENTIFY YOUR STRENGTHS AND WEAKNESSES

To determine your areas of strength and weakness and to get an idea of which concepts you need to review, take a full-length, accurate practice exam to serve as a diagnostic test. Practice exams for the ISEE can be found in Ivy Global's *ISEE Practice*.

Make sure you simulate test day conditions by timing yourself. Then, check your answers against the correct answers. Write down how many questions you missed in each section, and note the topics or types of questions you found most challenging. What was hard about the test? What did you feel good about? Did you leave a lot of questions blank because of timing issues, or did you leave questions blank because you did not know how to solve them? Reflecting on these questions, in addition to looking at your score breakdown, will help you determine your strengths, weaknesses, and areas for improvement.

CREATE A STUDY SCHEDULE

After determining your areas of strength and weakness, create a study plan and schedule for your ISEE preparation to review content. Work backward from your test date until you arrive at your starting date for studying. The number of weeks you have until your exam will determine how much time you can (and should) devote to your preparation. Remember, practice is the most important!

To begin, try using this sample study plan as a model for your own personalized study schedule.

SAMPLE STUDY PLAN

My test date is: _________________.

I have ____ weeks to study. I will make an effort to study ____ minutes/hours each night, and I will set aside extra time on _________________ to take timed sections.

I plan to take ____ full-length tests between now and my test date. I will study for ____ weeks and then take a practice test. My goal for this test is to improve my score in the following sections:

____

____

____

____

____

____

____

____

If I do not make this goal, then I will spend more time studying.

STUDY SCHEDULE				
Date	**Plan of Study**	**Time Allotted**	**Time Spent**	**Goal Reached?**
Jan. 1	Learn 5 words and review perimeter of polygons	1 hour	44 minutes	Yes, I know 5 new words and can calculate perimeter!
Jan. 3	Learn 5 words and review area of triangles	1 hour	1 hour	I know 5 new words, but I'm still confused about the area of triangles. I'll review this again next time and ask a teacher, tutor, or parent for help.

WHAT STRATEGIES CAN YOU LEARN TO USE DURING THE TEST?

Once you have grown accustomed to the ISEE through practice, you are ready to learn strategies to use during the ISEE. The following points will prepare you to take the test as cleverly and efficiently as possible:

1. Enter your answer choices correctly and carefully.
2. Pace yourself to manage your time effectively.
3. Learn a strategic approach for multiple-choice questions.

ENTERING ANSWER CHOICES

Whether you are taking a pencil-and-paper or a computer-based exam, you must follow the directions carefully to enter your answers. In school you probably take tests that, for the most part, do not ask you to enter your answers in a specific format. However, the ISEE streamlines the grading process by only reviewing the answers you have entered on your answer sheet or into the computer program. This means that any notes or work you have written on your scratch paper will not be reviewed, and you will only receive credit for entering your answers correctly.

On a computer-based exam, you will click an answer on the computer screen in order to enter your response. Follow the directions carefully to make sure your answer has been recorded. Within each section, you will be able to go back to questions earlier in the section and change your answers. You will also be able to skip questions and come back to them later. However, you will not be able to review questions from sections that come earlier or later in the exam; you will only be able to review your answers for the questions in the section you are currently working on. Make sure all of your answers have been entered correctly before your time is up for the section.

On a pencil-and-paper exam, you will enter your answers on a separate answer sheet. You must grid in your multiple-choice answers onto this sheet using an HB pencil to fill in the circle that corresponds to your answer. This sheet is scanned and scored by a highly sensitive computer. You will also write your Essay on separate lined pages of this answer sheet.

Since you have to take an additional step to record your answers, it is important that you avoid making gridding mistakes. Sadly, many students get confused and mismark their answer sheets. Remember, even if you arrive at the right answer, it is only correct and counted in your favor if you grid correctly on your answer sheet.

To grid correctly and carefully to maximize your points, consider the following tips:

Keep your answer sheet neat. Since your answer sheet is graded by a machine, your score is calculated based on what your marks look like. The machine cannot know what you really meant if you filled in the wrong bubble. Stray marks can harm your score, especially if you darken the correct answer but accidentally make a mark that confuses the machine! Avoid this and other errors by consulting the following image, which shows the difference between answers that are properly shaded and those that are not.

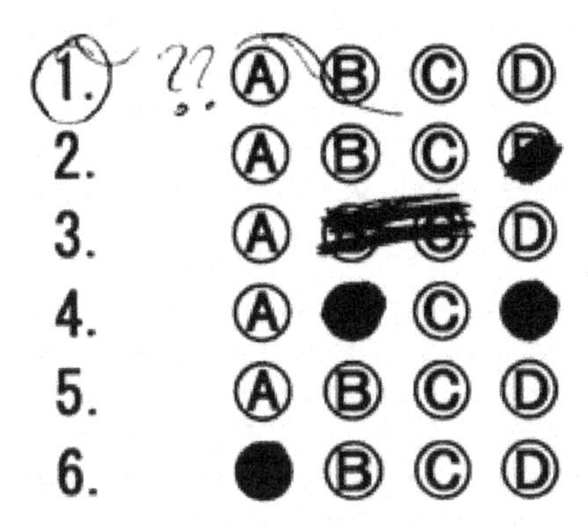

- Answer 1 is *wrong* because no answer is selected and there are stray marks.
- Answer 2 is *wrong* because choice (D) has not been darkened completely.
- Answer 3 is *wrong* because two answers have been selected.
- Answer 4 is *wrong* because two answers have been selected.
- Answer 5 is *neither right nor wrong* because it was left blank.
- Answer 6 is *right* because choice (A) has been darkened properly.

Train yourself to **circle your answer choice in your test booklet**. If you have time to go back and check your answers, you can easily check your circled answers against your gridded ones.

You should also **create a system for marking questions that you skipped** or that you found confusing (see the next section for more information about skipping questions). Try circling those question numbers only in your test booklet so that you can find them later if you want to solve them or check your work. Be aware of these questions when gridding answers on your answer sheet.

Finally, **grid your answers in batches of four, five, or six answer choices.** That way, you do not have to go back and forth between your test booklet and your answer sheet every minute. If you choose to use this strategy, keep an eye on the clock—you do not want to get to the end of the section and find you have not gridded any answers. Depending on how much time you have left to check your work (if you happen to finish early), you can either review every problem or spot-check a series of questions on your answer sheet against your test booklet.

TIME MANAGEMENT (PACING)

Manage your time effectively to boost your score. The ISEE has an element of time pressure, so it is important to keep moving on the exam rather than wasting your time on any single question.

You can come back to questions within each section of the ISEE. Each question is only worth one point, regardless of its difficulty. If you are stuck on a problem, you should make your best guess and move on to try to answer another problem. It makes more sense to answer as many questions as possible (and get as many points as possible) rather than spending all your time on one question. If you come across a question you want to come back to, circle it in your question booklet or mark it on your scratch paper if you are taking the computer based test. Remember not to make any stray marks on your answer sheet.

By moving quickly through each question of the section, you will ensure that: 1) you see every question in the section; 2) you gain points on questions that are easy for you; 3) you return to more challenging problems and figure out as many as you can with your remaining time. It is also important to note that you might not be able to answer several questions in each section if you are on the younger end of the testing group for your particular test level. In that case, you should make your best guess based on the information you do know, but shouldn't worry if the content is unfamiliar.

Even if you are unsure about a question and want to come back to it later, you should **always make a guess.** The ISEE doesn't take off any points for answering questions incorrectly, so you should never leave a question blank! Even if you guess a completely random answer, you have a small chance of gaining a point. If you can rule out one or two choices that you know are wrong, you have even better odds of guessing the right answer. Therefore, always make a guess on every question, even if you are planning to come back to it later. Before your time is up, you want to make sure that you have entered an answer for every question!

Follow this step-by-step process for moving through a section:

1. Look through the section and answer the questions that are easy for you. If a question seems difficult or is taking too long, make a guess in your answer sheet and circle the question in your test booklet to come back to later.
2. After answering all the easier questions, go back to the questions you have circled and spend some time working on ones that you think you might be able to solve. If you realize that the answer you originally guessed was incorrect, change that answer on your answer sheet.
3. If you have no idea how to solve a question, leave your best guess as your answer.
4. If you have any time remaining, check your work for the questions you solved.

STRATEGIES FOR MULTIPLE-CHOICE QUESTIONS

Apply universal strategies—prediction-making, Process of Elimination, back-solving, and educated guessing—to the multiple-choice sections. To illustrate the value of these strategies, read through the following example of a synonym question from the Verbal Reasoning section:

HAPPY:

(A) delighted
(B) unhappy
(C) crazy
(D) nice

Answer: (A). "Delighted" is the correct answer because it is the word that most nearly means "happy."

Regardless of whether the answer choices are easy, difficult, or somewhere in between, you can use certain tricks and tips to your advantage. To approach ISEE questions effectively, you need to step into the test makers' minds and learn to avoid their traps.

Make predictions. When you see a question, try to come up with an answer on your own before looking at the answer choices. You can literally cover the answer choices with your hand so that you must rely on your own intelligence to predict an answer instead of being swayed by answer choices that you see. If you look at the answer choices first, you might be tempted to pick an answer without thinking about the other options and what the question is asking you. Instead, make a prediction so that you understand the question fully and get a clear sense of what to look for in the answers. In the synonym example above, you could predict that a possible synonym for "happy" would be something like "glad."

Use the Process of Elimination. For each multiple-choice question, you must realize that the answer is right in front of you. To narrow down your answer choices, think about the potential incorrect answers and actively identify those to eliminate them. Even if you can eliminate just one answer, you will set yourself up for better odds of getting a correct answer if you decide to guess. For the synonym example above, test your prediction of "glad" against the answer choices and immediately eliminate "unhappy" since it is opposite in meaning. You can also probably eliminate "crazy" and "nice" since those words do not match your prediction. This leaves you with "delighted," which is the correct answer.

Try back-solving. This strategy is most useful on the math sections, especially when you are given a complicated, multi-step word problem. Instead of writing an equation, try plugging in the answer choices to the word problem. Take a look at the following question:

Catherine has a basket of candy. On Monday, she eats ½ of all the candy. On Tuesday, she eats 2 pieces. On Wednesday, she eats twice the amount of candy that she consumed on Tuesday. If she only has 4 pieces left on Thursday, how many pieces did she initially have?

(A) 12
(B) 14
(C) 16
(D) 20

To use back-solving, start with answer choice (C) and plug it into the word problem. If (C) is the correct answer, you are done. If not, you will then know whether you should test (B) or (D). When we start with 16 pieces of candy, we subtract 8 on Monday, then 2 more for Tuesday, and then 4 more for Wednesday. By Thursday, Catherine only has 2 pieces of candy left, which is less than the amount we wanted. Therefore, we know our answer has to be bigger, so we eliminate choices (A), (B), and (C) and try (D), which works.

(*Fun Fact:* If you think about it, you will have to plug in three answer choices at most to determine the right answer.)

Armed with these strategies, you might feel that the ISEE is starting to look more manageable because you now have shortcuts that will help you navigate the maze of questions quickly and cleverly.

Take a look at this example to practice using the strategies you just read about.

Because Kaitlin was -------- from her soccer game, she went to bed early.

(A) thrilled
(B) exhausted
(C) competitive
(D) inspired

1. Assess the question and recognize what it is testing. In this case, the question tests whether you can pick a word to complete the sentence.
2. Make a prediction. What about Kaitlin's soccer game would cause her to go to bed early? Maybe it wore her out, so we could look for something like "tired" to go in the blank.
3. Look for inaccurate answer choices and eliminate them. If Kaitlin were "thrilled," "competitive," and "inspired" as a result of her soccer game, this wouldn't explain why she had to go to bed early. Therefore, you can eliminate answers (A), (C), and (D).

4. Make an educated guess, or choose the best answer if you feel confident about the answer. Since you made a fantastic prediction and used Process of Elimination, you only have one choice left: (B). "Exhausted" is the correct answer—you just earned yourself a point!

HOW CAN YOU MANAGE YOUR STRESS?

If you have ever had a big test before, or an important sports match, play, or presentation, then you know what anxiety feels like. Even if you are excited for an approaching event, you might feel nervous. You might begin to doubt yourself, and you might feel as if your mind is racing while butterflies flutter in your stomach!

When it comes to preparing for the ISEE, the good news is that a little anxiety (or adrenaline) goes a long way. Anxiety is a natural, motivating force that will help you study hard in the days leading up to your test. That anxiety will also help you stay alert and work efficiently during the test.

Sometimes, however, anxiety might become larger than life and start to get the best of you. To prevent anxiety and nerves from clouding your ability to work effectively and believe in yourself, you should try some of the suggestions below. Many of these suggestions are good ideas to use in everyday life, but they become especially important in the final week before your test and on test day itself.

- **Relax and slow down.** To center yourself and ease your anxiety, take a big, deep breath. Slowly inhale for a few seconds and then slowly exhale for a few seconds. Shut your eyes and relax. Stretch your arms, roll your neck gently, crack your knuckles—get in the zone of Zen! Continue to breathe deeply and slowly until you can literally feel your body calm down.
- **Picture your goals.** Close your eyes or just pause to reflect on what you want to achieve on test day. Visualize your success, whether that means simply answering all the math questions or getting a top score and gaining acceptance into the school of your dreams. Acknowledge your former successes and abilities, and believe in yourself.
- **Break it down.** Instead of trying to study a whole section at once, break up your studying into small and manageable chunks. Outline your study goals before you start. For example, instead of trying to master the entire Reading Comprehension section at once, you might want to work on one type of passage at a time.
- **Sleep.** Make sure you get plenty of rest and sleep, especially the two nights leading up to your exam!
- **Fuel up.** Eat healthy, filling meals that fuel your brain. Also, drink lots of water to stay hydrated.
- **Take a break.** Put down the books and go play outside, read, listen to music, exercise, or have a good conversation. A good break can be just as restful as a nap. However, watching television will provide minimal relaxation.

On the night before the exam, study only lightly. Make a list of your three biggest fears and work on them, but don't try to learn anything new. Pick out what you are going to wear to the exam—try wearing layers in case the exam room is hotter or colder than you expect. Organize everything you need to bring. Know where the test center is located and how long it will take to get there. Have a nutritious meal and get plenty of sleep!

On the morning of the exam, let your adrenaline kick in naturally. Eat a good breakfast and stay hydrated; your body needs fuel to endure the test. Bring along several pencils and a good eraser. Listen carefully to the test proctor's instructions and let the proctor know if you are left-handed so you can sit in an appropriate desk. Take a deep breath and remember: you are smart and accomplished! Believe in yourself and you will do just fine.

QUANTITATIVE REASONING

CHAPTER 3

INTRODUCTION

SECTION 1

The ISEE Quantitative Reasoning Section tests your ability to reason mathematically. Unlike the Mathematics Achievement Section (see p. 129), it does not test the amount of math you have learned in school or your ability to perform calculations; instead, it tests how well you can use critical thinking, estimation, and logic skills to solve math problems. On the Lower Level ISEE, you will have 35 minutes to solve 38 **word problems**. On the Middle and Upper Level ISEE, you will have 35 minutes to solve 37 problems: 18-21 **word problems** and 14-17 **quantitative comparisons**. Each question will have 4 answer options, and you will need to pick the one option that best answers the question. Calculators, rulers, compasses, protractors, and other aids are not permitted on the ISEE.

HOW TO APPROACH THE QUANTITATIVE REASONING SECTION

Review the following test-taking strategies and study methods to help you prepare for the Quantitative Reasoning Section as a whole. Then, turn to the following sections on specific strategies for the word problems and quantitative comparison questions.

PACE YOURSELF

Don't spend too long on one question, but don't rush yourself. Start out with questions you can answer quickly, and make your best guess on questions that are taking too long to answer. Circle these questions so you can come back to them later if you have time at the end of the section. Remember that each question is worth only one point, so don't waste time struggling with a difficult question when you can answer three easier questions in the same amount of time. Make sure that you have time to make your best guess on every question.

MAKE EDUCATED GUESSES

The Quantitative Reasoning questions will never require tedious calculations, and sometimes you will not need to perform any calculations in order to arrive at the right answer. See if you can select an answer by estimating or using logical reasoning: are there any answer options that couldn't possibly be correct because they don't make sense? Cross those out! If you still don't know how to answer the question at this point, make your best guess among the answer choices that remain. Your odds of guessing the correct answer increase with the more answers you can eliminate.

WRITE DOWN YOUR PROCESS

Write down your work in your test booklet (or on the scratch paper provided during the computer-based test). Don't rely on mental math alone. It is so easy to make a careless mistake when you are trying to remember numbers in your head. Break complicated problems into steps and tackle one step at a time. Do you need to first find the area of a triangle, then the area of a square, and then compare the two using fractions? Write down these steps for yourself so you remember what to do next.

USE FIGURES AND DIAGRAMS

Trust and use the measurements that have been provided for any figures on the ISEE. Write in any other measurements that are given in the problem or that can be deduced from the information given. Are you working on a geometry problem and there is no figure provided? Draw your own! Are you working with negative numbers? Draw a number line! Drawings can be very helpful for organizing your thoughts and information.

CHECK YOUR WORK

If you have extra time, go back and check all of your work to make sure that you have not made any careless errors and that you have answered what each question is asking. Remember that there is no partial credit on this test—if you make a mistake or misread the question and you get a wrong answer, you will not receive any points for that question.

WORD PROBLEMS

PART 1

WORD PROBLEM STRATEGIES

SECTION 1

On the Lower Level Quantitative Reasoning section, you will see 38 word problems, and these will make up the entire section. On the Middle and Upper Level, you will see 18-21 word problems in the first half of the Quantitative Reasoning section. Continue reading about the best strategies for approaching this question type.

WHAT ARE WORD PROBLEMS?

Word problems are math questions in the form of sentences. They often describe a situation where some type of math is needed to arrive at a conclusion. Then, they ask you to pick the one answer that best represents this solution. Here is an example:

It takes Karen seven minutes to read one page in her textbook. At this rate, how long will it take her to read seven pages?

(A) 1 minute
(B) 7 minutes
(C) 14 minutes
(D) 49 minutes

This question is asking you to predict Karen's total reading time for seven pages, based on how quickly she normally reads. From the information given in the question, you know that it takes Karen seven minutes to read each page. Therefore, seven pages would take her 7×7 minutes to read. The correct answer is (D) 49 minutes.

Remember that every word problem question on the ISEE will have only **one correct answer**. For each question, make sure that you look through all 4 answer choices to double-check that you have really selected the correct answer. If it seems like multiple answers might be possible, re-read the question and remind yourself what it is asking you to solve. Only one answer will be the correct solution to the question as a whole. Continue reading for some strategies to help you select the best answer every time.

BASIC APPROACH

Math word problems involve a lot of reading comprehension! It can be tricky to find out what they mean and what they are asking you to solve. For each word problem, follow the basic steps below to arrive at the right answer quickly and efficiently.

READ THE QUESTION CAREFULLY

Read through the whole question. Don't assume you understand the question just by reading the first few words! Reading the whole question will help you avoid making assumptions that can lead to careless errors.

If you see unfamiliar or difficult-looking material, stay calm and keep reading until the end of the question. There might be more information in the question that will help you figure out the solution. If you still think a question is too difficult after you have finished reading the whole thing, then you should make your best guess, circle it in your question booklet, and come back to it if you have time. Don't get anxious that you couldn't find the correct answer to a question: not every student is expected to answer every question correctly, and some questions might be beyond your grade level.

Here is a simple example that we will work through to demonstrate these basic test-taking strategies. Read the whole question carefully:

A triangular park has sides that are 3 meters, 4 meters, and 5 meters long. If John wants to put a fence around the entire park, how many meters of fence will he need?

(A) 3
(B) 7
(C) 12
(D) 15

UNDERLINE KEY WORDS

Underline or circle any information given in the question that will help you solve it. Our example question should now look something like this:

A <u>triangular</u> park has sides that are <u>3 meters</u>, <u>4 meters</u>, and <u>5 meters long</u>. If John wants to put a fence <u>around the entire park</u>, <u>how many meters</u> of fence will he need?

IDENTIFY WHAT THE QUESTION IS ASKING

Ask yourself, "What is the question asking me to solve?" This is especially important for word problems. Sometimes the wording of a question can be confusing, so make it simpler for yourself and summarize in your own words what the question is asking for. Pay close attention to the key words you have underlined, and take a moment to remember their meanings as you summarize the question.

In our example question, you are being asked to find the length of fence that John would need to buy in order to build a fence around the entire park. How would you explain this in your own words? You might remember that the distance around a figure is called its "perimeter," so John really just needs to calculate the perimeter of the park.

DRAW A CHART OR DIAGRAM

Charts and diagrams are great tools to help you visualize the problem and organize your information. In our example question, you might try drawing a quick sketch of a triangle that would represent the park. Then, fill in any information you are given in the question. You can write in the lengths of all three sides:

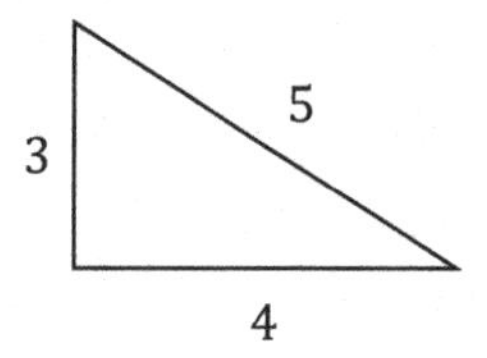

COME UP WITH A STRATEGY

Strategize the best way to solve the question. Sometimes finding the answer requires some thought if there are multiple steps involved. Think about all of the information provided in the question and how it is related. Think about where you have seen this type of question before, and what methods you have used to solve similar types of questions. If there is a formula that you know that could help, write it down.

Here's a strategy we could use to solve our example question.

- *We know*: the lengths of the sides of the park are 3 meters, 4 meters, and 5 meters.
- *We want*: the distance around the park, or its perimeter.
- *Our strategy*: add up the lengths of all three sides of the triangle.

$$perimeter = 3 + 4 + 5 = 12$$

Is our solution one of the answer choices? It is indeed! The answer is (C) 12.

CHECK YOUR ANSWER

Always check your work to make sure that you picked the best answer among all of the options the ISEE gave you! Double-check all of your arithmetic to make sure that you didn't make any careless errors.

Make sure that you solved for what the question was asking. For example, if the question asked you to solve for the triangle's perimeter, make sure you didn't solve for area.

Try to determine whether or not your answer seems reasonable based on context. For example, if the length of one side of the triangle is 3, the perimeter of the whole triangle cannot be 3, so answer (A) in our example is unreasonable.

Finally, check that you bubbled in the answer on your answer sheet correctly. It would be a shame to have solved the question correctly and not get credit!

PUTTING IT ALL TOGETHER

Here is another example question that is a bit more complicated. Use the same question-solving steps to try it out.

1. **Read the question:**

   The width of a rectangular field is one-quarter its length. If the length is 16, what is the perimeter of the field?

   (A) 4
   (B) 24
   (C) 36
   (D) 40

2. **Underline key words:**

   The <u>width</u> of a <u>rectangular</u> field is <u>one-quarter its length</u>. If the <u>length is 16,</u> what is the <u>perimeter</u> of the field?

3. **Ask yourself, "What is the question asking me to solve?"**
   Just like our first example, you are being asked to find the perimeter of the rectangle. Put this in your own words: the perimeter is the length of the outline of the rectangle.

4. **Draw a diagram.**
   Try drawing a quick sketch of a rectangle and fill in any information given in the question:

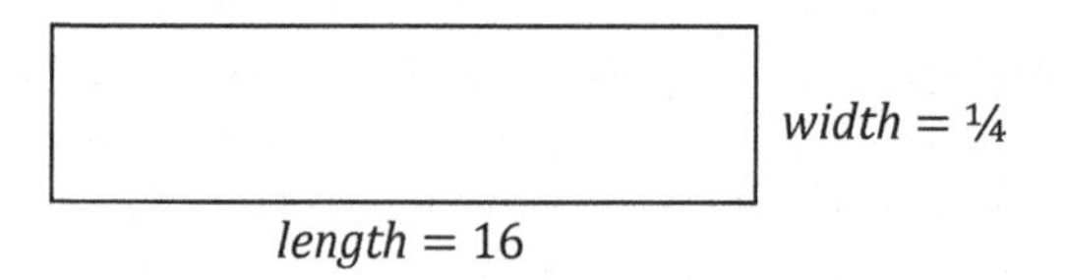

5. **Strategize a solution.**

   We know: length = 16

   $$\text{width} = \frac{1}{4}\text{ of length} = \frac{1}{4}\text{ of } 16 = \frac{1}{4} \times 16 = \frac{16}{4} = 4$$

   We want: the perimeter of the whole rectangle.

   Our strategy: we can use a formula that relates a rectangle's perimeter to its length and width.

   $$perimeter = (2 \times length) + (2 \times width)$$

   We can now plug in the values and solve:

   $$perimeter = (2 \times 16) + (2 \times 4) = 32 + 8 = 40.$$

If you did not remember this formula, look at the diagram again. To find the perimeter, we need to add up the lengths of the four sides of the rectangle. Our sides include two lengths and two widths, so here's how we would add them up:

$$perimeter = 16 + 4 + 16 + 4 = 40$$

There are often many different ways to solve a problem, so think creatively to find a strategy that works for you!

Exercise #1: For each of the sample questions below, (1) read the question, (2) underline key words, (3) determine what the question is asking you to solve, (4) draw a diagram if appropriate, and (5) strategize a solution. Then, check your answer with the answer key at the back of the book.

1. Northwood Elementary School has 3 clocks for every 5 doors. If there are a total of 40 clocks and doors at Northwood Elementary School, how many clocks are there?

   (A) 15
   (B) 20
   (C) 24
   (D) 25

2. Ben and Mari are playing a game. Mari gives Ben a number. Ben triples it and divides the result by 2. If Ben ends up with the number 9, what number did Mari give Ben?

   (A) 3
   (B) 6
   (C) 15
   (D) 18

3. Harry likes to play hockey on a team, play hockey video games at home, and watch hockey on TV. On Saturday, his team had a game that lasted 1.5 hours. When Harry got home, he played a hockey video game for 1 hour. At 8:00pm, he started watching a game that lasted 2.5 hours. What fraction of his day did Harry spend on hockey-related activities?

   (A) $^{3}/_{48}$
   (B) $^{5}/_{48}$
   (C) $^{1}/_{6}$
   (D) $^{5}/_{24}$

Questions 4 and 5 are Middle/Upper Level Only.

4. If 12% of a number is 6, then what is 60% of the same number?

   (A) 30
   (B) 40
   (C) 50
   (D) 60

5. Two circles with a radius of 6cm are drawn on a sheet of paper. If the circles intersect at least once, what is the longest possible distance between one point on one circle and another point on the other circle?

   (A) 6cm
   (B) 12cm
   (C) 18cm
   (D) 24cm

ADDITIONAL STRATEGIES

If you are stuck after working through the basic approach for a problem, here are some additional strategies that you can use. Try out these strategies in your practice questions so that you become familiar with them.

PROCESS OF ELIMINATION

It is worthwhile to guess on a question if you can eliminate any answer options that you know are wrong. So how do you eliminate wrong answers? Read the question and the answer choices, and determine whether any of them seem unreasonable. For example:

Which of the following fractions is less than $^1/_3$?

(A) $^4/_{18}$

(B) $^4/_{12}$

(C) $^3/_3$

(D) $^{12}/_9$

Even if you forget how to solve the question above, you can eliminate wrong answers. You know that $^1/_3$ is less than 1. Remember that an "improper fraction" has a numerator that is greater than its denominator, and any improper fraction is greater than 1. Because answer (D) is an improper fraction, it also must be greater than 1, so it can't be less than $^1/_3$. You can eliminate this choice right away.

You might also remember that a fraction with the same numerator and denominator is always equal to 1. Answer (C) has the same numerator and denominator, so it must be equal to 1 and can't be less than $^1/_3$. You can also eliminate answer (C).

If you don't know how to proceed with the arithmetic, you can guess between (A) and (B) and you will have pretty good odds of getting the correct answer. Or, you can look at answer (B) and reduce $^4/_{12}$ to $^1/_3$. Because the question is asking for a fraction that is less than $^1/_3$, (B) can't be the correct answer. You are left with only one possible answer: (A).

Exercise #2: For each question below, cross out answer choices that are definitely wrong without fully solving the question. Briefly note why you eliminated certain choices. Finally, solve the problem! Check your answers in the answer key at the end of the book.

1. The spinner below has five equal sections, each with a number. What is the probability of spinning a 3 or a 5?

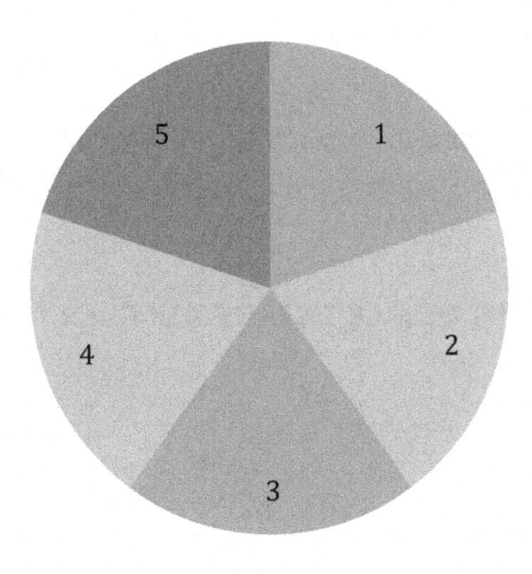

(A) 1/5 Eliminate? If so, why?

(B) 2/5 Eliminate? If so, why?

(C) 1/2 Eliminate? If so, why?

(D) 3/5 Eliminate? If so, why?

2. If four dozen chew toys are divided equally among two dozen dogs, how many chew toys will each dog get?

(A) 2 Eliminate? If so, why?
(B) 4 Eliminate? If so, why?
(C) 12 Eliminate? If so, why?
(D) 24 Eliminate? If so, why?

3. Which of the following numbers is divisible by 12?

(A) 549 Eliminate? If so, why?
(B) 578 Eliminate? If so, why?
(C) 624 Eliminate? If so, why?
(D) 754 Eliminate? If so, why?

Questions 4 and 5 are Middle/Upper Level Only.

4. Matt had an average of 83% on his first four math tests. What score would he have to average on his remaining two tests in order to have an 85% average on the 6 tests?

   (A) 85% Eliminate? If so, why?
   (B) 87% Eliminate? If so, why?
   (C) 89% Eliminate? If so, why?
   (D) 91% Eliminate? If so, why?

5. Jack's beanstalk is growing at a constant rate. The graph shows the height of Jack's beanstalk over time. What is the relationship between D (the day) and H (the height)?

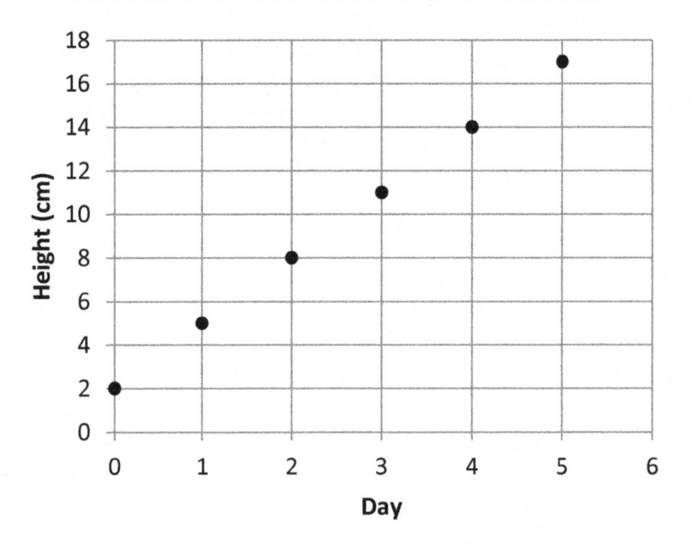

   (A) $H = 3D$ Eliminate? If so, why?
   (B) $H = -3D + 2$ Eliminate? If so, why?
   (C) $H = 2D + 3$ Eliminate? If so, why?
   (D) $H = 3D + 2$ Eliminate? If so, why?

GUESS AND CHECK

Sometimes you can narrow your choices down to one based on what seems reasonable, and then check to see if this is actually the correct answer. This is often true with geometry questions or problems where you can estimate. For example:

> Julia arrived at Jenny's house at 6:35 PM. Her mother picked her up at 8:04 PM. How long did Julia spend at Jenny's house?
>
> (A) 29 minutes
> (B) 1 hour, 9 minutes
> (C) 1 hour, 29 minutes
> (D) 2 hours, 9 minutes

We can guess an answer for this question by rounding the times. 6:35 PM is approximately 6:30 PM and 8:04 PM is approximately 8:00 PM. The time between 6:30 to 7:00 is half an hour, and the time from 7:00 to 8:00 is another hour. Therefore, the time between 6:30 to 8:00 is about an hour and a half.

Looking at the answer choices, this is very close to (C) 1 hour, 29 minutes, so you can guess that this is the right answer. If you're running out of time, you might want to circle (C) as your best guess and move on.

In order to check that (C) is actually the right answer, subtract 6:35 PM from 8:04 PM:

$$\begin{array}{r} 8:04 \\ \underline{-6:35} \end{array}$$

8 hours and 4 minutes is the same as 7 hours and 64 minutes. Use borrowing and re-write 8:04 as 7:64 so you can subtract properly:

$$\begin{array}{r} 7:64 \\ \underline{-6:35} \\ 1:29 \end{array}$$

Our estimation by rounding was close to the actual answer, and our guess was correct.

Now try the guess-and-check method for a more challenging question:

Figure $PQRS$ (drawn to scale) is a square with side length of 12. What is the area of the shaded region?

(A) 50
(B) 72
(C) 100
(D) 120

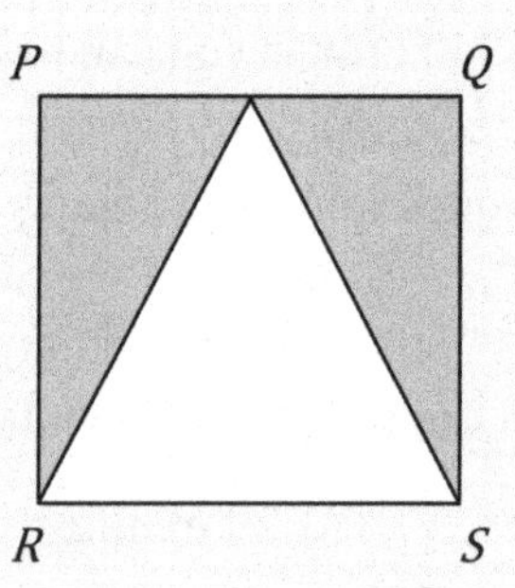

Because $PQRS$ is a square, its area is $12 \times 12 = 144$. We're told that the diagram is drawn to scale, and it looks like that the shaded area is approximately half of the area of the square. Based on this estimate, let's see if we can eliminate any answers that seem unreasonable. Answer (D) is too large, and so is (C). (A) seems too small because 50 is about 1/3 of 144. (B) seems about right, so we can circle (B) as our best guess.

Now we can check to see if (B) is actually correct. The area of the unshaded triangle is $1/2 \times base \times height = 1/2\,(12)(12) = 1/2\,(144) = 72$. Subtract this from the area of the square to find the shaded area: $144 - 72 = 72$.

Our initial estimate was exactly right! If you were short on time and didn't have time to check all of the calculations for this problem, you would have been correct with this guess.

Exercise #3: For each of the questions below, use guess-and-check to estimate the answer without calculating the answer exactly. Then, check to make sure your estimate is close to the exact answer. Check your work in the answer key in the back of the book.

1. A librarian has $400 with which to buy new books. If she buys books for $9 each, what is the greatest number of books she can buy?

2. There are 15 total cows and chickens on a farm. If the total number of legs for these animals equals 42, how many cows are there? *(**Upper Level Challenge:** can you find a way to do this with a system of equations?)*

3. Katie bought 4 cans of soup at $1.49 each and 8 cans of beans at $0.79 each. If she gave the cashier $15, how much change did she get back?

4. $11 + 29 + 39$ is closest to

   (A) $10 + 20 + 30$
   (B) $10 + 30 + 30$
   (C) $11 + 29 + 30$
   (D) $10 + 30 + 40$

5. If $x = 5.9$ and $y = 7.1$, then xy equals

   (A) 35.9
   (B) 41.89
   (C) 41.9
   (D) 42

PICKING NUMBERS

Sometimes an algebra question may seem difficult or abstract because it contains a lot of variables—those letters or symbols that stand for numbers. The quickest way to solve these questions is to simplify the algebra. However, you can also make any question more concrete by picking an easy number to work with and plugging in this number instead of a variable.

The "picking numbers" method is typically used to solve questions whose answer choices are algebraic expressions. For example, you might be asked to state someone's age or height "in terms of" variables, remainders, percentages, or fractions of variables. You might also be asked to determine whether an expression or variable is even or odd. Both of these situations are excellent times to use the "picking numbers" method. For example:

> Michelle is 3 years older than Tommy. If Tommy is t years old, then how old is Michelle, in terms of t?
>
> (A) $t + 3$
> (B) $t - 3$
> (C) $3t$
> (D) $t \div 3$

This example has variables in the answer choices, so we can use the "picking numbers" method. Pick an age for Tommy to replace t. Let's pick 10. (You could have chosen any number.) If Tommy is 10 years old, Michelle is 3 years older than Tommy, so Michelle is $10 + 3 = 13$ years old. The next step is to replace t with Tommy's age (10) in each of the answer choices:

(A) $10 + 3 = 13$
(B) $10 - 3 = 7$
(C) $3 \times 10 = 30$
(D) $10 \div 3 = 3\,^1/_3$

If Tommy is 10 years old, we've already determined that Michelle must be 13 years old. Therefore, answer (A) is correct.

Warning: If you replaced t with 1.5, you would find that Michelle is three times as old as Tommy. However, this is only true for this case! Try picking a different age for Tommy. Because this is not always true, $m = 3t$ is incorrect. Think about why that can never be true for an age problem. Have you ever heard of someone who is always three times as old as someone else?

Let's try another slightly more challenging example:

Nathan is three inches taller than Joseph, who is five inches shorter than Ethan. If e represents Ethan's height in inches, then how many inches tall is Nathan, in terms of e?

(A) $e + 4$
(B) $e + 2$
(C) e
(D) $e - 2$

This example has variables in the answer choices, so we can apply the "picking numbers" method. Let's say that Ethan is 50 inches tall, so $e = 50$. (You can choose any number and this method will still work. Try it!) If Ethan is 50 inches tall, we know that Joseph is five inches shorter, so Joseph is $50 - 5 = 45$ inches tall. Nathan is three inches taller than Joseph, so he is $45 + 3 = 48$ inches tall.

The question is asking for Nathan's height in terms of e. The next step is to replace e with Ethan's height (50) into each of the answer choices, and figure out which one matches Nathan's height (48):

(A) $50 + 4 = 54$
(B) $50 + 2 = 52$
(C) 50
(D) $50 - 2 = 48$

We know that Nathan's height is 48 inches when Ethan's height is 50 inches, so answer (D) is correct.

Exercise #4: For each question below, pick a number that will simplify the question. Then, use this number to solve the question. Check your answers in the back of the book.

1. At a barbecue, $^6/_{10}$ of the people had a hamburger and $^4/_{10}$ had a veggie burger. If there are twice as many veggie burgers in a box as hamburgers, and the organizers used 4 boxes of veggie burgers, how many boxes of hamburgers did they use?

2. Nina starts at floor x. She goes up 5 floors, then down 2 floors, up 7 floors, and down 3 floors. In terms of x, on what floor does she end up?

3. George draws a rectangle. He then draws another rectangle whose length is 9 times the length of his first rectangle and whose width is $^1/_3$ the width of his first rectangle. The second rectangle's area is how many times greater than the first rectangle's area? ($Area = length \times width$)

Questions 4 and 5 are Middle/Upper Level Only.

4. From 2000 to 2001, the population of fish in a pond grew by 10%. From 2001 to 2002, the population of fish declined by 5%. By what percent did the population of fish rise from 2000 to 2002?

5. If a certain maple tree grew by 3 feet and then doubled in height, it would be the same height as a certain red oak. What is the relationship between the height of the maple tree (m) and the height of the red oak (r)?

BACK-SOLVING

Back-solving is a method that allows you to work backwards from the multiple-choice answers you are given. Unlike the "picking numbers" method, you can only use back-solving if your answer choices don't include variables. When your answer choices are numbers, you can expect them to be given in order from largest to smallest or smallest to largest. Take one of the middle answers (B or C) and plug it into your problem. If it works, it is right. If not, you can usually determine whether to try a larger or smaller answer.

For example:

Two consecutive numbers have a sum of 13. What is the smaller of the two numbers?

(A) 5
(B) 6
(C) 7
(D) 8

Start with answer choice (C). If 7 is the smaller number, then the two consecutive numbers are 7 and 8, which have a sum of 15. The correct numbers must add up to 13, so we're looking for a starting number that is smaller. We'll try (B) next. If 6 is the smaller of the 2 numbers, then the two numbers are 6 and 7, which have a sum of 13! (B) is the right answer.

If (B) gave us a sum that was still larger than 13, we would have known that (A) was correct. If we started with answer (C) and it gave us a sum that was less than 13, we would have known that answer (D) was correct.

Here's another more challenging example:

Four consecutive multiples of 5 have a sum of 90. What is the greatest of these four numbers?

(A) 10
(B) 15
(C) 20
(D) 30

Start with answer (C). If 20 is the greatest of the four numbers, we need to find the next three multiples of 5 that are smaller than 20. These are 15, 10, and 5, so our four numbers would be 20, 15, 10, and 5. However, the sum of these four numbers is $20 + 15 + 10 + 5 = 50$. The correct numbers must add up to 90, so we know (C) is incorrect.

Because 90 is greater than 50, we know that the greatest of the four numbers must be larger than 20. Therefore, we'll try answer (D) next. If 30 is the greatest of the four numbers, then the numbers are 30, 25, 20, and 15. The sum of these four numbers is $30 + 25 + 20 + 15 = 90$. (D) is correct.

Exercise #5: For each of the following questions, use back-solving to select your answer. Then, check your answer in the answer key at the back of the book.

1. Pauline has a certain number of stickers. If she splits them evenly between herself and her 5 friends, there will be 3 left over. If she splits them evenly between herself and her 3 friends, there will be 1 left over. What could be the number of stickers that Pauline has?

   (A) 23
   (B) 33
   (C) 43
   (D) 53

2. When 58 is divided by 8, the remainder is the same as when 47 is divided by

   (A) 1
   (B) 3
   (C) 4
   (D) 6

3. Sue-Anne is stringing small beads onto a string. She has 12 beads on the string to start. If she wants to have a total of 47 beads on the string in 5 minutes, how many beads does she need to string per minute?

   (A) 7
   (B) 8
   (C) 9
   (D) 10

4. How many sevenths are there in $3\frac{4}{7}$?

   (A) 21
   (B) 24
   (C) 25
   (D) 28

5. If $a = 7$ and $b = 12$, what is the value of ab?

   (A) 5
   (B) 19
   (C) 84
   (D) 96

WORD PROBLEM PRACTICE QUESTIONS

SECTION 2

In this section, you will find 103 practice questions to prepare you for the types of quantitative comparison questions you might find on the ISEE. The Lower Level questions cover the full range of content that you will find on the Lower Level exam, as well as the easier content on the Middle and Upper Level exams. The Middle Level questions cover content that you will only find on the Middle and Upper Level exams. The Upper Level questions cover content that you will only find on the Upper Level exam.

Each question consists of a word problem followed by four answer choices. Look at the four answer choices given and select the best answer. Use the answer key at the back of the book to check your work.

LOWER LEVEL QUESTIONS

Use these questions to practice the full range of content that you will see on the Lower Level ISEE, as well as the easier content that you will see on the Middle and Upper Levels. Lower, Middle, and Upper Level students should attempt these questions.

1. Which fraction is the smallest?

   (A) $\frac{1}{2}$

   (B) $\frac{2}{3}$

   (C) $\frac{4}{9}$

   (D) $\frac{6}{18}$

2. A submarine was located 260 feet below sea level. The submarine then rose up 120 feet. What was its new altitude?

(A) 380 feet below sea level
(B) 140 feet below sea level
(C) 120 feet below sea level
(D) 140 feet above sea level

3. Sarah owns four puzzles, Anna owns six puzzles, and Bella owns three puzzles. What is the mean number of puzzles that the girls own?

(A) $2\frac{2}{3}$

(B) 3

(C) $4\frac{1}{3}$

(D) 5

4. If $3n + 5 = 17$, what is the value of n?

(A) 2
(B) 4
(C) 6
(D) 12

5. A bag contains 6 red markers, 9 yellow markers, 4 blue markers, and 5 green markers. If Pooja randomly picks a marker from the bag, what is the probability that she will pick a red marker?

(A) $\frac{1}{24}$

(B) $\frac{1}{6}$

(C) $\frac{1}{4}$

(D) $\frac{1}{3}$

6. What are the dimensions of a square with an area of 64 cm^2?
($A = s \times s$, where A = area and s = side length)

(A) 2 cm by 32 cm
(B) 8 cm by 4 cm
(C) 8 cm by 8 cm
(D) 16 cm by 16 cm

7. At a school basketball game, each ticket cost $5. If p represents the number of people who attended the game, what is the total amount of money that the school earned from ticket sales?

(A) 5 dollars
(B) $5 + p$ dollars
(C) $5p$ dollars
(D) $5p + 5$ dollars

8. The chart below shows the number of children with a cold or with the flu at three schools.

NUMBER OF SICK CHILDREN BY ILLNESS AND BY SCHOOL		
	Children with a Cold	**Children with the Flu**
School A	125	50
School B	55	30
School C	30	10

According to the chart above, for each school in the chart, the number of children with a cold is:

(A) greater than the number of children with the flu.
(B) equal to the number of children with the flu.
(C) less than the number of children with the flu.
(D) twice the number of children with the flu.

9. In the figure below, line segments MP and PQ both have a length of 6. If point N is the midpoint of MP, what is the distance between point N and point Q?

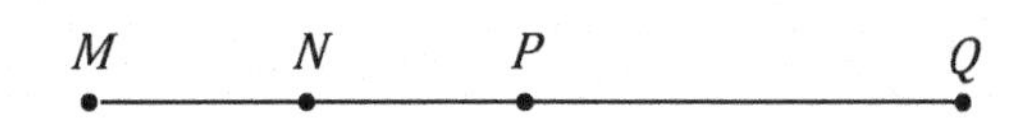

(A) 3
(B) 6
(C) 9
(D) 12

10. Sasha walked 5 blocks north, 6 blocks west, 5 blocks south, and 6 blocks east. If it took her an average of 3 minutes to walk one block, how long did her entire walk take?

    (A) 30 min.
    (B) 33 min.
    (C) 66 min.
    (D) 70 min.

11. If one of the students in the graph below were selected at random, what is the probability that he or she would own a cat?

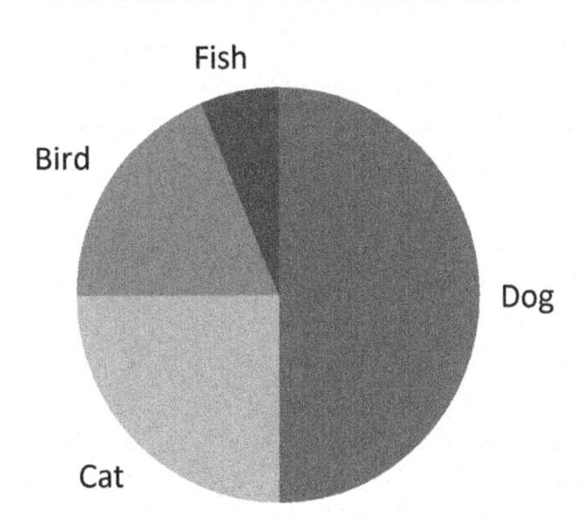

    (A) $\frac{1}{5}$
    (B) $\frac{1}{4}$
    (C) $\frac{1}{3}$
    (D) $\frac{1}{2}$

12. Use the pattern below to help answer the question.

$$1 \times 1 = 1$$
$$11 \times 11 = 121$$
$$111 \times 111 = 12{,}321$$

    What is the solution to $1{,}111 \times 1{,}111$?

    (A) 12,321
    (B) 12,341
    (C) 123,421
    (D) 1,234,321

13. John has 6 pencils. Rashmi tells him to guess how many pencils she has. She says she has fewer than 26 pencils, but she has more than four times as many pencils as John. How many pencils does Rashmi have?

    (A) 6
    (B) 12
    (C) 24
    (D) 25

14. In the figure below, a dog is tethered by a leash to a point on the edge of a barn. If the leash is 10 feet long, the dog will be able to reach all of the following points EXCEPT

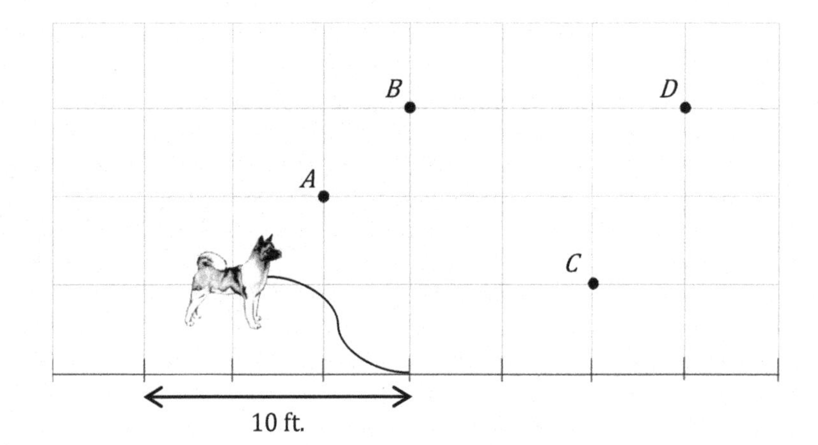

    (A) Point A
    (B) Point B
    (C) Point C
    (D) Point D

15. A triangle with a perimeter of $24z$ has two sides with lengths $6z$ and $10z$. What is the length of the third side of the triangle?

    (A) 8
    (B) 16
    (C) $8z$
    (D) $16z$

16. A box has 30 jellybeans of different colors. The probability of Eric choosing a blue jellybean from the box is 1 out of 2. How many blue jellybeans are in the box?

(A) 5
(B) 6
(C) 10
(D) 15

17. In the figure below, Gerry is connecting points on a grid to make a rectangle. If points L, M, and N are the first three corners of his rectangle, what will be the coordinates of the fourth corner?

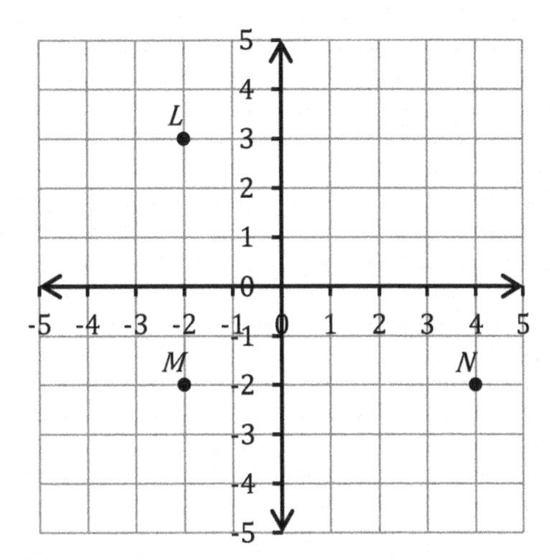

(A) $(-2,-2)$
(B) $(4,-2)$
(C) $(4,3)$
(D) $(3,4)$

18. If the shape below was rotated counter-clockwise 90 degrees, which shape would result?

(A) 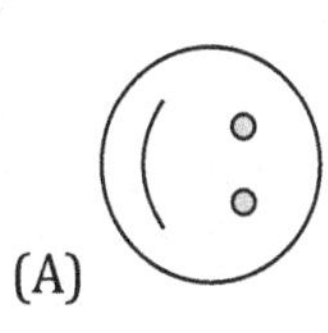

(C) 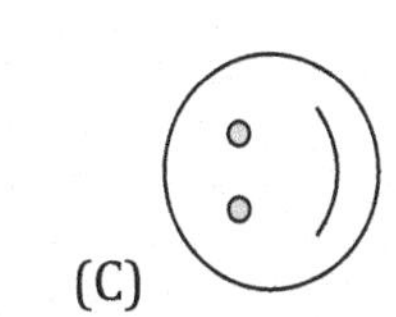

(B) 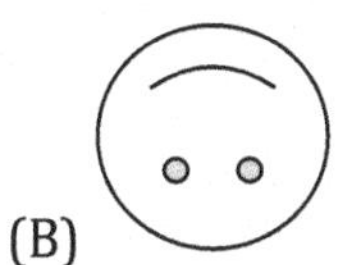

(D) 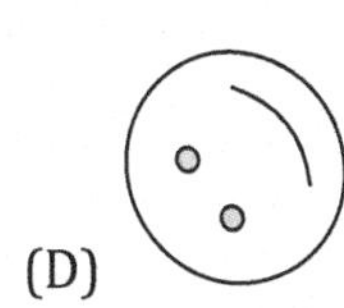

19. Which story would best fit the entire expression $3d \div 2$?

(A) Suraya bought three markers that cost d dollars each and then bought two more.
(B) Suraya bought three bags of sparkles with d sparkles in each bag.
(C) Suraya bought 3 boxes of toys with d toys in each box, and she divided the toys equally between her 2 nieces.
(D) Over a period of 2 days, Suraya ate 3 pizzas with d slices each.

20. A group of 70 students were asked to vote on their favorite type of ice cream, and the results are shown below.

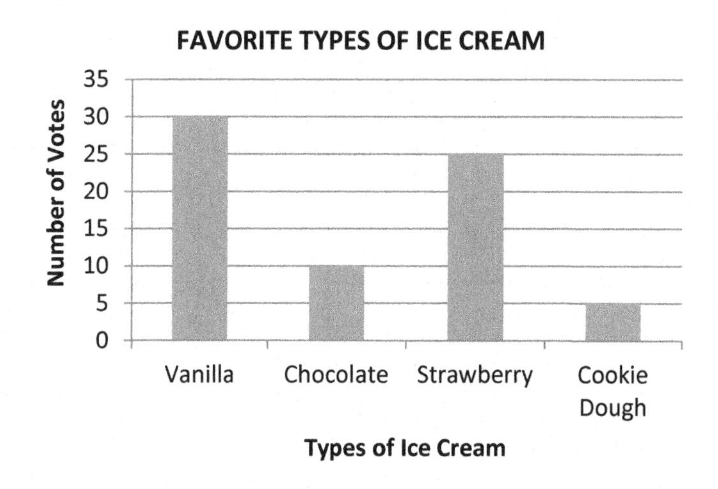

Based on this graph, which conclusion is true about the students' favorite ice cream flavors?

(A) Cookie dough is the most popular ice cream flavor among the students.
(B) Half the number of students who prefer strawberry prefer chocolate.
(C) The number of students who prefer vanilla equals the number of students who prefer cookie dough and strawberry combined.
(D) The average number of votes for each ice cream flavor was between 20 and 25.

21. There is a remainder of 2 when x is divided by 3, and there is also a remainder of 2 when x is divided by 4. Which of these numbers could be x?

(A) 6
(B) 14
(C) 15
(D) 18

22. If A represents the average number of slices of pizza that Adam ate each day from Monday to Sunday, which expression represents the total number of pizza slices that Adam ate over that time period?

(A) A
(B) 7
(C) $\frac{7A}{7}$
(D) $7A$

23. Use the diagram below to answer the question.

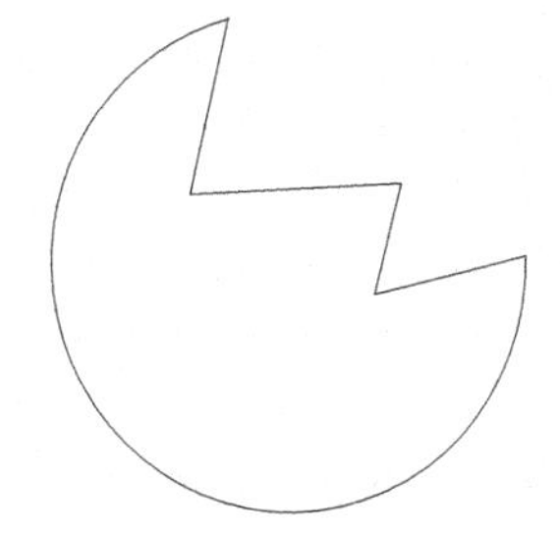

Which shape below would complete the circle?

(A)
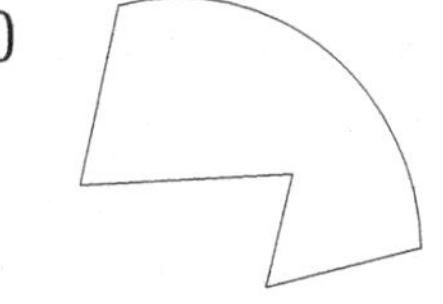

(C)

(B)
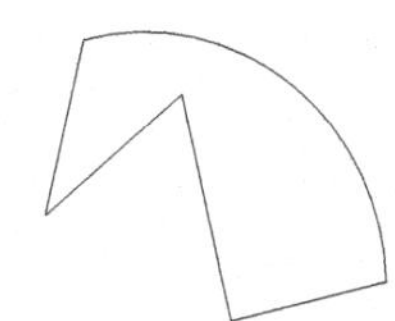

(D)

24. The glass below is partially filled with juice. If the volume of the juice is 2 in^3, what is the volume of the entire glass?

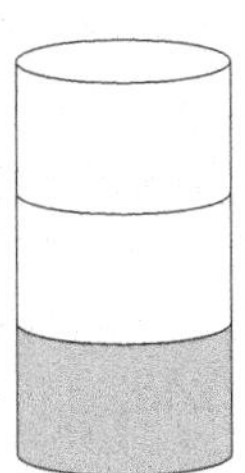

(A) 3 in^3
(B) 4 in^3
(C) 6 in^3
(D) 8 in^3

25. If Elias rolls a standard six-sided number cube, he has an equal chance of rolling any number from 1 through 6. What is the probability that he will NOT roll a 2?

(A) $\frac{1}{36}$

(B) $\frac{1}{6}$

(C) $\frac{5}{6}$

(D) $\frac{2}{3}$

26. If a rectangular sticker is 4 centimeters wide and 6 centimeters long, what is the smallest number of stickers that would completely cover a sheet of 20 cm by 72 cm paper?

(A) 36
(B) 45
(C) 60
(D) 80

27. The pentagon shown below can be folded along each of the four lines, labeled a through d. Along which line should Sonia fold the shape if she wants the sides to line up exactly?

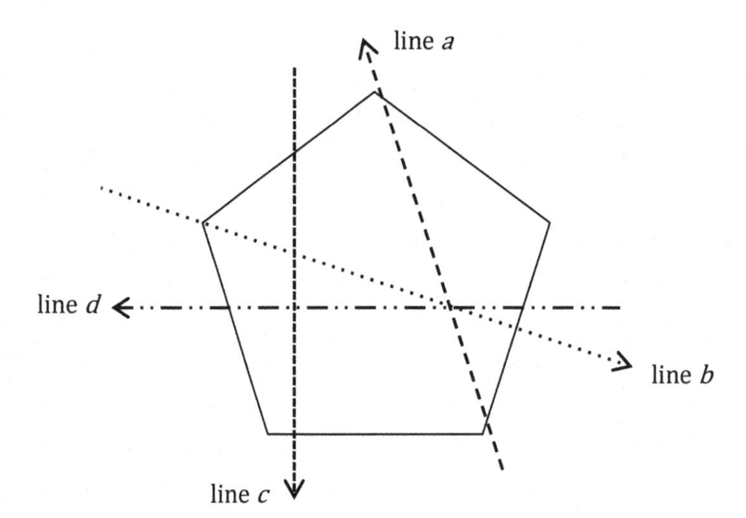

(A) line a
(B) line b
(C) line c
(D) line d

28. If this pattern continues, the fifth tree will have how many more branches than the fourth tree?

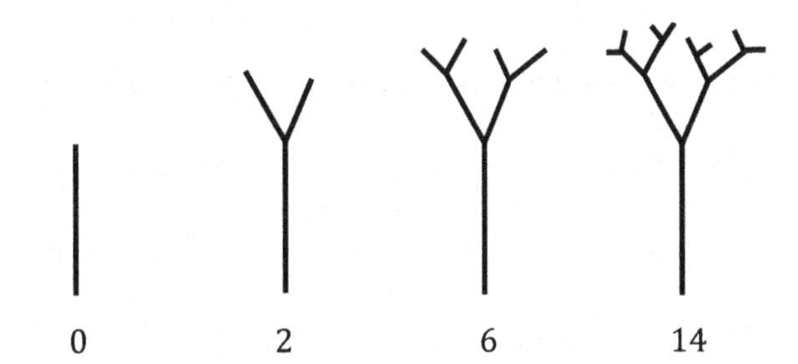

(A) 10
(B) 16
(C) 24
(D) 35

29. A flower shop had 3 roses, 3 tulips, and 4 carnations. John bought 1 rose and then decided to randomly choose another flower from those left at the shop. What is the probability that he will choose a carnation?

(A) $\frac{2}{5}$
(B) $\frac{4}{7}$
(C) $\frac{3}{9}$
(D) $\frac{4}{9}$

30. Which expression is equivalent to the expression $2(6x - 3)$?

(A) $6(x - 2)$
(B) $6(2x - 1)$
(C) $12x - 3$
(D) $12(x - 3)$

MIDDLE LEVEL QUESTIONS

Use these questions to practice the content that you will only see on the Middle Level and Upper Level ISEE. Only Middle and Upper Level students should attempt these questions.

1. What is the greatest integer less than $\frac{83}{6}$?

   (A) 11
   (B) 12
   (C) 13
   (D) 15

2. What is the sum of all the prime factors of 6?

   (A) 3
   (B) 5
   (C) 6
   (D) 12

3. Ms. Anderson's math class has 30 students. 60% of these students are boys, and 50% of these boys ride the bus to school. How many boys in Ms. Anderson's math class ride the bus to school?

   (A) 6
   (B) 7
   (C) 8
   (D) 9

4. When 6 is subtracted from four times a number L, the result is 26. Which of the following equations represents this statement?

   (A) $4L = 26 - 6$
   (B) $4L - 6 = 26$
   (C) $L - 6 = 26 \times 4$
   (D) $4(L - 6) = 26$

5. Jenny sleeps for 8 hours every day. How many days does she spend asleep over the course of one week?

(A) $\frac{1}{3}$

(B) $\frac{4}{3}$

(C) $2\frac{1}{3}$

(D) $2\frac{1}{8}$

6. Out of the 40 games a baseball team played in one season, it lost 15 games, tied 5 games, and won the remaining games. What was the ratio of the team's wins to losses?

(A) 2:1
(B) 4:3
(C) 5:3
(D) 40:15

7. Which of the following is equivalent to $\frac{1}{4} \times \frac{1}{4}$?

(A) $\frac{1^{1/2}}{4}$

(B) $\left(\frac{1}{4}\right)^2$

(C) $4^{\frac{1}{2}}$

(D) 4^2

8. What is the area, in square units, of the figure in the grid below?

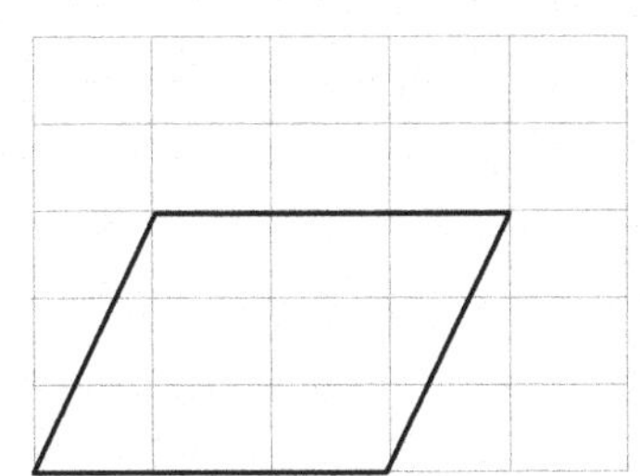

(A) 4
(B) 6
(C) 9
(D) 12

9. A student collects data on the average height in inches of four different plants. According to the chart below, which of the following is true?

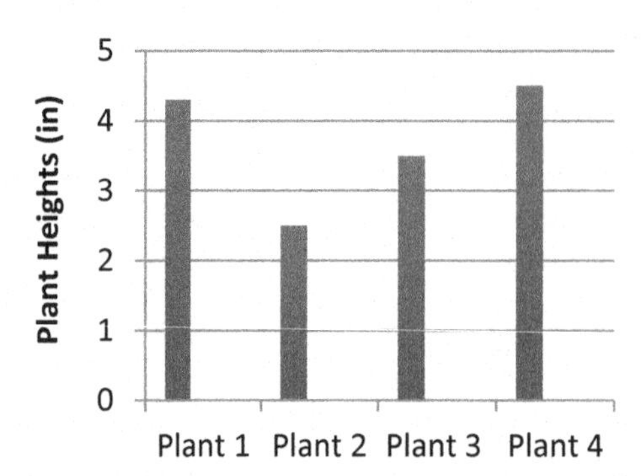

(A) The range of plant heights is greater than the height of Plant 4.
(B) The median plant height is between the heights of Plant 1 and Plant 3.
(C) The mode of the data is 2 inches.
(D) The mean plant height is equal to the height of Plant 2.

10. Use the equations below to help answer the question.

$$6n + 4 = 16$$
$$17 + 2m = 27$$

What is the sum of $3n + m$?

(A) 5
(B) 11
(C) 12
(D) 14

11. A coat is on sale for 60% off of $19.95. What is the new price of the coat, rounded to the nearest whole number?

(A) 4
(B) 5
(C) 8
(D) 10

12. When N is divided by 6, the result is 7 with a remainder of 3. What is the value of N divided by 5?

(A) 6
(B) 7
(C) 8
(D) 9

13. A rectangular flowerbed is one-fifth as wide as it is long. If the flowerbed is 3 meters long, what is its area, in square meters?

(A) $\frac{3}{5}$ m^2
(B) $\frac{3}{2}$ m^2
(C) $\frac{9}{5}$ m^2
(D) 2 m^2

14. A line segment drawn on a coordinate grid has one endpoint at $(2, 3)$. If the line segment is 5 units long, which of the following could be the coordinates of its second endpoint?

(A) $(2, 5)$
(B) $(5, 3)$
(C) $(3, 4)$
(D) $(7, 3)$

15. A worm is tunneling straight into a sphere-shaped apple, taking the most direct route to the center. The apple has a diameter of 10 centimeters. If the worm travels at 7 minutes per centimeter, how long will it take to reach the center of the apple?

(A) 17 minutes
(B) 35 minutes
(C) 63 minutes
(D) 70 minutes

16. If the largest of seven consecutive integers is 18, what is the average of the seven integers?

(A) 12
(B) 14
(C) 15
(D) 18

17. In eight years, Nicole will be twice as old as her sister Jenny was two years ago, and half the age that Nicole's mother was when she got married. If Nicole's mother got married when she was 28, what is the age difference between Nicole and Jenny?

(A) 2 years
(B) 3 years
(C) 6 years
(D) 9 years

18. If $c + d = 7$, then what is the value of $3(c + d) - 2$?

(A) 14
(B) 19
(C) 21
(D) 56

19. Alexis and her friends like to trade their jewelry with each other using the trading system below.

2 pairs of earrings = 1 ring
5 rings = 2 bracelets

Alexis wants to trade her earrings for one of her friend's bracelets. How many pairs of earrings must she give her friend?

(A) 2
(B) 3
(C) 5
(D) 7

20. Which number is closest to the square root of 39.5?

(A) 3.5
(B) 6.0
(C) 7.0
(D) 7.5

21. The table below shows the average speed at which Noor drove over three different parts of her road trip.

Time Period	Average Speed (miles per hour)
2:00 PM – 4:00 PM	20
4:00 PM – 5:00 PM	0
5:00 PM – 8:00 PM	50

How far did Noor drive altogether?

(A) 100 miles
(B) 150 miles
(C) 190 miles
(D) 220 miles

22. Which of the following is a multiple of 2, 3, and 5?

(A) 123,450
(B) 123,455
(C) 123,460
(D) 123,466

23. Team Blue played Team Red in a basketball game, but they lost the game with a score of 41 points. If 6 players played for Team Red, the average number of points each player must have scored was at least which of the following values?

(A) 4
(B) 6
(C) 7
(D) 10

24. Both Kate and Jim work at the Corner Ice Cream Shop. If Jim sells x ice cream cones and Kate sells $3x + 4$ ice cream cones, the average number of ice cream cones sold by each employee is equal to

(A) $2x + 4$

(B) $2x + 2$

(C) $\frac{3x}{2} + 4$

(D) $\frac{3x}{2} + 2$

25. What is the smallest number that can be added to 367 to produce a result divisible by 3?

(A) 1
(B) 2
(C) 3
(D) 4

26. The figure below shows a square game board with two shaded square areas. The sides of the game board are 10 inches long, and the sides of each of the shaded squares are 5 inches long. A coin was thrown at random and landed somewhere on the game board. What is the probability that it landed on one of the shaded squares?

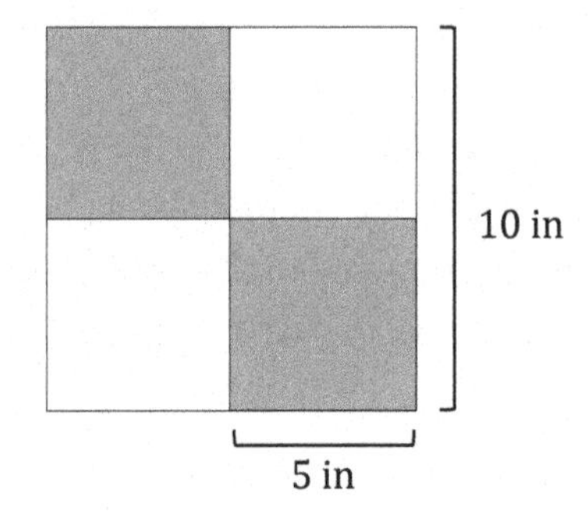

(A) 10%
(B) 25%
(C) 50%
(D) 75%

27. Which is a solution for n in the inequality $4n - 3 < 3n + 4$?

(A) $n > -7$
(B) $n \leq 7$
(C) $n > 1$
(D) $n < 7$

28. Susie's Superstore has 3 times as many wooden desks as plastic desks in its inventory. If the store only sells these two types of desks, which could be the total number of desks in stock?

(A) 10
(B) 25
(C) 38
(D) 44

29. There are x goldfish currently in a fish tank. If four more goldfish are added, there will be three times as many goldfish as there were last week, but only half as many as there were a year ago. Which expression represents the number of goldfish in the tank a year ago?

(A) $x + 4$
(B) $2(x + 4)$
(C) $(x + 4) \div 2$
(D) $(x + 4) \div 3$

30. The circle in the figure below fits exactly inside of a square. If the radius of the circle is $4p$, what is the area of the square? (Note: area of a circle $= \pi r^2$)

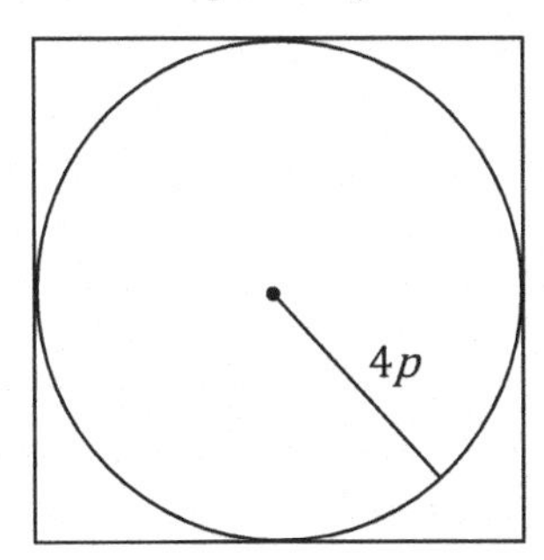

(A) $8p$
(B) $16p^2$
(C) $32p$
(D) $64p^2$

31. The median of five consecutive integers is 23. What is the value of the smallest of the five integers?

(A) 18
(B) 20
(C) 21
(D) 22

32. Which two expressions are equal in value?

(A) $\sqrt{9}$ and 2^2
(B) 2^3 and $\sqrt{16}$
(C) $\sqrt{14}$ and $2\sqrt{7}$
(D) $2\sqrt{4}$ and 4

33. Aliya bought a sweatshirt on sale for 40% off its original price and a hat at 30% off. If she spent $30 total and the hat originally cost $20, how much did she pay for the sweatshirt?

(A) $12
(B) $16
(C) $18
(D) $22

34. If the sum of 13 and twice a number P is less than the product of 4 and P, what is the lowest integer value for P that satisfies this expression?

(A) 6
(B) 7
(C) 13
(D) 14

35. At a bicycle rental store, Colleen can choose among 10 silver bikes, 8 red bikes, and 7 blue bikes. If Colleen chooses one bike randomly, what is the probability that she does NOT choose a silver bike?

(A) 33%
(B) 40%
(C) 50%
(D) 60%

36. Kyle has six more notebooks than Milly, and Milly has four more notebooks than twice the number that Samantha has. If S stands for the number of notebooks Samantha has, which expression represents the number of notebooks Kyle will have when he buys two more?

    (A) $2(S + 2)$
    (B) $2(S + 6)$
    (C) $2S + 6$
    (D) $4S + 2$

37. The graph below shows the populations of Towns A, B, and C between 1970 and 2010.

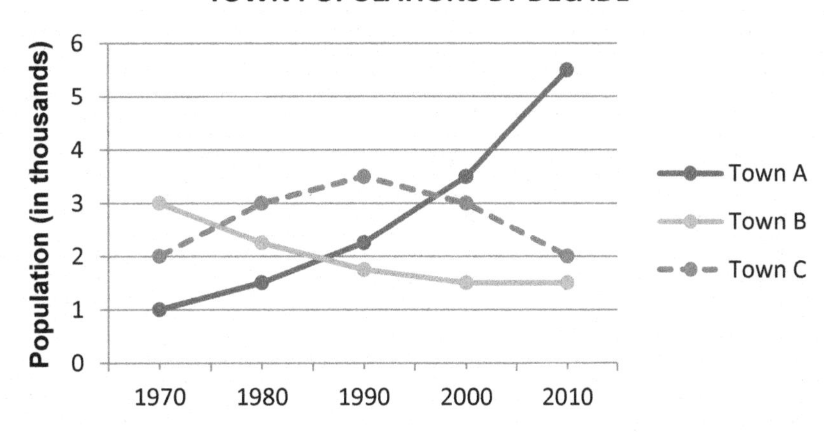

    If the population of Town C continues to decline at the same rate as it did between 2000 and 2010, in approximately which year will the town's population be zero?

    (A) 2012
    (B) 2015
    (C) 2020
    (D) 2030

38. In the figure below, the centers of four identical circles form the corners of a square. If the diameter of each circle is 6 cm, what is the area of the square?

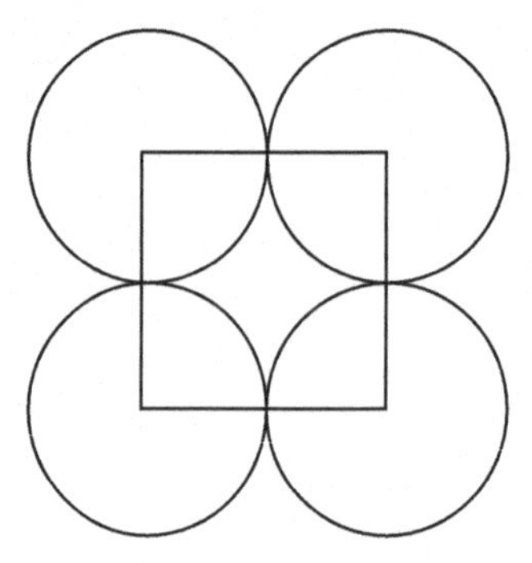

(A) 9 cm^2
(B) 24 cm^2
(C) 36 cm^2
(D) 144 cm^2

39. The square root of 85 falls between which two integers?

(A) 4 and 5
(B) 6 and 7
(C) 8 and 9
(D) 9 and 10

40. If $2N = N + 2$, then which of the following is NOT true?

(A) $N^3 = 8$
(B) $3N = 2N + 2$
(C) $N^2 - 1 = 5$
(D) $3N^2 = 12$

41. An isosceles triangle has an area of 12 in^2. The length of its base is multiplied by 3, and its height is divided by 4. What percent of the old area is the new area of the triangle?

(A) 30%
(B) 75%
(C) 120%
(D) 150%

42. $x - 3 = 5y + 4$. What is the value of the expression $x + 8$ in terms of y?

(A) $5y + 3$
(B) $5y + 7$
(C) $5y + 12$
(D) $5y + 15$

43. Three different positive integers have an average of 5. What is the largest possible value for any one of these integers?

(A) 5
(B) 11
(C) 12
(D) 15

44. If $h(z) = 5z^2$ what is the value of $h(2k)$?

(A) $4k$
(B) $20k$
(C) $4k^2$
(D) $20k^2$

45. Once folded, this will become a cube. If the cube is rolled, what is the probability that it will land with either the black or grey face up?

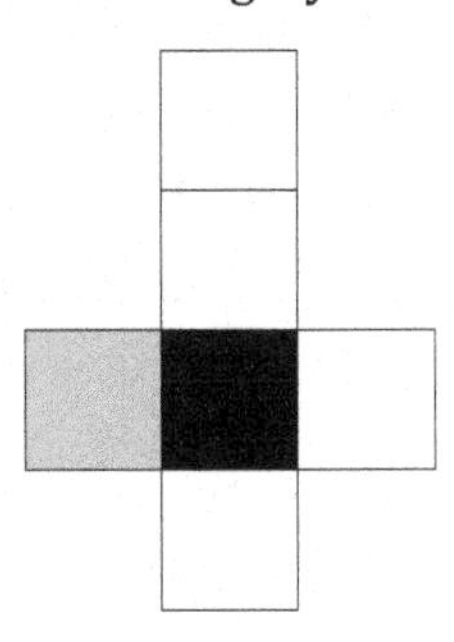

(A) $\frac{1}{4}$
(B) $\frac{3}{6}$
(C) $\frac{1}{3}$
(D) $1\frac{1}{6}$

46. The equation of a certain line is $y = 3(x - 2)$. Which of the following values is the greatest?

(A) The value of the y-intercept.
(B) The slope of the line.
(C) The value of the x-intercept.
(D) The y-intercept when $x = 4$.

47. A pond contains 4 green frogs and 3 yellow frogs. Each week, one frog is randomly selected from the pond and then returned back to the pond. What is the probability that a green frog will be selected two weeks in a row?

(A) $^9/_{49}$
(B) $^2/_7$
(C) $^4/_7$
(D) $^{16}/_{49}$

48. If N is a positive number, all of the following statements must be true EXCEPT

(A) $N - N = 0$
(B) $N \times \frac{1}{N} = 1$
(C) $N^1 = N$
(D) N^2 is an even number

UPPER LEVEL QUESTIONS

Use these questions to practice the most challenging difficulty level you will see on the Upper Level ISEE. Only Upper Level students should attempt these questions.

1. Anna sold her textbook for $20. James sold his textbook for $5 more than its original cost, and he made 30% more money in the sale than Anna did. What was the original cost of James's textbook?

   (A) $19.50
   (B) $21.00
   (C) $26.00
   (D) $32.00

2. A carton is two-thirds full of milk. If one liter of milk is poured out, the carton will be one-half full. How many liters of milk will the carton hold when full?

   (A) 3
   (B) 6
   (C) 9
   (D) 12

3. If Octagon 2 is similar to Octagon 1, which of the following statements is true?

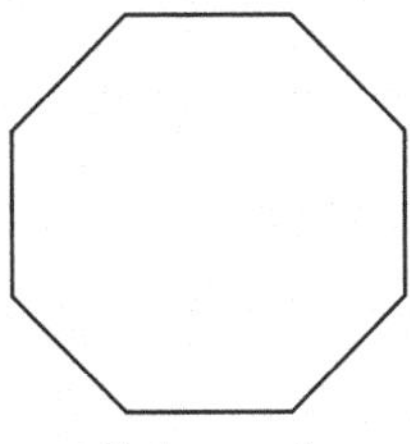

Octagon 1

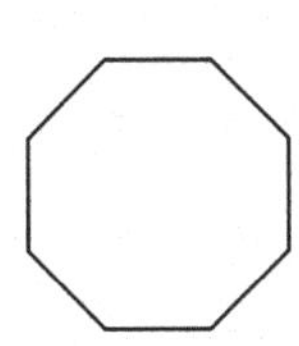

Octagon 2

   (A) The sum of the interior angles in Octagon 1 is greater than the sum of interior angles in Octagon 2.
   (B) The measure of each interior angle in Octagon 1 is equal to the measure of each corresponding interior angle in Octagon 2.
   (C) The length of the sides of Octagons 1 and 2 are equal.
   (D) The area of Octagons 1 and 2 are equal.

4. If the product of all integers from 1 to 300, exclusive, is x, then which expression represents the product of all integers from 1 to 302, exclusive?

(A) $x + 90{,}300$
(B) $x \times 90{,}300$
(C) $x \times 601$
(D) $x \times (301 + 302)$

5. Which integer is closest to $\sqrt{149}$?

(A) 10
(B) 11
(C) 12
(D) 13

6. A student art club has 48 members. The ratio of boys to girls is 3:5. One third of the girls in the art club are also on the tennis team. How many girls in the art club are NOT on the tennis team?

(A) 5
(B) 10
(C) 20
(D) 30

7. While training for a swim meet, Jennifer swims four laps at the following speeds: 2:20, 2:30, 2:35, and 2:15 minutes. If Jennifer wants to keep her median lap time the same, how fast must she swim her fifth lap?

(A) 2:15 min
(B) 2:20 min
(C) 2:25 min
(D) 2:30 min

8. Which expression is equivalent to $2(x^3 + 2x^2 - 2x - 4)$?

(A) $2x(x^2 - x - 1)$
(B) $(2x^2 - 4)(x + 2)$
(C) $(2x^3 + 2)(x^2 - 2)$
(D) $4(x^3 + x^2 - x - 2)$

9. After studying together in the city, Seira and Daine drove back to their own hometowns. Seira drove north at a speed of g miles per hour. Daine drove south at a speed of m miles per hour. How long did it take for Seira and Daine to be 90 miles apart?

(A) $\frac{90}{g}$

(B) $\frac{90}{m}$

(C) $\frac{g+m}{90}$

(D) $\frac{90}{g+m}$

10. A cylinder of height $\frac{1}{x}$ inches is constructed with Circle A as the base. If Circle A has an area of $a \times \pi \; in^2$, what is the volume of the new cylinder?
(Note: volume of a sphere is $\text{V} = r^2 2h\pi$)

(A) $a \times \frac{1}{x}$ in²

(B) $\frac{a}{h}$ in²

(C) $\frac{a \times \pi}{x}$ in²

(D) $a \times \pi \times x$ in²

11. What is the length of the line segment in the figure below?

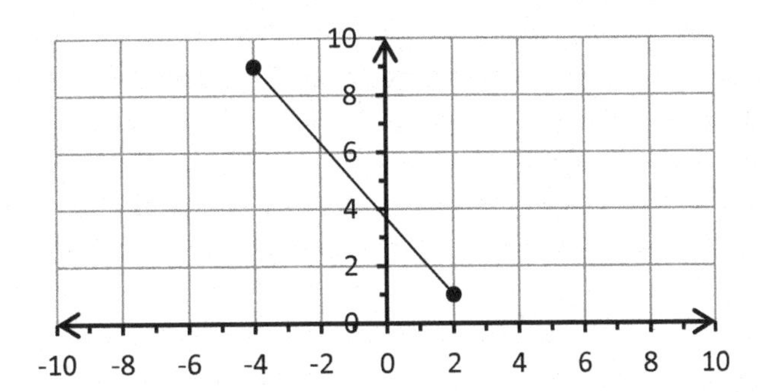

(A) 8 units
(B) 10 units
(C) 16 units
(D) 40 units

12. If the perimeter of a rectangle is 64 in, what is the largest area it could have?

(A) 87 in^2
(B) 120 in^2
(C) 128 in^2
(D) 256 in^2

13. If $b@ = 3b - 6$, what is $\left(\frac{y}{3}\right)@$?

(A) $3y - 3$
(B) $3y - 6$
(C) $y - 3$
(D) $y - 6$

14. Catalina wants to get an overall mean score of 80 in her math class. She knows that the sum of her scores from her first five tests was 405. What is the lowest score she can receive on her sixth test while still reaching her goal?

(A) 75
(B) 78
(C) 80
(D) 93

15. A container for orange juice is a centimeters wide, a centimeters long, and b centimeters tall. If one orange yields 20 cubic centimeters of juice, which expression represents how many oranges would produce enough juice to fill an entire container?

(A) $20ab$
(B) $20a^2b$
(C) $\frac{a^2b}{20}$
(D) $\frac{20a^2}{b}$

16. The graph below shows the distance Mina traveled during her walking trip as a function of the time she took.

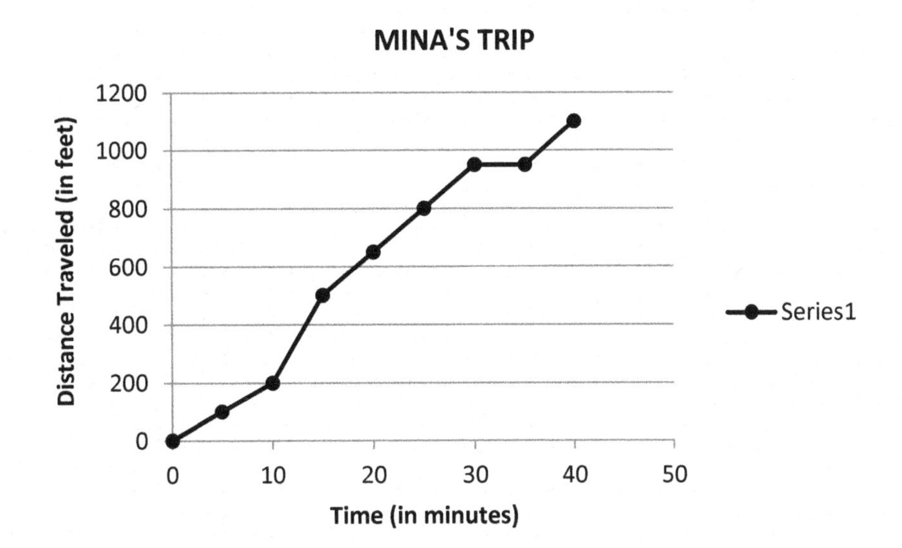

What was Mina's speed during the interval when she walked the fastest?

(A) 20 ft/min
(B) 30 ft/min
(C) 50 ft/min
(D) 60 ft/min

17. A student club has 16 members with 8 boys and 8 girls. To represent the club at an upcoming event, 2 members are randomly chosen, one at a time. What is the probability that both members chosen will be girls?

(A) $\frac{1}{2}$
(B) $\frac{1}{4}$
(C) $\frac{7}{15}$
(D) $\frac{7}{30}$

18. In the figure below, a cable is connected at one end to the ground, and at the other end to the top of a pole that is 80 feet away. If the cable is 100 feet long, what is the area of the triangle formed by the cable?

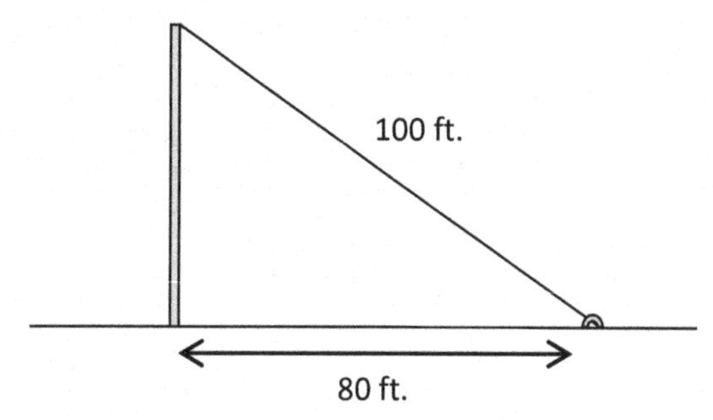

(A) 1200 ft^2
(B) 2400 ft^2
(C) 4800 ft^2
(D) 8000 ft^2

19. What is the value of the expression $(4)^{\frac{1}{2}} \times (2^3 + 2)$?

(A) 8
(B) 10
(C) 20
(D) 160

20. The vertices of Square $QRST$ bisect each of the four sides of Square $ABCD$. Which value is equivalent to the sum of the perimeters of Triangle QAR and Triangle SCT?

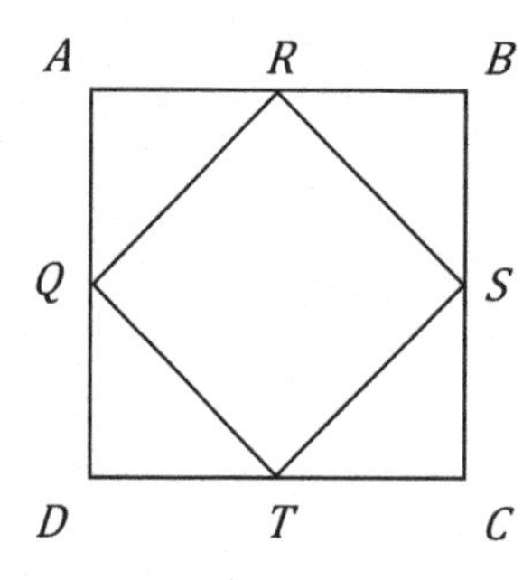

(A) The perimeter of Square $ABCD$.
(B) Twice the perimeter of Square $QRST$.
(C) The sum of the perimeters of Square $QRST$ and Square $ABCD$.
(D) The sum of the perimeters of Square $QRST$ and Square $ABCD$ divided by 2.

21. Charles can choose five numbers to put on the empty slots on his lottery ticket. All five numbers must be different, and each number must be greater than zero and only one digit. What is the probability that Charles will choose the correct combination of numbers?

(A) $\frac{1}{\left(\frac{1}{9/(9\times5)}\right)}$

(B) $\frac{1}{(9\times8\times7\times6\times5)}$

(C) $\frac{1}{(9\times8\times7\times6\times5\times4\times3\times2\times1)}$

(D) $\frac{1}{\left(\frac{9\times5}{5\times4\times3\times2\times1}\right)}$

22. x and y are both integers. If $-3 \leq x \leq -1$ and $1 \leq y \leq 3$ then which of the following expressions has the greatest value?

(A) $x^3 + y$
(B) $2x + y$
(C) $x^2 + y^2$
(D) $x^3 + y^2$

23. The perimeter of an isosceles triangle is 18 inches. If the area and all sides of the triangle are measured in whole inches, what is the greatest possible area of the triangle?

(A) 18 in^2
(B) 12 in^2
(C) 10 in^2
(D) 6 in^2

24. What is the value of the expression $8 \times (2^3 + 2^4 - 2^2) \div (32 \times (2^3 + 16))$?

(A) $2^8 - \frac{5}{3}$

(B) 7×2^5

(C) 2^7

(D) $\frac{5}{3} \times 2^{-3}$

25. A bag contains red, blue, and green tickets. The probability of picking a red ticket is 0.24 and the probability of picking a blue ticket is 0.16. What is the least number of tickets that could be in the bag?

(A) 5
(B) 25
(C) 50
(D) 100

QUANTITATIVE COMPARISONS

MIDDLE/UPPER LEVEL ONLY

PART 2

QUANTITATIVE COMPARISON STRATEGIES

SECTION 1

In the Middle and Upper Level Quantitative Reasoning section, you will see 14-17 quantitative comparison questions in the second half of this section. Continue reading about the best strategies for approaching this question type.

Note: Quantitative comparisons are not included on the Lower Level ISEE. If you are a Lower Level student, you should skip this section.

WHAT ARE QUANTITATIVE COMPARISONS?

Quantitative comparison questions give you values in two columns, Column A and Column B. These questions ask you to compare the values in the two columns and then select one of the following multiple-choice answers on your answer sheet:

(A) The quantity in Column A is greater.
(B) The quantity in Column B is greater.
(C) The two quantities are equal.
(D) The relationship cannot be determined from the information given.

These answer choices will be the same for every quantitative comparison question: either one of the columns will be greater (A or B), the two columns will be equal (C), or you will not be able to determine the relationship from the information given (D).

Here is an example:

Column A	Column B
$10 - (2 \times 6) \div 4 + 2$	$10 - 4 \div 1 \times 2 + 6$

This question is asking you to compare the values of each column and determine whether one is bigger than the other, whether the values are equal, or whether it's impossible to determine with the information provided. For this question, we can calculate the value of each column using the Order of Operations, and then compare the two results:

Column A	Column B
$10 - (2 \times 6) \div 4 + 2 =$	$10 - 4 \div 1 \times 2 + 6 =$
$10 - 12 \div 4 + 2 =$	$10 - 4 \times 2 + 6 =$
$10 - 3 + 2 = 9$	$10 - 8 + 6 = 8$

9 is greater than 8, so the correct answer is (A): the quantity in Column A is greater. (*To review the Order of Operations, see page 214*)

These answer options look a little strange, but remember that just like the rest of the ISEE, every quantitative comparison question will have only **one correct answer**. You will be able to determine that one column is greater than the other all of the time, or that the two columns are equal all of the time, or that the relationships could be different in different situations. Continue reading for some strategies to help you select the best answer every time.

APPROACHING QUANTITATIVE COMPARISONS

The quantitative questions seem tricky, but they don't actually test any new math concepts. Instead, they ask you to think a little outside of the box and apply your logical reasoning skills as well as the math you know. Here are some strategies to help you solve these questions confidently and efficiently.

KNOW WHAT THE ANSWER CHOICES MEAN

As we just saw, each quantitative comparison question has exactly the same answer choices:

(A) The quantity in Column A is greater.
(B) The quantity in Column B is greater.
(C) The two quantities are equal.
(D) The relationship cannot be determined from the information given.

Only one answer choice will be correct for each question. In order to understand these questions, it is important to learn what these answer choices mean and what you need to do in order to pick an answer.

In order to select answer choice (A) or (B), you'll need to prove to yourself that the quantity in one of the columns is greater *all of the time*. Similarly, in order to select answer choice (C), you'll need to prove that the quantities in the two columns are equal *all of the time*. If one of the two columns is sometimes greater but not always, or the two columns can be equal sometimes but not always, then the answer is (D)—you don't have enough information to determine the relationship.

Answer choice (D) is actually the easiest answer choice to prove. All you have to do is find one situation where one column is greater, and then find a second situation where that column is not greater. Because neither column is greater all of the time, you can rule out answers (A) and (B). Because the columns are not equal all of the time, you can also rule out answer (C)—and you know the answer must be (D). Here is an example:

Column A	Column B
x	10

The quantity in Column A is a variable (x), which stands for a number. Because the question doesn't tell you any information about what number x could be, it might stand for any number. If $x = 200$, it would be greater than 10, which is the value in Column B. However, if $x = 5$, it would be less than 10. Therefore, the answer is (D) because it is impossible to tell which value is greater.

Exercise #1: For each of the following example questions, the answer is (D): the relationship cannot be determined from the information given. Read each question carefully and explain why (D) is the answer. Have a trusted reader check your work.

1.

Column A	Column B
The number of bananas that can be purchased for 5 dollars	The number of oranges that can be purchased for 5 dollars

***Answer: (D).** My explanation:*

2.

Column A	Column B
Max's height	Max's dad's height

***Answer: (D).** My explanation:*

3.

Column A	Column B
The perimeter of an equilateral triangle	The perimeter of a square

***Answer: (D).** My explanation:*

---

4. A pair of jeans costs $40.

Column A	Column B
The cost of the jeans after an x% discount	$38

***Answer: (D).** My explanation:*

5. Mary draws two shapes: a pentagon and a hexagon.

Column A	Column B
The measure of the largest angle in the pentagon	The measure of the largest angle in the hexagon.

Answer: (D). *My explanation:*

SIMPLIFY THE QUESTION

It's much easier to compare the two columns in a quantitative comparison question if you **simplify** their values. For example, take a look at the question below:

Column A	Column B
$\frac{1}{2}+\frac{5}{6}$	3

Here you might decide to turn the value in Column A into a single fraction. $^1/_2$ is equal to $^3/_6$, so the expression in Column A is equal to 8/6:

Column A	Column B
$\frac{3}{6}+\frac{5}{6}=\frac{8}{6}$	3

You don't need to worry about dividing 8 by 6 to find the exact value of Column A. Because you know that 8/6 is only a little bigger than 6/6, you can estimate that the value in Column A is only a little bigger than 1. This value is definitely less than 3, so the answer is (B): the quantity in Column B is greater.

For some questions, it might be simpler to add, subtract, multiply, or divide the same number by the values in **both columns**. Think about the two columns as two sides of an inequality or an equation. You're not sure what sign is supposed to connect the two columns—it might be a greater-than sign (>), a less-than sign (<), or an equals sign (=). However, you know that you can add, subtract, multiply, or divide the two sides of any equation or inequality by the same positive number, and the equation or inequality will stay the same. (*See pages 257-270 for a review of equations and inequalities*).

Take another look at the previous example. After you found that Column A was equal to $^8/_6$, you could multiply both columns by 6:

Column A	Column B
$\frac{8}{6} \times 6 = 8$	$3 \times 6 = 18$

Now it is obvious that Column B has the greater value: 18 is much bigger than 8!

You can add or subtract both columns by any number or variable you choose, but it is important to remember that you can **only multiply or divide both columns by a positive number**. This is because the two columns might represent two sides of an inequality, and multiplying or dividing by a negative number would reverse the inequality. For example, let's say you started with the inequality $4 < 12$. Dividing both sides of this inequality by 4 would give $1 < 3$, which is a correct inequality. Dividing both sides of the same inequality by -4 would give $-1 < -3$, which is wrong! When you multiply or divide both sides of an inequality by a negative number, you have to reverse the inequality. Because of this complication, it's best to multiply and divide only by positive numbers. And because a variable might be positive or negative (or even zero), you should not multiply or divide by a variable.

Exercise #2: For each of the following example questions, simplify the values to solve the question. Check your answer in the answer key at the back of the book.

	Column A	Column B	Answer
1.	$\frac{17}{6}$	3	Ⓐ Ⓑ Ⓒ Ⓓ
2.	$\frac{1}{3} + \frac{2}{7}$	$\frac{1}{2}$	Ⓐ Ⓑ Ⓒ Ⓓ
3.	$\frac{2}{3} + \frac{1}{4}$	$\frac{8}{9}$	Ⓐ Ⓑ Ⓒ Ⓓ
4.	$\frac{1}{2} + \frac{1}{3} + \frac{1}{4}$	$\frac{3}{8} + \frac{5}{12}$	Ⓐ Ⓑ Ⓒ Ⓓ

PAY ATTENTION TO VARIABLES

If the question contains no variables, only numbers, then you will always be able to determine the relationship between the quantities in the two columns. Using estimation or calculation, you will be able to figure out if one of the values is bigger or smaller than the other, or if the two are equal. If your question contains variables, however, it might be trickier to figure out the relationship between the two columns. Here are some strategies to make this process easier.

Pay attention to **which variables** appear in each column. If the two columns contain different variables, they might stand for different numbers. For example:

Column A	Column B
$p + 8$	$2q + 2$

In this case, there is no way to know which value is bigger. p could be very small and q could be very big, or vice-versa. The answer is (D): the relationship cannot be determined from the information given.

If the two columns contain the same variable, you know that the variable stands for the same number in each expression. However, you may need to **simplify the expression** to see whether you can determine the relationship between the two columns. Use the distributive property to expand the expression, and then add or subtract like terms. (*See pages 247-258 for a review of algebraic expressions.*) For example, take a look at the question below:

Column A	Column B
$3(x + 4) + 5(x - 2)$	$8x + 2$

You need to simplify the expression in Column A in order to compare it to the expression in Column B. You would first expand this expression using the distributive property:

Column A	Column B
$3(x + 4) + 5(x - 2) =$ $3x + 12 + 5x - 10$	$8x + 2$

Then, you would add and subtract like terms:

Column A	Column B
$3x + 12 + 5x - 10 =$ $8x + 2$	$8x + 2$

Now that you have simplified Column A, you can see that the expressions in the two columns are identical. Because both expressions contain the same variable (x), you know that

x stands for the same number in both expressions. For example, if $x = 1$, both Column A and Column B will equal $8 \times 1 + 2 = 10$. If $x = 1000$, both Column A and Column B will equal $8 \times 1000 + 2 = 8002$. Because both columns will always be equal, the answer is (C): the two quantities are equal.

However, even if both columns contain the same variable, you still may not be able to determine which expression has the greater value. For example:

Column A	Column B
$x + 8$	$2x + 2$

You can simplify the question by subtracting 2 from both columns. Subtracting 2 from both sides of the inequality will not change the relationship between the value in Column A and the value in Column B:

Column A	Column B
$x + 8 - 2 =$ $x + 6$	$2x$

Similarly, subtracting x from both sides will not change the relationship:

Column A	Column B
6	x

Which is bigger, 6 or x? We don't know. For example, if $x = 0$, 6 is bigger. If $x = 10$, x is bigger. Finally, if $x = 6$, the two values are equal. This leaves us with answer (D): the relationship cannot be determined from the information given.

Exercise #3: For each of the following example questions, pay attention to the variables to solve the question. Check your answer in the answer key at the back of the book.

	Column A	Column B	Answer
1.	$m+7$	$n-4$	Ⓐ Ⓑ Ⓒ Ⓓ
2.	$x+3$	$x-5$	Ⓐ Ⓑ Ⓒ Ⓓ
3.	$2(x-3)$	$2x-3$	Ⓐ Ⓑ Ⓒ Ⓓ
4.	x^2+7	x^2+3	Ⓐ Ⓑ Ⓒ Ⓓ
5.	$3(x+6)$	$3x+18$	Ⓐ Ⓑ Ⓒ Ⓓ
6.	$5(x-2)+3(x-2)$	$2(4x-2)$	Ⓐ Ⓑ Ⓒ Ⓓ
7.	$3-(x-4)$	$x+7$	Ⓐ Ⓑ Ⓒ Ⓓ

PLUG IN NUMBERS

If you get stuck on a question involving algebra, try plugging in numbers to the expressions you are given. If you are smart about which numbers you pick, you can quickly eliminate several answer choices and point yourself towards the correct response. In order to make sure that you have accounted for all possibilities, plug in several extreme values: small numbers, large numbers, fractions, and zero.

For example, let's look at the last example again:

Column A	Column B
$x + 8$	$2x + 2$

If you weren't sure how to simplify these expressions so they are easier to compare, you could test out some values for x and then compare the results. Zero is often a good number to plug in. If $x = 0$, Column A is equal to 8 and Column B is equal to 2. It looks like Column A is bigger than Column B.

However, you should never pick an answer choice without testing some extreme values. Let's try 1000. If $x = 1000$, Column A is equal to $1000 + 8 = 1008$ and Column B is equal to $2 \times 1000 + 2 = 2002$. In this case, Column B is bigger than Column A. Because neither column is greater all of the time, we can conclude that the answer is (D): the relationship cannot be determined from the information given.

When you pick numbers to plug in, be careful what conclusions you draw. For example, if you started by plugging in 0 and then tried -1000, you would see that Column A is bigger than Column B both times. This might lead you to believe that the answer is (A), when you actually haven't tested enough values to see that the answer is (D). Remember that plugging in numbers can help you eliminate answer choices, but if you don't test enough values, it may not point you directly to an answer choice.

Plugging in numbers can also be helpful if your question involves two different variables. Here is an example:

$$x < y$$

Column A	Column B
$-x$	$3y$

First try plugging in zero for x. If $x = 0$, then Column A is equal to 0 and y is greater than 0:

$$0 < y$$

Column A	Column B
0	$3y$

If y is greater than 0, then $3y$ is certainly greater than 0. The value in Column B is greater.

Now try plugging in a negative number for x, like -5. If $x = -5$, then Column A is equal to 5, and y is greater than -5:

$$-5 < y$$

Column A	Column B
$-(-5) = 5$	$3y$

We already know that Column B is at least sometimes greater than Column A. Is there any value for y that would make Column B less than Column A? We'd have to find a value for y that is greater than -5, but smaller than 5 when multiplied by 3. What if y equals zero?

$$-5 < 0$$

Column A	Column B
5	0

If $y = 0$, Column B can sometimes be less than Column A. Because Column B is sometimes greater than and sometimes less than Column A, the answer is (D): the relationship cannot be determined from the information given.

Exercise #4: For each of the example questions below, plug in numbers to solve the question. Check your answer in the answer key at the back of the book.

	Column A	Column B	Answer
1.	$5x + 4$	$5x + 6$	Ⓐ Ⓑ Ⓒ Ⓓ

	Column A	Column B	Answer
2.	$2x - 5$	$3x + 10$	Ⓐ Ⓑ Ⓒ Ⓓ

	Column A	Column B	Answer
3.	$x^2 + 3$	$10x$	Ⓐ Ⓑ Ⓒ Ⓓ

4.

Column A	Column B	Answer
$x^2 + 3$	$-2x$	Ⓐ Ⓑ Ⓒ Ⓓ

---

5. $ab > cd$

Column A	Column B	Answer
$a + b$	$c + d$	Ⓐ Ⓑ Ⓒ Ⓓ

---

6. $0 < x < 1$

Column A	Column B	Answer
x^2	x^3	Ⓐ Ⓑ Ⓒ Ⓓ

Questions 7 and 8 are Upper Level Only.

7. $0 < x < 1$

Column A	Column B	Answer
$\sqrt{2x}$	$\sqrt{x}$	Ⓐ Ⓑ Ⓒ Ⓓ

---

8. $x \neq 0$

Column A	Column B	Answer
$\frac{1}{x}$	$\frac{1}{\sqrt{x}}$	Ⓐ Ⓑ Ⓒ Ⓓ

LOOK FOR SHORTCUTS

Some questions do not have to be solved all the way through. Instead, you can arrive at the correct answer by finding a shortcut, estimating, or making a smart guess. Here is an example:

Column A	Column B
23×97	17×93

You don't need to calculate the exact value in these two columns in order to determine which is greater. 23 is greater than 17 and 97 is greater than 93, so 23×97 must be greater than 17×93. The answer is (A): the quantity in Column A is greater.

Here is another example:

Column A	Column B
The number of 30 cent apples that can be purchased for 5 dollars	The number of 35 cent pears that can be purchased for 5 dollars

You could divide 30 cents into 5 dollars, and then divide 35 cents into 5 dollars. But the truth is that you don't need to know how many apples or pears 5 dollars can buy—all you need to know is whether you can buy more apples or pears. Since you have the same amount of money in both situations, common sense tells you that you can buy more of something that is cheaper. This means that you can buy more apples, so the answer is (A): the quantity in Column A is greater.

However, make sure you think about the question carefully! The test makers could try to trick you with a question like this:

Column A	Column B
The number of 17 cent baseball cards that can be purchased for 2 dollars	The number of 18 cent hockey cards that can be purchased for 2 dollars

In this case, the values in the two columns are actually equal! Although it seems logical that you'd be able to purchase more baseball cards because they are cheaper, if you try calculating the exact number you could buy, you'll end up with a decimal: $2 \div 0.17$ is about 11.76. Because you can only buy a whole number of sports cards, it doesn't matter that the cards in Column B cost one cent more. In both cases, you can only buy 11 cards with 2 dollars. The answer is (C): the two quantities are equal.

Exercise #5: For each of the example questions below, look for a shortcut to solve the question. Check your answer in the answer key at the back of the book.

	Column A	Column B	Answer
1.	$2000 - 1.7850$	$2000 - 1.7849$	Ⓐ Ⓑ Ⓒ Ⓓ
2.	16×0.39	0.389×16	Ⓐ Ⓑ Ⓒ Ⓓ
3.	The number of hours in a week	The number of seconds in half an hour	Ⓐ Ⓑ Ⓒ Ⓓ
4.	39×77	41×79	Ⓐ Ⓑ Ⓒ Ⓓ
5.	$\frac{2}{3} \times \frac{3}{4} \times \frac{4}{5} \times \frac{5}{6}$	$\frac{1}{3}$	Ⓐ Ⓑ Ⓒ Ⓓ
6.	$\frac{2}{3} + \frac{8}{9} + \frac{11}{12} + \frac{19}{20}$	$\frac{20}{5}$	Ⓐ Ⓑ Ⓒ Ⓓ
7.	$(-7)^2$	-7^2	Ⓐ Ⓑ Ⓒ Ⓓ

8. Tess cuts a 12cm string into several pieces of equal length. There are fewer than 10 pieces.

Column A	Column B	Answer
The length of each piece	1.2 cm	Ⓐ Ⓑ Ⓒ Ⓓ

QUANTITATIVE COMPARISON PRACTICE QUESTIONS

SECTION 2

In this section, you will find 105 practice questions to prepare you for the types of quantitative comparison questions you might find on the ISEE. The Middle Level questions cover the full range of content that you will find on the Middle Level exam, as well as a large portion of content that you will find on the Upper Level exam. The Upper Level questions cover content that you will only find on the Upper Level exam.

Using the information given in each question, compare the quantity in Column A to the quantity in Column B. All questions have these answer choices:

(A) The quantity in Column A is greater.
(B) The quantity in Column B is greater.
(C) The two quantities are equal.
(D) The relationship cannot be determined from the information given.

MIDDLE LEVEL QUESTIONS

Use these questions to practice the full range of content that you will see on the Middle Level ISEE, as well as a large portion of the content that you will see on the Upper Level ISEE. Both Middle and Upper Level students should attempt these questions.

1.

Column A	Column B
$-(-8+5)\times 3+4$	-5

2. A bridge is split into four different segments. Rickie has just ridden his bicycle across the first two segments, and is starting on the third segment.

Segment	Distance
Segment 1	195ft
Segment 2	300ft
Segment 3	150ft
Segment 4	335ft

Column A	Column B
The total distance Rickie has traveled across the bridge	The total distance left for Rickie to travel across the bridge

3. Students in a class are asked whether they prefer juice or water.

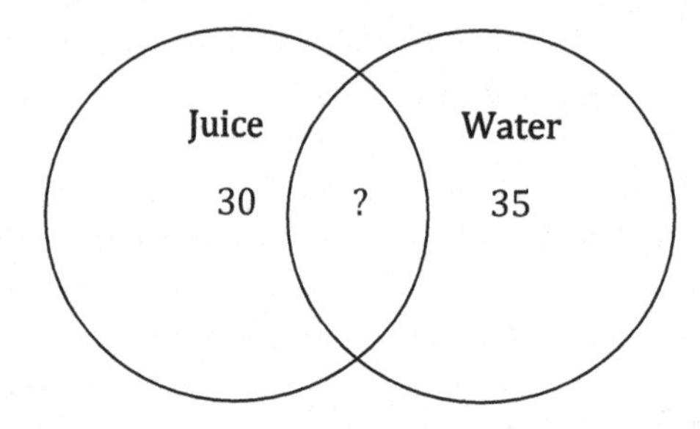

Column A	Column B
The number of students who prefer juice	The number of students who have no preference

4.

Column A	Column B
$\sqrt{100 - 36}$	$\sqrt{100} - \sqrt{36}$

5. The Northampton train takes 20 minutes to get from Northampton to Burberry, and the Southampton train takes 30 minutes to get from Southampton to Burberry. The Northampton train travels at 60 miles per hour, and the Southampton train travels at 50 miles per hour.

Column A	Column B
The distance from Northampton to Burberry	The distance from Southampton to Burberry

6. Gordon purchased a book and received \$0.94 change in quarters, dimes, and pennies. (Note: 1 penny $= \$.01$; 1 dime $= \$.10$; 1 quarter $= \$.25$)

Column A	Column B
12	The smallest number of coins that Gordon could receive

7. A and B are two side lengths of the rectangle below:

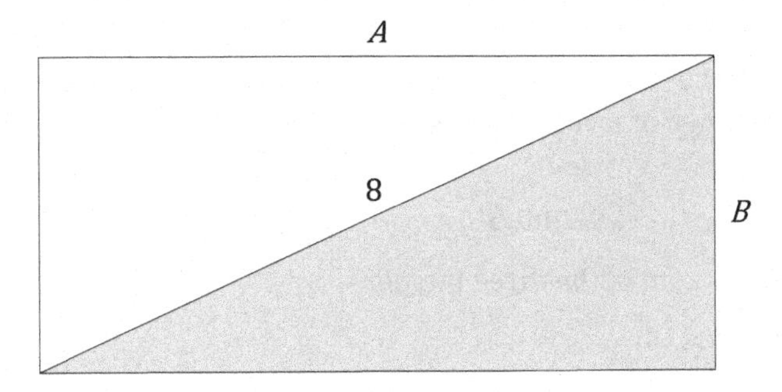

Column A	Column B
$\frac{A \times B}{2}$	The area of the shaded region

8. Ahmed has 5 shirts, 4 hats, and 3 ties. He chooses one shirt, one hat, and one tie to wear.

Column A	Column B
The number of combinations that Ahmed can choose.	12

---

9. Exam scores out of 55 for a class of 9 people are represented in the stem-and-leaf plot below:

Stem	Leaf
3	1 2 2
4	0 3 4
5	0 0 0

Column A	Column B
The mode of the scores	The mean of the scores

---

10. The average of three consecutive odd integers is 15.

Column A	Column B
The sum of the three integers	40

---

11. One eighth of the town's population was born in December.

Column A	Column B
The probability that a town citizen chosen at random was born in December	The probability that a town citizen chosen at random was born in February

12. Column A: $2 + 4 \times 5 - (3 + 1)$ — Column B: 19

---

13. Equation A: $3a - 2 = 6$

Equation B: $4b + 6 = 2$

Column A: a — Column B: b

---

14. Column A: $(-2)^4$ — Column B: 4^2

---

15. Column A: The slope of the line $0 = 6y - 12x + 8$ — Column B: The slope of the line $y = 2x - 9$

---

16. Postal Route A — Postal Route B

50 meters — 50 meters

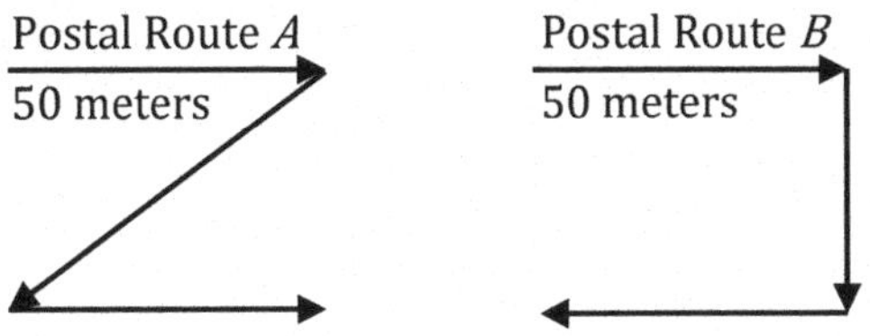

Column A: The total length of Route A — Column B: The total length of Route B

17. A spinner is divided into six sections: two quarters and four eighths.

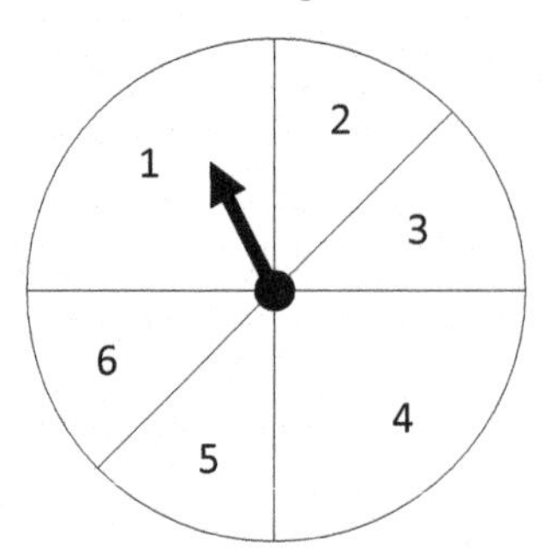

Column A	Column B
The probability that that the spinner will land on 1 or 4	The probability that the spinner will land on an even number

---

18. Tank A and tank B can both hold exactly 10 gallons of water. The tanks are being filled by two hoses that pump water at the same rate.

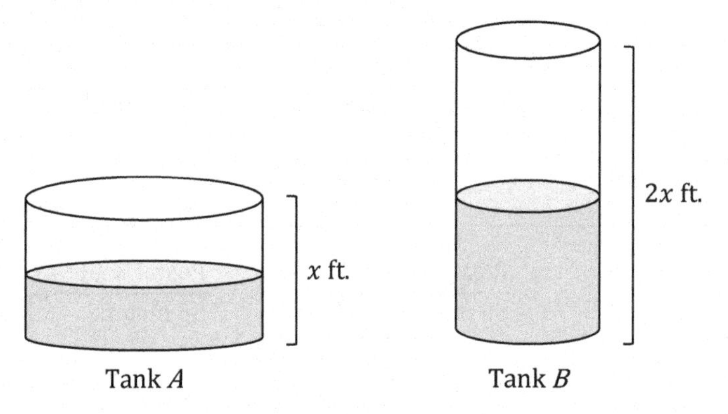

Column A	Column B
The amount of time it takes for Tank A's water level to rise by one inch	The amount of time it takes for Tank B's water level to rise by one inch

19. The histogram shows the number of pets owned by each student in a small class.

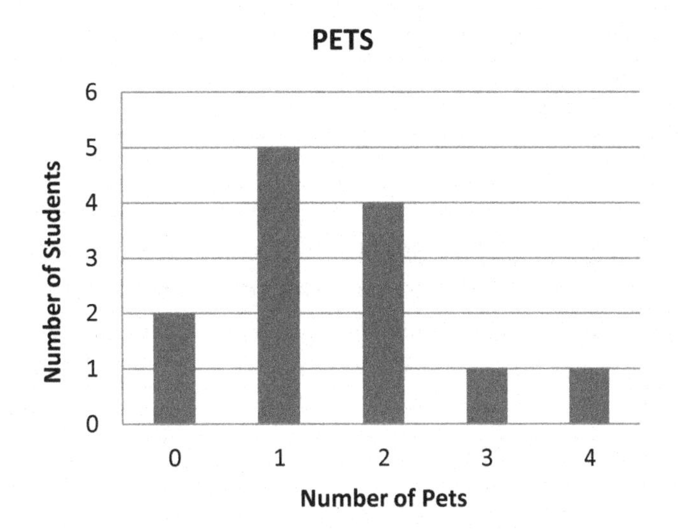

Column A	Column B
The mode of the data	The median of the data

20.

Column A	Column B
$\sqrt{3.2}$	$\sqrt{\frac{3}{2}}$

21.

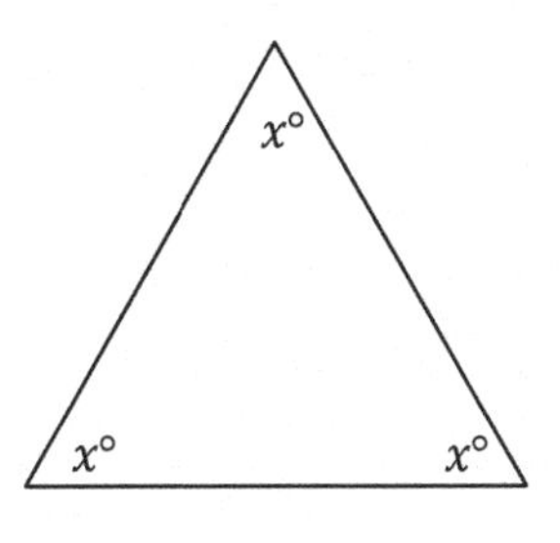

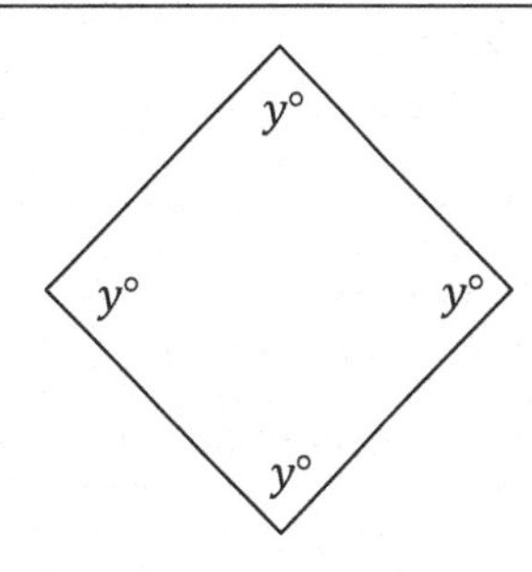

Column A	Column B
$3x$	$2y$

22. The expression $2x$ rounds to 8 when rounded to the nearest whole number.

Column A	Column B
x	3.7

---

23. To predict how two groups of people would vote on a proposal, samples of each group were surveyed to see if they would vote YES on the proposal. The surveyors used the results from these samples to predict the number of YES votes for the entire group.

Group	A	B
Number of YES votes	12	11
Predicted number of YES votes when an entire group votes	36	44

Column A	Column B
The percent of group A that was surveyed	The percent of group B that was surveyed

---

24. Use the table from question 23 to answer this question.

Column A	Column B
The total number of people in group A	The total number of people in group B

---

25. Marcus has two 6-sided number cubes, each with sides numbered from 1-6. He rolls them at the same time.

Column A	Column B
The probability that both cubes land on 6	The probability that one cube lands on 3 and one cube lands on 5

26. Three angles have measures of $a°$, $b°$, and $c°$:

$$a° = c°$$
$$a° + b° = 70°$$
$$a° + b° + c° = 90°$$

Column A	Column B
$a°$	$b°$

27.

Column A	Column B
$\sqrt{9^2} - (2^2 - 3) + 2$	10

---

28. James walks at 4 kilometers per hour. Joyce walks at 6 kilometers per hour. James lives 5 km away from school, and Joyce lives 8 km away from school.

Column A	Column B
Time required for James to walk to school	Time required for Joyce to walk to school

---

29.

Column A	Column B
The probability of rolling two 2s in a row with one six-sided number cube	The probability of rolling two 2s at the same time with two six-sided number cubes

30. The pattern shown below can be folded into a pyramid.

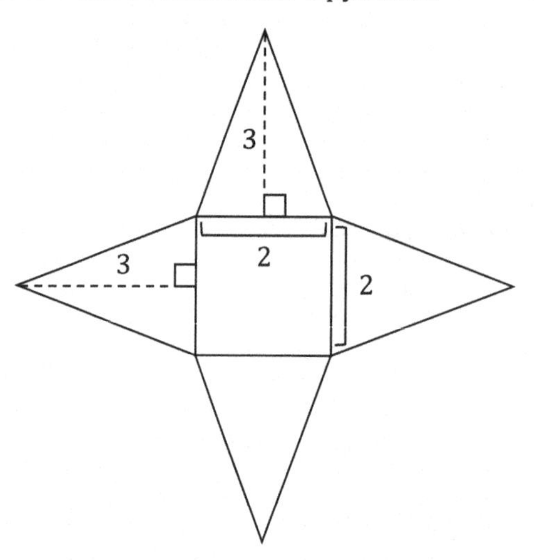

Column A	Column B
The surface area of a cube whose volume is 8	The surface area of the pyramid above

---

31. Skylar has a baseball, a marble, and a bowling ball and wants to trade them with Xiao. Xiao is willing to trade them using the following values.

$$1\ baseball = 5\ marbles$$
$$1\ bowling\ ball = 8\ baseballs$$

Column A	Column B
The number of marbles equivalent to 3 bowling balls	116

---

32. There are 24 students in John's class. The class buys 8 pies that are all the same size. Ishmael eats 1 half of a pie and Cindy eats 1 third of a pie. The remaining pies are divided equally between the other 22 students.

Column A	Column B
The amount of pie that Cindy eats	The average amount of pie per student remaining after Ishmael and Cindy eat their pie

33. As a delivery company increases its number of deliveries, shipping costs decrease per delivery.

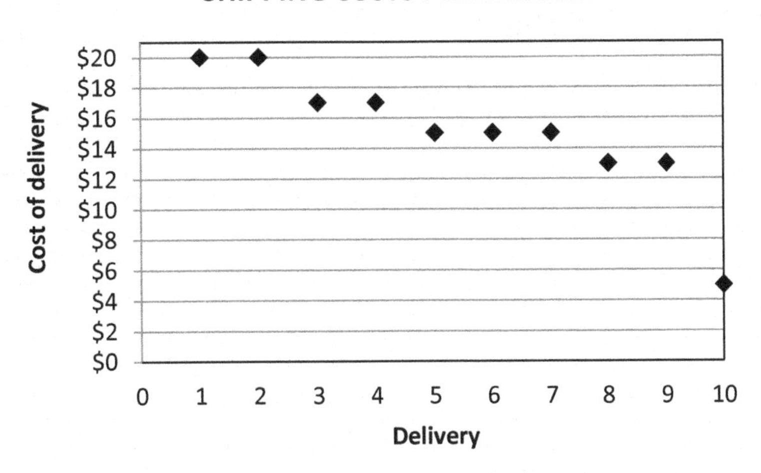

Column A	Column B
The median cost per delivery	The cost of the 5th delivery

34.

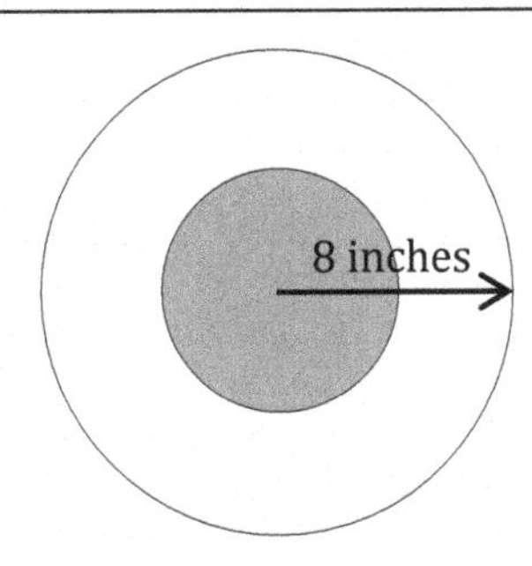

$$Circumference\ of\ circle = 2\pi r$$
$$Area\ of\ a\ circle = \pi r^2$$

Column A	Column B
The circumference of the inner circle	The area of the outer circle

---

35. $y = 2x - 2$

Column A	Column B
The value of x when $y = 8$	The value of y when $x = 2$

36. On Tuesday, Store B had 20% lower prices for jeans than Store A. On Wednesday, Store A decreased its prices for jeans by 10%. On Thursday, Store A decreased its prices for jeans by another 10%.

Column A	Column B
The price of Store B's jeans on Tuesday	The price of Store A's jeans on Thursday

---

37.

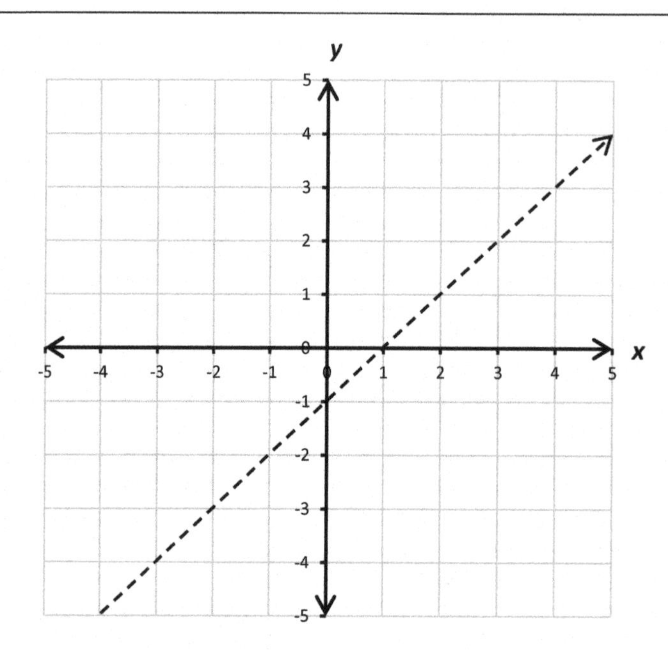

Column A	Column B
The slope of the dashed line	The slope of a line passing through $(-2, -4)$ and $(-1, -2)$

---

38. 13 tickets are shuffled. Each of the tickets has a number between 0 and 99 and Maria chooses a ticket at random.

Column A	Column B
The probability of choosing a single digit number	The probability of choosing a double digit number

39. Column A: $\frac{1}{3}(k-10)$ | Column B: $\frac{1}{3}k-10$

Column A	Column B
$\frac{1}{3}(k-10)$	$\frac{1}{3}k-10$

---

40. Grace interviewed 30 people in her neighborhood to ask if they own cats or dogs. Every person she interviewed owns a cat, a dog, or both.

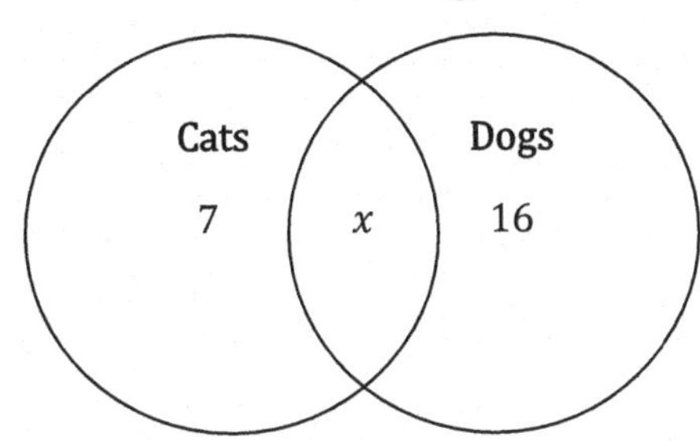

Column A	Column B
The value of x	9

41.

Column A	Column B
The slope of the line segment connecting points $(0,5)$ and $(2,-5)$	The slope of the line $y-5x=5$

---

42. In 2012, a village had a population of 17 people, and 1 of those people has a September birthday. In 2013, the village's population increased by 3 people.

Column A	Column B
The percentage of people in the village in 2013 with September birthdays	15%

43. Triangle 1 is translated and rotated on the coordinate plane below, and its final position is represented as Triangle 1'

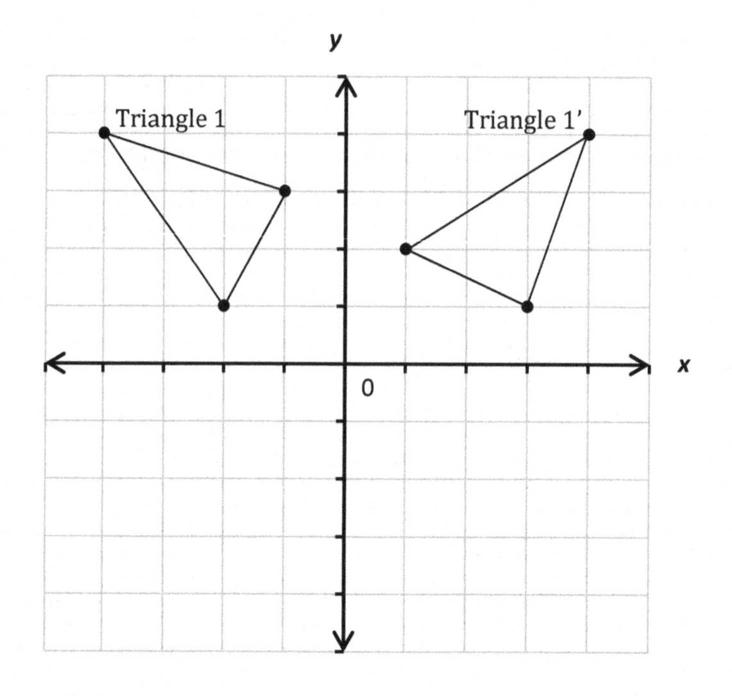

Column A	Column B
Area of Triangle 1'	Area of Triangle 1

44.

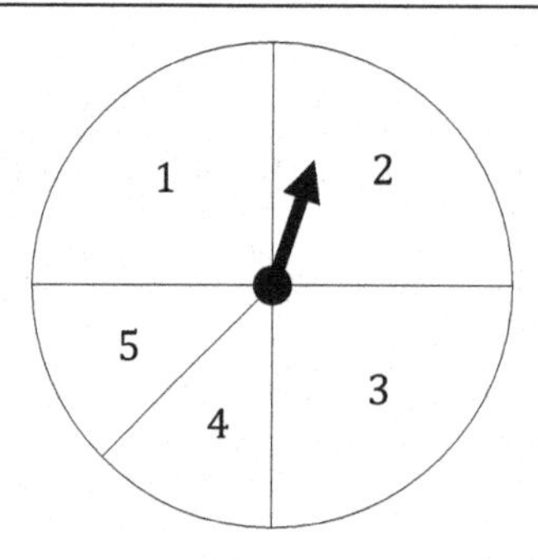

The spinner shown above is spun once and lands on one of the sections, which are numbered 1-5.

Column A	Column B
The probability of landing on an even number	The probability of landing on an odd number

45. Samantha paddles her canoe at a rate of 3 feet per second, but it takes her 20 minutes to set up her canoe. Cooper swims at a rate of 1 foot per second and can begin swimming immediately. They both have 30 minutes to travel as far as they can.

Column A	Column B
The distance that Samantha travels in feet	The distance that Cooper travels in feet

---

46.

$$\frac{x}{2} - 3 = 7$$

$$6 = 14 - 2y$$

Column A	Column B
x	y^2

---

47. Use the figure below to answer the question.

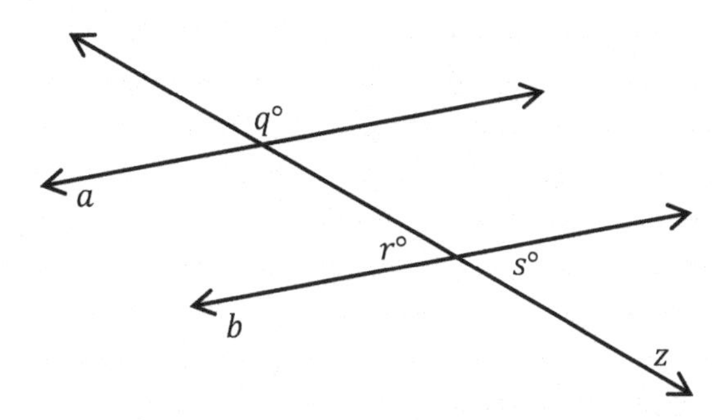

Parallel lines a and b are intersected by line z.

Column A	Column B
$q + r$	$q + s$

48. The original price of a shirt was $20.00

Column A	Column B
The final cost of the shirt after a 30% discount	The final cost of the shirt after it was put on sale for 20% off, and then on clearance for another 10% off of the sale price

---

49. Line w passes through coordinates $(0,12)$ and $(4,8)$.

Column A	Column B
The slope of line w	The slope of the line perpendicular to line w

---

50.

Figure 1

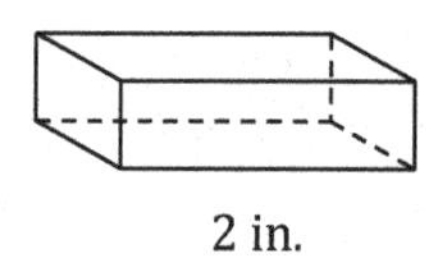

$V = 8$ inches^3

Figure 2

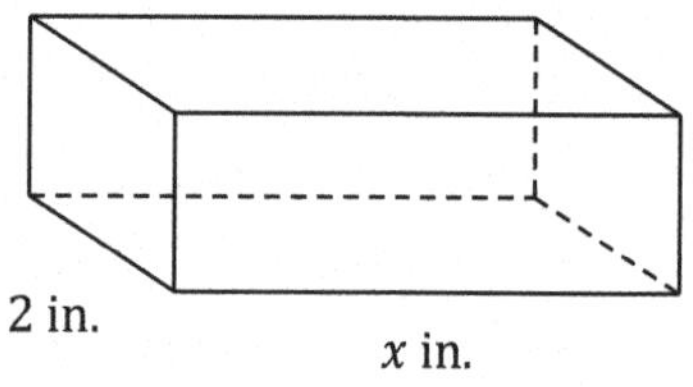

2 in.

x in.

$V = 64$ inches^3

Column A	Column B
x	16 inches

---

51. Martha's class has two boys for every girl.

Column A	Column B
The ratio of girls to boys in the class	30%

52. Students at two schools were interviewed about their reading preferences. A representative sample of students at each school was interviewed in order to predict the preferences of the whole student body. The percent of students who were interviewed and these students' responses are shown in the table below.

School	Interlocken	Geld
Percent interviewed	50%	25%
Students who prefer fiction	40	6
Students who prefer nonfiction	30	20

Column A	Column B
The predicted total number of students who prefer fiction at Interlocken	The predicted total number of students who prefer nonfiction at Geld

---

53. The equation for line d is $y = mx + a$

The equation for line s is $y = \frac{1}{3}x + b$

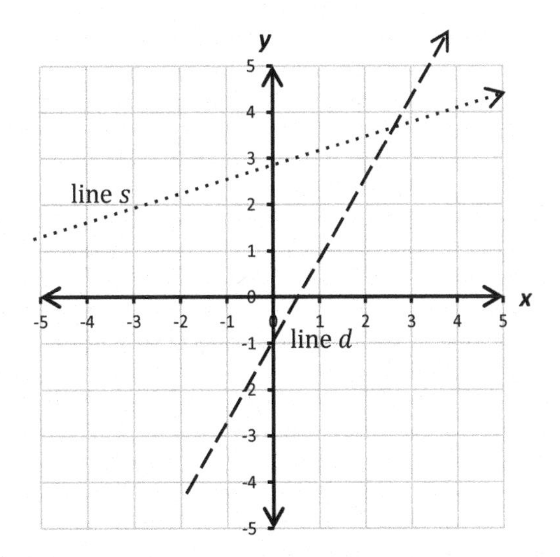

Column A	Column B
The value of a	The value of b

54.

Column A	Column B
0.03×10^{22}	2232×10^{17}

55.

$$12 < 3x < 18$$

Column A	Column B
5	x

---

56. Walter rolled a 2 on a six-sided number cube. He then rolled the number cube a second time.

Column A	Column B
The probability that Walter will have an average of 3 for the two numbers he rolls	The probability that Walter will roll a 2 the second time

---

57.

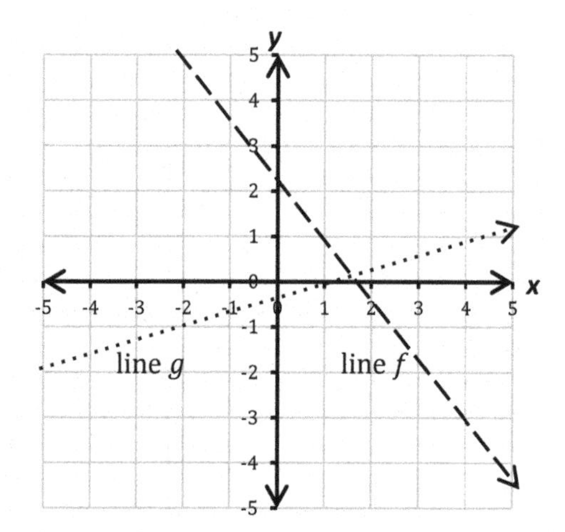

$\boldsymbol{m}$ represents the rate at which the y value of a line increases as the x value increases.

Column A	Column B
$\boldsymbol{m}$ of line f	$\boldsymbol{m}$ of line g

58. A board is divided evenly into squares that are numbered 1-100. A bean bag is randomly thrown at the board. Casey gets a point if the bean bag lands on a square with an odd number. Jordan gets a point if the bean bag lands on a square with an even number, or a number ending in 5.

Column A	Column B
The probability of Casey getting a point	The probability of Jordan getting a point

---

59.

Column A	Column B
The slope of the line perpendicular to $y = \frac{1}{2}x - 2$	The slope of $y = 2x - 2$

---

60. The high school math team buys sweatshirts for its members. An individual sweatshirt costs $10.00, but a standard discount is applied to the cost of each sweatshirt when the team buys more than one sweatshirt at a time. The discount applied is x%. The table below shows the cost of three different sweatshirt orders.

Number of sweatshirts	Total cost of sweatshirts
1	$10.00
4	$38.00
2	$19.00

Column A	Column B
The value of x	5

61. Bellville has a population of 9 people and an average of 3 vehicles per person. André, from a different city, has 6 vehicles.

Column A	Column B
The average number of vehicles per person in Bellville if André moves to Bellville.	3.2 vehicles/person

---

62.

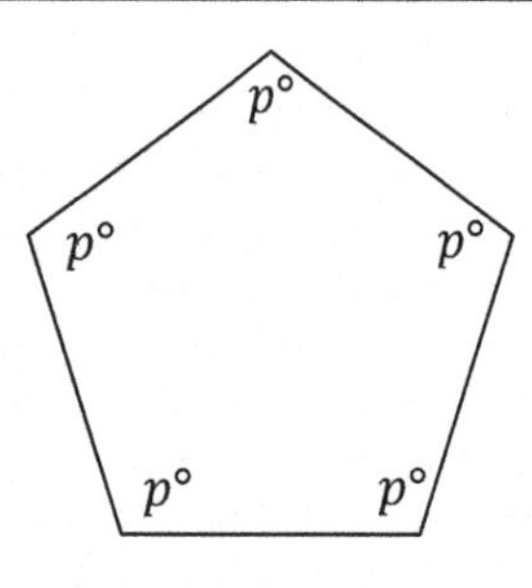

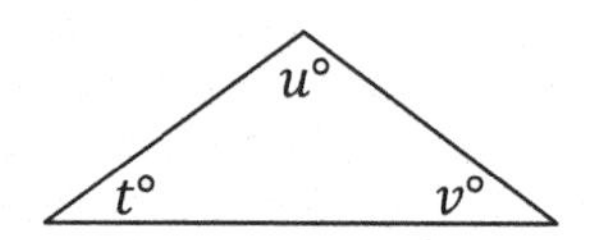

Column A	Column B
$5p$	$3(t + u + v)$

---

63. The equation for line m is $-4x = 6 - 2y$.

Column A	Column B
The slope of line m	The y-intercept of line m

UPPER LEVEL QUESTIONS

Use these questions to practice the most challenging difficulty level you will see on the Upper Level ISEE. Only Upper Level students should attempt these questions.

1.

Column A	Column B
2^{4y}	4^{2y}

---

2. Cone A has a radius of 4 cm and a height of 3 cm. Cone B has a radius that is $^1/_2$ that of Cone A, and a height that is three times that of Cone A. (The formula for the volume of a cone is $^1/_3\,\pi r^2 h$.)

Column A	Column B
Volume of Cone A	Volume of Cone B

---

3. A bag is full of nickels, dimes, and quarters. The probability of randomly selecting a nickel from the bag is $^1/_{10}$. (Note: 1 nickel = \$.05; 1 dime = \$.10; 1 quarter = \$.25)

Column A	Column B
The probability of randomly selecting a nickel and then a dime	The probability of randomly selecting a quarter and then a nickel

---

4. The product of three consecutive integers is 120.

Column A	Column B
The least of the three consecutive integers.	5

5.

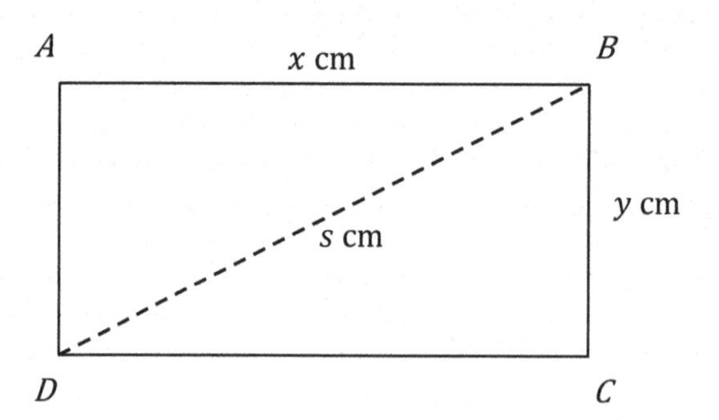

All angles that appear to be right angles are right angles.

Column A	Column B
s^2	$x^2 + y^2$

---

6. The graph below shows a function $f(x)$.

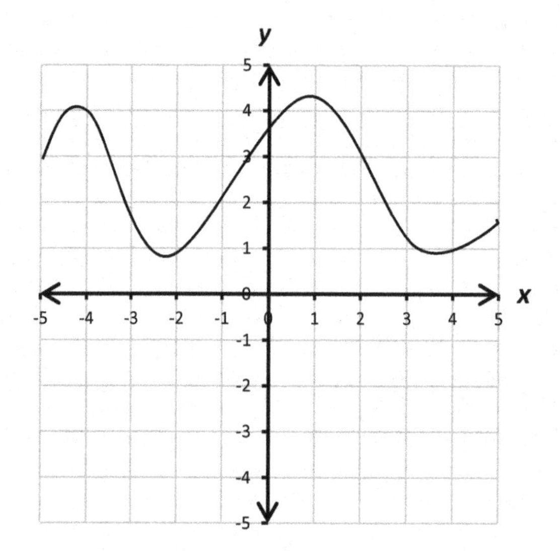

Column A	Column B
$f(0)$	$f(3)$

7. Jane has $2.20 in her pocket, consisting only of quarters and dimes. There are four times as many quarters as dimes. (Note: 1 dime = $\$.10$; 1 quarter = $\$.25$)

Column A	Column B
The total value of the dimes	$0.80

---

8. There are 60 marbles evenly divided into three colors: red, orange, and blue. Haji randomly picks 6 marbles.

Column A	Column B
The probability that all of his marbles are red	The probability that 2 of his marbles are blue

---

9.

Column A	Column B
$3^2 + 9^3$	$2^3 + 3^6$

10.

Column A	Column B
$(4x^8 - 9y^{10})$	$(2x^4 - 3y^5)(2x^4 + 3y^5)$

11. The rectangle below shows the route that Jonathan drives every day, beginning and ending at "Home." The dashed line shows a shortcut that Jonathan used one day.

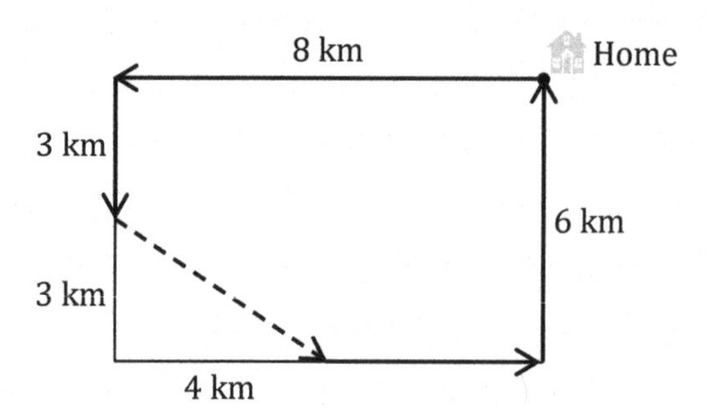

Column A	Column B
The distance Jonathan saved by taking the shortcut home instead of the regular route	5km

---

12.

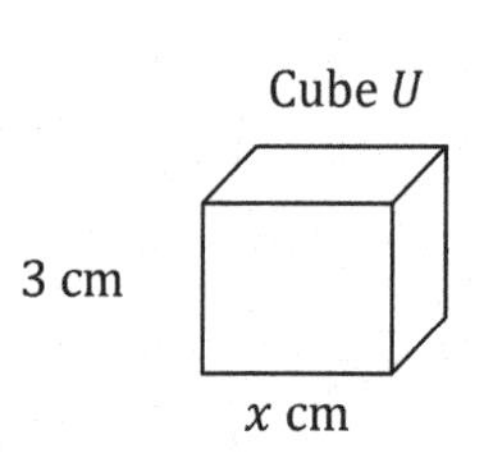

Cube W

$2x$ cm

Column A	Column B
The value of the surface area of cube W, in cm^2	The value of the volume of cube W, in cm^3

---

13. Use the function $f(x) = x^2 - (2 + x)$ to make the following comparison.

Column A	Column B
$f(0)$	$f(-2)$

14. x is an integer less than zero.

Column A	Column B
x^3	x^2

---

15. Elizabeth's jewelry case contains 2 pairs of gold earrings and 2 pairs of silver earrings. She puts one gold earring on her ear, and then randomly selects another earring.

Column A	Column B
The probability that both earrings are gold	The probability that one earring is gold and one earring is silver

---

16.

Column A	Column B
The measure of one interior angle of a regular hexagon	The sum of all the interior angles of a triangle

---

17.

$$-2h = 1$$

Column A	Column B
$\left(\frac{1}{4}\right)^h$	$(4)^h$

---

18. Sally wants to buy a chocolate bar from Bill. Bill bought the chocolate bar from a store at 10% off the regular price, and he is selling the bar to Sally at 10% more than the price he paid.

Column A	Column B
Regular price of the chocolate bar	The price Sally pays for the chocolate bar

19. The circle C shown below is reflected across the y-axis, creating circle C' whose center is at point (x, y).

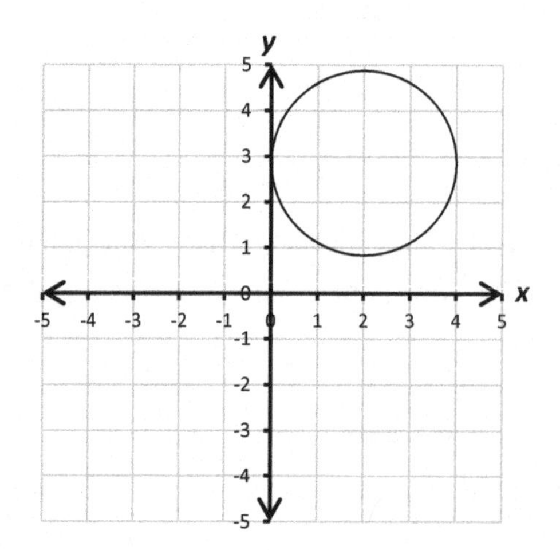

Column A	Column B
x	y

---

20. x is an odd integer that is greater than zero.

Column A	Column B
$(-7)^{2x}$	$(4)^x$

---

21. Triangle J is similar to triangle K, and both are right triangles.

Triangle J

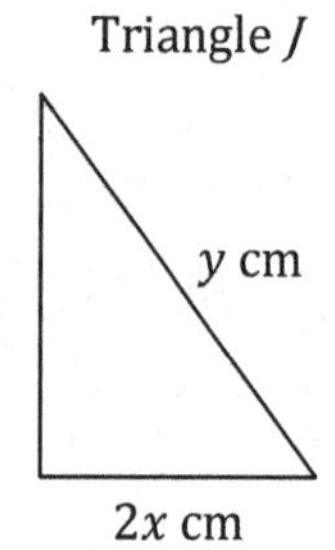

Triangle K

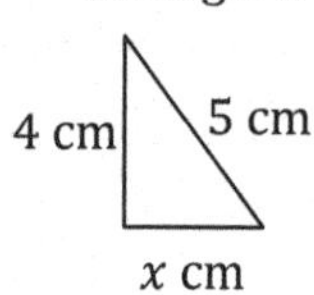

Column A	Column B
The value of $3x$	The value of y

22. x is a non-zero integer.

Column A	Column B
$(x-2x)(x+2x)$	(x^4-4x^2)

---

23. Debbie's wallet contains 5 quarters, 2 dimes, and 1 nickel. She takes three coins out of her purse, one at a time. (Note: 1 penny = $\$.01$; 1 dime = $\$.10$; 1 quarter = $\$.25$)

Column A	Column B
The probability that the three coins add up to \$0.55	The probability that the three coins add up to \$0.25

---

24. s is a factor of t and b is a factor of c.

Column A	Column B
$s+b$	$s+t$

---

25. A cone has a height of 1 cm and a radius of 6 cm. The cone's volume is equal to 3x cm^3 an the area of the cone's circular bas is equal to 3y cm^2. Note: the formula for the volume of a cone is $\frac{1}{3}\pi r^2 h$

Column A	Column B
x	y

26.

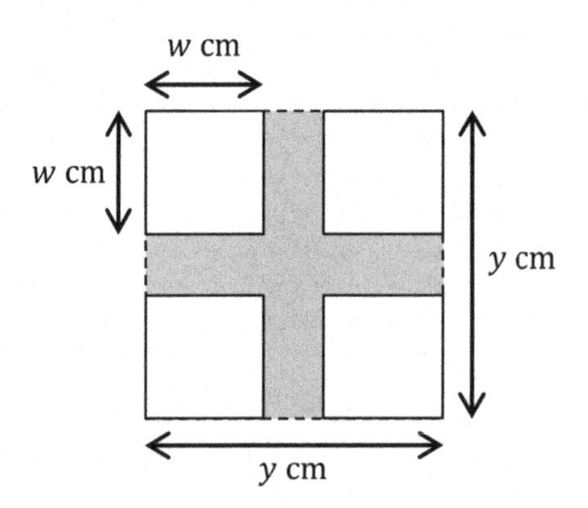

$w > 0$ and $y > 0$

In the figure above, the area between four identical squares is shaded gray.

Column A	Column B
The area of the shaded region	$(y - 2w)(y + 2w)$

---

27. x is a positive integer.

Column A	Column B
$(x^3)^0$	$\left(\frac{1}{x}\right)^2$

---

28. A circle C has an area that is twice its circumference.

Column A	Column B
The radius of circle C	5

29. Rachel has 10 cards that are numbered 0-9. She randomly selects one card from the pile, and uses its number as the tens place in a 2-digit number. Without replacing the first card, she then randomly selects another card and uses its number as the ones place in the same 2-digit number. The first card she selects has the number 5.

Column A	Column B
The probability that her 2-digit number will be greater than 55	The probability that her 2-digit number will be less than 55

---

30. x is an integer less than zero.

Column A	Column B
$\left(\frac{1}{10}\right)^x$	10^x

---

31. The circular target in the figure below is made up of three concentric circles. The entire target has a diameter of 16 inches, and the radius of each concentric circle is half as large as that of the next largest circle.

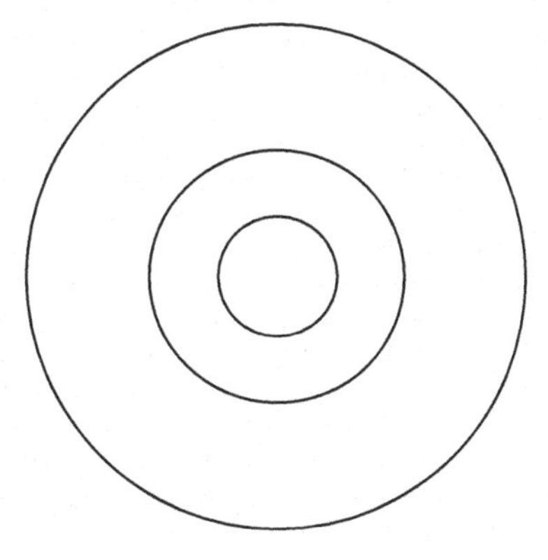

Column A	Column B
The circumference of the largest circle	The circumference of the smallest circle plus the circumference of the middle circle

32. A circle's diameter is increased by 15%. It is then decreased by 15%.

Column A	Column B
The original area of the circle	The final area of the circle

---

33. Jessica has 8 bottles of blue nail polish, 4 bottles of red nail polish, and 2 bottles of yellow nail polish. Each bottle is a different shade of color. Jessica wants to paint her nails using one shade of yellow, one shade of red, and one shade of blue. She randomly selects three nail polishes one at a time, without replacing the previous selection before choosing the next.

Column A	Column B
The probability that she chooses a yellow shade, then a red shade, then a blue shade	The probability that she chooses a blue shade, then a red shade, then a yellow shade

---

34.

Column A	Column B
x^{2x+8}	$(2x+8)^x$

---

35. x and y are both integers that are greater than zero.

Column A	Column B
$(3x^2 + 1)(2y - 1)$	3

36. Circle C is tangent to line k at the origin. The center of circle C is at point $(-3, 3)$.

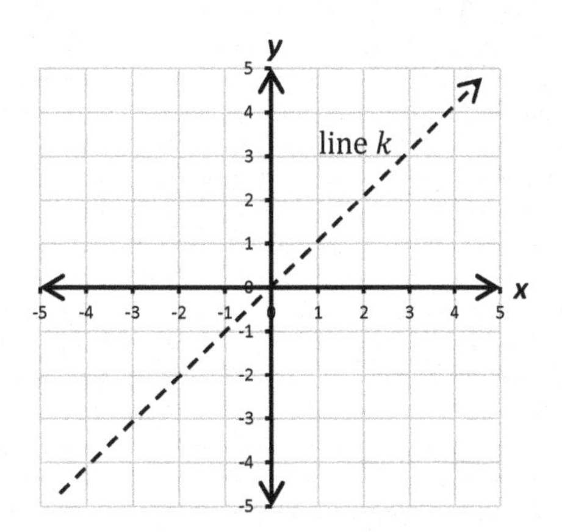

Column A	Column B
The radius of circle C	3

---

37. A large cube M has side lengths of m units. A smaller cube, R, with side lengths of r units, is cut out and removed from cube M.

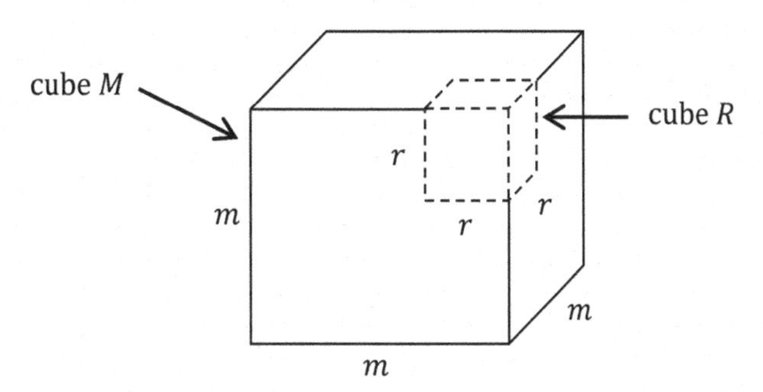

Column A	Column B
The surface area of the original cube	The surface area of the solid when cube R is removed from cube M

38. Use the figure from question 37 to answer this question.

Column A	Column B
The volume of the solid when cube R is removed from cube M	$(m + r)(m^2 + mr + r^2)$

---

39. Point $(0, -4)$ is the center of a circle.

Column A	Column B
The area of the circle if point (0,0) is on the circle	The area of the circle if it is tangent with the line $y = -9$

40.

Column A	Column B
$8i^2$	$(3i)^{-4}$

MATH ACHIEVEMENT

CHAPTER 4

INTRODUCTION

SECTION 1

The following review covers all of the math concepts commonly tested on the Lower, Middle, and Upper levels of the ISEE, including arithmetic, algebra, geometry, and data interpretation. Each section begins with fundamental content appropriate for all levels, followed by more detailed and advanced content tailored to the Middle and Upper Levels. If you are a Lower Level student, stop when you reach the Middle and Upper Level content. If you are a Middle or Upper Level student, make sure you review the fundamental content before moving on to the more advanced concepts.

Remember that the concepts tested at each level of the ISEE span a wide range of grade levels, so you may see content that you haven't learned yet in school. Work through the material appropriate to your grade level. Review the topics you are familiar with first, before moving on to topics that are new or unfamiliar.

Each section is followed by review questions. Attempt the questions appropriate to your level, and the check your work using the answer key at the back of the book. Practice answering questions quickly and accurately, and spend extra time reviewing concepts that you find difficult. Make flashcards for information that you need to memorize and drill yourself on this information frequently.

ARITHMETIC

PART 1

NUMBERS AND OPERATIONS

ALL LEVELS

SECTION 1

Look over the definitions of the number properties in the table below. In this section, we will explore what these definitions mean and how to use them.

NUMBER PROPERTIES		
Word	**Definition**	**Examples**
Integer	Any negative or positive whole number	-3, 0, 5, 400
Positive	Greater than zero	2, 7, 23, 400
Negative	Less than zero	-2, -7, -23, -400
Even	Divisible by two	4, 18, 2002, 0
Odd	Not evenly divisible by two	3, 7, 15, 2001
Factor	An integer that evenly divides into a number	3 and 4 are factors of 12.
Multiple	The result of multiplying a number by an integer	36 and 48 are multiples of 12.
Prime	Only divisible by itself and 1	3, 5, 7, 11, 19, 23
Composite	Divisible by numbers other than itself and 1	4, 12, 15, 20, 21
Consecutive	Whole numbers that follow each other in order	2, 3, 4, 5, 6 ...

INTEGERS

An **integer** is any positive or negative whole number. Fractions and decimals are not integers. **Zero** is an integer, but is neither positive nor negative.

OPERATIONS

An **operation** is a fancy name for a process that changes one number into another. The most common operations are addition, subtraction, multiplication, and division. Know the following vocabulary related to operations:

OPERATIONS		
Word	**Definition**	**Examples**
Sum	The result of adding numbers	The sum of 3 and 4 is 7.
Difference	The result of subtracting numbers	The difference between 5 and 2 is 3.
Product	The result of multiplying numbers	The product of 6 and 4 is 24.
Quotient	The result of dividing numbers	The quotient when 40 is divided by 5 is 8.
Remainder	The amount left over when a number cannot be evenly divided by another number	When 11 is divided by 2, the result is 5 with a remainder of 1.

Students are not allowed to use a calculator on the ISEE. As a result, you will need to be able to solve arithmetic calculations quickly and accurately on paper. In order to make sure that you have mastered all of the basics of long addition, subtraction, multiplication, and division, look through the review below and try the drills that follow.

ADDITION

To add large numbers, break up the question into parts based on the **place** of the digits. Each digit in a number has a place value, as shown in the following chart. For a more complete chart including place values with decimals, see Section 6.

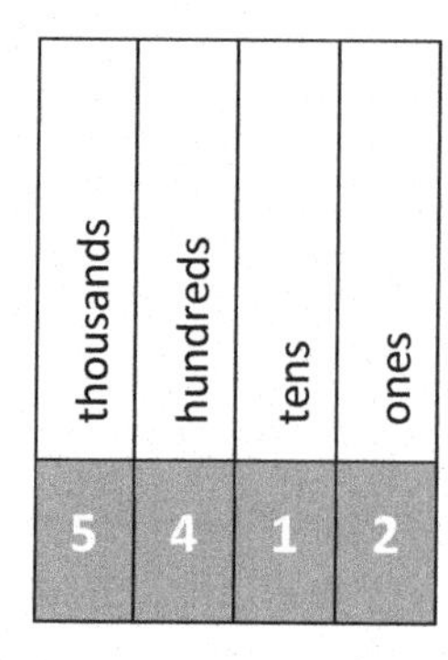

For the number 5,412 above, 5 is in the thousands place, 4 is in the hundreds place, 1 is in the tens place, and 2 is in the ones place.

Use your knowledge of place values to add large numbers by hand. For example, if you had the question:

$$\begin{array}{r} 32 \\ +\,14 \\ \hline \end{array}$$

First add the ones place digits together, and then add the tens place digits together. 2 and 4 are both in the ones place, and $2 + 4 = 6$. 3 and 1 are both in the tens place, and $3 + 1 = 4$. Therefore, your answer will be:

$$\begin{array}{r} 32 \\ +\,14 \\ \hline 46 \end{array}$$

Always start from the rightmost column and move to the left when you are adding.

Recall that sometimes you will need to use **carrying** in addition problems. For example, look at the following problem:

$$\begin{array}{r} 45 \\ +\,17 \\ \hline \end{array}$$

Your ones place digits are going to add up to a double-digit number: $5 + 7 = 12$.

If you have a double digit number when you add two numbers together in a column, you will need to use carrying. In this case, you will take the ones digit from 12, which is 2, and place it under the ones digit column. Then you will "carry" the tens digit, which is 1, over the top of the tens digit column.

$$\begin{array}{r} 1 \\ 45 \\ +17 \\ \hline 2 \end{array}$$

Finally, you will add together all of the digits in the tens column, including the 1 that you carried over. $1+4+1=6$, so your answer will be:

$$\begin{array}{r} 1 \\ 45 \\ +17 \\ \hline 62 \end{array}$$

If you are adding together larger numbers, you may have to carry multiple times. For example:

$$\begin{array}{r} 11 \\ 7658 \\ +1571 \\ \hline 9229 \end{array}$$

SUBTRACTION

In subtraction, just like in addition, focus on the place of the digits. Start subtracting the digits in the ones place and then move to the left. For example, if you had the question:

$$\begin{array}{r} 85 \\ -23 \\ \hline \end{array}$$

You would start by subtracting the ones place digits, which are 5 and 3, and then subtract the tens place digits, which are 8 and 2. $5-3=2$ and $8-2=6$. Therefore, your answer will be:

$$\begin{array}{r} 85 \\ -23 \\ \hline 62 \end{array}$$

Sometimes in subtraction problems, the digits in your first number will be smaller than the digits in your second number. For example:

$$\begin{array}{r} 34 \\ -18 \\ \hline \end{array}$$

As you can see, in our ones place column, 4 is smaller than 8. Therefore, you will need to use **borrowing.** You will need to "borrow" from the tens place digit in order to continue with your subtraction.

34 is the same thing as 3 tens and 4 ones. We can borrow from the 3 tens in order to make our ones place larger than 8. To do this, take one of the 3 tens and add it to the 4 ones, turning the 3 tens into 2 tens and the 4 ones into 14:

$$\begin{array}{r} \mathit{2}\ \mathit{14} \\ \cancel{3}\,4 \\ -\,1\,8 \\ \hline \end{array}$$

14 is larger than 8, so we can subtract the digits in our ones and tens columns as usual. $14 - 8 = 6$ and $2 - 1 = 1$, so:

$$\begin{array}{r} \mathit{2}\ \mathit{14} \\ \cancel{3}\,4 \\ -\,1\,8 \\ \hline 1\,6 \end{array}$$

Some problems will require you to borrow multiple times. For example:

$$\begin{array}{r} 8762 \\ -\,3914 \\ \hline \end{array}$$

We can solve this problem step-by-step, starting with the ones place column and moving to the left.

Our first number has a ones place digit that is smaller than the ones place digit of our second number. As a result, we will need to borrow from the 6 tens in the tens place:

$$\begin{array}{r} \mathit{5}\ \mathit{12} \\ 8\ 7\ \cancel{6}\ \cancel{2} \\ -\,3\ 9\ 1\ 4 \\ \hline 4\ 8 \end{array}$$

In our hundreds place, our first number is also smaller than our second number, so we will need to borrow from the 8 in our thousands place. After we have subtracted all of the columns, we can come up with our final answer:

$$\begin{array}{r} \mathit{7}\ \mathit{17}\quad\ \ \\ \cancel{8}\ \cancel{7}\ 6\ 2 \\ -\,3\ 9\ 1\ 4 \\ \hline 4\ 8\ 4\ 8 \end{array}$$

MULTIPLICATION

You should be very comfortable multiplying whole numbers from 1 to 12 in your head. If you have trouble remembering your **multiplication table**, put this information on flashcards and quiz yourself regularly.

MULTIPLICATION TABLE

	1	**2**	**3**	**4**	**5**	**6**	**7**	**8**	**9**	**10**	**11**	**12**
1	1	2	3	4	5	6	7	8	9	10	11	12
2	2	4	6	8	10	12	14	16	18	20	22	24
3	3	6	9	12	15	18	21	24	27	30	33	36
4	4	8	12	16	20	24	28	32	36	40	44	48
5	5	10	15	20	25	30	35	40	45	50	55	60
6	6	12	18	24	30	36	42	48	54	60	66	72
7	7	14	21	28	35	42	49	56	63	70	77	84
8	8	16	24	32	40	48	56	64	72	80	88	96
9	9	18	27	36	45	54	63	72	81	90	99	108
10	10	20	30	40	50	60	70	80	90	100	110	120
11	11	22	33	44	55	66	77	88	99	110	121	132
12	12	24	36	48	60	72	84	96	108	120	132	144

To solve multiplication problems with larger numbers, rely on your knowledge of the multiplication table for smaller numbers. For example, let's look at this problem:

$$\begin{array}{r} 17 \\ \times\ 6 \\ \hline \end{array}$$

Even though you probably do not have your 17 times tables memorized, you can still easily solve this problem by breaking it down into parts. In this problem, take the number 6 and multiply it first by the ones place, and then by the tens place of the larger number (17).

First, multiply 6 by 7, which is the number in the ones place. Recall from your multiplication table that $6 \times 7 = 42$. Since 42 is a two-digit number, we will need to carry the 4:

$$\begin{array}{r} \mathit{4}\ \, \\ 17 \\ \times\ \ 6 \\ \hline 2 \end{array}$$

Then, we will multiply 6 by 1, which is the number in the tens place. Afterwards, we will add 4, the number that we carried. $6 \times 1 + 4 = 10$, so our final answer will be:

$$\begin{array}{r} \mathit{4}\ \, \\ 17 \\ \times\ \ 6 \\ \hline 102 \end{array}$$

Now take a look at a slightly more complicated problem:

$$\begin{array}{r} 45 \\ \times 13 \\ \hline \end{array}$$

In this problem, our second number has two digits. We will need to go through the multiplication process for each digit separately. Let's start with the ones digit, which is 3, and ignore the tens digit for now.

Just like we did in our first example, we'll multiply 3 first by the ones place, followed by the tens place. 5 is the number in the ones place, and $3 \times 5 = 15$. Since we have a two-digit number, we will need to carry the 1. We'll then multiply by 4, which is the number in the tens place, and add the number we carried. $3 \times 4 + 1 = 13$, so we get:

$$\begin{array}{r} \mathit{1}\ \ \, \\ 45 \\ \times\ 13 \\ \hline 135 \end{array}$$

But we're not done yet! Now that we have finished with the "3" in "13", we need to work on the "1." We'll start a new line under the answer. The "1" in 13 is really a "10", because 13 is the same thing as 1 ten plus 3 ones. In order to make our multiplication problem reflect that our "1" is really a "10," we will need to add a zero under our answer:

$$\begin{array}{r} 45 \\ \times\ 13 \\ \hline 135 \\ 0 \end{array}$$

After we have added the zero, we'll multiply 1 first by the ones place, followed by the tens place. 5 is in the ones place, and $1 \times 5 = 5$. 4 is in the tens place, and $1 \times 4 = 4$. Therefore, we are left with:

$$\begin{array}{r} 45 \\ \times\ 13 \\ \hline 135 \\ 450 \end{array}$$

To get our final answer, we need to add the two lines together:

$$\begin{array}{r} 45 \\ \times\ 13 \\ \hline 135 \\ +\ 450 \\ \hline 585 \end{array}$$

Our final answer is 585.

When you are multiplying even larger numbers, remember to always add another zero when you start a new line. For example:

$$\begin{array}{r} 524 \\ \times\ 212 \\ \hline 1048 \\ 5240 \\ +\ 104800 \\ \hline 111088 \end{array}$$

VIDEO

1.1 MULTIPLICATION

Watch at http:// videos.ivyglobal.com

DIVISION

In order to divide with large numbers, you can also apply your knowledge of the multiplication table.

For example, let's see how we would divide 2406 by 3:

$$3\overline{)2406}$$

To solve this problem, we need to take 3 and divide it into each number, one at a time. Unlike multiplication, however, we're going to work from left to right. 3 does not divide evenly into 2, which is the digit farthest to the left. As a result, we will move onto the next digit, and try to divide 3 into 24.

3 does divide evenly into 24. Recall from your multiplication tables that $3 \times 8 = 24$. We'll therefore write "8" above the "4" in "24." To check our work, we'll multiply 3×8 again, and write the product below "24." We'll then subtract to see what remainder we get:

```
     8
 3)2406
  -24
   --
    0
```

$24 - 24 = 0$, so we'll write "0" as the remainder to finish this step.

In the next step, we'll bring down the next number in 2406, which is 0, and write this next to the remainder from our last step:

```
     8
 3)2406
  -24↓
   --
    00
```

Our new number is "00," which is the same thing as 0. We'll then divide 3 into this number. 3 goes into 0 zero times. Following the same process as above, we'll therefore write "0" above the tens place over the division symbol and multiply by 3 to check our work:

```
     80
 3)2406
  -24↓
   --
    00
   - 0
    --
     0
```

Finally, we'll bring down our last number, which is 6, and we'll divide 3 into this number. Recall that $3 \times 2 = 6$. 3 divides into 6 two times, so we'll write "2" above the division symbol and check whether we have a remainder:

```
     802
 3)2406
  -24↓|
   --  |
    00 |
    -0↓
    --
     06
     -6
     --
      0
```

3 divides evenly into 2406, so there is no remainder. Our final answer is 802.

In some cases, your divisor will not divide evenly into your dividend. In such a case, you will be left with a remainder. Let's look at the following example:

$$4\overline{)6571}$$

Starting with the first number to the left, we see that 4 goes into 6 only once without going over, but it doesn't go into 6 evenly. $4 \times 1 = 4$, and when we subtract 4 from 6, we will have a remainder of 2:

$$\begin{array}{r} 1 \\ 4\overline{)6571} \\ -4 \\ \hline 2 \end{array}$$

When we bring down the next number, 5, we'll write this next to the remainder and get a new number, 25. 4 goes into 25 six times because $4 \times 6 = 24$. We'll write "6" above the hundreds place over the division symbol. $25 - 24 = 1$, so here we will be left with a remainder of 1:

$$\begin{array}{r} 16 \\ 4\overline{)6571} \\ -4\downarrow \\ \hline 25 \\ -24 \\ \hline 1 \end{array}$$

Our next step is to bring down the next number, 7, and write this next to our remainder to get 17. 4 goes into 17 four times because $4 \times 4 = 16$. We'll write "4" above the tens place over the division symbol. $17 - 16 = 1$, so we have a remainder of 1 again:

$$\begin{array}{r} 164 \\ 4\overline{)6571} \\ -4\downarrow \\ \hline 25 \\ -24\downarrow \\ \hline 17 \\ -16 \\ \hline 1 \end{array}$$

Finally, we will bring down the last number, 1, and write this next to our remainder to get 11. 4 goes into 11 two times because $4 \times 2 = 8$. We'll write "2" above the division symbol. $11 - 8 = 2$, so we have a remainder of 3.

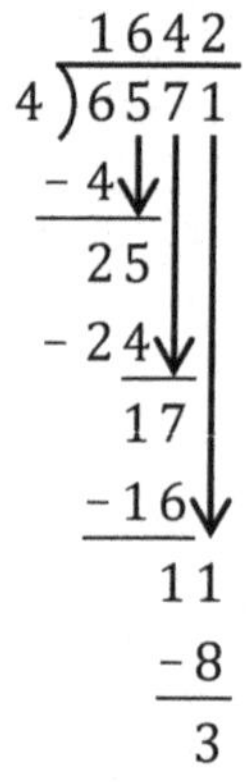

```
   1642
4)6571
 - 4↓
   25
 - 24↓
    17
  - 16↓
     11
     -8
      3
```

Because we have no more numbers to bring down, our final answer is 1,642 with a remainder of 3. We can write this remainder as "R3" above the division line:

```
   1642 R3
4)6571
```


PRACTICE QUESTIONS: NUMBERS AND OPERATIONS

On the next few pages, you'll find several sets of basic arithmetic drill questions. On the ISEE, it is very important to be able to add, subtract, multiply, and divide short and long numbers quickly and accurately by hand. Try to complete these drills as quickly as you can. When you are finished, check your answers.

ADDITION DRILLS						
27 + 3	13 + 9	39 + 2	10 + 7	42 + 8	75 + 6	98 + 7
67 + 23	72 + 35	18 + 49	37 + 14	68 + 41	99 + 27	32 + 85
55 + 12	82 + 44	32 + 16	63 + 14	18 + 99	75 + 75	69 + 64
78+98=	39+42=	18+54=	37+84=	28+18=	90+40=	22+53=
125 + 5	534 + 9	639 + 1	832 + 7	422 + 9	799 + 1	502 + 3
648 + 22	331 + 86	510 + 27	396 + 19	421 + 90	307 + 21	517 + 17
392 + 184	739 + 717	402 + 184	492 + 391	246 + 184	582 + 909	521 + 486
329 428 + 186	42 593 + 204	821 12 + 947	82 194 + 53	529 438 + 167	625 14 + 39	527 941 + 368

SUBTRACTION DRILLS						
13 − 2	62 − 5	41 − 9	73 − 1	64 − 4	94 − 7	40 − 3
72 − 52	81 − 59	54 − 37	90 − 31	84 − 73	29 − 17	40 − 27
99 − 42	58 − 39	56 − 38	84 − 27	91 − 57	30 − 22	73 − 15
86−42=	72−65=	62−43=	95−78=	48−43=	81−72=	57−31=
613 − 5	749 − 7	397 − 9	942 − 3	264 − 4	481 − 9	285 − 7
849 − 31	762 − 40	492 − 32	781 − 39	267 − 69	843 − 85	328 − 57
752 − 321	481 − 278	473 − 327	849 − 212	747 − 381	604 − 518	582 − 175
391 286 − 73	847 41 − 316	904 269 − 79	798 280 − 142	359 90 − 21	740 380 − 242	867 329 − 415

ADDITION AND SUBTRACTION DRILLS						
76 + 15	34 + 76	54 − 14	90 − 32	86 + 55	86 − 55	99 − 33
67 − 31	89 + 41	76 − 66	54 − 31	22 + 16	87 − 59	33 + 99
66+42=	31−27=	54−29=	49+96=	38+57=	27+64=	75−35=
52−36=	96−43=	21+68=	53+94=	92−61=	42+53=	49+77=
6 7 + □ □ 8 2	7 2 − □ □ 1 3	3 2 + □ □ 6 4	□ □ + 6 7 9 9	□ □ − 7 6 1 2	3 □ − □ 1 2 1	□ 4 + 2 □ 5 5
□ 4 − 3 □ 3 6	6 □ + □ 2 8 6	□ 7 + 3 1 □ 0 □	□ □ − 2 3 4 7	□ 9 + 3 □ 7 1	□ 2 − 6 □ 8	5 4 + □ 3 7 □
341 − 142	529 + 671	904 − 731	641 − 232	804 + 321	922 − 344	798 + 421
5 2 □ − 3 □ 1 □ 0 4	1 4 □ + □ 2 3 □ 0 □ 8	2 □ 9 − □ 4 7 □ 1 □	□ 3 4 + 8 □ 7 □ 7 5 □	□ □ 4 + 3 7 8 6 0 □	7 □ 7 − □ 3 □ 2 7 8	□ 5 6 + 3 4 □ 4 9 7
32 + 64 − 25	78 − 29 + 93	65 + 31 − 19	90 + 22 − 78	320 − 245 + 980	975 − 629 + 528	802 − 492 + 375

MULTIPLICATION DRILLS						
6×8=	9×6=	3×4=	2×12=	5×9=	3×6=	7×12=
3×7=	6×3=	2×7=	6×0=	8×2=	7×9=	5×4=
9×5=	8×4=	4×7=	12×8=	10×5=	11×3=	6×4=
12×11=	3×9=	4×9=	5×3=	11×9=	2×8=	7×7=
6×2=	12×9=	8×8=	8×7=	12×4=	9×9=	10×6=
19 × 4	22 × 9	35 × 7	76 × 3	38 × 8	24 × 6	65 × 2
53 × 97	86 × 51	63 × 54	11 × 22	59 × 77	20 × 65	95 × 38
477 × 7	904 × 3	285 × 8	876 × 9	337 × 5	273 × 4	489 × 6
395 × 44	411 × 97	530 × 64	214 × 55	503 × 84	375 × 70	339 × 83
783 × 904	899 × 974	318 × 814	657 × 165	847 × 322	555 × 396	286 × 862

DIVISION DRILLS						
8÷4=	12÷6=	12÷4=	12÷3=	10÷2=	4÷2=	18÷3=
18÷6=	20÷10=	15÷3=	21÷7=	20÷5=	16÷2=	25÷5=
21÷3=	30÷5=	18÷2=	15÷5=	24÷4=	20÷4=	18÷9=
35÷5=	24÷6=	32÷4=	42÷6=	26÷2=	40÷4=	24÷8=
54÷9=	48÷8=	42÷7=	55÷5=	64÷8=	36÷6=	48÷6=
5)6 R=	3)7 R=	4)9 R=	4)10 R=	3)8 R=	2)9 R=	7)10 R=
5)22 R=	3)20 R=	6)25 R=	6)39 R=	8)67 R=	4)34 R=	5)43 R=
5)435	3)762	7)455	8)392	6)756	2)748	9)711
11)748	8)432	3)297	4)260	7)455	5)785	9)684

MULTIPLICATION AND DIVISION DRILLS

6÷3=	6×3=	8÷2=	8×2=	36÷6=	6×6=	64÷8=
10÷5=	10×5=	9÷3=	9×3=	81÷9=	9×9=	7×7=
56 × 4	98 × 6	37 × 2	86 × 8	30 × 3	82 × 6	39 × 7
5)785	3)912	7)462	8)400	6)612	2)852	9)1008
5)34 R=	3)52 R=	6)17 R=	6)45 R=	8)64 R=	4)25 R=	5)52 R=
8×□=40	□×7=63	□×7=7	□×9=0	3×□=27	6×□=48	9×□=36
□÷7=6	60÷□=5	□÷4=24	□÷6=24	12÷□=4	□÷9=6	12÷□=6
81÷□=9	7×□=56	□×4=36	□×12=36	42÷□=6	6×□=18	□÷5=8
744 × 72	843 × 21	904 × 50	371 × 52	987 × 47	382 × 82	426 × 18

PROPERTIES OF OPERATIONS

ALL LEVELS

SECTION 2

In the previous section, we learned that addition, subtraction, multiplication, and division are all **operations:** processes that change one number into another. Each of these operations has important properties that you will need to know for the ISEE.

COMMUTATION

Addition and multiplication obey the property of **commutation,** which means that you can switch the order of the numbers that you are adding or multiplying. You might have heard the word "commute" in the context of "commuting to work" or "commuting to school," where it means to move from one place to another. When we talk about the property of commutation, we mean that we can move around the numbers we are adding or multiplying and the result will be the same.

Imagine that you are buying a candy bar that costs $1.15, and you have one dollar, one dime, and one nickel. $1 plus 10 cents plus 5 cents adds up to $1.15, so you'll get your candy bar once you have given all of your money to the store clerk. However, it doesn't matter in what order you give the clerk your money. You could give her the dime first, then the nickel, then the dollar bill:

10¢ + 5¢ + $1 = $1.15

Or, you could give her the dollar bill first, then the dime, then the nickel:

$1 + 10¢ + 5¢ = $1.15

In both cases, the clerk will still see that you have the same amount of money, and you'll get your candy bar.

Therefore, it doesn't matter in what order you add two, three, or even 100 numbers—because of the property of commutation, the result will be the same.

Just like with addition, it doesn't matter in what order you multiply together two, three, or even 100 numbers—the result will be the same. For example, imagine that you are a store clerk and you need to give a customer 5 cents in change. You can either give her 1 nickel or 5 pennies, and the result will be the same:

$1 \times$ (5¢) $= 5$¢

$5 \times$ (1¢) $= 5$¢

We know that these two quantities are the same because 1×5 and 5×1 both equal 5. Therefore, you can multiply numbers in different orders, and you'll still get the same product.

Unlike addition and multiplication, commutation is *not* a property of subtraction and division. **Order matters** when you are subtracting or dividing. For example, $10 - 1$ is definitely not the same thing as $1 - 10$. Similarly, $20 \div 5$ is not the same thing as $5 \div 20$.

Here is an example:

Which of the following is NOT equal to 6?

(A) 2×3
(B) 3×2
(C) $18 \div 3$
(D) $3 \div 18$

Answers (A) and (B) both equal 6 because multiplication obeys the property of commutation: 2×3 is the same thing as 3×2. However, answers (C) and (D) do not both equal 6, because order matters in division. $18 \div 3$ is equal to 6, but $3 \div 18$ is not. Therefore, answer choice (D) is the right answer.

ASSOCIATION

Addition and multiplication also obey the property of **association**, which means that it doesn't matter how you group together the things you are adding or multiplying. If something is "associated" with something else, it means that the two things are connected or grouped together.

In math, we show that two numbers are grouped together by using **parentheses**: ( ). When you see numbers inside parentheses, you should think of them as a separate group of numbers in your calculation. Always **calculate numbers in parentheses first**, so you can figure out the sum, difference, product, or quotient of the group of numbers. Then, you can use this result in the rest of your calculation.

When we talk about the property of association, we mean that it doesn't matter what numbers are grouped together with parenthesis when we add or multiply. We can make different groups with the same numbers, and the result of adding or multiplying will be the same.

Remember the example above, where you were paying a store clerk a dollar, a nickel, and a dime to buy a candy bar? This time, imagine that you gave her the dollar in one hand, and you gave her the dime and the nickel in another hand. The dime and the nickel will be grouped together, and we can represent this by putting the dime and nickel in parentheses:

$$\$1 + (10¢ + 5¢) = \$1.15$$

What if you gave her the dollar and dime in one hand, and the nickel in another? The parenthesis would be different, but the sum would still be the same:

$$(\$1 + 10¢) + 5¢ = \$1.15$$

When you are adding numbers, you can change the grouping of the numbers that are being added, and the result will be the same.

Now imagine that you wanted to give two of your friends three dimes each. How many cents would you need? You could write this as a multiplication problem. You have two groups of three dimes each, so you would multiply a group of three dimes by two:

$$(3 \times 10¢) \times 2 = 60¢$$

3×10 is equal to 30, so each friend gets 30 cents. You are giving money to 2 of your friends, so you'll need $30 \times 2 = 60$ cents.

What if you wanted to give three of your friends two dimes each? This time each friend gets a different number of dimes: you have three groups of two dimes each. However, all you need to do is move the parentheses in your multiplication problem:

$$3 \times \left(10¢ \times 2 \right) = 60¢$$

10×2 is equal to 20, so each friend gets 20 cents. You are giving money to 3 of your friends, so you'll need $20 \times 3 = 60$ cents—exactly the same amount of money as before!

When you are multiplying numbers, you can change the grouping of the numbers that are being multiplied, and the result will be the same.

Just like commutation, association is *not* a property of subtraction and division. Your **groups of numbers matter** when you divide or subtract. Remember that you always solve the calculation in the parentheses first, so grouping your numbers differently might mean that you are subtracting or dividing in a different order. Subtracting or dividing in a different order will change the result you get. For example:

$$(4 - 2) - 1 =$$
$$2 - 1 = 1$$

In the subtraction problem above, the result was 1. However, if we move the parentheses, we'll have to solve the subtraction problem in a different order:

$$4 - (2 - 1) =$$
$$4 - 1 = 3$$

Because we subtracted in a different order, the result was 3 instead of 1. Grouping our numbers differently gave us a different result.

In division, grouping numbers differently can also give you a different result:

$$(8 \div 2) \div 2 =$$
$$4 \div 2 = 2$$

$$8 \div (2 \div 2) =$$
$$8 \div 1 = 8$$

To summarize, you can group together numbers in different ways when you add or multiply, but moving the parentheses can change your calculation when you subtract or divide. If you move the parentheses and end up subtracting or dividing in a different order, you will not have the same result.

Here's another example:

Which of the following is NOT correct?

(A) $(■+▲)+●=■+(▲+●)$

(B) $(■×■×▲)=■×(■×▲)$

(C) $●-(●-▲)=(●-●)-▲$

(D) $■×(■×◆)=(■×■)×◆$

This question is asking whether each answer choice shows two equal sums, differences, or products. If you look at each answer choice, you'll notice that the calculations on each side of the equals sign are the same except for the parentheses. Because of the property of association, you know that it doesn't matter where you put parentheses when you are adding or multiplying. Therefore, you know that the sums shown in answer choice (A) are equal, and the products in answer choices (B) and (D) are also equal. However, you also know that it matters where you put parentheses when you subtract. Because the differences shown in answer choice (C) have different groups of numbers in parentheses, you will subtract in a different order. Therefore, the differences are not equal, and (C) is the right answer.

DISTRIBUTION

Distribution is another property of multiplication involving parentheses. "Distribution" means sharing or spreading something out. When we talk about the distributive property in mathematics, we are talking about "distributing" a number that is being multiplied by a group of numbers. Sometimes you might multiply one number by a group of numbers being added or subtracted in parentheses. In this case, you will get the same result if you multiply that number by each of the other numbers separately (you "share" or "distribute" it), and then add or subtract the products.

Here's an example:

$$5 \times (3 + 1) = ?$$

To solve this calculation using the steps we've already discussed, we'll first add together the numbers in parentheses: $3 + 1 = 4$. Then, we'll multiply this sum by 5:

$$5 \times (3 + 1) =$$
$$5 \times 4 = 20$$

Our answer is 20.

However, we can also solve this calculation using distribution. To do this, we'll distribute the number we're multiplying—5—over the numbers in parentheses. We'll multiply 5 by each one of them separately, and then we'll add together the products. Here's what it looks like:

$$5 \times (3 + 1) =$$
$$5 \times 3 + 5 \times 1 =$$
$$15 + 5 = 20$$

We arrived at the same answer: 20!

Here's another example:

Which of the following is equal to ■×(▲+●)?

(A) (■×▲)+●
(B) ■×▲+■×●
(C) ■×▲×●
(D) ■+▲+■+●

This question is multiplying one shape by two other shapes in parentheses, so we can use distribution to find an equivalent answer. Answer choice (B) is correct because it shows the process of distribution: the square is multiplied by the triangle and the circle separately, and then the products are added together.

Answer choice (D) is incorrect because the square is *added* to the triangle and circle separately, instead by being multiplied. Answer choice (C) is incorrect because the shapes are just being multiplied by each other with no addition. Answer choice (A) is incorrect because the parentheses have been moved, changing the grouping of shapes. You can change the groupings of numbers when you are adding or multiplying, but you can't change them when you are both adding *and* multiplying.

ORDER OF OPERATIONS

The **Order of Operations** for addition, subtraction, multiplication, and division brings together the properties of commutation, association, and distribution. Use the following order when you have many operations to calculate:

1. Calculate any operations inside parentheses (groups).
2. Multiply and divide from left to right.
3. Add and subtract from left to right.

For instance, let's solve this calculation:

$$3 + 7 \times (6 - 4) - 8 \div 2$$

1. Calculate the numbers inside parentheses:

$$3 + 7 \times (\mathbf{6 - 4}) - 8 \div 2 =$$

$$3 + 7 \times \mathbf{2} - 8 \div 2$$

2. Multiply and divide from left to right:

$$3 + \mathbf{7 \times 2} - \mathbf{8 \div 2} =$$

$$3 + \mathbf{14} - \mathbf{4}$$

3. Add and subtract from right to left:

$$3 + 14 - 4 = 13$$

(*See page 216 for the complete Order of Operations for the Middle/Upper Level only.*)

OPERATIONS WITH EVEN AND ODD NUMBERS

Remember that an **even number** is a number that can be evenly divided by 2, and an **odd number** cannot be evenly divided by 2. This means that an odd number will have a remainder when you try to divide by 2, and an even number will have no remainder.

Here's a fun fact about even and odd numbers. You can predict whether the sum or product of two numbers will be even or odd:

- even + even = even
- odd + odd = even
- odd + even = odd

- even × even = even
- odd × odd = odd

- odd $\times$ even $=$ even

Test this on any pair of numbers you can find, and you'll see that it is always true!

PRACTICE QUESTIONS: PROPERTIES OF OPERATIONS

For questions 1-10, identify whether the equations below are CORRECT or INCORRECT. Explain your answer using the properties of commutation, association, and distribution.

1. $\triangle + \bigcirc = \bigcirc + \triangle$

2. $\diamond + (\diamond + \square) = (\diamond + \diamond) + \square$

3. $\triangle - \square - \diamond = \square - \triangle - \diamond$

4. $\diamond \times \bigcirc + \diamond \times \square = \diamond \times (\bigcirc + \square)$

5. $\diamond \div (\triangle \div \square) = (\diamond \div \triangle) \div \square$

6. $\square \times (\bigcirc + \bigcirc + \bigcirc) = \square \times \bigcirc + \square \times \bigcirc + \square \times \bigcirc$

7. $\square + \bigcirc + \triangle \times \bigcirc = (\square + \triangle) \times \bigcirc$

8. $\bigcirc + \square + \triangle + (\square - \triangle) = \bigcirc + (\square + \triangle) + (\square - \triangle)$

9. $\triangle \div \square + \square \div \bigcirc = \triangle \div (\square + \square) \div \bigcirc$

10. $\square + (\triangle \div \bigcirc) = (\triangle \div \bigcirc) + \square$

Use the Order of Operations to solve questions 11-16.

11. $3 + 7 - 6 =$

12. $4 \times (8 - 3) + 13 =$

13. $3 \times 2 + (8 - 6) \div 2 =$

14. $(2 - 1) \times (6 + 2) \div 2 =$

15. $6 \div 2 + 3 \times 3 - 2 + (8 - 5) \times 2 =$

16. $(7 + 3) \div 2 + 8 \times 5 - 2 + 3 \times 2 \times (2 + 1) =$

The expressions in questions 17-24 show operations involving even and odd numbers. Identify whether the result will be even or odd.

17. even × even

18. odd + even

19. even × odd

20. odd + odd

21. odd + odd + odd

22. even × odd × even

23. (odd + even) × odd

24. (even + even) × (odd + odd)

FACTORS AND MULTIPLES

ALL LEVELS

SECTION 3

A number is **divisible** by another number if the result of division is a whole number. For instance, 12 is divisible by 3 because $12 \div 3 = 4$ with nothing left over. Because 12 is divisible by 3, we can say that 3 is a **factor** of 12. Because 3 multiplied by a whole number is 12, we can say that 12 is a **multiple** of 3.

12 is not evenly divisible by 7, because 7 goes into 12 once with 5 left over. The amount left over is called a **remainder**. We can say that $12 \div 7 = 1$ with a remainder of 5.

Because there is a remainder, 7 is not a factor of 12, and 12 is not a multiple of 7.

FINDING FACTORS

When you are trying to find all of the factors of a number, organize them in pairs, starting with 1. Here is how we would find all of the factors of 12:

$$1 \times 12 = 12$$
$$2 \times 6 = 12$$
$$3 \times 4 = 12$$

12 has six factors: 1, 2, 3, 4, 6, and 12.

VIDEO
1.2 FINDING FACTORS
Watch at http://videos.ivyglobal.com

Here are some quick ways to test whether one number is divisible by another:

DIVISIBILITY RULES		
Divisible by ...	**When ...**	**Example**
2	The last digit is divisible by 2 (the number is even)	4028 is divisible by 2 because 8 is divisible by 2.
3	The sum of the digits is divisible by 3	465 is divisible by 3 because 4 + 6 + 5 = 15, which is divisible by 3.
4	The number formed by the last two digits is divisible by 4	340 is divisible by 4 because 40 is divisible by 4.
5	The last digit is 0 or 5	750 is divisible by 5 because it ends in 0.
6	The number is even and the sum of the digits is divisible by 3	1044 is divisible by 6 because it is even and 1 + 0 + 4 + 4 = 9, which is divisible by 3.
9	The sum of the digits is divisible by 9	1296 is divisible by 9 because 1 + 2 + 9 + 6 = 18, which is divisible by 9.
10	The last digit is 0	3390 is divisible by 10 because it ends in 0.

VIDEO
1.3 DIVISIBILITY RULES
Watch at http://videos.ivyglobal.com

FINDING MULTIPLES

Any number has an infinite number of multiples, because you can keep multiplying the number by bigger integers to get bigger multiples. Here is how we would find the first three multiples of 12:

$$12 \times 1 = 12$$
$$12 \times 2 = 24$$
$$12 \times 3 = 36$$

The first three multiples of 12 are 12, 24, and 36.

Notice that any number is a multiple of itself, because any number multiplied by 1 is itself. Any number is also a factor of itself, because any number can be divided by itself to give a quotient of 1.

PRIME AND COMPOSITE NUMBERS

A **prime** number is a number that has only two factors: itself and 1. A prime number is not divisible by any other integers. 1 is not a prime number, because it only has one factor: 1! 2 is the only even prime number. Here is a list of the first ten prime numbers:

- 2, 3, 5, 7, 11, 13, 17, 19, 23, 29...

A **composite** number is a number that has more than two factors. Composite numbers are not prime numbers because they are divisible by three or more integers. For example, 15 is a composite number because it is divisible by 1, 15, 3, and 5.

FACTOR TREES AND PRIME FACTORS

Draw a **factor tree** to find the prime factors of any integer. Start with any two factors of that integer. Then, find two factors of each of these numbers. Continue drawing branches until you end up with all prime numbers at the end of your tree. These are your **prime factors.**

For example, we can draw a factor tree for 72 by starting with the factors 8 and 9:

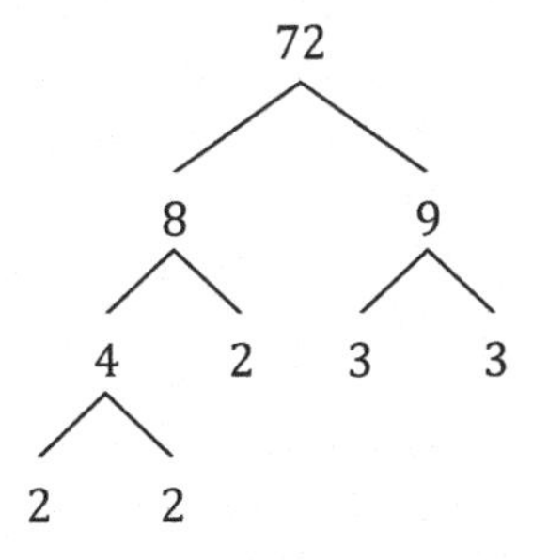

Based on this tree, we see that 72 is the product of the prime factors 2, 2, 2, 3, and 3. We can test this out by multiplying these prime factors together: $2 \times 2 \times 2 \times 3 \times 3 = 72$.

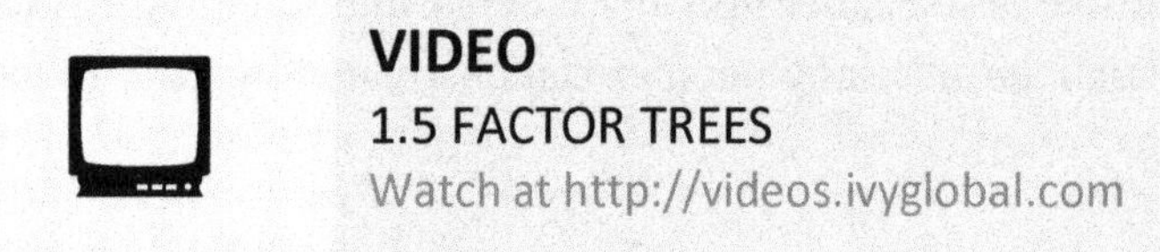

VIDEO
1.5 FACTOR TREES
Watch at http://videos.ivyglobal.com

GREATEST COMMON FACTOR (GCF)

The **greatest common factor (GCF)** of two integers is the largest integer that is a factor of both integers. For example, 8 is the GCF of 16 and 24. To find the GCF of two numbers, first find their prime factors using factor trees:

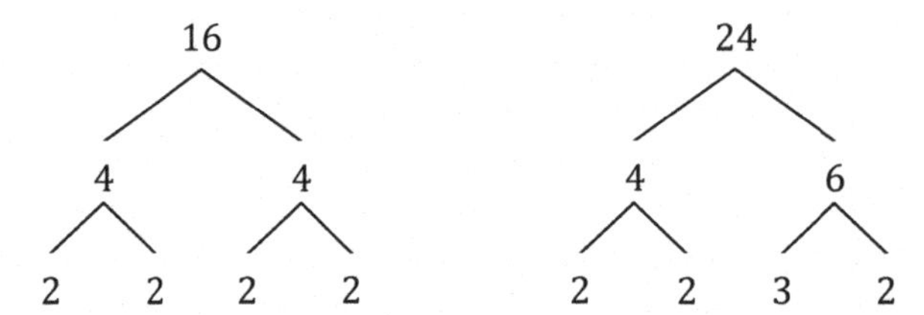

Based on these prime factors, we can see that 16 and 24 share three 2s. Multiply these shared prime factors together to find their GCF: $2 \times 2 \times 2 = 8$.

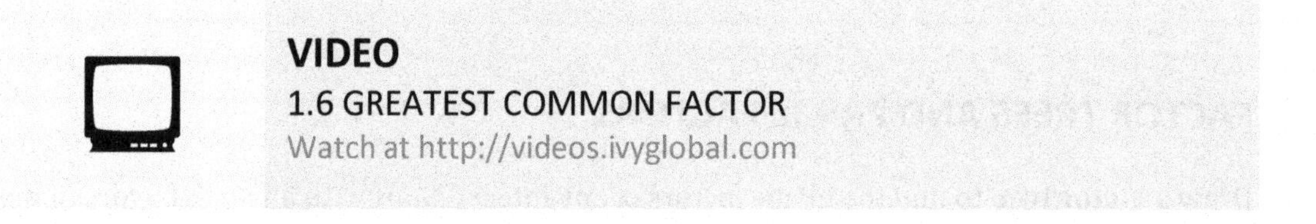

VIDEO
1.6 GREATEST COMMON FACTOR
Watch at http://videos.ivyglobal.com

LEAST COMMON MULTIPLE (LCM)

The **least common multiple (LCM)** of two integers is the smallest integer that is a multiple of both integers. For example, 48 is the LCM of 16 and 24. To find the LCM of two numbers, start by creating factor trees. Then, multiply the factors that appear the most number of times in each factor tree.

For instance, we can show the prime factors of 16 and 24 in a Venn Diagram:

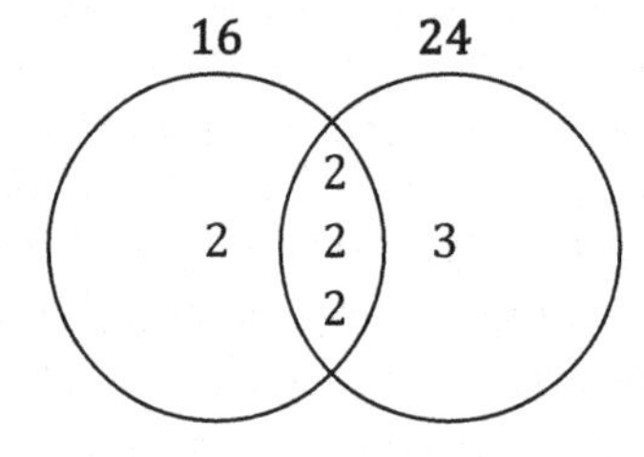

In total, four 2s and one 3 appear in these prime factors, excluding repeats. Therefore, the LCM of 16 and 26 is $2 \times 2 \times 2 \times 2 \times 3 = 48$.

VIDEO

1.7 LEAST COMMON MULTIPLE

Watch at http://videos.ivyglobal.com

PRACTICE QUESTIONS: FACTORS AND MULTIPLES

1. List the first 4 multiples of 2:

2. List the first 5 multiples of 7:

3. List all of the factors of 10:

4. List all of the factors of 48:

5. List all of the prime numbers between 10 and 20:

6. Is 216 divisible by 4?

7. Is 3972 divisible by 3?

8. Is 3972 divisible by 9?

9. Is 123456789 divisible by 6?

10. What is the remainder when 5 is divided by 2?

11. What is the remainder when 35 is divided by 3?

12. What is the remainder when 7 is divided by 7?

13. Find all of the prime factors of 18:

14. Find all of the prime factors of 34:

15. Find all of the prime factors of 84:

16. Find the greatest common factor of 36 and 45:

17. Find the greatest common factor of 1 and 2:

18. Find the least common multiple of 10 and 6:

19. Find the least common multiple of 15 and 5:

20. Let ☼x represent the number of distinct factors of any number x. For example, ☼$6 = 4$ because 6 has four distinct factors: 1, 2, 3 and 6. What is ☼9?

FRACTIONS

ALL LEVELS

SECTION 4

A fraction can be thought of in two ways. First, it is another way to represent division. When we write $\frac{3}{4}$, we mean three divided by four. But more importantly, a fraction represents a portion of a whole. The number on top is called the **numerator**, which represents the part. The number on the bottom is called the **denominator**, which represents the whole. In the fraction $\frac{3}{4}$, 3 is the numerator and 4 is the denominator. This fraction means that our whole has been divided into four equal pieces, and we are selecting three of them.

$$\frac{part}{whole} = \frac{numerator}{denominator}$$

For example, in the picture below, we've cut a pie into three equal pieces and picked one of those pieces. Because we've picked 1 part out of 3, 1 is our numerator and 3 is our denominator:

1/3

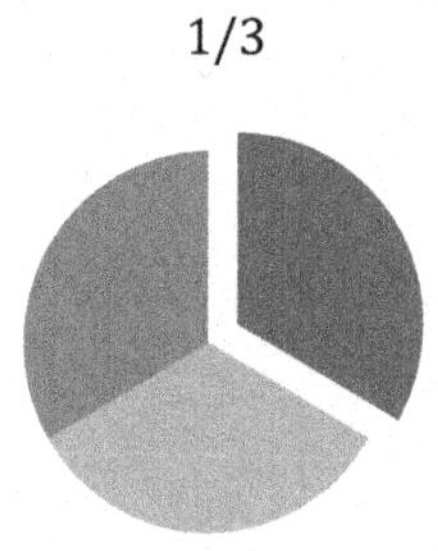

Here's another picture. This time, we've divided our pie into *four* equal pieces. We're still picking one of them, so 1 is still our numerator. However, there are four pieces to choose from, so 4 is our denominator:

1/4

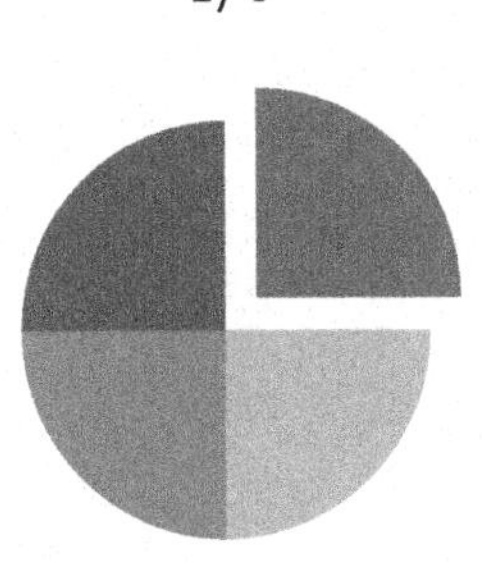

A whole number can also be written as a fraction with any denominator! Think about this in terms of division. To write the number 2, we could write $\frac{2}{1}$ (two divided by one), $\frac{4}{2}$ (four divided by two), $\frac{6}{3}$ (six divided by three), and so on. Anything divided by itself is one, so we can write 1 as $\frac{2}{2}$, $\frac{3}{3}$, $\frac{4}{4}$, etc.

EQUIVALENT FRACTIONS AND REDUCING FRACTIONS

Equivalent fractions have exactly the same value, but are written in different ways. For example, we can write one third as $\frac{1}{3}$, which represents one out of three pieces. We can also write it as $\frac{2}{6}$, which represents two out of six pieces. The picture below shows that these two fractions are equivalent. If you were eating these pieces of pie, you would have the same amount of pie regardless if whether you were eating $\frac{1}{3}$ or $\frac{2}{6}$:

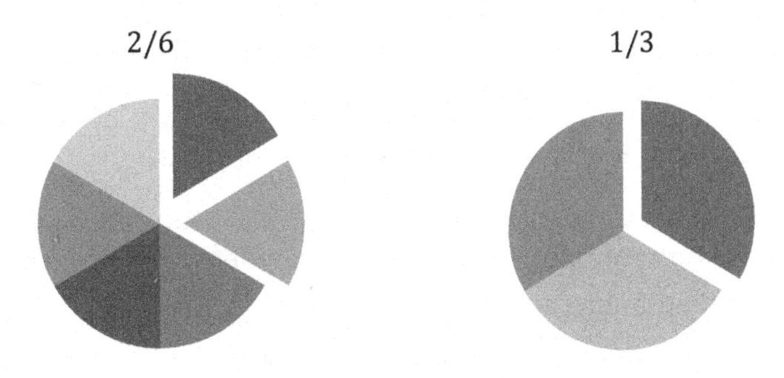

To find equivalent fractions, multiply both the numerator and denominator by the same number:

$$\frac{1}{3} = \frac{1 \times 2}{3 \times 2} = \frac{2}{6}$$

Reducing fractions means doing this process backwards. When your numerator and denominator share a common factor, reduce your fraction by dividing the top and bottom by this number:

$$\frac{2}{4} = \frac{2 \div 2}{4 \div 2} = \frac{1}{2}$$

A fraction is reduced to its **lowest terms** when the numerator and denominator no longer share any common factors—when you have the smallest possible denominator. In the example above, $\frac{1}{2}$ is in lowest terms because there is no number that divides into both 1 and 2.

VIDEO
1.8 INTRO TO FRACTIONS
Watch at http://videos.ivyglobal.com

COMPARING FRACTIONS

When fractions have the **same numerator**, they can be placed in order from least to greatest by ordering their denominators from greatest to least. Or, to put them in order from greatest to least, order the denominators from least to greatest.

For example:

Order the following fractions from least to greatest:

$$\frac{6}{2}, \frac{6}{7}, \frac{6}{1}, \frac{6}{3}$$

All of these fractions have the same numerator, 6. To order them from least to greatest, put the fractions in the order where the denominators are ordered from greatest to least. The result is $\frac{6}{7}, \frac{6}{3}, \frac{6}{2}, \frac{6}{1}$.

When fractions have the **same denominator**, you can determine their order from least to greatest by ordering their numerators from *least to greatest.* Or, to put them in order from greatest to least, order the numerators from greatest to least.

For example:

Order the following fractions from least to greatest:

$$\frac{7}{15}, \frac{3}{15}, \frac{12}{15}, \frac{8}{15}$$

All of these fractions have the same denominator, 15. To order them from least to greatest, put the fractions in the order where the numerators are ordered from least to greatest. The result is $\frac{3}{15}, \frac{7}{15}, \frac{8}{15}, \frac{12}{15}$.

To compare fractions that do not have the same numerator or denominator, you first need to convert them into equivalent fractions with the same denominator. Once the fractions have the same denominator, your smallest fraction will have the smallest numerator, and your largest fraction will have the largest numerator.

For example, to compare the fractions $\frac{5}{6}$ and $\frac{7}{9}$, find a denominator that will work for both of these fractions. Often, the easiest denominator to use is the least common multiple of both denominators. The least common multiple of 6 and 9 is 18, so we will convert both of these fractions into equivalent fractions with a denominator of 18:

$$\frac{5}{6} = \frac{5 \times 3}{6 \times 3} = \frac{15}{18}$$

$$\frac{7}{9} = \frac{7 \times 2}{9 \times 2} = \frac{14}{18}$$

15 is bigger than 14, so we can see that $\frac{5}{6}$ is bigger than $\frac{7}{9}$.

VIDEO

1.9 COMPARING FRACTIONS

Watch at http://videos.ivyglobal.com

ADDING AND SUBTRACTING FRACTIONS

You can only add or subtract two fractions when they have the same denominator. To add or subtract two fractions with different denominators, you first need to convert them to equivalent fractions with the same denominator. Then, you can add or subtract the numerators. For example:

$$\frac{3}{4} + \frac{2}{3}$$

To add $\frac{3}{4}$ and $\frac{2}{3}$, we need to find the least common denominator of both fractions. In this case, 12 would be the best number to use. Then, we need to re-write these fractions with 12 as the denominator:

$$\frac{3}{4} = \frac{3 \times 3}{4 \times 3} = \frac{9}{12}$$

$$\frac{2}{3} = \frac{2 \times 4}{3 \times 4} = \frac{8}{12}$$

Now that both fractions have the same denominator, we can add them by adding their numerators:

$$\frac{3}{4} + \frac{2}{3} = \frac{9}{12} + \frac{8}{12} = \frac{17}{12}$$

If we wanted to subtract these fractions, we would go through the same process and then subtract the numerators:

$$\frac{3}{4} - \frac{2}{3} = \frac{9}{12} - \frac{8}{12} = \frac{1}{12}$$

VIDEO

1.10 ADDING AND SUBTRACTING FRACTIONS

Watch at http://videos.ivyglobal.com

MIXED NUMBERS AND IMPROPER FRACTIONS

A **mixed number** is a combination of a whole number and a fraction. For instance, $1\frac{2}{5}$ is a mixed number that means "1 and 2 fifths," or "1 plus 2 fifths." To add or subtract mixed numbers, we must convert them to **improper fractions**, which are fractions where the numerator is bigger than the denominator. Here's how:

- First, write your mixed number as an addition problem: $1\frac{2}{5} = 1 + \frac{2}{5}$
- Then, convert your whole number into a fraction with the same denominator. 1 is the same as 5 fifths, so we can write: $1 + \frac{2}{5} = \frac{5}{5} + \frac{2}{5}$
- Then, add the two fractions by adding their numerators: $\frac{5}{5} + \frac{2}{5} = \frac{7}{5}$. This improper fraction is the same as the mixed number $1\frac{2}{5}$.

To go backwards and convert an improper fraction into a mixed number, you need to remember that a fraction can also mean division. Divide the numerator by the denominator to get a whole number and a remainder. This remainder becomes the numerator of your new fraction.

For example, $\frac{13}{6}$ means 13 divided by 6, which is 2 with a remainder of 1. Therefore, we would write the mixed number $2\frac{1}{6}$.

VIDEO

1.11 MIXED NUMBERS AND IMPROPER FRACTIONS

Watch at http://videos.ivyglobal.com

MULTIPLYING AND DIVIDING FRACTIONS

Multiplying fractions is very easy. Simply multiply the numerators and the denominators:

$$\frac{4}{5} \times \frac{3}{7} = \frac{4 \times 3}{5 \times 7} = \frac{12}{35}$$

VIDEO

1.12 MULTIPLYING FRACTIONS

Watch at http://videos.ivyglobal.com

To divide one fraction by another, you multiply by the **reciprocal** of the second fraction, which is a fancy word for the upside-down version of this fraction. Flip the second fraction upside-down and multiply straight across:

$$\frac{4}{5} \div \frac{3}{7} = \frac{4}{5} \times \frac{7}{3} = \frac{4 \times 7}{5 \times 3} = \frac{28}{15}$$

VIDEO

1.13 DIVIDING FRACTIONS

Watch at http://videos.ivyglobal.com

PRACTICE QUESTIONS: FRACTIONS

1. What fraction of the shape below is shaded?

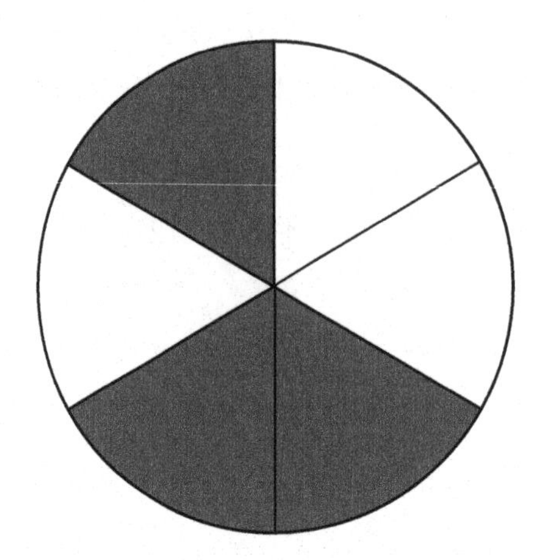

2. What fraction of the shape below is shaded?

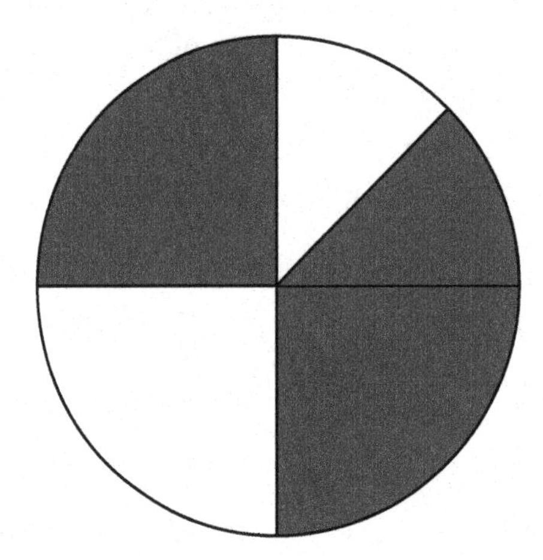

3. Reduce $\frac{16}{48}$ to lowest terms:

4. Reduce $\frac{12}{32}$ to lowest terms:

5. Re-write $\frac{3}{4}$ with a denominator of 12:

6. Re-write $\frac{3}{5}$ with a denominator of 25:

For questions 7-10, put the fractions in order from greatest to smallest:

7. $\frac{9}{7}, \frac{4}{7}, \frac{1}{7}, \frac{12}{7}$

8. $\frac{5}{2}, \frac{5}{8}, \frac{5}{3}, \frac{5}{6}$

9. $\frac{12}{8}, \frac{4}{8}, \frac{1}{8}, \frac{10}{8}$

10. $\frac{3}{8}, \frac{3}{2}, \frac{3}{3}, \frac{3}{7}$

11. Which is bigger, $\frac{4}{7}$ or $\frac{7}{10}$?

12. Which is bigger, $\frac{3}{5}$ or $\frac{5}{9}$?

13. $\frac{2}{3} + \frac{4}{5} =$

14. $\frac{2}{5} + \frac{4}{3} =$

15. $\frac{4}{5} - \frac{1}{2} =$

16. $\frac{8}{9} - \frac{3}{4} =$

17. $1\frac{5}{6} + \frac{1}{12} =$

18. Write $1\frac{2}{3}$ as an improper fraction:

19. Write $3\frac{1}{7}$ as an improper fraction:

20. Write $\frac{10}{3}$ as a mixed number:

21. Write $\frac{9}{5}$ as a mixed number:

22. $\frac{3}{8} \times \frac{1}{4} =$

23. $\frac{5}{8} \div \frac{2}{3} =$

24. $1\frac{3}{5} \times \frac{1}{2} =$

25. $4\frac{6}{7} \div 2 =$

RATIOS

ALL LEVELS

SECTION 5

While a fraction represents a relationship between a part and a whole, a **ratio** represents a relationship between two or more parts. For instance, a ratio might compare the number of girls to the number of boys in a class, or the amount of sugar to the amount of water in a recipe. A ratio can be expressed verbally, using a colon, or using a numerator and a denominator like a fraction:

- The ratio of boys to girls is 2 to 3.
- The ratio of boys to girls is 2:3.
- The ratio of boys to girls is $\frac{2}{3}$.

CONVERTING BETWEEN RATIOS AND FRACTIONS

You will sometimes be asked to convert between ratios and fractions. Remember that the two numbers in a ratio are both parts, while the denominator in a fraction represents the whole. Therefore, you need to add both parts together to find your new denominator. For example:

> The ratio of boys to girls in a class is $\frac{2}{3}$. If there are 12 girls in the class, what is the fraction of boys in the class?

You can write this as an equation. If the ratio of boys to girls in the class is $\frac{2}{3}$, the fraction of boys in the class is $\frac{2}{2+3} = \frac{2}{5}$. The fraction of girls in the class is $\frac{3}{2+3} = \frac{3}{5}$.

WORD PROBLEMS WITH RATIOS

You may need to use your knowledge of equivalent fractions to solve word problems involving ratios. For example:

The ratio of boys to girls in a class is $\frac{2}{3}$. If there are 12 girls in the class, what is the number of boys in the class?

You can write this as an equation:

$$\frac{boys}{girls} = \frac{2}{3} = \frac{?}{12}$$

This equation is asking you to re-write the ratio $\frac{2}{3}$ with a denominator of 12. To do this, multiply both the numerator and the denominator by the same number to find the equivalent ratio:

$$\frac{boys}{girls} = \frac{2 \times 4}{3 \times 4} = \frac{8}{12}$$

If the ratio of boys to girls is $\frac{2}{3}$ and there are 12 girls in the class, there must be 8 boys in the class.

VIDEO

1.14 INTRO TO RATIOS

Watch at http://videos.ivyglobal.com

CROSS-MULTIPLYING: MIDDLE AND UPPER LEVEL ONLY

In examples like the one above where two ratios are set equal to each other, you can also solve for the missing variable by **cross-multiplying**:

$$\text{If } \frac{a}{b} = \frac{c}{d}, \text{ then } ad = cb.$$

For example:

A recipe calls for a ratio of 2 teaspoons of cinnamon for every 3 teaspoons of sugar. If you want to add 7 teaspoons of cinnamon, how much sugar do you need?

First, set up an equation and let x represent the amount of sugar:

$$\frac{2}{3} = \frac{7}{x}$$

Then, cross-multiply and solve:

$$2x = 21$$
$$x = 10.5$$

For 7 teaspoons of cinnamon, you need 10.5 teaspoons of sugar.

(See Part 2 for more information about solving algebraic equations.)

PRACTICE QUESTIONS: RATIOS

For questions 1-4, consider the following information:

A class library has 200 books, of which 20 are history books and 30 are math books.

1. What is the ratio of history books to math books?

2. What is the ratio of history books to non-history books?

3. What fraction of the library's books are math books?

4. If the library adds 50 new books, what would be the ratio of new books to old books?

5. Jenny bought a bag of gummy worms and hard candies. In the bag, the ratio of gummy worms to hard candies is 3 to 5. What is the fraction of hard candies in the bag?

6. A school has a student-teacher ratio of 15 to 1. If the school has 22 teachers, how many students are at the school?

7. A recipe says to add a ratio of 3 cups of water to every 2 cups of rice. If John adds 6 cups of rice, how much water should he add?

For questions 8-11, consider the following information:

Mrs. Markle has a jar of green, red, and blue marbles on her desk. In the jar, the ratio of green to red to blue marbles is 3:2:4.

8. What is the ratio of green marbles to non-green marbles?

9. What is the fraction of blue marbles in the jar?

10. If there are 12 red marbles, how many green marbles are in the jar?

11. If there are 12 red marbles, how many total marbles are in the jar?

12. If 12 inches are equivalent to 30.48 centimeters, and there are 36 inches in one yard, how many centimeters are equivalent to one yard?

13. A store sells flour in 1-pound bags, which cost $1.50, and 5-pound bags, which cost $3.50. If Dominique needs to buy 10 pounds of flour, how much money will she save by buying 5-pound bags instead of 1-pound bags?

14. Monica has a wooden board 27 centimeters long. She needs to cut the board into two pieces whose lengths are in a ratio of 4:5. How long should she make the smallest piece?

15. The instructions for Kevin's plant fertilizer said to dissolve 1 packet of fertilizer in 2.5 cups of water. If Kevin is using 6 cups of water, how many packets of fertilizer does he need?

16. Amy can read 10 pages of her textbook in 15 minutes. How many pages can she read in 40 minutes?

17. If a fruit stand sells 5 kilograms of apples for $6.75, how many kilograms of apples can Carlos buy for $2.70?

Question 18 is Middle and Upper Level Only.

18. The tax on a car valued at $30,000 is $1,200. If there is a $2,000 tax on a second car and the same tax rate applies, what is the value of the second car?

DECIMALS

ALL LEVELS

SECTION 6

Decimals are another way of writing fractions without using a numerator or a denominator. In the decimal system, digits to the right of the decimal point represent fractions with a denominator of 10, 100, 1000, and so on. These digits fall into the tenths, hundredths, and thousandths place values. For instance, the number 351.748 could be read as "three hundred and fifty one, and seven tenths, four hundredths, and eight thousandths" based on the place values of its digits:

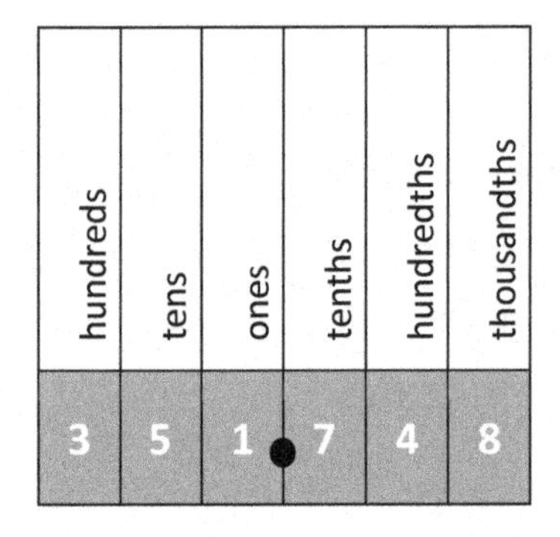

You would arrive at this number by adding the following fractions:

$$351.748 = 300 + 50 + 1 + \frac{7}{10} + \frac{4}{100} + \frac{8}{1000}$$

Another way of looking at decimals is on a **number line**, a visual representation of the divisions between numbers. Let's place 351.75 on the number line below. First, since 351.5 is halfway between 351 and 352, it would look like this on the number line:

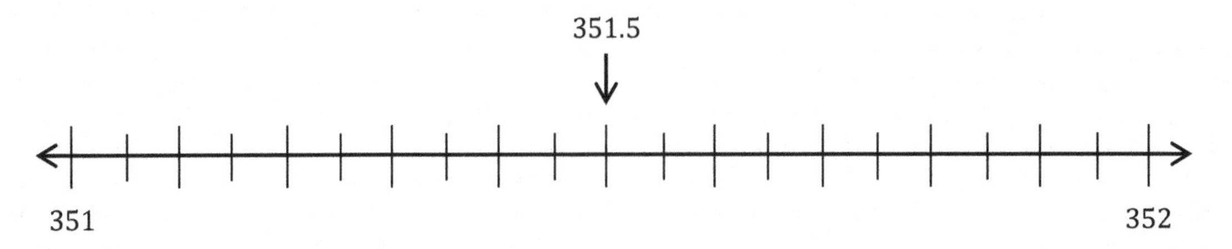

If you count the big tick marks between 351 and 352, you can see that 351.5 is positioned at the 5th tick mark. This means that each big tick mark represents a tenth, or 0.1. 351.5 is positioned at the 5th tick mark because it is 5 tenths, or 0.5, greater than 351.

What number is halfway between 351.5 and 352? We know that each big tick mark stands for 0.1, so we can write in the rest of the labels for these tick marks between 351.5 and 352. The halfway point is the small tick mark between 351.7 and 351.8:

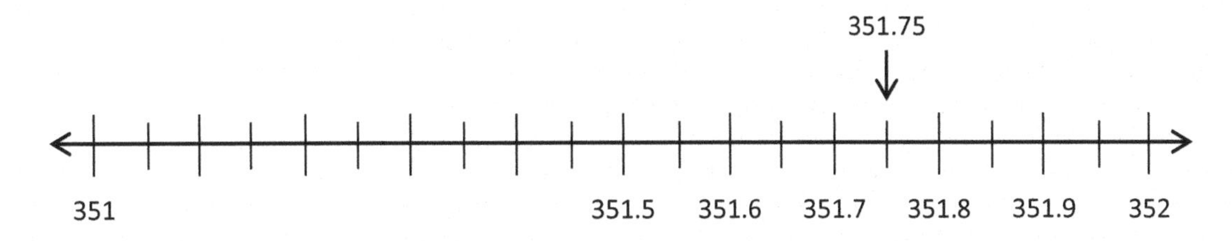

This small tick mark is halfway between two large tick marks, so it represents half of a tenth, or half of 0.1. Half of one tenth is equal to one twentieth, which is the same as 5 hundredths or 0.05. Because this small tick mark is 0.05 greater than 351.7, it represents 351.75.

ADDING AND SUBTRACTING DECIMALS

To add or subtract numbers with decimals, make sure you line up the decimal point:

$$\begin{array}{r} 8.51 \\ +\,17.34 \\ \hline 25.85 \end{array} \qquad \begin{array}{r} 10.25 \\ -2.11 \\ \hline 8.14 \end{array}$$

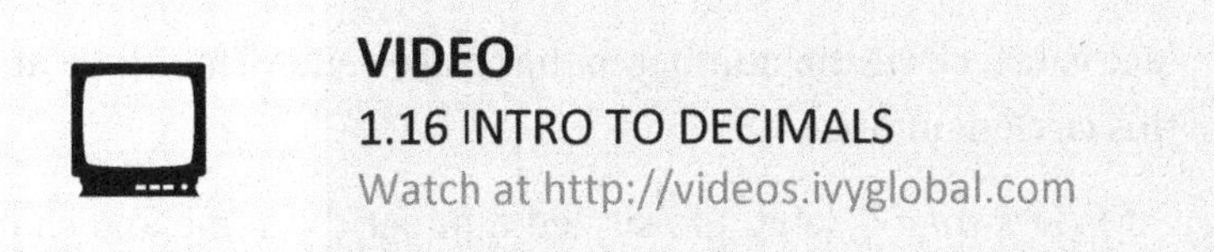

VIDEO
1.16 INTRO TO DECIMALS
Watch at http://videos.ivyglobal.com

MULTIPLYING AND DIVIDING DECIMALS

To multiply decimals, it doesn't matter whether your decimal points are lined up. Line up your two numbers in the most convenient way, and multiply as normal. Then, count the number of total digits to the right of the decimal point in both numbers, and move over the decimal point in your answer this many spaces:

$$\begin{array}{r} 1.52 \\ \times\,0.4 \\ \hline 0.608 \end{array} \qquad \begin{array}{r} 50 \\ \times\,0.11 \\ \hline 5.50 \end{array}$$

To divide decimals, you want to make sure that the number outside of the long division symbol is an integer. To do this, move the decimal point over the same number of spaces for both numbers and divide as usual. It is okay if you still have a decimal point in the number underneath the long division symbol. Re-write this decimal point in exactly the same position on top of the long division symbol, where you will put your answer:

$$0.2\overline{)3.432} = 2\overset{17.16}{\overline{)34.32}}$$

If you run out of spaces to move your decimal point in the number underneath the long division symbol, just add an appropriate number of zeros:

$$3.25\overline{)13.00} = 325\overset{4}{\overline{)1300}}$$

VIDEO
1.17 MULTIPLYING AND DIVIDING DECIMALS
Watch at http://videos.ivyglobal.com

ROUNDING DECIMALS

Rounding is a method we use to simplify a number. It is useful when we are trying to estimate, or make a rough calculation. We can round a number to any place value that is convenient, such as the nearest tenth, hundredth, or hundred.

To round a number to any place value, circle the number in that place value. Then, look at the digit directly to the right of this circled number.

- If the digit to the right is less than 5, keep the circled number the same and change all digits to the right of this number to zero.
- If the digit to the right is equal to or greater than 5, add 1 to the circled number and change all digits to the right of this number to zero.

For example:

Round 5412.798 to the nearest hundred.

First, locate the number in the hundreds place and circle it. This is the number 4. Then, look at the digit directly to its right, which is the digit 1. 1 is less than 5, so keep 4 the same and change all numbers to its right to zero. The answer is 5400.000.

As another example:

Round 2318.76 to the nearest tenth.

First, locate the number in the tenths place and circle it. This is the number 7. Then, look at the digit directly to its right, which is the digit 6. Because 6 is greater than 5, we are going to add 1 to our circled number, 7:

$$7 + 1 = 8$$

All of the numbers to the right of this number will be changed to zeros. The answer is 2318.80.

Here is one more example:

Round 152.97 to the nearest tenth.

The number 9 is in the tenths place. The digit to the right of this 9 is a 7. Since 7 is greater than 5, we add 1 to the 9:

$$9 + 1 = 10$$

But we can't put 10 into the tenths place, since 10 isn't a single-digit number. Instead, we put a 0 into the tenths place, and carry the 1 over into the ones place. Our final answer is 153.00.

In order to estimate or simplify an arithmetic problem, we can round all of the numbers and then perform the operation on the simplified numbers. The answer should be a good estimate of the real answer.

For example, to add 23 to 56, you can round each number to the nearest ten. $20 + 60 = 80$ is a simpler problem. The real answer is 79, so our estimate is close.

CONVERTING BETWEEN FRACTIONS AND DECIMALS

There are two ways to convert from a fraction to a decimal. The short way, which will work for a lot of fractions but not all of them, is to convert your fraction into an equivalent fraction with a denominator of 10, 100, or 1000. Then, re-write this fraction as a decimal:

$$\frac{11}{20} = \frac{11 \times 5}{20 \times 5} = \frac{55}{100} = 0.55$$

The long way, which will work for all fractions, is to treat your fraction as a long division problem and divide your numerator by your denominator:

$$20\overline{)11.00} \quad 0.55$$

To convert from a decimal to a fraction, re-write your decimal as a fraction with a denominator of 10, 100, or 1000. Then, reduce to lowest terms:

$$0.68 = \frac{68}{100} = \frac{68 \div 4}{100 \div 4} = \frac{17}{25}$$

VIDEO

1.18 CONVERTING BETWEEN FRACTIONS AND DECIMALS

Watch at http://videos.ivyglobal.com

PRACTICE QUESTIONS: DECIMALS

1. What number corresponds with the circle on the number line below?

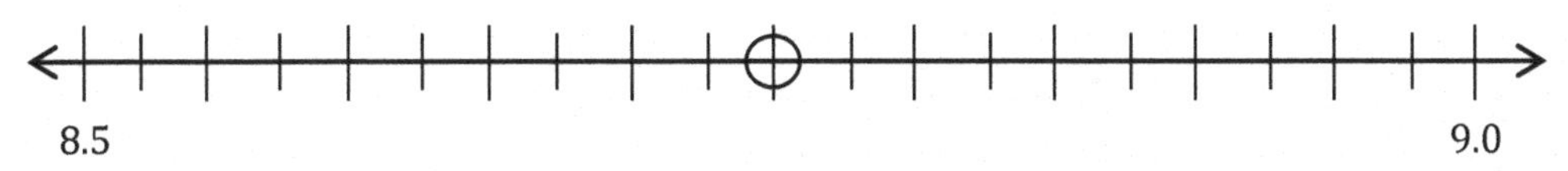

2. What number corresponds with the circle on the number line below?

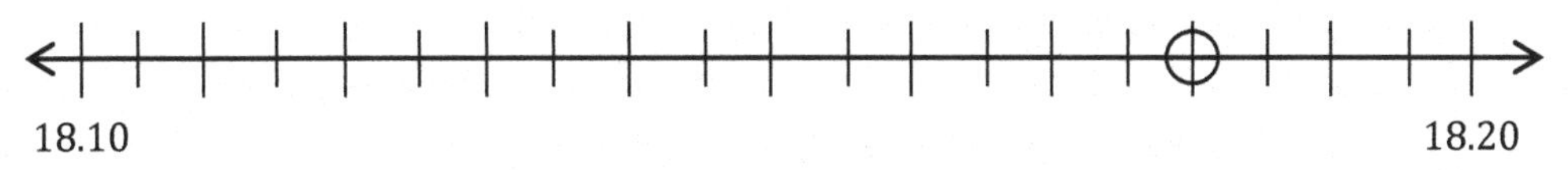

3. $1.25 + 4.75 =$

4. $3.65 + 4.7 =$

5. $7.4 - 1.02 =$

6. $15.42 + 0.675 =$

7. $3.78 - 2.5 =$

8. $5.36 - 0.005 =$

9. $4 \times 6.7 =$

10. $115.5 \times 0.4 =$

11. $8 \div 1.6 =$

12. $0.8 \div 16 =$

13. $8.68 \times 3.3 =$

14. $4.2 \div 0.7 =$

15. $15.96 \div 3.8 =$

For questions 16-18, round each number to the nearest tenth:

16. 29.061

17. 3189.5204

18. 40.976

For questions 19-21, round each number to the nearest thousand:

19. 58421.3

20. 75002

21. 948.42

22. Write $\frac{7}{8}$ as a decimal:

23. Write $\frac{9}{50}$ as a decimal:

24. Write $\frac{3}{25}$ as a decimal:

25. Write $\frac{19}{40}$ as a decimal:

26. Write 0.25 as a fraction:

27. Write 0.6 as a fraction:

28. Write 0.35 as a fraction:

WORD PROBLEMS

ALL LEVELS

SECTION 7

Many questions on the ISEE ask you to solve a word problem with your knowledge of math and logic. We've already discussed many word problems that involve arithmetic, fractions, ratios, decimals, and percents. In this section, we'll look at a few more concepts that are helpful for solving ISEE word problems.

TIME

In math problems involving time, you will be dealing with seconds, minutes, hours, days and weeks. These quantities of time are related to each other as follows:

- There are 60 seconds in a minute.
- There are 60 minutes in an hour.
- There are 24 hours in a day.

The day is divided into 24 hours. These 24 hours are split into two 12-hour periods denoted by AM (morning hours) and PM (night hours). Be sure to pay attention to whether the question states AM or PM! The format used to represent time has a colon separating the hours from minutes with AM or PM following. For example, 12:34 PM represents the time twelve hours and 34 minutes in the afternoon. *Important!* Remember that midnight is 12:00 AM and noon is 12:00 PM.

Remember the following facts about days, weeks, months, and years:

- There are 7 days in a week.
- There are 30 days in the months of April, June, September, and November.
- There are 31 days in the months of January, March, May, July, August, October, and December.
- There are usually 28 days in February, but every four years there is a "leap year" where February has 29 days.
- There are usually 365 days in a year. Can you guess how many days are in a leap year?

RATE

Some word problems will ask you about time, distance, and **rate**. Rate is a measure of how something changes over time. A speed like "miles per hour" is an example of a rate: this tells you how many miles you are traveling in one hour.

If you know the rate (how quickly you are traveling) and the time spent traveling, then you can calculate the distance you will cover. Distance is always equal to rate multiplied by time:

$$Distance = Rate \times Time$$

For example:

A train travels at 60 miles per hour. How many miles will it travel in 2 hours?

60 miles per hour is the train's rate, and it is traveling for a total of 2 hours. Therefore, we can find the distance it will travel by multiplying 60 by 2:

$$Distance = 60\ mph \times 2hrs = 120\ miles$$

The train will travel 120 miles in 2 hours.

Here is another example:

Armin lives one mile away from the grocery store. If it takes him 15 minutes to walk to the store, he walks at a speed of how many miles per minute?

In this problem, we know Armin's distance and his time, but we need to find his rate. If distance is equal to rate multiplied by time, then we can find Armin's rate by dividing his distance by his time:

$$Rate = Distance \div Time$$

In Armin's case, we would divide his distance (1 mile) by his time (15 minutes) to find his rate in miles per minute:

$$Rate = 1\ mile \div 15\ mins = \frac{1}{15}\ miles/minute$$

Armin walks at a rate of $\frac{1}{15}$ miles per minute.

MONEY

When dealing with questions involving money amounts, it is important to pay attention to the location of the decimal point. Always write your dollar amounts with two digits to the right of the decimal. For example, if you wanted to say that you have 5 dollars, you would write it as $5.00, showing two digits on the right of the decimal. If you had 5 dollars and 25 cents, it would be written as $5.25. When you are doing addition and subtraction problems involving money, make sure you line up your decimal points so that you don't mix up your place values.

You should be familiar with the following coins and how much they are worth:

COIN	VALUE
Penny	$0.01
Nickel	$0.05
Dime	$0.10
Quarter	$0.25
Dollar	$1.00

UNITS

Units are standard quantities of measurement. Seconds, minutes, hours, and days are all units of time. Dollars and cents are units of money. A dozen is a unit that refers to a group of 12 things. Eggs are frequently sold by the dozen— that is, in groups of 12.

There are two systems of units frequently used to measure mass, length, and volume. The **imperial system** is used frequently in the United States. The imperial system measures weight in pounds (abbreviated *lb*), and it uses the following units to measure length:

- Inch
- Foot: 12 inches
- Yard: 3 feet
- Mile: 5,280 feet

The imperial system uses the following units to measure volume:

- Cup

- Pint: 2 cups
- Quart: 2 pints (4 cups)
- Gallon: 4 quarts (16 cups)

The **metric system** is very important to learn because it is used more commonly internationally and in the scientific community. In the metric system, mass is measured in grams, length is measured in meters, and volume is measured in liters. Each of these units can be abbreviated as *g* for grams, *m* for meters and *l* for liters.

The metric system also has prefixes, or different word beginnings, that indicate different multiples of 10. These prefixes can be combined with any of the units (grams, meters, or liters) to result in the multiplied amounts:

- Kilo = 1000
- Hecto = 100
- Deca = 10
- Deci = 1/10
- Centi = 1/100
- Milli = 1/1000

For example, a kilometer is 1000 meters, a decaliter is 10 liters, and a milligram is 1/1000 of a gram, or 0.001 grams.

Each prefix also has a short form that is combined with the unit to make writing simpler.

- Kilo: k
- Hecto: h
- Deca: D
- Deci: d
- Centi: c
- Milli: m

Instead of writing "kilogram," we can write the abbreviation "kg." Instead of "millimeter," we can write "mm." Questions on the ISEE may be written in abbreviations, so it is important to know what these mean.

Here's a quick way to remember the correct order of prefixes. If you write out the prefix abbreviations from biggest to smallest, you'll get

k h D d c m

A common phrase to remember this order is **K**ing **H**enry **D**ied **D**rinking **C**hocolate **M**ilk.

The ISEE may also ask you to convert between different prefixes. As you move up the list of prefixes, the next unit is 10 times greater than the unit below it. As you move down the list, the next unit is one-tenth the unit above it. To move from one prefix to another, set up a ratio between the two units. For example:

How many meters are equal to 16 kilometers?

From our chart above, we know that one kilometer equals 1,000 meters. To figure out how many meters equal 16 kilometers, we can set up the following ratios:

$$\frac{meters}{kilometers} = \frac{1000}{1} = \frac{?}{16}$$

$$\frac{meters}{kilometers} = \frac{1000 \times 16}{1 \times 16} = \frac{16{,}000}{16}$$

Because there are 1,000 meters in 1 kilometer, there must be 16,000 meters in 16 kilometers.

PATTERNS

ISEE word problems may also involve **patterns**, or lists that follow a rule. This rule tells you what to do to get the next item in the pattern. For example, the counting numbers follow a pattern where you take the first number 1, and you add one to get the second number 2. Then you add one to this number to get the third number 3, and so on.

A pattern involving numbers is called a **sequence**, and the numbers in the pattern are called **terms**. Two types of sequences are described below:

- A number may be *added* to each term to get the next term. For example, if we start with the number 5 and add 2 to get 7, then add 2 to 7 to get 9, and continue adding 2, we get the sequence 5, 7, 9, 11, 13. In this sequence, 5 is the first term, 7 is the second term and 13 is the fifth term of the sequence.
- Each term may also be *multiplied* by a number to get the next term. For example, if we start with the number 5 and multiply it by 2 to get 10, and then multiply 10 by 2 to get 20, and keep multiplying by 2, we get the sequence 5, 10, 20, 40, 80.

Both types of sequences can be increasing or decreasing. If you are asked to determine a specific term in a sequence, you must first figure out the rule that is being used.

If you have an "adding sequence," look for the constant number that is added to each term to get the next one. This can be found by subtracting any number in the list from the number after it. For example:

How would you find the next number in the list below?

$$2, 5, 8, 11, 14$$

To determine the rule in this sequence, we can subtract any two consecutive numbers in the list. For example, we can calculate $5 - 2 = 3$, or $11 - 8 = 3$, or $14 - 11 = 3$. This tells us the rule for this sequence: add 3 to any term in the sequence and you'll find the next term.

Now that we know the rule, we can find the next number in the sequence by adding 3:

$$14 + 3 = 17$$

The next number in this sequence is 17.

If the list is a "multiplying sequence," look for the constant number that each term is multiplied by. This can be found by dividing any term by the term before it.

For example:

What comes next in the sequence below?

$$125, 25, 5, 1$$

To determine the rule in this sequence, we can divide any of the terms by the term before it. For example, we can calculate $\frac{25}{125} = \frac{1}{5}$ or $\frac{5}{25} = \frac{1}{5}$. This tells us the rule for this sequence: multiply any term in the sequence by $\frac{1}{5}$, and you'll find the next term. Equivalently, divide any term in the sequence by 5, and you'll find the next term.

Now that we know the rule, we can find the next number in the sequence by multiplying the last number by $\frac{1}{5}$:

$$1 \times \frac{1}{5} = \frac{1}{5}$$

The next number in this sequence is $\frac{1}{5}$.

If you are trying to determine whether a sequence is produced by adding or multiplying, try out both of these methods and see which one works for all of the terms that you are given.

ESTIMATING

We have focused so far on getting *exactly* the right answer for any ISEE word problem. Sometimes, however, we are asked to **estimate** an answer. Estimating is a process for guessing an approximate answer without calculating it exactly.

For example, let's look at the question below:

> If 171 potatoes cost 255 dollars, approximately how much does one potato cost?

We know that 171 potatoes cost 255 dollars. In order to figure out how much one potato costs, we'll need to divide 255 dollars by 171:

$$\frac{255}{171}$$

171 doesn't divide into 255 neatly, so we need to **estimate** what this would equal in decimal form. To make this equation more user-friendly, we can round to numbers that are easier to divide. We want to round to the closest numbers we can find to help us solve the equation.

We know that 171 is close to 170, and 255 is close to 260. Using the numbers 170 and 260, we can more easily estimate the price per potato:

$$\frac{260}{170} =$$

How did this simplify things? Both of these numbers now end in 0, which means they are both multiples of 10. Therefore, we can reduce this fraction by dividing both the numerator and the denominator by 10:

$$\frac{260}{170} = \frac{26 \div 10}{17 \div 10} = \frac{26}{17}$$

Now we're only dividing 26 by 17. To see how many times 17 goes into 26, let's multiply 17 by some integers until we reach a number greater than 26:

$$17 \times 1 = 17$$

$$17 \times 2 = 34$$

26 is greater than 17 but less than 34, so we know our number must be between 1 and 2. In fact, 26 is almost exactly halfway between 17 and 34, so our number should be about halfway between 1 and 2. Therefore, we can guess that the answer is approximately 1.5.

Here's a summary of how we found this. In the equation below, the symbol $\approx$ means "is approximately equal to:"

$$\frac{255\ dollars}{171\ potatoes} \approx \frac{260\ dollars}{170\ potatoes} \approx 1.5\ dollars/potato$$

To check that we have estimated the right answer, we can multiply our 171 potatoes by \$1.50. If our answer is close to \$255, then we know that we have made a good estimate:

$$171 \times \$1.50 = \$256.50$$

This is very close to \$255, so our estimate is good.

PRACTICE QUESTIONS: WORD PROBLEMS

1. Thomas arrived at the park 18 minutes before noon. His sister arrived at the park 25 minutes later. At what time did his sister arrive at the park?

2. A play started at 8:30 PM and ended at 10:09 PM. How long was the play?

3. It takes two and a half hours to drive to the zoo. If Sam's family wants to arrive at the zoo when it opens at 10:15 AM, at what time should they leave home?

4. If a train is moving 50 miles per hour, what is the distance that it will travel in 3 hours?

5. When you walk your dog, you walk 0.5 miles away from your house and 0.5 miles back to your house. If you leave your house at 12:15PM and walk at a speed of 3 miles per hour, at what time will you return home?

For questions 6-10, write the total dollar and cent amount for the following combinations of coins:

6. Four dollars, 8 dimes, 3 nickels, 8 pennies

7. 8 dollars, 9 quarters, 6 dimes, 7 nickels, 2 pennies

8. 7 quarters, 6 nickels, 8 pennies

9. One $20 bill, 6 dollars, 8 quarters, 5 dimes, 5 pennies

For questions 10-13, write a combination of coins that would equal the following totals:

10. $0.45

11. $2.64

12. $1.03

13. $3.57

14. After spending $15.92 on a skateboard, Joe has $2.08 left. How much money did Joe have before he bought the skateboard?

15. Corwin has $32.55 to spend on hamburgers. If each hamburger costs $7.00, how many hamburgers can Corwin buy?

16. Raquel divides the money in her piggybank by 3 and adds $7. The result is $15. How much money did Raquel start with?

17. Jean earns $12 per hour. She was paid $444.00 for this week of work. How many hours did she work this week?

18. 25 kilograms is equal to how many grams?

19. 478 milliliters is equal to how many liters?

20. Cleo measured a length of string equal to 0.047 km. If she cuts the string into equal pieces that are each 50 cm long, how many pieces will she have?

21. What number comes next in the pattern below?

    37, 41, 45, 49, 53, ___

22. What is the missing number in the pattern below?

    64, 32, 16, ___, 4, 2

23. On his first day at school, Tommy made 1 friend. On his second day, he made 3 friends. On his third day, he made 9 friends, and on his fourth day, he made 27 friends. If this pattern continues, how many friends will Tommy make on his fifth day of school?

24. Gita sorted her marbles into bags. She placed 3 marbles in the first bag, 4 marbles in the second bag, 6 marbles in the third bag, and 9 marbles in the fourth bag. If she continued this pattern, how many marbles did she put in the sixth bag?

25. There are 155 children who have 31 marbles each. If the children pool their marbles together and divide them all evenly among 11 lucky parents, approximately how many marbles will each parent receive?

PERCENTS

MIDDLE/UPPER LEVEL ONLY

SECTION 8

A **percent** is another way of expressing a fraction with a denominator of 100. The word "percent" means "out of 100." For example, 30% means "30 out of 100."

CONVERTING AMONG PERCENTS, FRACTIONS, AND DECIMALS

A percent can always be re-written as a fraction with a denominator of 100. Write your percent as the numerator, 100 as the denominator, and reduce to lowest terms:

$$30\% = \frac{30}{100} = \frac{3}{10}$$

A percent is easily re-written as a decimal. Because your percent represents a certain number of hundredths, write this number in the hundredths place:

$$30\% = 30 \text{ hundredths} = 0.30 \text{ or } 0.3$$

Similarly, it is very simple to convert a decimal into a percent. Just multiply your decimal by 100 (move the decimal point over two places) and add a percent sign:

$$0.45 = 45\%$$

There are two ways to convert a fraction into a percent. The fast way, which will work for some fractions, is to convert your fraction into an equivalent fraction with a denominator of 100. Your numerator then becomes your percent:

$$\frac{13}{20} = \frac{13 \times 5}{20 \times 5} = \frac{65}{100} = 65\%$$

The slower way, which will work for all fractions, is to first convert the fraction into a decimal using long division, and then convert your decimal into a percent:

$$20\overline{)13.00} = 0.65$$

$$0.65 = 65\%$$

VIDEO

1.19 INTRO TO PERCENTS

Watch at http://videos.ivyglobal.com

COMMON EQUIVALENCIES

You should learn the most common equivalent fractions, decimals, and percents given in the chart below. The horizontal line above a decimal digit means that it repeats indefinitely.

FRACTION, DECIMAL, AND PERCENT EQUIVALENCIES		
Fraction	**Decimal**	**Percent**
$\frac{1}{2}$	0.5	50%
$\frac{1}{4}$	0.25	25%
$\frac{3}{4}$	0.75	75%
$\frac{1}{3}$	$0.\bar{3}$	$33.\bar{3}\%$
$\frac{2}{3}$	$0.\bar{6}$	$66.\bar{6}\%$
$\frac{1}{5}$	0.2	20%
$\frac{2}{5}$	0.4	40%
$\frac{3}{5}$	0.6	60%
$\frac{4}{5}$	0.8	80%
$\frac{1}{8}$	0.125	12.5%

SOLVING PERCENT PROBLEMS

In order to solve word problems involving percents, you will need to be very skilled at converting among percents, decimals, and fractions. Be sure you are entirely comfortable with this process before moving on to word problems.

For example, consider the following question:

> On his last science test, Adam answered 15 questions correctly and 5 questions incorrectly. He did not leave any questions blank. What percent of the questions did he answer correctly?

There are two ways to solve this question. First, you could write a fraction that represents the number of questions he answered correctly out of the total number of questions on the test, and then convert this fraction into a percent. Because he answered 15 questions correctly and there were 20 questions on the test, you would write:

$$\frac{15}{20} = \frac{15 \times 5}{20 \times 5} = \frac{75}{100} = 75\%$$

Or, you could convert this fraction into a decimal using long division, and then convert that decimal into a percent:

$$20\overline{)15.00} = 0.75$$

$$0.75 = 75\%$$

Either way, you find that Adam answered 75% of the questions correctly.

You may also be asked to find a certain percent of a number. In this case, remember that the word "of" means "multiply." Convert your percent into a fraction or decimal, and then multiply by your given number.

For example, consider the following question:

> As a special promotion, all clothes at a certain boutique are now discounted 40%. If the regular price of a dress at this boutique is \$80, what is the discounted price?

You can find 40% of \$80 in two ways. First, you could convert 40% into a fraction, and then multiply this fraction by \$80:

$$40\% = \frac{40}{100} = \frac{40 \div 20}{100 \div 20} = \frac{2}{5}$$

$$\frac{2}{5} \times \$80 = \frac{\$160}{5} = \$32$$

You could also convert 40% into a decimal and then multiply by $80:

$$40\% = \frac{40}{100} = 0.40 = 0.4$$

$$\begin{array}{r} \$80 \\ \times\ 0.4 \\ \hline \$32.0 \end{array}$$

You have now found that 40% of $80 is $32. However, the dress is 40% off of the original price, which means that you have to subtract $32 from $80 to find the discounted price:

$$\$80 - \$32 = \$48$$

The discounted price of the dress is $48.

Note: You could also have observed that if the dress is discounted by 40%, the new price must be 60% of the original price. If you convert 60% into a decimal and then multiply by 80, you'll get $0.6 \times 80 = 48$. This is the same value that we got above.

VIDEO
1.20 SOLVING PERCENT PROBLEMS
Watch at http://videos.ivyglobal.com

SOLVING PERCENT PROBLEMS WITH ALGEBRA (UPPER LEVEL ONLY)

Some percent problems will require you to set up an algebraic equation (*see Part 2 for more information about solving algebraic equations*). In this case, remember that the word "of" means "multiply," and use x to represent the missing percent or amount.

For example, consider the following problem:

> A book has been discounted 25%, which means that the discounted price is $3 lower than the original price. What was the original price of the book?

Based on this information, we can write the following sentence:

$3 is 25% of the original price of the book.

Now we need to put this sentence into an algebraic equation. "Is" means "equals," "of" means "multiply," and we will let x represent the unknown original price of the book:

$$\$3 = 25\% \times x$$

Then, convert 25% into a fraction or decimal, and solve for x:

$$\$3 = 0.25x$$

$$x = \$12$$

The original price of the book was $12.

VIDEO

1.21 SOLVING PERCENT PROBLEMS WITH ALGEBRA

Watch at http://videos.ivyglobal.com

PRACTICE QUESTIONS: PERCENTS

For all questions involving fractions, reduce fractions to lowest terms.

1. Write 60% as a fraction:

2. Write 37% as a decimal:

3. Write 85% as a fraction:

4. Write 29% as a decimal:

5. Write 0.73 as a percent:

6. Write 0.326 as a percent:

7. Write $\frac{3}{5}$ as a percent:

8. Write $\frac{11}{25}$ as a percent:

9. Write $\frac{5}{8}$ as a percent:

10. What is 80% of 45?

11. What is 70% of 90?

12. What is 37% of 300?

13. What is 25% of 60% of 500?

14. Amanda's class has 11 girls and 9 boys. What percent of the class are boys?

15. John has gray, blue, black, and white shirts in his drawer. If he has 4 gray shirts, 3 blue shirts, 6 black shirts, and 7 white shirts, what percent of his shirts are black?

16. Kevin's class has 30 students. If 40% of the students own pets, how many students do not own pets?

17. A CD is on sale for 25% off of the regular price. If the regular price is $16.40, how much is the sale price?

18. Out of all of the jelly beans in a jar, 30% are green. Of the green jelly beans, 75% are lime-flavored. If there are 400 total jelly beans in the jar, how many are lime-flavored?

Questions 19-20 are Upper Level Only.

19. Elise answered 90% of the questions on her math exam correctly. If she answered 2 questions incorrectly and skipped 3 questions, how many total questions were on the exam?

20. In an appliance store, a refrigerator is on sale for 35% off of the original price. If the discounted price is $130, what was the original price?

NEGATIVE NUMBERS

MIDDLE/UPPER LEVEL ONLY

SECTION 9

Positive numbers are greater than zero. **Negative numbers** are smaller than zero and have a negative sign (–) in front of them. They are found to the left of zero on a number line. Zero itself is neither positive nor negative:

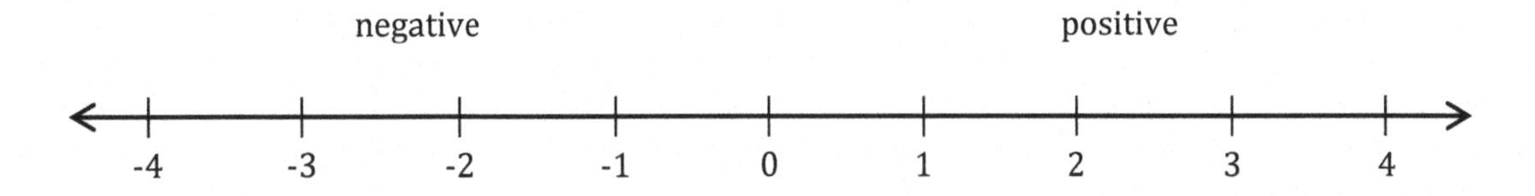

You might ask why negative numbers are useful. It is true that we rarely talk about quantities smaller than zero. However, we frequently use negative numbers when talking about losses, deficits, or decreases in quantities over time. For instance, we could say, "There was a – 3° change in temperature between 4pm and 9pm." This means that the temperature dropped 3°. Or, your bank statement for your checking account could read – $50. This means that you have a deficit of $50: you accidentally spent $50 more than you had in your checking account, and you owe money to the bank!

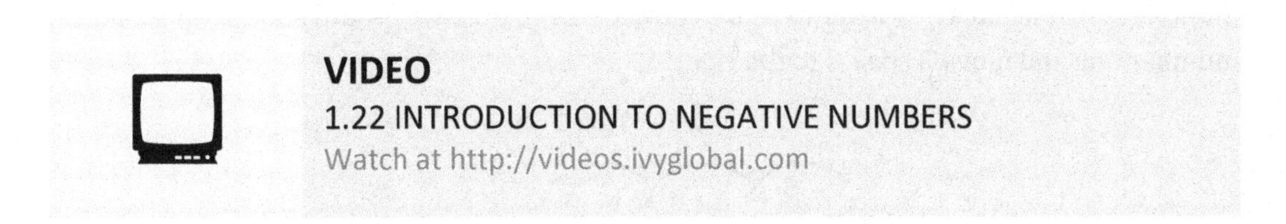

VIDEO
1.22 INTRODUCTION TO NEGATIVE NUMBERS
Watch at http://videos.ivyglobal.com

ADDING AND SUBTRACTING NEGATIVE NUMBERS

It is easiest to visualize addition and subtraction with negative numbers if you use a number line.

To add a positive number, you need to move right a certain number of places on the number line. For instance, if we wanted to add $-2 + 5$, we would start with – 2 on the number line and move 5 places to the right:

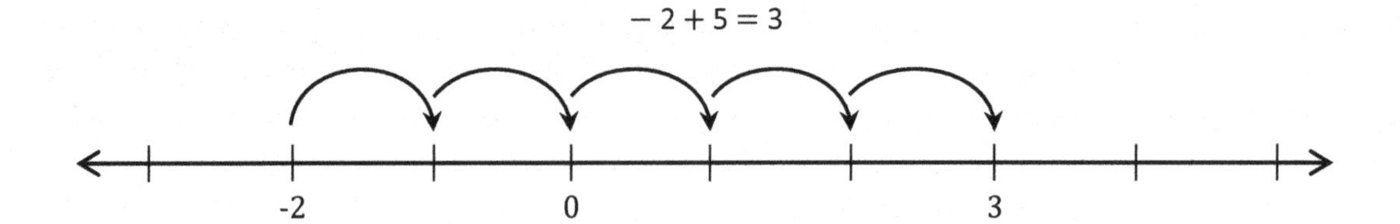

To subtract a positive number, you need to move left a certain number of places on the number line. For instance, if we wanted to subtract $-1 - 3$, we would start with -1 on the number line and move 3 places to the left:

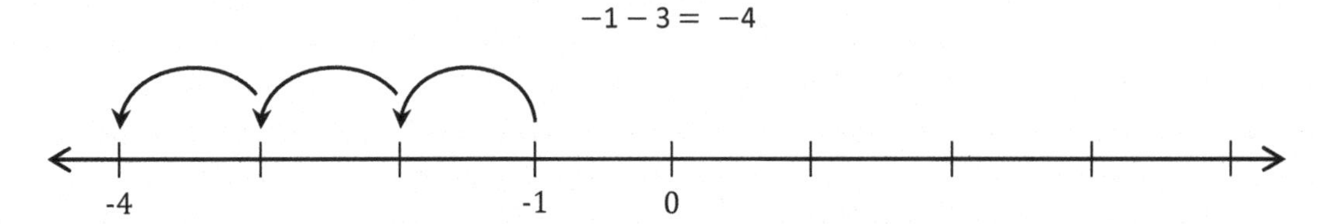

To add a negative number, you actually need to move a certain number of spaces left on the number line—adding a negative number is the same thing as subtracting a positive number! For instance, if we wanted to add $4 + (-2)$, we would start with 4 on the number line and move 2 spaces to the left:

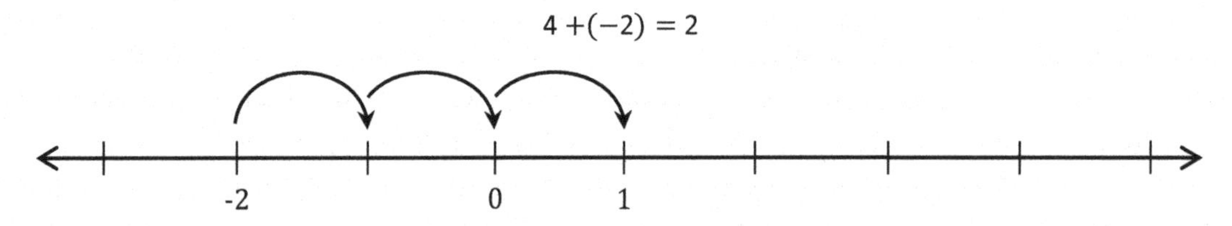

Similarly, to subtract a negative number, you need to move a certain number of spaces right on the number line—subtracting a negative number is the same thing as adding a positive number! For instance, if we wanted to subtract $-2 - (-3)$, we would start with -2 on the number line and move 3 spaces to the right:

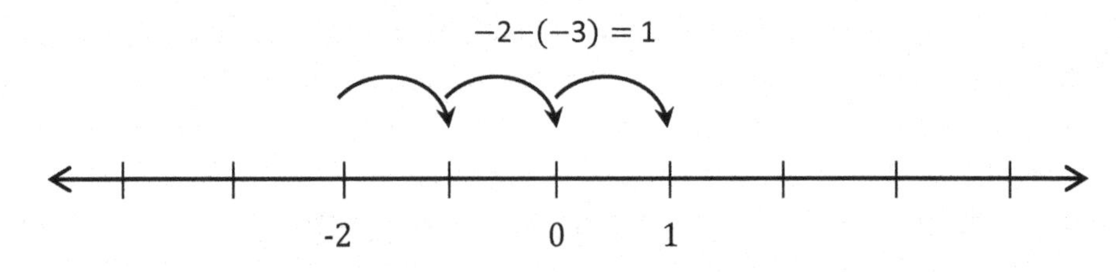

To add or subtract negative numbers without a number line, follow these three rules:

- To add two numbers with the same sign, add the numbers as usual and keep their sign:

$$7 + 13 = 20 \qquad\qquad -7 + (-13) = -20$$

- To add two numbers with different signs, subtract the two numbers and keep the sign of the number that is farthest away from zero:

$$5 + (-4) = +(5 - 4) = 1 \qquad -6 + 2 = -(6 - 2) = -4$$

- To subtract any two numbers, flip the sign of the second number to its opposite, and then add the two numbers:

$$-4 - 5 = -4 + (-5) = -9 \qquad 17 - (-4) = 17 + 4 = 21$$

VIDEO
1.23 ADDING AND SUBTRACTING NEGATIVE NUMBERS
Watch at http://videos.ivyglobal.com

MULTIPLYING AND DIVIDING NEGATIVE NUMBERS

Multiplying and dividing negative numbers is simpler than adding or subtracting. Multiply and divide as usual, then determine the sign of the product or quotient. If both of your numbers have the same sign, the product or quotient will be positive. If the numbers have different signs, the product or quotient will be negative:

- positive × positive = positive

  $3 \times 4 = 12$

- negative × negative = positive

  $-3 \times (-4) = 12$

- positive × negative = negative

  $3 \times (-4) = -12$

- negative × positive = negative

  $-3 \times 4 = -12$

- positive ÷ positive = positive

  $10 \div 5 = 2$

- negative ÷ negative = positive

  $-10 \div (-5) = 2$

- positive ÷ negative = negative

  $10 \div (-5) = -2$

- negative ÷ positive = negative

  $-10 \div 5 = -2$

VIDEO
1.24 MULTIPLYING AND DIVIDING NEGATIVE NUMBERS
Watch at http://videos.ivyglobal.com

PRACTICE QUESTIONS: NEGATIVE NUMBERS

1. $-10+8=$

2. $5+(-15)=$

3. $-4-7=$

4. $3-(-9)=$

5. $-1+(-6)=$

6. $144+(-214)=$

7. $9-(-9)=$

8. $-8-(-2)=$

9. $14+(-14)=$

10. $-100+8100=$

11. $6\times(-3)=$

12. $-5\times(-7)=$

13. $-24\div 4=$

14. $8\times(-5)=$

15. $18\div(-2)=$

16. $-32\div(-4)=$

17. $-12 \times 2 =$

18. $-45 \div (-3) =$

19. $-120 \div 20 =$

20. $-25 \times (-4) =$

EXPONENTS AND ROOTS

MIDDLE/UPPER LEVEL ONLY

SECTION 10

An **exponent** indicates that a number is being multiplied by itself. The exponent is the small raised number to the right of the **base**:

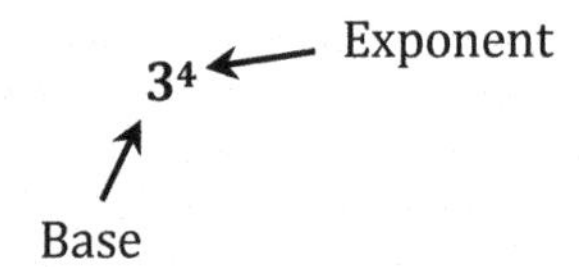

For this example, we would read "three to the power of four." **Squaring** a number means raising it to the power of two, and **cubing** a number means raising it to the power of three.

HOW TO USE EXPONENTS

The exponent tells you how many times the base is being multiplied by itself. For example, 3^4 means that three is being multiplied by itself four times: $3^4 = 3 \times 3 \times 3 \times 3 = 81$.

You can apply an exponent to a negative number, a fraction, and even a variable, and it will work the same way. For example, $\left(\frac{1}{4}\right)^2$ means to multiply $\frac{1}{4}$ by itself twice: $\left(\frac{1}{4}\right)^2 = \frac{1}{4} \times \frac{1}{4} = \frac{1}{16}$.

Zero raised to any positive power is equal to zero: $0^3 = 0 \times 0 \times 0 = 0$.

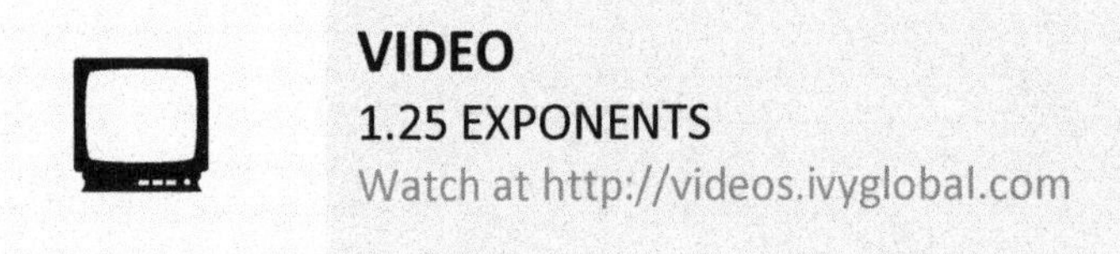

VIDEO

1.25 EXPONENTS

Watch at http://videos.ivyglobal.com

ROOTS

A **root** is the opposite of an exponent. A root is indicated by a **radical** placed over a **radicand**. This tells us that the radicand is the product of some other number multiplied by itself a certain number of times:

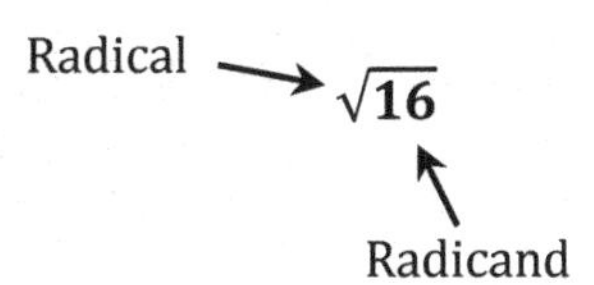

For instance, the **square root** of a number is the opposite of squaring a number. The square root of a number is always positive. To find a square root of a number underneath a radical, ask yourself, "What number can be multiplied by itself to produce the number in the question?" For example:

$$\sqrt{16} = 4 \text{ because } 4^2 = 4 \times 4 = 16$$

Similarly, the **cube root** of a number is the opposite of cubing a number. A cube root (or fourth root, fifth root, etc.) is indicated by a small raised number to the left of the radical:

$$\sqrt[3]{27} = 3 \text{ because } 3^3 = 3 \times 3 \times 3 = 27$$

You can take the square root (or cube root, or any root) of a fraction by taking the root of the numerator and the denominator separately:

$$\sqrt{\frac{16}{25}} = \frac{\sqrt{16}}{\sqrt{25}} = \frac{4}{5}$$

All of the roots we've seen above equal an integer or a fraction. However, sometimes we have to work with imperfect roots, which don't resolve to an integer or a common fraction. In this case, it is useful to estimate the result. We can estimate a root by finding the two perfect squares on either side of the imperfect root.

For example. $\sqrt{5}$ is an imperfect root. On either side of $\sqrt{5}$, the two closest perfect squares are $\sqrt{4}$ and $\sqrt{9}$. Because 5 is closer to 4, we can estimate that $\sqrt{5}$ is closer to $\sqrt{4}$. We know that $\sqrt{4} = 2$, so we can estimate that $\sqrt{5}$ is a number fairly close to 2—for instance, 2.2. We can check this estimate by multiplying 2.2 by 2.2, which is equal to 4.84. Because this is very close to 5, we can estimate that:

$$\sqrt{\mathbf{5}} \approx 2.2$$

VIDEO

1.26 ROOTS

Watch at http://videos.ivyglobal.com

ORDER OF OPERATIONS WITH EXPONENTS AND ROOTS

In Section 2, we introduced the Order of Operations for addition, subtraction, multiplication, and division. Here is the complete **Order of Operations** including exponents:

1. Simplify any expressions inside parenthesis
2. Simplify any exponents or roots
3. Multiply and divide from left to right
4. Add and subtract from left to right

These six steps (Parenthesis, Exponents, Multiplication, Division, Addition, and Subtraction) can be remembered by the mnemonic PEMDAS or the phrase "Please Excuse My Dear Aunt Sally."

For example, let's solve this complicated expression:

$$3 + 7 \times (6 - 4)^2 - 8 \div 2$$

1. Simplify the parenthesis:

$$3 + 7 \times (6 - 4)^2 - 8 \div 2 = 3 + 7 \times (2)^2 - 8 \div 2$$

2. Simplify the exponents:

$$3 + 7 \times (2)^2 - 8 \div 2 = 3 + 7 \times 4 - 8 \div 2$$

3. Multiply and divide from right to left:

$$3 + 7 \times 4 - 8 \div 2 = 3 + 28 - 4$$

4. Add and subtract from right to left:

$$3 + 28 - 4 = 27$$

VIDEO

1.27 ORDER OF OPERATIONS

Watch at http:// videos.ivyglobal.com

RULES FOR EXPONENTS AND ROOTS (UPPER LEVEL ONLY)

If you are multiplying two expressions with the same base, add their exponents:

$$4^2 \times 4^7 = 4^{2+7} = 4^9$$

Similarly, if you are dividing two expressions with the same base, subtract their exponents:

$$\frac{5^6}{5^2} = 5^{6-2} = 5^4$$

If you are raising an exponent to another power, multiply the two exponents:

$$(2^3)^2 = 2^6$$

So far, these rules apply only to expressions with the same base. If you have two different bases with two different exponents, you cannot use these rules to simplify your exponents. However, if you are multiplying or dividing two different bases with the *same* exponent, you can multiply or divide the two bases and keep this exponent:

$$3^2 \times 4^2 = (3 \times 4)^2 = 12^2$$
$$30^3 \div 5^3 = (30 \div 5)^3 = 6^3$$

Note that there is no way to simplify your exponents if you are adding or subtracting two numbers with exponents. These rules only apply to multiplication, division, or raising an exponent to another power. For example, $2^2 + 2^3$ is NOT equal to 2^5:

$$2^2 + 2^3 = 2 \times 2 + 2 \times 2 \times 2 = 4 + 8 = 12$$
$$2^5 = 2 \times 2 \times 2 \times 2 \times 2 = 32$$

In order to use these rules with roots, we need to convert them into exponential form. We can re-write roots as **fractional exponents**. If we are taking the nth root of a number, it's the same thing as raising that number to the power of $\frac{1}{n}$. For example, the square root of x is equal to $x^{\frac{1}{2}}$, and the cube root of x is equal to $x^{\frac{1}{3}}$.

Here is an example:

Simplify $\sqrt[4]{x} \times x^2$.

First, we'll re-write $\sqrt[4]{x}$ using exponential form. We're taking the 4th root of x, so this is the same as raising x to the power of $\frac{1}{n}$:

$$\sqrt[4]{x} \times x^2 = x^{1/4} \times x^2$$

Now, we'll use our exponent rules to simplify this expression. We're multiplying two expressions with the same base, so we can add their exponents:

$$x^{1/4} \times x^2 = x^{\left(\frac{1}{4}+2\right)} = x^{\frac{9}{4}}$$

The expression is equal to $x^{9/4}$.

Here is another example:

Simplify $\sqrt[3]{9} \times \sqrt[3]{3}$.

We saw that we can multiply two expressions with different bases but the same exponent by multiplying their bases. In this question, we're taking the cubed root of 9 and 3. Because taking the cubed root of a number is the same as raising that number to the power of $\frac{1}{3}$, these two expressions are being raised to the same exponent. Therefore, we can multiply them together by multiplying 9 and 3:

$$\sqrt[3]{9} \times \sqrt[3]{3} = \sqrt[3]{(9 \times 3)} = \sqrt[3]{27} = 3$$

The cubed root of 27 is 3, so 3 is the value of this expression.

We just saw that we can have fractional exponents. We can also have **negative exponents**. A negative exponent means that your expression is the *reciprocal* of the positive expression. For example, x^{-2} is the reciprocal of x^2 :

$$x^{-2} = \frac{1}{x^2}$$

Here is another example:

What is the value of 3^{-3}?

3^{-3} is the reciprocal of 3^3, so we write it as $\frac{1}{3^3}$:

$$3^{-3} = \frac{1}{3^3} = \frac{1}{(3 \times 3 \times 3)} = \frac{1}{27}$$

3^{-3} is equal to $\frac{1}{27}$.

Finally, exponents obey certain rules with the number zero. As we saw before, zero raised to any positive power equals zero. Zero can't be raised to a negative power because you can't take the reciprocal of zero—you can't divide by zero!

Any nonzero number raised to the **power of zero** is equal to 1. For example, $1^0 = 5^0 = (-12)^0 = 1$. Some people say that 0^0 is also equal to 1, and others consider it undefined.

VIDEO
1.28 RULES FOR EXPONENTS
Watch at http://videos.ivyglobal.com

VIDEO
1.29 RULES FOR ROOTS
Watch at http://videos.ivyglobal.com

SCIENTIFIC NOTATION (UPPER LEVEL ONLY)

Scientists and mathematicians often use an exponential notation to write out very large and very small numbers. This is called **scientific notation**, which displays a number as a product of a decimal and 10 raised to some integer power. The decimal must have exactly one digit to the left of the decimal place.

We know that we can write 10 as 10^1. Similarly, we can write 100 as 10^2, 1000 as 10^3, and so on. If we wanted to write a very large number, we could write it as a product of 10 to a positive exponent. For example, we know that 2891 is equal to 2.891×1000. Because we know that 1000 is equal to 10^3, we can write:

$$2891 = 2.891 \times 10^3$$

The expression 2.891×10^3 is the scientific notation for the number 2891. In order to convert back from scientific notation, we "undo" 10^3 by moving the decimal point 3 spots to the right:

$$2.891 \times 10^3 = 2891$$

Similarly, we can write numbers less than 1 as a product of 10 to a negative exponent. For example, $0.1 = \frac{1}{10}$, which is the reciprocal of 10^1. Therefore, we can write $0.1 = 10^{-1}$. Similarly, $0.01 = \frac{1}{100}$, which is the reciprocal of 10^2, so we can write $0.01 = 10^{-2}$. As our negative exponents get smaller, we just add more zeroes after the decimal point: $0.001 = 10^{-3}$, $0.0001 = 10^{-4}$, and so on.

A number like 0.002891 could be expressed as 2.891×0.001. Because $0.001 = 10^{-3}$, we can also write this as:

$$0.002891 = 2.891 \times 10^{-3}$$

In order to convert 2.891×10^{-3} back from scientific notation, we "undo" 10^{-3} by moving the decimal point 3 spots to the left:

$$2.891 \times 10^{-3} = 0.002891$$

Here are some more examples of scientific notation:

$10000 = 1 \times 10^4$	$28910 = 2.8910 \times 10^4$
$1000 = 1 \times 10^3$	$2891 = 2.891 \times 10^3$
$100 = 1 \times 10^2$	$289 = 2.89 \times 10^2$
$10 = 1 \times 10^1$	$28 = 2.8 \times 10^1$
$1 = 1 \times 10^0$	$2 = 2 \times 10^0$
$1/10 = 0.1 = 1 \times 10^{-1}$	$0.28 = 2.8 \times 10^{-1}$
$1/100 = 0.01 = 1 \times 10^{-2}$	$0.028 = 2.8 \times 10^{-2}$
$1/1000 = 0.001 = 1 \times 10^{-3}$	$0.0028 = 2.8 \times 10^{-3}$
$1/10000 = 0.0001 = 1 \times 10^{-4}$	$0.00028 = 2.8 \times 10^{-4}$

PRACTICE QUESTIONS: EXPONENTS AND ROOTS

1. $7^2 =$

2. $2^4 =$

3. $5^3 =$

4. $1^5 =$

5. $\left(\frac{2}{3}\right)^3 =$

6. $\left(\frac{1}{2}\right)^4 =$

7. $(-10)^3 =$

8. $(-9)^2 =$

9. $\sqrt{100} =$

10. $\sqrt{36} =$

11. $\sqrt[3]{8} =$

12. $\sqrt[3]{64} =$

13. $\sqrt{\frac{4}{9}} =$

14. $\sqrt{\frac{1}{49}} =$

15. Estimate the value of $\sqrt{12}$.

16. Estimate the value of $\sqrt[3]{60}$.

17. $5^2 - 3 \times 4 =$

18. $8^2 - 3 \times (-4) =$

19. $3 + 8^2 - (6 - 4) \times 12 =$

20. $10^2 - (4 - 3) \times 100 =$

21. $32 + 2^5 \div 16 =$

22. $-3 + (1 - 7)^2 \div 3^2 =$

23. $6 \times \sqrt{9} - (7^2 - 40) =$

24. $\sqrt{(3 + 5)^2} - (6 \times 7 - 34) =$

25. $\sqrt{(9 + 1)^2 \div 4} =$

26. $3 \times (-2)^2 + 15 \div 3 - (2 + 14) =$

Questions 27-45 are Upper Level Only.

27. $2^2 \times 2^5 =$

28. $5^7 \div 5^5 =$

29. $\left(\frac{1}{3}\right)^2 \times \left(\frac{1}{3}\right)^3 =$

30. $(4^2)^2 =$

31. $(2^3)^4 =$

32. $\sqrt{5} + 4\sqrt{5} =$

33. $4\sqrt{2} - 3\sqrt{2} =$

34. $\sqrt{18} \div \sqrt{2} =$

35. $2\sqrt{3} \times 2\sqrt{12} =$

36. $\left(\sqrt[3]{9}\right)^3 =$

37. $2^{-3} =$

38. $4^{-2} \times 4^2 \times 4^0 =$

39. $\frac{a^4bc}{ab^2c^3} =$

40. $\sqrt[5]{x} \times \sqrt[5]{x^4} =$

For questions 41-45, write the number in scientific notation.

41. 26.235

42. 262.35

43. 0.26235

44. 0.0026235

45. 2623500

IMAGINARY NUMBERS

UPPER LEVEL ONLY

SECTION 11

In the last section, we reviewed how to find a square root: we look for a value that, when multiplied by itself, will give us the number under the square root sign. Normally, it is impossible to take the square root of a negative number. Even when you square a negative number, you end up with a positive result. Therefore, there isn't a way to work backwards and find a real number that is the square root of a negative number.

However, sometimes it is helpful to "imagine" that we can take the square root of a negative number and use this in our calculations. We can do this by introducing the unit i, which stands for the square root of -1:

$$i = \sqrt{-1}$$
$$i^2 = -1$$

Because a number like i does not exist in the set of real numbers, we call it an **imaginary number**. In equations and calculations that involve imaginary numbers, we can use i as a placeholder for $\sqrt{-1}$.

SIMPLIFYING EXPRESSIONS WITH i

In an expression that involves imaginary numbers, we can simplify the square root of any negative number by using i. For example:

Simplify $\sqrt{-25}$ in terms of i.

Because of the rules of exponents and roots, we can re-write $\sqrt{-25}$ as the product of $\sqrt{-1}$ and $\sqrt{25}$:

$$\sqrt{-25} = \sqrt{-1} \times \sqrt{25}$$

Why are we able to do this? Remember that multiplying two numbers raised to the same power is the same thing as raising the product of those two numbers to that power.

Therefore, multiplying the square roots of -1 and 25 is the same thing as taking the square root of $-1 \times 25 = -25$.

Now we can simplify our expression by plugging in i:

$$\sqrt{-1} \times \sqrt{25} = i \times \sqrt{25} = 5i$$

$\sqrt{-25}$ can be expressed as $5i$.

Here is another example:

Simplify $5 \times \frac{6\sqrt{-16}}{60}$ in terms of i.

First, we multiply and reduce this fraction:

$$5 \times \frac{6\sqrt{-16}}{60} = \frac{30\sqrt{-16}}{60} = \frac{\sqrt{-16}}{2}$$

Then, we re-write the square root as the product of two square roots:

$$\frac{\sqrt{-16}}{2} = \frac{\sqrt{-1} \times \sqrt{16}}{2}$$

And finally, we plug in i:

$$\frac{\sqrt{-1} \times \sqrt{16}}{2} = \frac{i \times \sqrt{16}}{2} = \frac{4i}{2} = 2i$$

Our final answer is $2i$.

We know that the square of i is -1, but now let's look at what happens when we raise i to another exponent. For example, what happens when we take the cube of i? We can substitute $\sqrt{-1}$ for i in order to work out the equation:

$$\begin{aligned} i^3 &= (\sqrt{-1})^3 \\ &= \sqrt{-1} \times \sqrt{-1} \times \sqrt{-1} \\ &= -1 \times \sqrt{-1} \\ &= -1 \times i \\ &= -i \end{aligned}$$

The square of i is -1, but the cube of i is $-i$.

Here is a chart showing the values of i raised to some other exponents:

$i^0 = 1$
$i^1 = i$
$i^2 = -1$
$i^3 = -i$
$i^4 = 1$

Using this table, how can we determine what i^5 is equal to?

We know that $i^4 = 1$ and $i^5 = i^4 \times i$. Plugging in these values, we can write:

$$i^5 = 1 \times i = i$$

Therefore, i^5 is the same thing as i, or $\sqrt{-1}$.

PRACTICE QUESTIONS: IMAGINARY NUMBERS

Express the following expressions as real numbers when possible and in terms of *i* only when the equation is not defined in the real number set. Remember $\sqrt{-1}$ does not exist in the real number set and must be expressed in terms of i.

1. $\sqrt{-16} =$

2. $\sqrt{-49} =$

3. $\sqrt{-64} =$

4. $\sqrt{-100} =$

5. $i^3 =$

6. $i^4 =$

7. $i^6 =$

8. $i^7 =$

9. $\sqrt{-9} =$

10. $i \times \sqrt{-9} =$

11. $\frac{4}{2} \times \sqrt{-5} \times \sqrt{5} =$

12. $i^3 \times \sqrt{-4} =$

13. $3 + \sqrt{-64} =$

14. $i^6 \times \sqrt{-36} =$

PART 1 REVIEW

ARITHMETIC

In this section, you will find 40 practice questions to review the arithmetic content tested on the ISEE's Math Achievement section. The Lower Level questions cover the arithmetic content that you will find on the Lower Level section, as well as the easier arithmetic content on the Middle and Upper Level sections The Middle Level questions cover content that you will only find on the Middle and Upper Level sections. The Upper Level questions cover content that you will only find on the Upper Level section.

Each question is followed by four suggested answers. Read each question and then decide which one of the four suggested answers is best.

LOWER LEVEL QUESTIONS

Use these questions to practice the arithmetic content that you will see on the Lower Level Math Achievement section, as well as the easier arithmetic content that you will see on the Middle and Upper Levels. Lower, Middle, and Upper Level students should attempt these questions.

1. An artist is drawing the following shapes on a sidewalk.

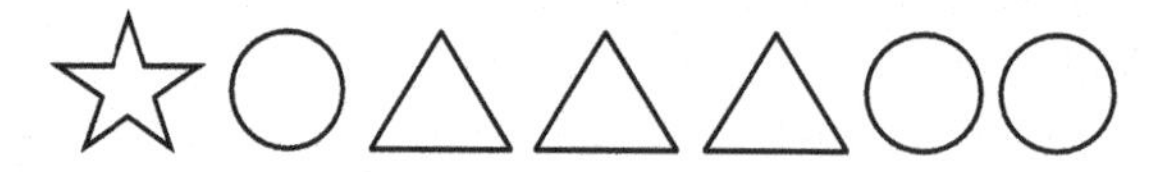

What fraction of the shapes are circles?

(A) $^1/_7$
(B) $^2/_7$
(C) $^3/_7$
(D) $^2/_3$

2. Mei Mei is trying to estimate 1.45×3.99. What is the best way to estimate this number?

(A) 1×4
(B) 1×3
(C) 1.5×4
(D) 1.5×3

3. Which expression is equal to the expression $3 + (2 - 1) \times (3 + 2) \times 2$?

(A) $3 + 2 - 1 \times 3 + 2 \times 2$
(B) $(3 + 2 - 1 \times 3 + 2 \times 2)$
(C) $3 + 5 \times 2$
(D) $4 \times 3 + 2 \times 2$

4. $468.3 \div 31.2$ is closest to

(A) 1.5
(B) 15
(C) 150
(D) 15000

5. Jan ate half a pie. After Jan finished, Rogelio then ate half of the amount that was remaining. How much of the pie was left after Rogelio finished eating?

(A) $^1/_2$
(B) $^1/_4$
(C) $^1/_8$
(D) $^2/_3$

6. What is the least prime number greater than 30?

(A) 31
(B) 32
(C) 35
(D) 39

7. Which is the value of the expression $5 \div (15 - 5) + 5 \times 3 - 2/4$?

(A) 15
(B) 28.5
(C) 16
(D) $^{15}/_{4}$

8. Which of the following numbers is NOT prime?

(A) 2
(B) 3
(C) 5
(D) 9

9. Sheila purchased two erasers, five pencils, and milk at a store. The prices were listed on the store's flyer as $0.22 per eraser, $0.14 per pencil, and $3.79 for milk. What was the total cost of Sheila's purchase?

(A) $4.15
(B) $4.17
(C) $4.93
(D) $3.79

10. $\frac{1}{100} + \frac{2}{200} + \frac{3}{300} =$

(A) $\frac{6}{6{,}000{,}000}$

(B) $\frac{1}{100}$

(C) $\frac{3}{100}$

(D) $\frac{6}{100}$

11. What is the value of the expression $\frac{1}{2} \times 6 + 2\frac{2}{3} - \frac{1}{6}$?

(A) $3\frac{3}{7}$

(B) $5\frac{1}{2}$

(C) 5

(D) 9

12. Which best summarizes the equation $\frac{10}{5} = 2$?

(A) I have ten toys and four friends. If I give a toy to each friend, how many toys will I still have?
(B) I have ten friends and want to share five toys with each of them. How many friends get a toy?
(C) I have two toys that I want to share with ten friends. Does every friend get a toy?
(D) I have ten toys that I want to share with five friends. If I share the toys equally among my friends, how many toys will each friend get?

13. Derek bought 1.2 pounds of apples at $0.40 per pound, 2.5 pounds of oranges at $1.20 per pound, and 1.3 pounds of bananas at $0.50 per pound. How much did he spend in total?

(A) $2.59
(B) $4.13
(C) $6.32
(D) $17.55

14. The peak of Mount Everest is about 29,030 feet above sea level, and the lowest point in the Dead Sea is about 1,310 feet below sea level. What is the difference in elevation between the lowest point of the Dead Sea and the peak of Mount Everest?

(A) 1,310 feet
(B) 27,720 feet
(C) 29,160 feet
(D) 30,340 feet

15. Which term best describes the following set of numbers?

$$\{4, 6, 9, 10, \ldots\}$$

(A) composite numbers
(B) even numbers
(C) odd numbers
(D) prime numbers

MIDDLE LEVEL QUESTIONS

Use these questions to practice the content that you will only see on the Middle Level and Upper Level ISEE. Only Middle and Upper Level students should attempt these questions.

1. At 8:00am, the temperature was –10 degrees. If the temperature dropped 13 degrees over the next 12 hours, what was the temperature at 8:00pm?

   (A) – 23°
   (B) – 13°
   (C) – 3°
   (D) 23°

2. $\sqrt{\left(\frac{64}{4}\right)}$

   (A) $^{1}/_{16}$
   (B) 2
   (C) 4
   (D) 16

3. A museum exhibit charges $15.25 for an adult ticket and $9.50 for a child ticket. If 500 adults and 120 children visit the exhibit, the museum's ticket sales will total

   (A) $5,890
   (B) $7,625
   (C) $8,765
   (D) $9,455

4. Kathy works 3.5 hours a day on Mondays, Wednesdays and Fridays and 4.5 hours a day on Tuesdays and Thursdays. She is paid $10.20 per hour. If Kathy does not work on Saturdays or Sundays, how much does she earn in one week?

   (A) $35.70
   (B) $81.60
   (C) $163.20
   (D) $198.90

5. A calculator has a price of $40, not including tax. After a 13% sales tax is applied, what will be the total cost of the calculator?

(A) $5.20
(B) $41.30
(C) $45.20
(D) $53.00

6. If Q is an even number, which of the following expressions must be odd?

(A) Q^2
(B) $Q - Q$
(C) $Q - 3$
(D) $Q + 2$

7. During a chemistry experiment, a solution contained in a beaker was initially measured at 25 degrees Celsius. The beaker was then placed on a hot plate, and the temperature rose 7 degrees. Next, the beaker was submerged in an ice bath, and the temperature dropped 41 degrees. The final temperature of the solution was

(A) – 16 degrees
(B) – 9 degrees
(C) 32 degrees
(D) 73 degrees

8. On his last chemistry test, Mark answered 85% of the questions correctly and did not skip any questions. If there were 120 questions on the test, how many did he answer incorrectly?

(A) 15
(B) 18
(C) 35
(D) 102

9. If K has a factor of 15, K must also have what other factor(s)?

(A) 5 only
(B) 3 and 5
(C) 0, 3 and 5
(D) 1, 3, and 5

10. $(8 - 17) \times 6 - \frac{1}{2} \times 4 =$

(A) -198
(B) -56
(C) 6
(D) 54

11. Three consecutive multiples of 6 have a sum of 126. What is the greatest of these numbers?

(A) 36
(B) 42
(C) 48
(D) 60

12. 3 is 10% of

(A) 0.3
(B) 10
(C) 30
(D) 300

13. $2^6 =$

(A) 6^2
(B) 8^2
(C) 16^2
(D) 4^4

14. A fast-food chain currently sells 8-ounce hamburgers. If the chain increases the weight of its hamburgers by 25%, the new hamburgers will weigh

(A) 4 ounces
(B) 8.25 ounces
(C) 10 ounces
(D) 12 ounces

15. 100 students attended a school carnival. If 60% of the students were less than 10 years old and 75% of the students were over 6 years old, how many children were between 6 and 10 years old?

(A) 15
(B) 35
(C) 45
(D) 75

UPPER LEVEL QUESTIONS

Use these questions to practice the most challenging difficulty level you will see on the Upper Level ISEE. Only Upper Level students should attempt these questions.

1. Between 1980 and 1990, the population of deer in a national park increased by 40%. Between 1990 and 2000, the deer population increased by 20%. The deer population in 2000 was how many times greater than the deer population in 1980?

   (A) 0.6
   (B) 1.6
   (C) 1.68
   (D) 168

2. A pair of jeans is on sale for 60% off the original price. If the discounted price is $27.50, the original price was

   (A) $11.15
   (B) $45.83
   (C) $68.75
   (D) $74.58

3. Anthony drove 53 kilometers. If 1 mile corresponds to about 1.6 kilometers, approximately how many miles did Anthony drive?

   (A) 16
   (B) 21
   (C) 33
   (D) 57

4. $(\sqrt{5})^4$

   (A) 2.2
   (B) 2.5
   (C) 5
   (D) 25

5. If 55% of N is 11, what is N% of 46?

(A) 5.1
(B) 6.1
(C) 9.2
(D) 25.3

6. On a property valued at $310,000, the property tax is $24,800. A second property is valued at $340,000 with the same property tax rate. Including tax, the second property is how much more expensive than the first?

(A) $30,000
(B) $32,400
(C) $33,480
(D) $57,270

7. $\sqrt{1200} =$

(A) $60 \times \sqrt{2}$
(B) $20 \times \sqrt{3}$
(C) $4 \times \sqrt{30}$
(D) $3 \times \sqrt{40}$

8. The value of a coin collection increased 8% in the first year and 15% in the second year. By what percent did the collection's value increase over the entire two-year period?

(A) 1.2%
(B) 7%
(C) 23%
(D) 24.2%

9. Which of the following expressions is NOT equal to 7?

(A) $7^5 - 7^4$
(B) $\left(\sqrt[3]{7}\right)^3$
(C) $7^4 \times \frac{1}{7^3}$
(D) $\sqrt{7} \times \sqrt{7}$

10. $\frac{-i^2}{\sqrt{-1}}$ is best expressed as:

(A) $\frac{1}{i}$

(B) $-\frac{i}{\sqrt{-1}}$

(C) $-\frac{1}{i}$

(D) $\frac{\sqrt{i}}{i}$

ALGEBRA

PART 2

BASIC ALGEBRA

ALL LEVELS

SECTION 1

Algebra is a branch of mathematics that uses letters to stand for numbers. These letters, called **variables**, represent numbers that are unknown. Any letter—x, y, a, b, N, Q, etc.—can be used to stand for unknown numbers. You can add, subtract, multiply or divide these variables just as you would any other number—the only difference is that you are working with letters!

BASIC ALGEBRA STRATEGIES

In some algebra questions, you could be given the value of a letter in the question, and will need to plug in this value to find the answer. For example, look at the following question:

If $a = 3$, what is $a + 4$?

This question is telling you that the letter "a" stands for the number 3. To solve the question, plug in 3 where you see "a":

$$a + 4$$
$$3 + 4 = 7$$

Replacing the letter "a" with the number "3," we solve a normal addition problem and find the answer: 7.

Here's another example:

If $b = 5$ and $c = 6$, what is $c - b$?

This question is telling you that the letter "b" stands for the number 5, and the letter "c" stands for the number 6. To solve the question, plug in 6 where you see "c" and 5 where you see "b":

$$\overset{c\,-\,b}{6 - 5} = 1$$

We can now solve a normal subtraction problem and find the answer: 1.

FINDING A MISSING NUMBER

Some algebra problems may ask you to "work backward" and find the missing number in an equation. For example, look at the question below:

$$6 + \square = 20$$

To find the missing number that goes in the box, ask yourself, "What plus 6 is equal to 20?" The answer is 14:

$$6 + \mathbf{14} = 20$$

Instead of a box, the missing number in an equation might be represented by a letter. In this case, all you need to do is work backward to find what number this letter is standing for. For example, look at the question below:

If $4 \times N = 8$, what is the value of N?

To find the number that N is standing for, ask yourself, "What can I multiply by 4 to get a result of 8?" The answer is 2:

$$4 \times \mathbf{2} = 8$$

Therefore, we know that the value of N must be 2.

VIDEO

2.1 INTRO TO ALGEBRA

Watch at http://videos.ivyglobal.com

FORMULAS AND WORD PROBLEMS

Algebra is very useful for solving word problems. For example:

John is building a rectangular patio in his backyard. If the patio must be 9 feet long, how wide should John make the patio so it has an area of exactly 36 square feet?

Because you know the area of a rectangle is equal to length multiplied by width, you can write an algebraic equation with the symbol x representing the width of the patio:

$$Area = length \times width$$
$$36 = 9 \times x$$

Based on this equation, you see that you need to divide 36 by 9 in order to find x, the width of the patio:

$$x = 36 \div 9$$
$$x = 4$$

Therefore, John should make the patio 4 feet wide.

Not all word problems will be as simple as plugging numbers into a formula. You will need to know some quick ways of translating plain English into the language of mathematics. The following chart gives some examples:

TRANSLATING ENGLISH INTO MATHEMATICS		
Word/Phrase	**Translation**	**Symbol**
is, was, has, will be	equals	$=$
more, total, increased by, exceeds, gained, older, farther, greater, sum	addition	$+$
less, decreased, lost, younger, fewer, difference	subtraction	$-$
of, product, times, each	multiplication	$\times$
for, per, out of, quotient	division	$\div$
at least	greater than or equal to	$\geq$
at most	less than or equal to	$\leq$
what, how much, a number	variable	x, y, N, etc.

For example, consider the question below:

Five less than three times a number is equal to seven. What is the number?

Let's write this as an algebraic equation using our translation chart above. If we let our unknown number be x, then "three times a number" means $3x$, and "five less" means we need to subtract 5. This whole expression equals 7:

$$3x - 5 = 7$$

$x = 4$ because $3 \times 4 - 5 = 12 - 5 = 7$. Therefore, we know our missing number must be 4.

As another example, consider the following word problem:

Each person in a certain town owns an average of 2 vehicles. If there are 1280 personal vehicles registered in the town, what is the town's population?

Let's write this as an equation, with the variable p representing the number of people. We can assume that each person owns exactly 2 vehicles. Because "each" means "multiply," the number of vehicles in the town would be equal to 2 times the number of people. There are 1280 vehicles in the town, so we would write:

$$1280 = 2p$$

What times 2 is equal to 1280? In order to solve this, we need to divide 1280 by 2:

$$p = 1280 \div 2$$
$$p = 640$$

Based on this equation, the town's population must be 640.

VIDEO

2.2 ALGEBRAIC WORD PROBLEMS

Watch at http:// videos.ivyglobal.com

INPUT AND OUTPUT FUNCTIONS

On the ISEE, you might also be asked to write your own formula to show how one set of numbers or variables is transformed into another set of numbers or variables. This type of formula is called a **function**. For every input you are given, you will need to find a rule that generates its output. Here is an example:

A calculator is given an input. It performs the same series of operations on each input and creates an output number, as shown in the table below. What is the output for an input of 6?

Input	Output
2	6
3	8
5	12
7	16
10	22

In this question, A calculator takes an input number and adds, subtracts, multiplies, or divides in order to arrive at an output number. The question says that the calculator performs the same series of operations on each input number, so all you have to do is figure out what those operations are.

Let's look at the first input and output. If you start with the number 2, there are many ways to arrive at the number 6. For example, you could add 4, multiply by 3, or multiply by 2 and then add another 2:

Input	Rule?	Output
2	$+4=$ $\times 3=$ $\times 2+2=$	6

Any of these operations might be the rule that the calculator uses to generate its outputs (and there are many other possibilities, too). We can write these rules more generally like this:

- $input + 4 = output$
- $input \times 3 = output$
- $input \times 2 + 2 = output$

In order to answer the question, we need to see which rule works for all of the inputs and outputs in the table we are given. Let's test out the first rule: $input + 4 = output$.

Does this rule work for the second input and output in our table?

Input	Rule?	Output
3	$+4=$	7

If we used this rule to add 4 to 3, our output would be 7. However, the output in the table is 8. Because this rule gets the output wrong, it does not describe what the calculator does.

Let's test out the second rule: $input \times 3 = output$. Does this rule give us an output of 8 for an input of 3?

Input	Rule?	Output
3	$\times 3=$	9

No! 9 is the wrong output, so this rule doesn't work, either. Let's try the third rule: $input \times 2 + 2 = output$.

Input	Rule?	Output
3	$\times 2+2=$	8

This rule gives us the correct output! In order to be sure that we have the right answer, we need to make sure that it also works for all of the other numbers in the table. Let's test it out:

Input	Rule?	Output
5	$\times 2+2=$	12
7	$\times 2+2=$	16
10	$\times 2+2=$	22

This rule gives us the right outputs for all of the numbers in the table, so we have figured out what the calculator does.

Now we can answer the question: "What is the output for an input of 6?" All we have to do is put the number 6 into the rule we have created:

Input	Rule?	Output
6	$\times 2 + 2 =$	14

Because we know that we've used the same rule that the calculator is using, we can figure out that 14 is the output for an input of 6.

PRACTICE QUESTIONS: BASIC ALGEBRA

1. If $N = 2$, what is the value of $N + 8$?

2. If $P = 6$, what is the value of $P + 7$?

3. If $m = 30$, what is the value of $m - 3$?

4. If $y = 10$, what is the value of $y - 10$?

For questions 5-12, solve each problem using the following information:

$$a = 4,\ b = 2, \text{and } c = 8$$

5. $a + 4 =$

6. $b + 10 =$

7. $c - 3 =$

8. $a + b =$

9. $a \times 5 =$

10. $c \div 2 =$

11. $a \times b =$

12. $a - b + c =$

For questions 13-18, fill in the missing number:

13. $4 - \square = 2$

14. $\square \times 7 = 14$

15. $\square - 8 = 10$

16. $\square \div 4 = 3$

17. $8 + \square = 14$

18. $\square + 6 = 15$

19. If $4 + N = 7$, then $N =$

20. If $18 - p = 4$, then $p =$

21. If $Q \times 2 = 8$, then $Q =$

22. If $15 \div x = 3$, then $x =$

23. The quotient of 45 and a number is equal to nine. What is the number?

24. The sum of twice a number and three is equal to nineteen. What is the number?

25. Adam has four more than twice as many marbles as John. If John has 5 marbles, how many marbles does Adam have?

26. On Tuesday, a store sold twice as many scarves as it did on Monday. On Wednesday, the store sold 10 more scarves than it did on Tuesday. If M represents the number of scarves sold on Monday, which of the following expressions represents the number of scarves sold on Wednesday?

    (A) $M + 10$
    (B) $M - 10$
    (C) $2M + 10$
    (D) $2M - 10$

27. If seven less than three times N is equal to 14, then what is the value of two times N?

28. During their last soccer game, Erin scored three less than twice as many goals as Jennifer did. If J represents the number of goals that Jennifer scored, which of the following expressions shows the total number of goals scored by Erin?

(A) $3 - 2J$
(B) $3 + 2 + J$
(C) $2J + 3$
(D) $2J - 3$

29. Mark is one year younger than Janet. Janet is twice Amanda's age. If Amanda is 9 years old, how old is Mark?

30. Joe has two more pencils than Derek. If Joe buys 3 more pencils, he will have twice as many pencils as Derek. How many pencils does Derek have?

For questions 31-32, use the following information:

The table below shows the inputs and outputs of a machine.

Input	Output
6	12
3	6
2	4

31. What is the output for an input of 9?

32. What is the input for an output of 14?

For questions 33-34, use the following table:

Input ⇩	**Output** ☆
9	4
7	3
5	2
3	1

33. What is the value of ☆ when ⇩ is equal to 13?

34. What is the value of ⇩ when ☆ is equal to 7?

Use the following table to find the rule.

Input ○	**Output** ▱
2	12
6	24
7	27

35. What is the rule for the function?

EXPRESSIONS

MIDDLE/UPPER LEVEL ONLY

SECTION 2

An algebraic **expression** is a mathematical "phrase" containing numbers, variables, and operations. In the example below, $9 \times x$ (which can also be written as $9x$) is an algebraic expression. There is no equals sign in an algebraic expression.

An algebraic expression is made up of **terms**, which are variables and/or numbers multiplied together. When a number is put right in front of a variable, it means the variable is being multiplied by that number—you don't have to write a multiplication sign. This number is called the **coefficient**.

Coefficient → $9x$ ← Variable

Term

An expression with one term only, like the one above, is called a **monomial**. The expression $4x + 6$ has two terms and is called a **binomial**. Any expression with one or more terms is called a **polynomial**.

VIDEO
2.3 EXPRESSION TERMINOLOGY
Watch at http:// videos.ivyglobal.com

PLUGGING IN

You may be given the value of one or more variables and be asked to solve an algebraic expression based on these values. Plug these values into your expression and follow the Order of Operations.

For instance, take a look at the following problem:

If $x = 2$ and $y = 3$, what is the value of $x^2 - 3y + 11$?

Plug in 2 for x and 3 for y, and use the Order of Operations to solve:

$$
\begin{aligned}
&2^2 - 3 \times 3 + 11 \\
&= 4 - 3 \times 3 + 11 \\
&= 4 - 9 + 11 \\
&= 6
\end{aligned}
$$

ADDING AND SUBTRACTING LIKE TERMS

You can simplify an algebraic expression by adding or subtracting like terms. **Like terms** have the same variable, raised to the same power. For example, $4x$ and $6x$ are like terms. The terms y^2 and $3y^2$ are also like terms. However, y and y^2 are not like terms because only one has been squared. Similarly, x^2 and y^2 are not like terms because they are two different variables.

To add or subtract like terms, add or subtract their coefficients. For example:

What is the sum of $4N$ and $6N$?

To solve this question, add 4 and 6: $4N + 6N = 10N$

Remember that when a variable does not have a coefficient, it is the same thing as having a coefficient of one. The term N^2 is the same as $1N^2$, but we don't normally bother writing a coefficient of one. For example:

Subtract N^2 from $3N^2$.

You would solve this by subtracting 1 from 3: $3N^2 - N^2 = 2N^2$

You can think of adding like terms as similar to adding groups of objects. For example:

Emil had a bag of 3 apples and 4 oranges. He then bought another 5 apples and 3 oranges. How many apples and oranges does Emil have now?

To calculate your total, you add the numbers of apples together and the numbers of oranges together: 8 apples and 7 oranges. However, you can't add 3 apples to 3 oranges because these are two different types of fruit! Just as you can only add or subtract similar objects, you can only add or subtract like terms in algebra.

What if you are adding or subtracting expressions with more than one term? You would add or subtract the like terms, and leave any remaining terms as they are. For example:

Add $P^2 + 6$ and $2P^2 + P - 4$.

$$\boldsymbol{P^2} + 6 + \boldsymbol{2P^2} + P - 4 = \boldsymbol{3P^2} + P + 2$$

We have two pairs of like terms: P^2 and $2P^2$, and 6 and -4. Add these like terms together, and keep the term P the way it is.

VIDEO

2.4 SIMPLIFYING EXPRESSIONS WITH ADDITION AND SUBTRACTION

Watch at http:// videos.ivyglobal.com

USING THE DISTRIBUTIVE PROPERTY

To multiply expressions, you need to remember the **distributive property**. According to the distributive property, multiplying a number by a sum of two other numbers in parentheses is the same as multiplying by each number separately and then adding:

$$a(b + c) = ab + ac$$

For example:

Multiply the expression $3x + 2$ by the number 6.

To solve, use the distributive property: $6(3x + 2) = 6 \times 3x + 6 \times 2 = 18x + 12$

The distributive property also works for division. Dividing a sum of two numbers by another number is the same as dividing each number separately and then adding:

$$\frac{b + c}{a} = \frac{b}{a} + \frac{c}{a}$$

For example:

Divide the expression $4y - 8$ by the number 2.

To solve, divide each term by 2:

$$\frac{4y-8}{2}=\frac{4y}{2}-\frac{8}{2}=2y-4$$

FACTORING EXPRESSIONS

Factoring is the opposite of distribution. To factor a polynomial, find the greatest common factor that all of your terms have in common. Then, work backwards to take this factor out of your expression: write your factor multiplied by a polynomial in parentheses, and make sure that all of the terms inside of the parentheses multiplied by the factor generate the polynomial that you started out with.

For example:

Factor out $5x^2-10x+5$.

In the expression above, all of your terms have a common factor of 5. Pull this factor out of your expression and determine what would be left over in parentheses:

$$5x^2-10x+5=5(x^2-2x+1)$$

To test whether you have factored correctly, use the distributive property to work backwards. Multiply your factor by the terms inside the parentheses and make sure that you get the same polynomial you started out with.

VIDEO
2.5 FACTORING EXPRESSIONS
Watch at http:// videos.ivyglobal.com

USING EXPONENT RULES AND FOIL (UPPER LEVEL ONLY)

To multiply two monomials, you can use your knowledge of exponent rules to multiply terms with the same base.

For example:

What is the product of x^2 and x^3?

To solve this problem, you would add the two exponents: $x^2\times x^3=x^{2+3}=x^5$

Similarly, to divide two terms in an equation that have the same base, you can subtract their exponents.

For example:

Find the quotient: $4y^5 \div 2y^2$

In the example above, you would first divide the coefficients of each term, and then divide the variables themselves: $4y^5 \div 2y^2 = (4 \div 2)y^{5-2} = 2y^3$

If your terms do not have the same base, you can't add or subtract their exponents. Write the product or quotient of the individual terms:

What is the product of $x^2$and y^2?

Your terms do not have the same base, so write out the product with the individual terms: $x^2 \times y^2 = x^2y^2$.

To multiply two binomials, use the **FOIL** method: multiply the First terms, the Outer terms, the Inner terms, and the Last terms. Then, combine like terms.

For example:

What is the product of $(x + 2)(3x + 4)$?

To expand this expression, we'll first multiply together the first terms in the parenthesis (x and $3x$), then the outer terms (x and 4), then the inner terms (2 and $3x$), and finally the last terms (2 and 4). Then, we'll add them together and combine last terms:

$$(x + 2)(3x + 4)$$

$$= (x \times 3x) + (x \times 4) + (2 \times 3x) + (2 \times 4)$$
$$= 3x^2 + 4x + 6x + 8$$
$$= 3x^2 + 10x + 8$$

VIDEO

2.6 SIMPLIFYING EXPRESSIONS WITH MULTIPLICATION AND DIVISION

Watch at http:// videos.ivyglobal.com

FACTORING TRINOMIALS (UPPER LEVEL ONLY)

Some questions on the Upper Level ISEE will ask you to fully factor a trinomial. A **trinomial** is an expression with three terms. $x^2 + 6x + 8$ is an example of a trinomial. To fully factor this expression, we want to write it as two binomials multiplied together:

$$x^2 + 2x - 8 = (x - 2)(x + 4)$$

How do we do this? We just need some more information about trinomials. Trinomials can be written as $\boldsymbol{ax^2} + \boldsymbol{bx} + \boldsymbol{c}$, where a is the coefficient of x^2, b is the coefficient of x, and c is the constant number. In the example above, $a = 1$, $b = 2$, and $c = -8$. When we factor a trinomial, we write the product of two binomials that each have x and a constant number. The two constant numbers should have a product of c and a sum of b. Both positive and negative numbers are possible.

For the example above, remember that $b = 2$ and $c = -8$. We're looking for two numbers that have a product of -8 and a sum of 2. Let's first look for two numbers that have a product of -8. There are several possibilities:

$$-1 \times 8 = -8$$

$$-8 \times 1 = -8$$

$$-2 \times 4 = -8$$

$$-4 \times 2 = -8$$

Which pair of numbers has a sum of 2? Only -2 and 4:

$$-2 + 4 = 2$$

Therefore, our two numbers are -2 and 4. To plug them into our binomials, we add them to x:

$$\big(x + (-2)\big)(x + 4) = (x - 2)(x + 4)$$

We can then check that we have factored correctly by using FOIL to multiply the two binomials:

$$(x - 2)(x + 4) = x^2 + 4x - 2x - 8 = x^2 + 2x - 8$$

Because these two binomials multiply to the expression we started out with, we know we have factored correctly.

FACTORING TRINOMIALS WITH A COEFFICIENT (UPPER LEVEL ONLY)

In the example we saw above, a—the coefficient of the squared variable—was equal to 1. However, what if a is equal to another number? First, check whether you can factor this number out of the entire expression, and then simplify the factored expression. Let's look at an example we've seen already:

Factor out $5x^2 - 10x + 5$.

In this example, $a = 5$. We started by pulling 5 out of the entire expression:

$$5x^2 - 10x + 5 = 5(x^2 - 2x + 1)$$

Now, we can use the method we've just learned to factor the quadratic expression in parentheses. We're looking for two numbers have a product of 1 and a sum of -2. Let's try -1 and -1:

$$5(x^2 - 2x + 1) = 5(x - 1)(x - 1)$$

We know that we've factored correctly because when we multiply these binomials together using FOIL, we arrive back at the original expression:

$$5(x - 1)(x - 1) = 5(x^2 - x - x + 1) = 5(x^2 - 2x + 1)$$

However, what happens when you can't factor out a from the entire expression? You need to leave a as a coefficient of x inside one of your binomials:

$$ax^2 + bx + c = (ax + ?)(x + ?)$$

To complete our binomials, we're still looking for two numbers with a product of c. However, this time the two numbers need to have a sum of b when the second one is multiplied by a.

Here is an example:

Factor out $3x^2 - 5x - 2$.

In this example, $a = 3$, but it isn't a common factor that we can pull out of the entire expression. Therefore, we need to leave it as a coefficient of x inside one of our binomials:

$$3x^2 + 5x - 2 = (3x + ?)(x + ?)$$

First, we need to find two numbers that have a product of -2. Two pairs of numbers are possible: 2 and -1, or 1 and -2. Then, we need to pick the pair of numbers that has a sum of 5 when the second number is multiplied by 3. At first, it doesn't look like our first pair will work:

$$2 + 3 \times (-1) = -1$$

But what if we switched the order?

$$(-1) + 3 \times 2 = 5$$

This works! We just have to plug these numbers into our binomials, with -1 as our first number and 2 as our second number:

$$3x^2 + 5x - 2 = (3x - 1)(x + 2)$$

Then, we can check whether we've factored correctly by using FOIL to multiply the binomials together:

$$(3x - 1)(x + 2) = 3x^2 + 6x - x - 2 = 3x^2 + 5x - 2$$

We're back at our original expression, so we know that we have factored correctly.

FACTORING A DIFFERENCE OF SQUARES (UPPER LEVEL ONLY)

Expressions such as $x^2 - 25$ are called a difference of squares because two squared numbers are being subtracted:

$$x^2 - 25 = x^2 - 5^2$$

To factor a difference of squares, remember the following formula:

$$a^2 - b^2 = (a + b)(a - b)$$

Here is an example:

Factor out $x^2 - 25$.

Because we know that 25 is equal to 5^2, we can apply the difference of squares formula. Here, a equals x and b equals 5:

$$x^2 - 25 = (x + 5)(x - 5)$$

If we use FOIL to multiply these binomials together, we find that we're back at our original difference of squares:

$$(x + 5)(x - 5) = x^2 - 5x + 5x - 25 = x^2 - 25$$

Here is another example:

Factor out $x^2 - y^4$.

Remember that you can write y^4 as $(y^2)^2$. Therefore, you can use the difference of squares formula to factor this expression, with a equal to x and b equal to y^2:

$$x^2 - y^4 = (x + y^2)(x - y^2)$$

Multiplying the two binomials together, we see that we've factored correctly:

$$(x + y^2)(x - y^2) = x^2 - xy^2 + xy^2 - y^4 = x^2 - y^4$$

PRACTICE QUESTIONS: EXPRESSIONS

1. If $x = 5$, what is the value of $3x - 4$?

2. If $N = -2$, what is the value of $N^2 + 4N$?

3. If $a = 6$ and $b = 1$, what is the value of $7a - 20b$?

4. If $P = 3$ and $Q = 4$, what is the value of $2P^2 + 3Q - 4P$?

For questions 5-10, simplify the expressions by adding or subtracting like terms.

5. $2N + 3N =$

6. $x + 8x =$

7. $4a^2 - 2a^2 =$

8. $4h - 3h + 7 =$

9. $N + M + 2N =$

10. $3x^2 - y^2 - 2x^2 + 4y^2 =$

For questions 11-18, use the distributive property to multiply or divide the expressions.

11. $3(x^2 + 12) =$

12. $2(a^2 - 2a + 3b^2) =$

13. $x^2(2x + 8) =$

14. $5y(3y^2 - 2y + 10) =$

15. $(3g + 9) \div 3 =$

16. $(16x^2 + 24x) \div 4x =$

17. Factor the expression $16y + 4z$:

18. Factor the expression $3x^2 - 9x + 12$:

Questions 19-35 are Upper Level Only.

For questions 19-22, simplify the expressions.

19. $a^2 \times a^7 =$

20. $x^3y^2 \times x^2y =$

21. $\frac{x^{10}}{x^7} =$

22. $\frac{a^4bc}{a^2b^2c^3} =$

For questions 23-26, multiply the two binomials.

23. $(x + 5)(x + 2) =$

24. $(y - 4)(y + 10) =$

25. $(3a + 1)(a + 8) =$

26. $(4x + y)(x - 2y) =$

For questions 27-35, completely factor the expressions.

27. $x^2 - 3x - 28 =$

28. $3x^2 - 12x - 15 =$

29. $-2x^2 + 4x - 2 =$

30. $2x^2 + 15x + 22 =$

31. $x^2 - 1 =$

32. $x^2 - 36 =$

33. $5x^2 - 80 =$

34. $p^4 - 16 =$

35. $x^2 + 5xy + 6y^2 =$

EQUATIONS

MIDDLE/UPPER LEVEL ONLY

SECTION 3

An algebraic **equation** tells you that two expressions are equal to each other. In our backyard patio example in Section 1, we came up with a very simple equation telling us that $9x$ was equal to 36:

$$9x = 36$$

To solve an algebraic equation, we need to find a value for x that makes the equation true. For the equation above, we found that $x = 4$ because $9 \times 4 = 36$.

What if our equation is a little more complicated? Take a look at the equation below:

$$3x - 2 = 13$$

For this equation, we need to find a value for x that, when we multiply by 3 and subtract 2, equals 13. This equation takes a little more thought, but we soon find that $x = 5$ because $3 \times 5 - 2 = 13$.

Always check your answer! To do this, plug your answer back into the equation and check whether it makes the equation true.

MANIPULATING EQUATIONS

For many complicated algebraic equations, you will not be able to figure out the answer in your head; you will need to use a method to manipulate your equation and solve for the unknown variable. Your goal is always to **isolate** your variable—that is, to get your variable by itself on one side of the equation, and all of your numbers on the other side of the equation. To do this, work backwards to "undo" all of the operations that are being performed on your variable until you can get it by itself.

There is one important rule to remember when working with equations: whatever you do to one side of the equation, you must also do to the other! If you violate this rule, the two sides of your equation will no longer be equal. For example, let's consider this (obviously) true equation:

$$4 = 4$$

If you add a number to one side of your equation but not to the other, the two sides are no longer equal:

$$4 = 4$$
$$4 + 2 \neq 4$$

You need to add the same number to both sides of your equation so they remain equal:

$$4 + 2 = 4 + 2$$

Let's see how this works with the equation we solved earlier:

$$3x - 2 = 13$$

On the left side of the equation, x is being multiplied by 3, and 2 is being subtracted from the product. We need to "undo" each of these operations by adding and dividing numbers to both sides of our equation. First, we "undo" the subtraction by adding 2 to each side:

$$3x - 2 = 13$$
$$3x - 2 + 2 = 13 + 2$$
$$3x = 15$$

Then, we "undo" the multiplication by dividing each side by 3:

$$\frac{3x}{3} = \frac{15}{3}$$

$$x = 5$$

What if our equation has variables on both sides? First, we need to get all of the variables onto one side of the equation and combine like terms. Then, we can isolate our variable by adding, subtracting, multiplying, and dividing the same numbers on both sides of our equation.

For example, consider the equation:

$$5a - 7 = 2a - 1$$

To solve for a, we first need to get all of our variables on one side of the equation by subtracting $2a$ from each side:

$$5a - 7 = 2a - 1$$
$$5a - 2a - 7 = 2a - 2a - 1$$
$$3a - 7 = -1$$

Then, we can "undo" the subtraction by adding 7 to each side:

$$3a - 7 + 7 = -1 + 7$$
$$3a = 6$$

And finally, we "undo" the multiplication by dividing each side by 3:

$$\frac{3a}{3} = \frac{6}{3}$$

$$a = 2$$

To test if we got the right answer, we can plug this number back into our equation to make sure that the equation holds true:

$$5a - 7 = 2a - 1$$
$$5 \times 2 - 7 = 2 \times 2 - 1$$
$$10 - 7 = 4 - 1$$
$$3 = 3$$

Because 3 does clearly equal 3, we know that our answer is correct.

VIDEO

2.7 INTRO TO EQUATIONS

Watch at http:// videos.ivyglobal.com

SOLVING SYSTEMS OF EQUATIONS (UPPER LEVEL ONLY)

A **system of equations** is a group of equations that go together. For example:

$$\begin{cases} x + y = 3 \\ 2x - y = 12 \end{cases}$$

In the earlier equations we have been looking at, each equation only has one variable (x). If a single equation had two variables (such as x and y), you would not be able to find the exact value of each variable. However, if you have two equations and two variables, you can use both equations to find the value of x and y. There are two methods for solving systems of equations: substitution and elimination.

Let's take a look at the example above:

$$\begin{cases} x + y = 3 \\ 2x - y = 12 \end{cases}$$

To solve this system of equations using the **substitution** method, first choose a variable to isolate in either equation. Let's try isolating y in the first equation. To isolate y, subtract x from both sides of the equation:

$$x + y - x = 3 - x$$

$$y = 3 - x$$

We've found that y is equal to the value of $3 - x$. We can then substitute this value into the second equation by writing it instead of y:

$$2x - \boldsymbol{y} = 12$$

$$2x - (\mathbf{3} - \boldsymbol{x}) = 12$$

Now we have a single equation with only one variable (x), so we can solve this equation for x:

$$2x - (3 - x) = 12$$

$$2x - 3 + x = 12$$

$$3x - 3 = 12$$

$$3x - 3 + 3 = 12 + 3$$

$$3x = 15$$

$$x = 5$$

Now that we know that $x = 5$, we can plug this value of x into either of our original two equations to solve for y. Let's plug this into our first equation:

$$\boldsymbol{x} + y = 3$$

$$\mathbf{5} + y = 3$$

$$5 + y - 5 = 3 - 5$$

$$y = -2$$

We've found that $x = 5$ and $y = -2$. We can check that we've solved this system of equations correctly by plugging these values back into our original two equations and verifying that they are true:

$$5 + (-2) = 3$$

$$2 \times 5 - (-2) = 12$$

Both of these equations are true, so we have solved this system of equations correctly.

You can also solve this system of equations using the **elimination** method. The elimination method allows us to cancel variables by adding or subtracting the two equations. In our example above, if we add the two equations together, the y's will cancel each other out:

$$\begin{array}{rr} & x + y = 3 \\ + & 2x - y = 12 \\ \hline & 3x \quad\;\; = 15 \end{array}$$

We now have one single equation in which we can solve for x:

$$3x = 15$$
$$x = 5$$

Then, we plug this value for x back into one of our two original equations to solve for y, following the same steps we used above.

Why are we allowed to add or subtract two equations? Recall the rule for manipulating equations: whenever you add or subtract something to one side of an equation, you must also add or subtract *the same value* to the other side of the equation. When we added together our two equations, we added the left side of the first equation to the left side of the second equation, and right side of the first equation to the right side of the second equation. Because the left side and right sides of the first equation are equal, we effectively added the same value to both sides of the second equation!

PRACTICE QUESTIONS: EQUATIONS

For questions 1-20, solve for x:

1. $x + 8 = 44$

2. $2x = 16$

3. $5 - x = 12$

4. $5x = -45$

5. $x \div 3 = 4$

6. $11x = 22$

7. $\frac{1}{2}x = 5$

8. $18 \div x = 6$

9. $4x - 2 = 18$

10. $-5x + 5 = 35$

11. $7x - 3 = 6x + 8$

12. $4.5x = -63$

13. $x + 14 = 3x - 4$

14. $10x - 5 = x + 22$

15. $4x = -90 + x$

16. $8 - 3.2x = 6 - 3x$

17. $x \div 3 = x - 16$

18. $20 - 2x = \frac{1}{2}x$

19. $4(x - 5) = x + 1$

20. $3x + 42 = 2(4x + 11)$

Questions 21-26 are Upper Level Only.

For questions 21-24, solve the systems of equations:

21. $\begin{cases} x = 5 + y \\ x + 3y = 13 \end{cases}$

22. $\begin{cases} 2m - n = -1 \\ 3m + n = 6 \end{cases}$

23. $\begin{cases} 5p + 6 = q \\ 4p + 9q = 5 \end{cases}$

24. $\begin{cases} 2x + y = 21 \\ 3x + 3y = 36 \end{cases}$

For questions 25-26, use the following information:

At a candy store, two chocolate eggs and one gummy worm cost 25 cents total. One chocolate egg and two gummy worms cost 20 cents total.

25. What is the cost of one chocolate egg?

26. What is the cost of one gummy worm?

For questions 27-28, use the following information:

A theater charges different prices for adult and child tickets. On Friday, the theater sold 60 adult and 20 child tickets, for a total of $700. On Saturday, the theater sold 50 adult and 10 child tickets, for a total of $550.

27. How much does one adult ticket cost?

28. How much does one child ticket cost?

INEQUALITIES

MIDDLE/UPPER LEVEL ONLY

SECTION 4

An **inequality** is a mathematical statement comparing two unequal quantities. We represent inequalities using the following symbols:

INEQUALITY SYMBOLS	
$>$	greater than
$<$	less than
$\geq$	greater than or equal to
$\leq$	less than or equal to

For example:

11 is greater than 6.

Using a "greater than" symbol, we would write this as $11 > 6$.

An algebraic inequality states that a certain algebraic expression is greater than or less than another quantity. For instance:

An unknown quantity, x, is less than 3.

We can express this statement with a "less than" symbol: $x < 3$.

There are many possible solutions for this inequality. For example, x might equal 1, 2, 0.5, –4, –6, 0, or any other number less than three.

If you have a more complex inequality, treat this inequality like an equation and find the simplest range of solutions for your variable. For example:

$$4N \geq 24$$

You would read this as "4 times N is greater than or equal to 24." You need to divide by four in order find what N alone is greater than or equal to:

$$4N \geq 24$$
$$N \geq 6$$

If 4 times N is greater than or equal to 24, than N can be any value greater than or equal to 6.

VIDEO
2.8 INTRO TO INEQUALITIES
Watch at http:// videos.ivyglobal.com

RULES FOR INEQUALITIES

As with an equation, you can add or subtract the same number from both sides of an inequality and still preserve the inequality. For example:

$$x + 3 > 7$$

To solve this problem, we would subtract 3 from both sides of the inequality to solve for x:

$$x + 3 > 7$$
$$x + 3 - 3 > 7 - 3$$
$$x > 4$$

You have to be more careful when multiplying or dividing. Multiplying or dividing both sides of an inequality by a positive number preserves the inequality, but multiplying or dividing by a negative number reverses the inequality. For example, consider the following inequality:

$$5 > 3$$

We can multiply both sides of this inequality by a positive number, and the inequality is still true:

$$5 > 3$$
$$5 \times 4 > 3 \times 4$$
$$20 > 12$$

However, if we multiply both sides by a negative number, we get a false result:

$$5 > 3$$
$$5 \times (-4) > 3 \times (-4)$$
$$-20 > -12 \textit{ Wrong!}$$

Therefore, we need to reverse the inequality when multiplying or dividing by a negative number:

$$5 > 3$$
$$5 \times (-4) < 3 \times (-4)$$
$$-20 < -12$$

Let's try a more complex algebraic inequality:

$$-4x + 1 > 3$$

We approach this like an equation, and "undo" the addition by subtracting 1 from both sides:

$$-4x + 1 > 3$$
$$-4x + 1 - 1 > 3 - 1$$
$$-4x > 2$$

Then, we "undo" the multiplication by dividing both sides by –4, remembering to reverse the inequality because we are dividing by a negative number:

$$\frac{-4x}{-4} < \frac{2}{-4}$$

$$x < -1/2$$

Therefore, x can be any number less than $-\frac{1}{2}$. We can check our solution by picking a possible value for x and plugging it back into the original inequality. In this case, let's have x equal –1:

$$-4x + 1 > 3$$
$$-4 \times (-1) + 1 > 3$$
$$4 + 1 > 3$$
$$5 > 3$$

Because 5 is greater than 3, we know we have solved our inequality correctly.

INEQUALITIES ON A NUMBER LINE

Algebraic inequalities are sometimes represented using lines, rays, line segments, and circles on a number line. A shaded ray or line segment represents all of the possible solutions for the inequality. Circles show whether numbers at the end of a line segment are part of the solution set. If a circle is shaded in completely, it means the number is included in the solution set: it is a possible solution for the inequality. If a circle is unshaded, it means the number is excluded from the solution set: it is not a possible solution for the inequality. When you see an inequality with the signs $\leq$ or $\geq$, the inequality will be represented with a shaded circle on the number line. When you see an inequality with the signs $<$ or $>$, the inequality will be represented with an open circle on the number line.

Here is an example:

Show the possible solutions for $x > 1$ on a number line.

All numbers greater than 1 are possible solutions for this inequality, so you would draw a shaded ray extending to the right of 1. The number 1 is not a possible solution for this inequality, so you would draw an unshaded circle over the number 1:

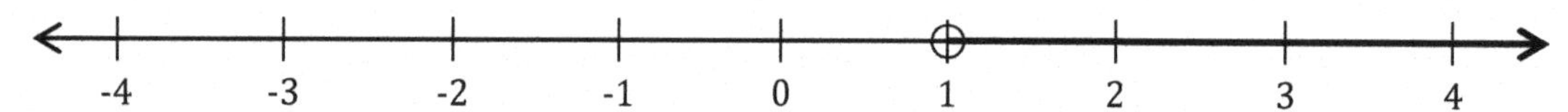

Here is another example:

Show the possible solutions for $x \leq -4$ on a number line.

All numbers less than or equal to -4 are possible solutions for this inequality, so you would draw a shaded ray extending to the left of -4. The number -4 is also a possible solution for this inequality, so you would draw a shaded circle over -4:

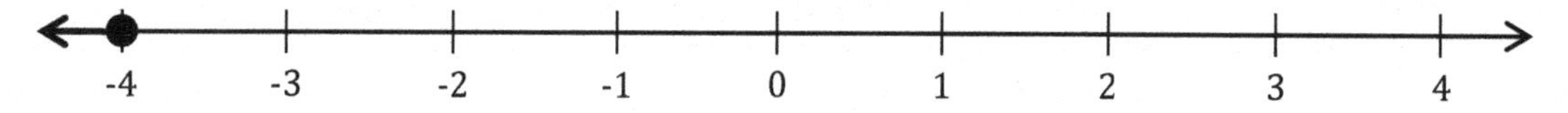

PRACTICE QUESTIONS: INEQUALITIES

1. If $x < 6$, can -1 be a possible value for x?

2. If $P \geq 4$, can 3 be a possible value for P?

3. If $N < 15$, can -10 be a possible value for N?

4. If $q \geq 10$, can 10 be a possible value for q?

5. If $2y \geq 20$, give one possible value for y:

6. If $d - 5 < 9$, give one possible value for d:

7. If $3 < a < 13$, give one possible value for a:

8. If $4x \leq 16$, give one possible value for x:

9. If $N + 2 \geq 9$, give one possible value for N:

10. If $3z > 27$, give one possible value for z:

Solve for x:

11. $7x \geq 21$

12. $x - 4 > 8$

13. $x + 16 \leq 15$

14. $-3x < 45$

15. $4x - 10 > -2$

16. $8 - 5x \leq -27$

17. $9x - 20 > 5x$

18. $3x + 7 \leq x + 1$

19. $16 < 4x < 24$

20. $23 \leq 7x + 2 \leq 37$

For questions 21-23, write an inequality that corresponds with the diagram:

21. 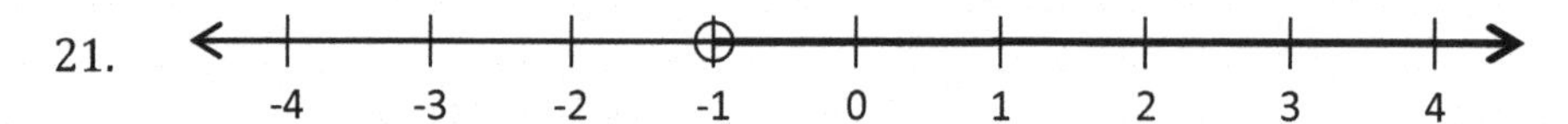

22. 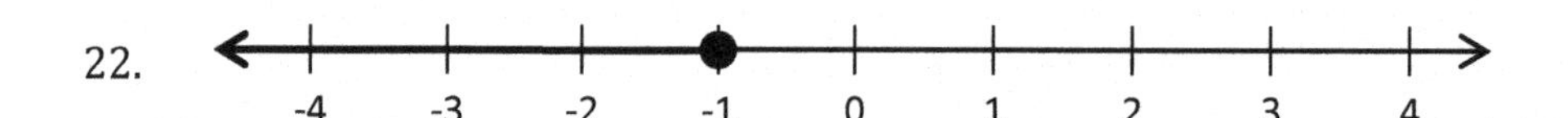

23. 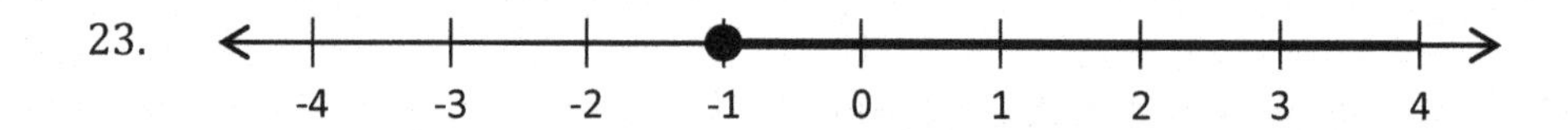

STRANGE SYMBOLS

MIDDLE/UPPER LEVEL ONLY

SECTION 5

The ISEE sometimes uses strange symbols—stars, bubbles, smiley faces, etc.—to represent relationships among numbers and variables. These symbols always have a formula or rule that clearly shows what the relationship is. To solve a strange symbol question, simply look for the rule, and figure out what numbers you need to plug in.

For example, consider the following question:

For any numbers N and M, $N♦M = 2N + 3M$. What is the value of $4♦1$?

In this question, the ISEE has used the symbol ♦ to represent a set of operations to perform on two numbers. The rule tells us that "one number ♦ another number means two times the first number plus three times the second number." Therefore, we only need to plug in 4 for the first number and 1 for the second number to answer the question:

$$4♦1 = 2 \times 4 + 3 \times 1 = 11$$

STRANGE SYMBOLS AND ALGEBRA

Strange symbol questions may also involve more complicated algebra. For example, consider the following question:

For any number x, $⇧x = 2x - 4$. If $⇧h = 4$, what is the value of h?

This complicated-looking question is just an algebra problem in disguise. The rule tells you that to "⇧" a number means to multiply the number by 2 and subtract 4. Therefore, to find $⇧h$, all we need to do is plug h into the rule:

$$⇧h = 2h - 4$$

We know that this expression must also equal 4, because the prompt tells us that $⇧h = 4$.

Therefore, we can write a simple algebraic equation:

$$2h - 4 = 4$$

Working backwards, we can see that

$$2h = 8$$

And therefore,

$$h = 4$$

Remember, to solve a strange symbol question, all you need to do is look for the rule and figure out what numbers or variables to plug in.

VIDEO
2.9 STRANGE SYMBOLS
Watch at http:// videos.ivyglobal.com

PRACTICE QUESTIONS: STRANGE SYMBOLS

1. For any number x, ✪$x = 5x + 7$. What is the value of ✪6??

2. For any number y, □$y = 3y^2$. What is the value of □2 + □3?

3. For any number a, 🡻$a = 2a^2 - 1$. What is the value of 🡻4?

4. For any non-zero number N, ¤$N = \frac{10}{N}$. What is the value of ¤5 × ¤1??

5. For any numbers g and h, g⌘$h = 5g - h$. What is the value of 5⌘13?

6. For any numbers j and k, j ✓$k = 2 + jk$. What is the value of (-7)✓2?

7. For any non-zero numbers m and n, m☺$n = \frac{2m}{n}$. What is the value of 8☺4?

8. For any number z, ♦$z = 4z - 6$. What is the value of ♦3 × ♦4?

9. For any positive numbers P and Q, P⅄$Q = \sqrt{P + Q}$. What is the value of 9⅄16?

10. For any positive number m, ❖m is equal to the number of prime numbers less than m. What is the value of ❖20?

11. If y is a negative number, let ✧$y = 4y + 7$. If y is zero or a positive number, let ✧$y = 3y^2$. What is the value of ✧3 + ✧(-5)?

12. For any number z, ◎$z = 5z + 14$. If ◎$x = 4$, what is the value of x?

13. For any number y, ➢$y = y^2 + 1$. What is the value of ➢➢3?

14. For any number N, ⊖$N = \frac{8}{6-N}$. If ⊖$P = 2$, what is the value of P?

15. For any number Q, ▲$Q = 2^Q$. What is the value of ▲▲1?

16. If x is a positive number, let ☼$x = \sqrt{x}$. If x is zero or a negative number, let ☼$x = x^2$. What is the value of ☼☼(-45)?

17. For any non-zero numbers a and b, $a\triangle b = \frac{2a}{b}$. If $3\triangle 4 = x\triangle 2$, what is the value of x?

ABSOLUTE VALUE

UPPER LEVEL ONLY

SECTION 6

The **absolute value** of a number is its distance away from zero on a number line. To show that we are taking the absolute value of a quantity, we write two vertical bars around to the quantity.

Here is an example:

What is $|5|$?

The two vertical bars around the number 5 mean the question is asking us to find the absolute value of 5. In other words, what is the distance between 5 and zero on a number line? 5 is 5 units away from zero, so its absolute value is 5:

$$|5| = 5$$

Here is another example:

What is $|4 - 7|$?

This question is asking us to find the absolute value of 4-7. First, we need to solve for the quantity within the absolute value bars:

$$|4 - 7| = |-3|$$

Now, we need to find the absolute value of -3. What is the distance between -3 and zero on a number line? -3 is 3 units away from zero, so its absolute value is 3:

$$|-3| = 3$$

Therefore, $|4 - 7| = 3$.

The absolute value of a number is always positive or zero. Any number will either be a positive distance away from zero, or it will be zero units away (if the number is equal to zero).

ABSOLUTE VALUE EQUATIONS

On the ISEE, you may need to solve an absolute value equation using algebra. Here is an important rule to remember:

- If $|x| = a$, then $x = a$ or $x = -a$.

For example:

If $|x| = 4$, then what values are possible for x?

This question is asking us to find any values of x that have an absolute value of 4. Only two values are possible: 4 and -4. Both of these numbers are 4 units away from zero on the number line, so they both have an absolute value of 4. Therefore:

If $|x| = 4$, then $x = 4$ or $x = -4$.

Here is another example:

Solve $|x - 5| = 4$.

We know that there are two numbers with an absolute value of 4: these are 4 and -4. Therefore, the quantity $x - 5$ could either be equal to 4 or -4. We can solve each of these equations separately to find the two possible values of x:

$$x - 5 = 4 \qquad\qquad x - 5 = -4$$
$$x = 9 \qquad\qquad x = 1$$

We have two solutions: $x = 1$ or $x = 9$.

We could also write this solution as $x = 5 \pm 4$. This leads to an important observation: $|x - a| = b$ means "x is b away from a." In our example above, $|x - 5| = 4$ means x is 5 units away from 4.

ABSOLUTE VALUE INEQUALITIES

You may need to solve an absolute value inequality on the ISEE. Here are two rules for absolute value inequalities:

- If $|x| < a$, then $-a < x < a$.
- If $|x| > a$, then $x < -a$ or $x > a$.

For example:

If $|x| \leq 3$, then what values are possible for x?

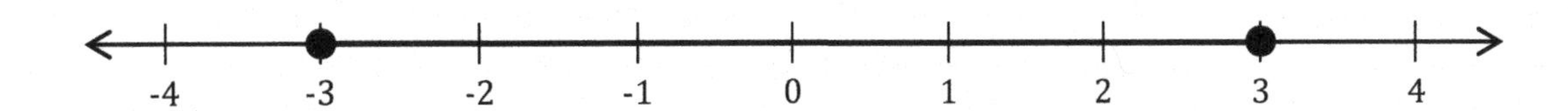

The inequality tells us that the distance between x and 0 is less than or equal to 3. Think of a dog tied to a post at the 0 mark on the number line. The dog's leash is 3 feet long. The dog can go up to the 3-foot mark to the right, and up to the -3-foot mark to the left:

All numbers between -3 and 3, inclusive, have a distance from zero that is 3 units or less. Therefore:

$$\text{If } |x| \leq 3, \text{ then } -3 \leq x \leq 3.$$

Here is another example:

If $|x| > 2$, then what values are possible for x?

Now imagine that someone has put up a circular fence on the number line, with the zero mark at the center. This fence has a radius of 2 feet so that it reaches the 2-foot mark and the -2-foot mark. A dog (without a leash) is outside this fence. The dog can approach this fence from either direction, but cannot stand where the fence is standing:

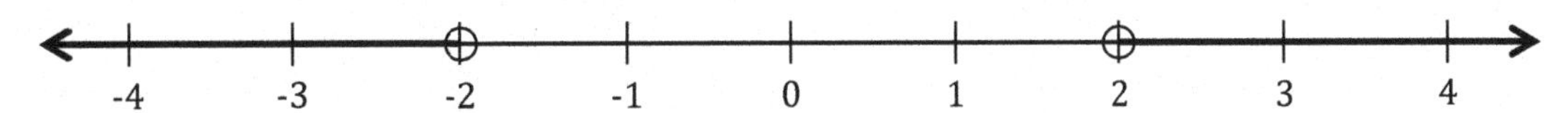

Like the dog, all numbers less than -2 and greater than 2 have a distance from zero that is greater than 2 units. Therefore:

$$\text{If } |x| > 2, \text{ then } x < -2 \text{ or } x > 2.$$

What about a question like this?

Solve $|x - 2| \leq 3$.

We know that all quantities between -3 and 3, inclusive, have an absolute value less than or equal to 3. Therefore, the quantity $x-2$ must be between -3 and 3, inclusive:

$$-3 \leq x-2 \leq 3$$
$$-1 \leq x \leq 5$$

x must be between -1 and 5, inclusive: $-1 \leq x \leq 5$.

Remember that $|x-a| = b$ means "x is b away from a." Similarly:

- $|x-a| < b$ means "x is less than b away from a."
- $|x-a| \leq b$ means "x is within b of a."
- $|x-a| > b$ means "x is more than b away from a."
- $|x-a| \geq b$ means "x is at least b away from a."

If we look at our solution above, we can see that this is true: $|x-2| \leq 3$ means that x is within 2 units of 3.

Here is one more example:

A manufacturer of cereal will discard all boxes weighing less than 18.5 oz. and more than 21.5 oz. What absolute value inequality represents all weights x that will be discarded?

This question is asking us to work backwards and find an absolute value inequality that represents a certain range of possible box weights. The question asks us to use the variable x to represent these box weights. According to the question, there are two ranges of x where a box will be discarded: if x is less than 18.5 oz. or x is more than 21.5 oz. We can sketch these ranges on a number line:

20 is exactly in between 18.5 and 21.5, so these ranges include all numbers that are more than 1.5 oz. away from 20. In other words, the manufacturer throws out any box that is more than 1.5 oz. away from 20 oz., which is likely the standard weight.

How would we write this as an absolute value inequality? Remember that $|x-a| > b$ means "x is more than b away from a." Therefore, we can write "x is more than 1.5 away from 20" as $|x-20| > 1.5$.

PRACTICE QUESTIONS: ABSOLUTE VALUE

1. $|-3| =$

2. $|100| =$

3. $|7 - 6| =$

4. $|0| =$

5. $|2 - 7| =$

6. $|15 - 18| =$

Define all values for x:

7. $|x - 3| = 2$

8. $|3 - x| = 2$

9. $-|x - 5| = -2$

10. $-|x - 3| < -5$

11. $|6 - x| < 5$

12. $|3 + x| > 20$

13. $|4 + x| \leq 23$

14. $|x - 11| \geq 7$

15. $|2 - x| = 9$

16. $|x + 7| < 4$

17. $|2x - 9| > 3$

18. The students in Mr. Brown's class are an average of 1.6 meters tall. The tallest student is 1.8 meters, and the shortest student is 1.4 meters tall. What absolute value inequality represents all heights x of the students?

19. At the McGregor family reunion, the ages of the family members ranged from 3 to 95. What absolute value equation represents both ages x of the youngest and oldest family members?

20. A certain cat is very picky about temperature. He complains if the temperature is more than 5°F away from 72°F. What absolute value inequality represents all temperatures x for which the cat complains?

MATRICES

UPPER LEVEL ONLY

SECTION 7

A **matrix** is a two dimensional array of numbers. Think of an array as a set of slots to put numbers in. For example, a cash register has spaces for dollar, 5 dollar, 10 dollar, and 20 dollar bills. Each bill has a space that is set aside for it, and they are in a row. Now imagine that in addition to having slots left to right, there are also slots up and down. This would be a two-dimensional matrix, with both rows and columns.

In math, matrices are written in square brackets with numbers arranged in rows and columns. For example, let's take a look at this matrix:

$$\begin{bmatrix} 3 & 4 \\ 0 & -1 \end{bmatrix}$$

This matrix has two rows and two columns, so we can call it a 2×2 matrix. Similarly, a 2×3 matrix would have two rows and three columns, and a 3×2 matrix would have three rows and two columns.

MATRIX ADDITION AND SUBTRACTION

We can add and subtract two matrices to generate a new matrix. When adding or subtracting, you must first check to see whether the two matrices have the same number of rows and columns. A 2×2 matrix must always be added to another 2×2 matrix, a 3×3 matrix must always be added to another 3×3 matrix, and so on.

Let's take a look at this sample question:

$$\text{If } A = \begin{bmatrix} 2 & -3 \\ 3 & 0 \\ 1 & 5 \end{bmatrix} \text{ and } B = \begin{bmatrix} 1 & -3 \\ 3 & 1 \\ 1 & 2 \end{bmatrix}, \text{ what is } A + B?$$

The matrix called "A" has 3 rows and 2 columns, so A is a 3×2 matrix. The matrix called "B" also has 3 rows and 2 columns, so B is also a 3×2 matrix. Because A and B have the same number of rows and columns, we can add the two matrices.

To add the two matrices together, all we have to do is add the corresponding values in each row and column. The sums of these values go into the corresponding slots of a new 3×2 matrix:

$$\begin{bmatrix} 2 & -3 \\ 3 & 0 \\ 1 & 5 \end{bmatrix} + \begin{bmatrix} 1 & -3 \\ 3 & 1 \\ 1 & 2 \end{bmatrix} = \begin{bmatrix} 2+1 & -3+(-3) \\ 3+3 & 0+1 \\ 1+1 & 5+2 \end{bmatrix} = \begin{bmatrix} 3 & -6 \\ 6 & 1 \\ 2 & 7 \end{bmatrix}$$

Adding A and B gave us the matrix $\begin{bmatrix} 3 & -6 \\ 6 & 1 \\ 2 & 7 \end{bmatrix}$.

Here is an example of subtraction:

If $A = \begin{bmatrix} 0 & 2 & 3 \\ -4 & 0 & 8 \end{bmatrix}$ and B=$\begin{bmatrix} 4 & 2 & 3 \\ -5 & 0 & 2 \end{bmatrix}$, what is $A - B$?

There are 2 rows in A and 3 columns in A, so A is a 2×3 matrix. There are also 2 rows in B and 3 columns in B, so B is also a 2×3 matrix. Because A and B have the same dimensions, we can subtract them. We subtract the corresponding values in each row and column, and enter these into a new 2×3 matrix:

$$\begin{bmatrix} 0 & 2 & 3 \\ -4 & 0 & 8 \end{bmatrix} - \begin{bmatrix} 4 & 2 & 3 \\ -5 & 0 & 2 \end{bmatrix} = \begin{bmatrix} 0-4 & 2-2 & 3-3 \\ -4-(-5) & 0-0 & 8-2 \end{bmatrix} = \begin{bmatrix} -4 & 0 & 0 \\ 1 & 0 & 6 \end{bmatrix}$$

Therefore, subtracting B from A gave us the matrix $\begin{bmatrix} -4 & 0 & 0 \\ 1 & 0 & 6 \end{bmatrix}$.

Let's look at another example:

If $A = \begin{bmatrix} 2 & -3 \\ 3 & 0 \\ 1 & 5 \end{bmatrix}$ and $B = \begin{bmatrix} 0 & 2 & 3 \\ -4 & 0 & 8 \end{bmatrix}$, what is $A + B$?

There are 3 rows and 2 columns in A, so A is a 3×2 matrix. There are 2 rows and 3 columns in B, so B is a 2×3 matrix. Because A and B have different dimensions, we cannot add them. This expression is **undefined** and therefore unsolvable.

MATRIX MULTIPLICATION

Multiplying two matrices is a little more complicated than adding and subtracting. First, we multiply **row by column**: we multiply the values in the rows of the first matrix by the values in the columns of the second matrix in pairs. Then, we add these products together.

Let's see how we would use these steps to solve the following question:

$$\text{If } A = \begin{bmatrix} 3 & 4 \\ 0 & -1 \end{bmatrix} \text{ and } = \begin{bmatrix} 0 & 5 \\ 1 & -1 \end{bmatrix}, \text{ what is } A \times B?$$

In order to multiply $A \times B$, the first step is to multiply row by column. We'll start by multiplying the values in the first row of matrix A by the values in the first column of matrix B. In other words, we're multiplying the values circled in the equation below:

$$\begin{bmatrix} 3 & 4 \\ 0 & -1 \end{bmatrix} \times \begin{bmatrix} 0 & 5 \\ 1 & -1 \end{bmatrix}$$

$$3 \times 0 = 0$$

$$4 \times 1 = 4$$

Then, we add together these two products:

$$0 + 4 = 4$$

Because we multiplied the first row by the first column, we'll put this value in the first row and the first column of our new matrix:

$$\begin{bmatrix} 4 & \\ & \end{bmatrix}$$

Next, we multiply the values in the first row of matrix A by the values in the second row of matrix B. In other words, we're multiplying the values circled below:

$$\begin{bmatrix} 3 & 4 \\ 0 & -1 \end{bmatrix} \times \begin{bmatrix} 0 & 5 \\ 1 & -1 \end{bmatrix}$$

$$3 \times 5 = 15$$

$$4 \times (-1) = -4$$

Then, we add together these two products:

$$15 + (-4) = 11$$

Because we multiplied the first row by the second column, we'll put this value in the first row and the second column of our new matrix:

$$\begin{bmatrix} 4 & 11 \\ & \end{bmatrix}$$

Now it's time to multiply the values in the second row of matrix A. We'll start multiplying these by the values in the first row of matrix B:

$$\begin{bmatrix} 3 & 4 \\ 0 & -1 \end{bmatrix} \times \begin{bmatrix} 0 & 5 \\ 1 & -1 \end{bmatrix}$$

$$0 \times 0 = 0$$

$$(-1) \times 1 = -1$$

We add together these two products:

$$0 + (-1) = -1$$

And we put this sum in the second row and the first column of our new matrix:

$$\begin{bmatrix} 4 & 11 \\ -1 & \end{bmatrix}$$

To finish our matrix, we'll multiply the values in the second row of matrix A by the values in the second row of matrix B:

$$\begin{bmatrix} 3 & 4 \\ 0 & -1 \end{bmatrix} \times \begin{bmatrix} 0 & 5 \\ 1 & -1 \end{bmatrix}$$

$$0 \times 5 = 0$$

$$-1 \times (-1) = 1$$

We add together these two products:

$$0 + 1 = 1$$

And we put this sum in the second row and the second column of our new matrix:

$$\begin{bmatrix} 4 & 11 \\ -1 & 1 \end{bmatrix}$$

Now that we have multiplied all of the rows by all of the columns in our two matrices, our final product is complete. Here is a summary of what we did:

$$\begin{bmatrix} 3 & 4 \\ 0 & -1 \end{bmatrix} \times \begin{bmatrix} 0 & 5 \\ 1 & -1 \end{bmatrix} =$$

$$= \begin{bmatrix} 3 \times 0 + 4 \times 1 & 3 \times 5 + 4 \times (-1) \\ 0 \times 0 + (-1) \times 1 & 0 \times 5 + (-1) \times (-1) \end{bmatrix}$$

$$= \begin{bmatrix} 4 & 11 \\ -1 & 1 \end{bmatrix}$$

WHICH MATRICES CAN YOU MULTIPLY?

In the example above, we saw that each row in matrix A was multiplied by a corresponding row in matrix B. Because we multiplied a 2×2 matrix with another 2×2 matrix, the result remained a 2×2 matrix.

Let's think of another situation—what would happen if we tried to multiply a 3×2 matrix with another 3×2 matrix? Let's look at the two hypothetical matrices below:

$$\begin{bmatrix} a & b \\ c & d \\ e & f \end{bmatrix} \times \begin{bmatrix} g & h \\ i & j \\ k & l \end{bmatrix}$$

If we started multiplying the first row of the first matrix (values a and b) by the first column of the second matrix (values g, i, and k), we would have an unmatched value. That is, there would be nothing to multiply with k. This result is therefore not possible—we can't multiply a 3×2 matrix with another 3×2 matrix.

This means that we can't always multiply two matrices that have the same dimensions. In order to multiply two matrices, the number of the columns in the first matrix must match the number of rows in the second matrix. This means that a 3×2 matrix can be multiplied by a 2×3 or a 2×5 matrix, but cannot be multiplied by another 3×2 matrix. For example:

$$\begin{bmatrix} g & h \\ i & j \\ k & l \end{bmatrix} \times \begin{bmatrix} a & b & c \\ d & e & f \end{bmatrix} \text{ is defined and therefore possible}$$

$$\begin{bmatrix} a & b & c \\ d & e & f \end{bmatrix} \times \begin{bmatrix} g & h \\ i & j \\ k & l \end{bmatrix} \text{ is defined and therefore possible}$$

$$\begin{bmatrix} a & b \\ c & d \\ e & f \end{bmatrix} \times \begin{bmatrix} g & h \\ i & j \\ k & l \end{bmatrix} \text{ is undefined and therefore impossible}$$

After determining the number of rows and the number of columns in both matrices, look at the **middle** numbers. If they match, then the two matrices can be multiplied.

[3 × **2**] and [**2** × 3] is defined

[2 × **3**] and [**3** × 5] is defined

[3 × **2**] and [**3** × 2] is **undefined**

MATRICES: PRACTICE QUESTIONS

For questions 1-3, use the following information:

Two matrices' dimensions are defined as follows: Matrix A has 3 rows and 9 columns, and Matrix B has 9 rows and 3 columns.

1. Can you multiply these matrices together?

2. Can you add these matrices together?

3. Can you subtract Matrix B from Matrix A?

For questions 4-13, add, subtract, or multiply the matrices. Write "Undefined" if the operation is not possible.

4. $\begin{bmatrix} 1 & 0 & -1 \\ 0 & -1 & 2 \end{bmatrix} + \begin{bmatrix} 1 & 3 & 1 \\ 4 & 2 & 0 \\ 1 & 0 & -1 \end{bmatrix} =$

5. $\begin{bmatrix} 0 & 1 & 1 \\ -4 & 0 & 2 \end{bmatrix} - \begin{bmatrix} 4 & 2 & 3 \\ -5 & 0 & 2 \end{bmatrix} =$

6. $\begin{bmatrix} 1 & 0 & 2 \\ -2 & 4 & 2 \\ 1 & 1 & 2 \end{bmatrix} - \begin{bmatrix} 4 & 2 & 3 \\ -5 & 0 & 2 \end{bmatrix} =$

7. $\begin{bmatrix} 0 & 5 \\ 1 & -1 \end{bmatrix} + \begin{bmatrix} 3 & 4 \\ 0 & -1 \end{bmatrix} =$

8. $\begin{bmatrix} 2 \\ 3 \\ 1 \end{bmatrix} + \begin{bmatrix} 0 \\ -1 \\ 1 \end{bmatrix} =$

9. $\begin{bmatrix} 0 & 5 \\ 1 & -1 \end{bmatrix} - \begin{bmatrix} 3 & 4 \\ 0 & -1 \end{bmatrix} =$

10. $\begin{bmatrix} 0 & 5 \\ 1 & -1 \end{bmatrix} \times \begin{bmatrix} 3 & 4 \\ 0 & -1 \end{bmatrix} =$

11. $\begin{bmatrix} 5 & 3 \\ 0 & 0 \\ -1 & 1 \end{bmatrix} \times \begin{bmatrix} 2 & 5 \\ -1 & 4 \\ 2 & -8 \end{bmatrix} =$

12. $\begin{bmatrix} 1 & 0 & -1 \\ 0 & -1 & 2 \end{bmatrix} \times \begin{bmatrix} 1 & 3 & 1 \\ 4 & 2 & 0 \\ 1 & 0 & -1 \end{bmatrix} =$

13. $\begin{bmatrix} 1 & 3 & 1 \\ 4 & 2 & 0 \\ 1 & 0 & -1 \end{bmatrix} \times \begin{bmatrix} 1 & 0 & -1 \\ 0 & -1 & 2 \end{bmatrix} =$

PART 2 REVIEW

ALGEBRA

In this section, you will find 40 practice questions to review the algebra content tested on the ISEE's Math Achievement section. The Lower Level questions cover the algebra content that you will find in the Lower Level section, as well as the easier algebra content on the Middle and Upper Level sections. The Middle Level questions cover content that you will only find in the Middle and Upper Level sections. The Upper Level questions cover content that you will only find in the Upper Level section.

Each question is followed by four suggested answers. Read each question and then decide which one of the four suggested answers is best.

LOWER LEVEL QUESTIONS

Use these questions to practice the algebra content that you will see on the Lower Level Math Achievement section, as well as the easier algebra content that you will see on the Middle and Upper Levels. Lower, Middle, and Upper Level students should attempt these questions.

1. If the sum of a number and 3 is equal to 9, what is the number?

   (A) 6
   (B) 9
   (C) 12
   (D) 27

2. If $3K = 15$, then what is the value of K?

   (A) 3
   (B) 5
   (C) 12
   (D) 18

3. Lucy wants to put 6 jellybeans on top of each of the 12 cupcakes she is baking. If J represents the total number of jellybeans, which equation would tell how many total jellybeans she needs?

(A) $J = 12 \div 6$
(B) $J + 6 = 12$
(C) $J = 6 \times 12$
(D) $J = 6 + 12$

4. The difference between three times a number and six is zero. What is the number?

(A) 0
(B) 1
(C) 2
(D) 3

5. If $P = 4$, then what is the value of $7P$?

(A) $7 - 4$
(B) 7×4
(C) $7 \div 4$
(D) 74

6. What is the value of n if $16 - n = 8$?

(A) 2
(B) 8
(C) 16
(D) 24

7. Jane baked two muffins less than twice the number of muffins Adam baked. If m represents the number of muffins Adam baked, then which expression represents the number of muffins that Jane baked?

(A) $2m$
(B) $2m - 2$
(C) $2m + 2$
(D) $2m - 4$

8. Use the following table to find the equation:

Input ☾	Output ◇
4	2
8	3
20	6

What is rule for this function?

(A) ☾ 2 =

(B) ☾ ÷ 2 =

(C) ☾ ÷ 5 + 2 =

(D) ☾ ÷ 4 + 1 =

9. If $x > 2$, then which of the following numbers is a possible value of x?

(A) 0
(B) 1
(C) 2
(D) 3

10. Suzy knows that James has five more than three times the number of marbles in the kitchen sink. She estimates that there are between 15 and 20 marbles in the sink. What is the fewest number of marbles that James could have?

(A) 15
(B) 20
(C) 50
(D) 65

11. If $S = 2$, then what is the value of $7S - 5$?

(A) 19
(B) 9
(C) 14
(D) 2

12. Use the equations to answer the question:

$$13 - m = 10$$
$$3 \times l = 15$$

What is the difference between l and m?

(A) 5
(B) 3
(C) 2
(D) 0

13. A convenience store charges $\$G$ for each pack of gum and $\$C$ for each chocolate bar. If Sandy bought two packs of gum and three chocolate bars, then which expression shows how many dollars she spent?

(A) $2G + 3C$
(B) $5 \times (G + C)$
(C) $G + 2 + C + 3$
(D) $2 \times 3 + G \times C$

14. Ranjeet wrote down a whole number that is less than twice as large as a whole number between 2 and 5. When Stephanie tried to guess the number, Ranjeet told her that the number was found between 6 and 20. What is Ranjeet's number?

(A) 6
(B) 7
(C) 8
(D) 13

15. Use the equations to answer the question:

$$3 \times g = 12$$
$$6 + f = 4$$

What is $g \div f$?

(A) 2
(B) 4
(C) 3
(D) 6

MIDDLE LEVEL QUESTIONS

Use these questions to practice the content that you will only see on the Middle Level and Upper Level ISEE. Only Middle and Upper Level students should attempt these questions.

1. In the equation $5x - 10 = 3x + 8$, what is the value of x?

   (A) 1
   (B) 6
   (C) 9
   (D) 18

2. If $-3 \leq \square < 5$, then which of the following numbers is NOT a possible value of $\square$?

   (A) -3
   (B) 0
   (C) 3
   (D) 5

3. Randy drove for three hours at an average speed of S miles per hour. He then drove for two hours at an average speed of 25 miles per hour. Which expression shows how many miles Randy drove in total?

   (A) $S \div 3 + 50$
   (B) $5(S + 25)$
   (C) $50 - 3S$
   (D) $50 + 3S$

4. In the equation $\frac{P}{18} = \frac{4}{24}$, what is the value of P ?

   (A) 2
   (B) 3
   (C) 6
   (D) 9

5. The weight of a car in kilograms, y, is determined by the size of its engine in cubic inches, x, according to the formula $y = 0.65x + 400$. What is the meaning of 400 in this formula?

(A) For every 600 cubic inches of space, the car weighs 0.65×400 kilograms more.
(B) For every 1 kilogram of weight, the car is 0.65 cubic inches larger.
(C) If the car is without an engine, it weighs 400 kilograms.
(D) When the engine is 0.65 cubic inches large, the car weighs 400 kilograms.

6. If 10■ = 15✸, then what is the value of 2■ ?

(A) 3✸
(B) 5✸
(C) 15✸ – 2
(D) 15✸ – 10

7. The Pioneer swim team has 20 members. Every year, each member contributes 10 cupcakes to the annual bake sale. At last year's bake sale, the swim team made $300 in cupcake sales. If the swim team wants to make twice as much money from cupcakes this year, how much should they charge for each cupcake?

(A) $1.50
(B) $2.00
(C) $3.00
(D) $6.00

8. If $3q + 8 = 29$, then what is the value of q^2 ?

(A) 7
(B) 25
(C) 49
(D) 81

9. An aquarium starts out with F fish, and the fish spawn every week. For every fish in the aquarium at the beginning of a week, two new fish are spawned by the end of the week. Which expression represents the total number of fish in the aquarium at the end of six weeks, assuming no fish die?

(A) $F \times 2^5$
(B) $F \times 2^6$
(C) $12F$
(D) $F + 2^5 + 2^4 + 2^3 + 2^2$

10. If $\bigcirc y = 5y - 5$, what is the value of $\bigcirc 4$?

(A) 4
(B) 12
(C) 15
(D) 20

11. The expression $7a + 14ab - 3a - 4a + 6a^2 - 2ab$ is equivalent to which expression?

(A) $6a^2 - 6ab + 7b$
(B) $6a^2 + 12ab + 14a$
(C) $6a^2 + 12ab$
(D) $6a^2 - 9ab$

12. If $x = -2, y = 5$, and $z = -4$, what is the value of the expression $x^2 + \frac{5}{y} - z$?

(A) -9
(B) -7
(C) 8
(D) 9

13. Rosa earns $D per hour, and Emmanuel earns $15 per hour. If Emmanuel works 30 hours, then which expression shows how many hours Rosa needs to work in order to earn the same amount as Emmanuel?

(A) $30(15 - D)$
(B) $450D$
(C) $D(30 \div 15)$
(D) $450 \div D$

14. In the equation $a + 4 = 6 - b$, what is the value of $a + b$?

(A) 2
(B) 4
(C) 10
(D) 24

15. Which is equivalent to the expression $-3x(-5xy + 7z)$?

(A) $35xy - 37xz$
(B) $-15xy^2 - 21x$
(C) $15x^2y - 21xz$
(D) $35x^2y - 21xz$

UPPER LEVEL QUESTIONS

Use these questions to practice the most challenging difficulty level you will see on the Upper Level ISEE. Only Upper Level students should attempt these questions.

1. Which is equivalent to the expression $12g^2 - 24gh + 8g$?

   (A) $4(3g - 6h + 2g)$
   (B) $4g(3 - 6h + 2g)$
   (C) $4g(3g - 6h + 2)$
   (D) $8g(4g - 3h + 1)$

2. The number of mice in an apartment building is directly proportional to the number of apartment residents, and increases at a rate equal to six times the number of residents. If there are currently 66 mice in the apartment building, how many mice will be in the building if seven new residents move in?

   (A) 73
   (B) 102
   (C) 108
   (D) 114

3. If $2c - 2 > 3(c + 4)$, then which of the following is not a possible value of c?

   (A) -28
   (B) -20
   (C) -16
   (D) -14

4. The expression $\frac{9a^7b^2c^4}{3a^3c^5}$ is equivalent to which expression?

   (A) $\frac{a^4b^2}{c}$
   (B) $\frac{3a^4b^2}{c}$
   (C) $\frac{3a^4b}{c}$
   (D) $\frac{a^4b^2}{3c}$

5. Jason earns $8 per hour for the first eight hours of work each day, and $12 per hour for any additional daily work over eight hours. Charlotte earns $10 per hour,

regardless of how many hours she works each day. One Tuesday, Jason and Charlotte worked the same number of hours and earned $166 combined. How many hours did each of them work?

(A) 7
(B) 8
(C) 9
(D) 10

6. Which expression is equivalent to the expression $\frac{1}{2}(2h-4)(3h-2)$?

(A) $6h^2 - 12h + 8$
(B) $6h^2 - 16h + 4$
(C) $3h^2 - 8h + 4$
(D) $3h^2 + 8h - 4$

7. Which describes all values of y for which $|2y-5| \leq 3$?

(A) $1 \leq y \leq 4$
(B) $1 \leq y \text{ or } y \geq 4$
(C) $1 \geq y \geq 4$
(D) $1 \geq y \text{ or } y \leq 4$

8. For what real value(s) of x does $\frac{x^2-16}{x-2} = 0$?

(A) $x = 4$ only
(B) $x = 4$ and $x = 2$
(C) $x = 4$ and $x = -4$
(D) $x = 2, x = 4$, and $x = -4$

9. If $x^2 - 25 = xy + 5y$ and $x \neq -5$, then which expression is equal to y?

(A) $x - 5$
(B) $x - 25$
(C) $x - \frac{25}{x}$
(D) $\frac{x}{5} - 25$

10. What is the result of the expression $\begin{bmatrix} 1 & 2 \\ 0 & -1 \end{bmatrix} + \begin{bmatrix} 0 & 1 \\ 2 & 0 \end{bmatrix}$?

(A) $\begin{bmatrix} 1 & 3 \\ 0 & 2 \end{bmatrix}$

(B) $\begin{bmatrix} 1 & 3 \\ 2 & -1 \end{bmatrix}$

(C) $\begin{bmatrix} 2 & 2 \\ -2 & 0 \end{bmatrix}$

(D) $\begin{bmatrix} 4 & 1 \\ -2 & 0 \end{bmatrix}$

GEOMETRY

PART 3

LINES AND ANGLES

ALL LEVELS

SECTION 1

A **line** is a straight, one-dimensional object: it has infinite length but no width. Between any two points, you can draw exactly one line that stretches in both directions forever. For instance, between the points A and B below, you can draw the line $\overleftrightarrow{AB}$. We name a line by drawing a horizontal bar with two arrows over two points on the line.

LINE SEGMENTS AND MIDPOINTS

A **line segment** is a portion of a line with a finite length. The two ends of a line segment are called endpoints. To name a line, we identify two points on the line, and we draw a horizontal bar with arrows above the letters for those two points. For instance, in the figure below, the points M and N are the endpoints of the line segment $\overline{MN}$.

The point that divides a line segment into two equal pieces is called its **midpoint**. In the figure below, the point Q is the midpoint of the line segment $\overline{PR}$.

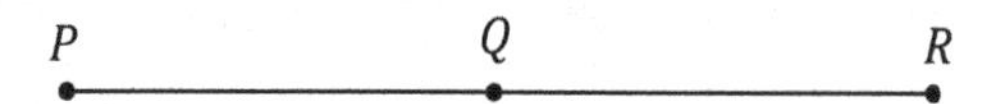

Because Q is the midpoint, it divides the segment into two equal pieces. Therefore, we know that $PQ = QR$.

You might be asked to find the length of a line segment based on the sum of its parts, or to find the length of one part of a line segment based on its total length. For example, consider the following question:

In the figure below, B is the midpoint of $\overline{AC}$ and C is the midpoint of $\overline{AD}$. If $AD = 12$, what is the length of $\overline{AB}$?

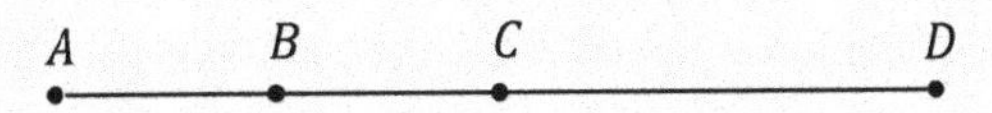

If C is the midpoint of $\overline{AD}$, this means that C divides $\overline{AD}$ into two equal segments: $AC = CD$. We're told that $AD = 12$, which means that $AC = 6$ and $CD = 6$.

We also know that B is the midpoint of $\overline{AC}$, which means that $AB = BC$. If $AC = 6$, we know that $BC = 3$ and $AB = 3$.

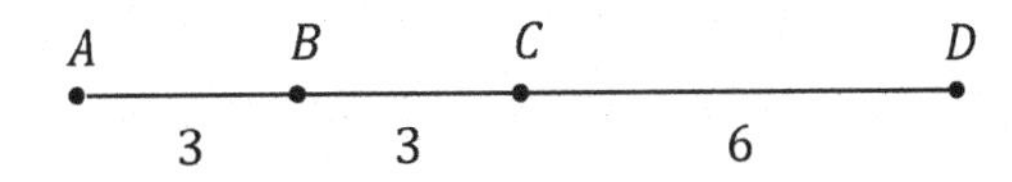

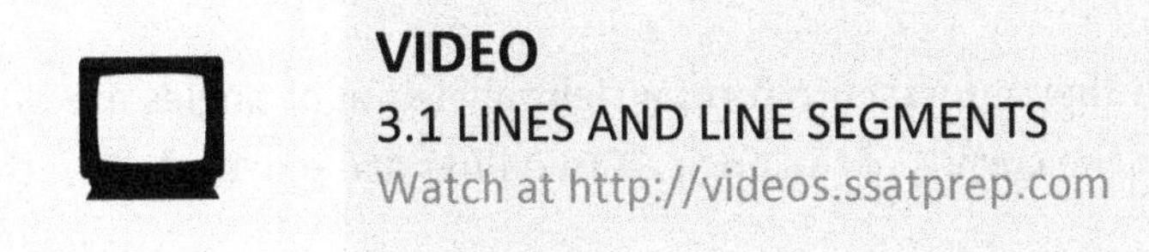

VIDEO
3.1 LINES AND LINE SEGMENTS
Watch at http://videos.ssatprep.com

ANGLES

An **angle** is formed when two lines or line segments intersect. The point where the lines meet is called the **vertex** of the angle, and the two sides of the angle are called the **legs**. An angle can be named either with a single letter representing its vertex, or by three letters representing three points that define the angle: a point on one of its legs, the vertex, and a point on the other leg. When naming an angle using three points, the vertex should always be in the middle. For example, the angle below can be called $\angle RST$ or simply $\angle S$:

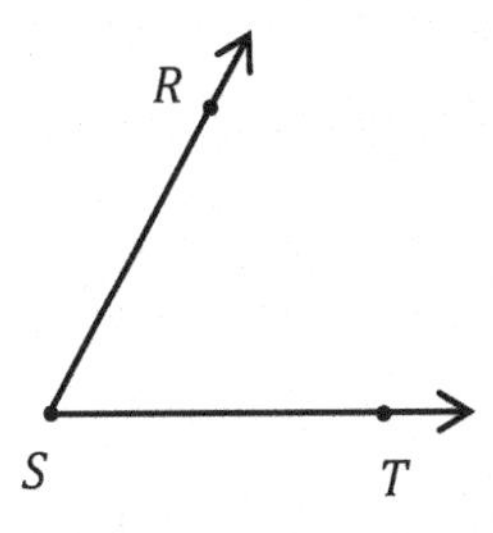

Angles are measured in degrees from 0° to 360°, which represents a full circle. Angles can be classified according to their degree measurements. An **acute** angle measures less than 90°.

- A **right** angle measures exactly 90°.
- An **obtuse** angle measures between 90° and 180°.
- A **straight** angle measures exactly 180°.

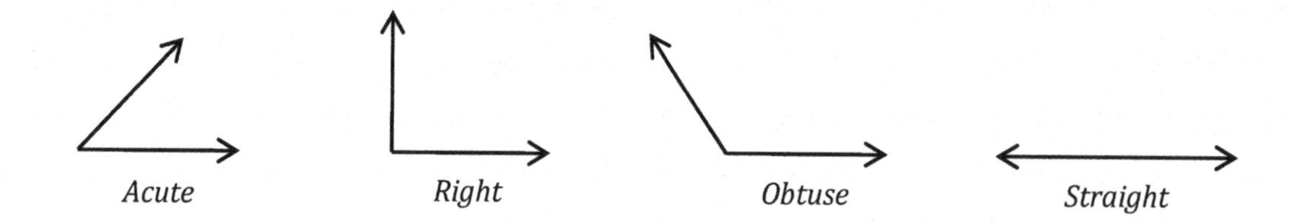

Two angles that have equal measures are called **congruent**.

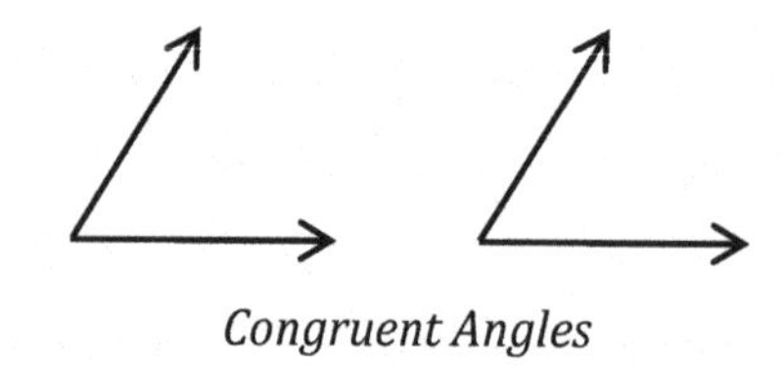

Congruent Angles

PERPENDICULAR AND PARALLEL LINES

Two lines are **perpendicular** if they intersect to form a right angle. Right angles are often designated by a small square in the corner of the angle. If two lines are **parallel**, then they will never intersect.

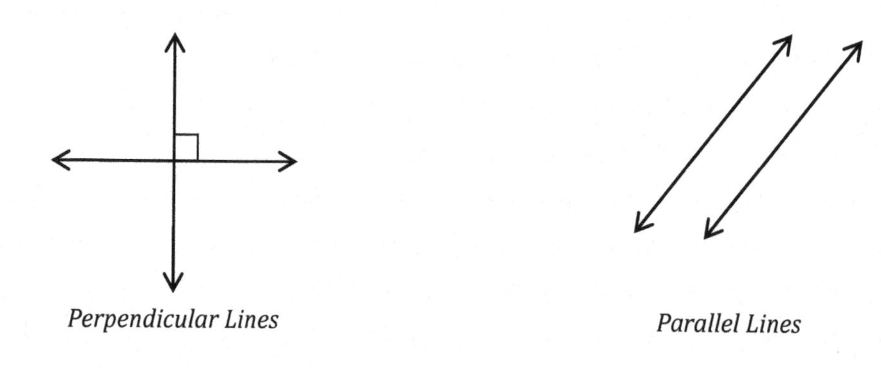

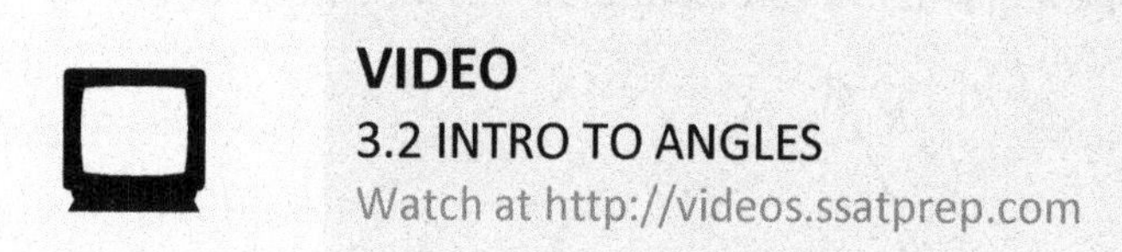

VIDEO
3.2 INTRO TO ANGLES
Watch at http://videos.ssatprep.com

ANGLE SUMS (MIDDLE/UPPER LEVEL ONLY)

Here are some facts to know about angle sums:

- The sum of any number of angles that form a straight line is 180°.
- The sum of any number of angles around a point is 360°.
- Angles that add up to 90° are called **complementary** angles.
- Angles that add up to 180° are called **supplementary** angles.

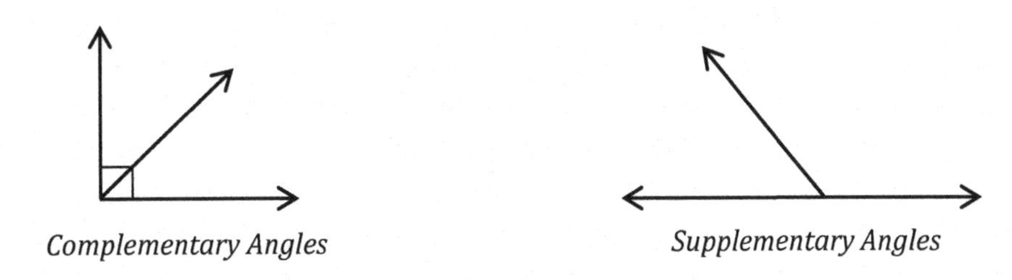

A line that **bisects** an angle divides it into two equal parts. In the figure below, line $\overleftrightarrow{BD}$ bisects $\angle ABC$ and divides it into two congruent angles, $\angle ABD$ and $\angle DBC$:

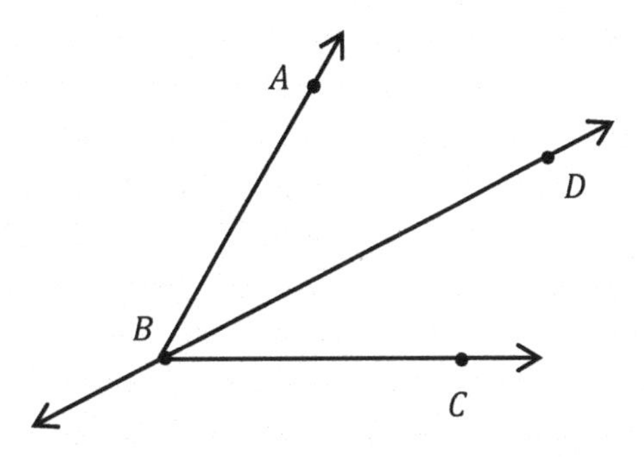

You may be asked to find the sum of several angles, or find the measure of one angle based on the sum of several angles. For example, consider the following question:

In the figure below, four angles intersect to form a straight line. If $\angle GFH$ and $\angle HFJ$ are complementary, and line $\overleftrightarrow{FK}$ bisects $\angle JFL$, what is the measure of $\angle KFL$?

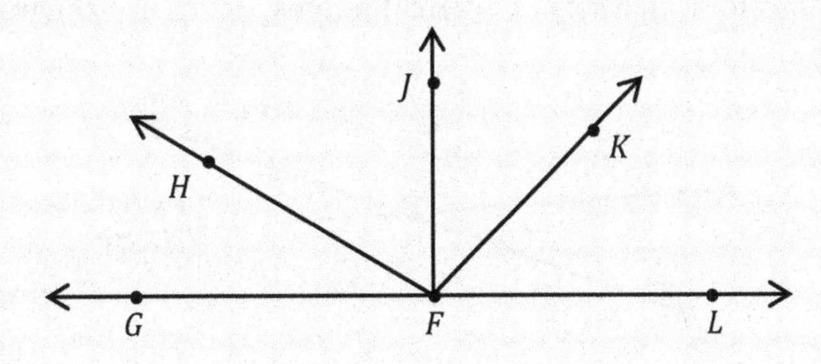

We know that any number of angles forming a straight line add up to 180°. Therefore, we can write:

$$\angle GFH + \angle HFJ + \angle JFK + \angle KFL = 180°$$

We are also told that $\angle GFH$ and $\angle HFJ$ are complementary, which means that they add up to 90°:

$$\angle GFH + \angle HFJ = 90°$$

If $\angle GFH$ and $\angle HFJ$ add up to 90°, this means that $\angle JFK$ and $\angle KFL$ also add up to 90°:

$$90° + \angle JFK + \angle KFL = 180°$$

$$\angle JFK + \angle KFL = 180° - 90° = 90°$$

Finally, we are told that line $\overleftrightarrow{FK}$ bisects $\angle JFL$, which means that $\angle JFK$ and $\angle KFL$ are congruent. If $\angle JFK$ and $\angle KFL$ are congruent and add up to 90°, then $\angle KFL$ must equal $90° \div 2 = 45°$.

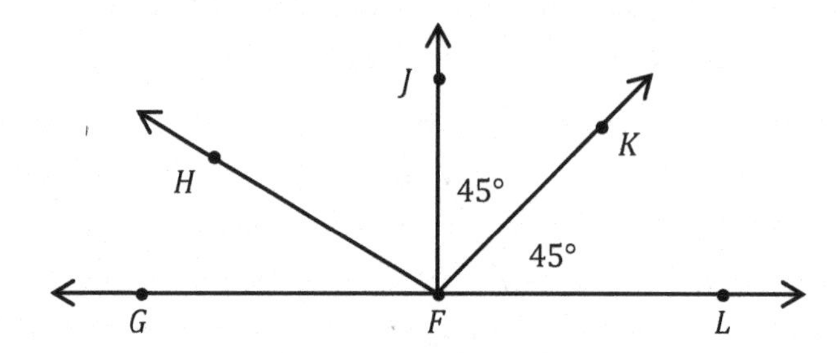

VIDEO

3.3 ANGLE SUMS

Watch at http://videos.ssatprep.com

PROPERTIES OF INTERSECTING LINES (UPPER LEVEL ONLY)

Two intersecting lines form two sets of **vertical angles**, which are congruent. In the figure below, $a = d$ and $b = c$.

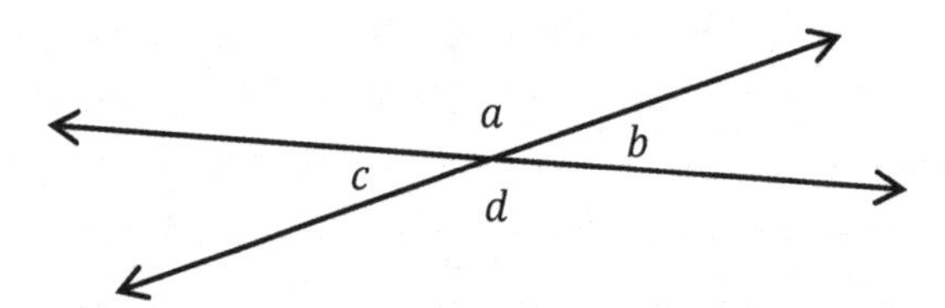

If a third line (**transversal**) intersects a pair of parallel lines, it forms eight angles, as in the following figure.

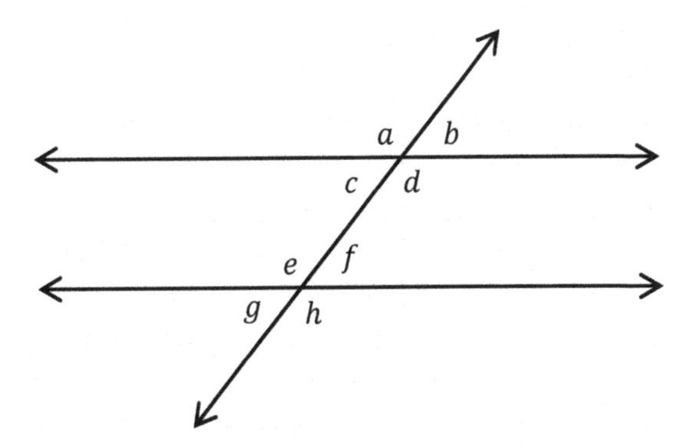

Know the following properties of transversals:

- The pairs of **corresponding angles** are congruent: $a = e,\ b = f,\ c = g,$ and $d = h$.
- The pairs of **alternate interior angles** are congruent: $c = f$ and $d = e$.
- The pairs of **alternate exterior angles** are congruent: $a = h$ and $b = g$.
- The pairs of **same side interior angles** are supplementary: $c + e = 180°$ and $d + f = 180°$.

For example, consider the following question:

In the figure below, line m and line n are parallel, and line p bisects $\angle RST$. What is the value of x?

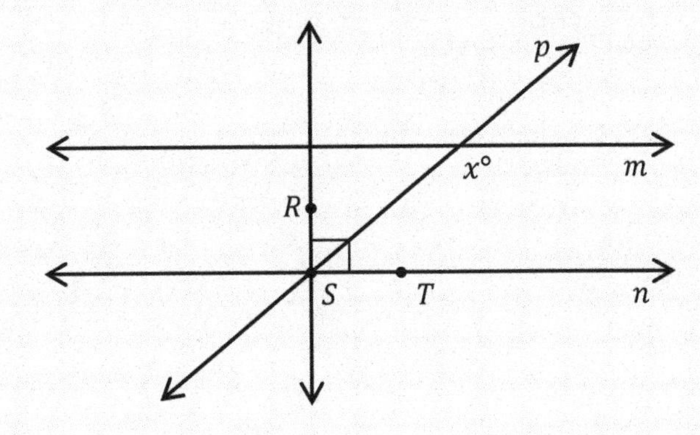

Based on the figure, we can see that $\angle RST$ is right angle and therefore measures 90°. If line p bisects this angle, it must divide it into two angles measuring 45° each. We can label these on the figure.

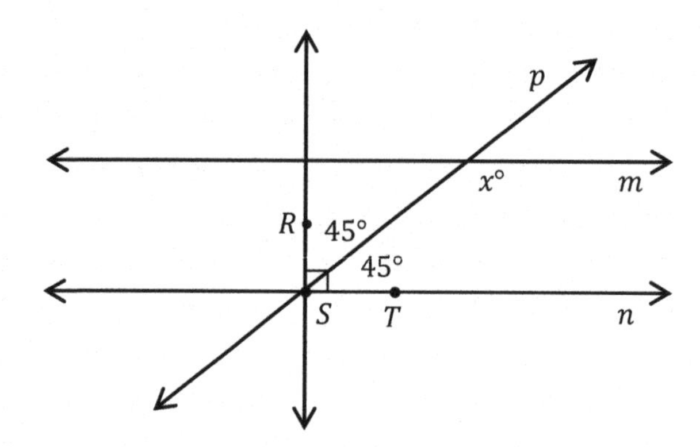

Because line p intersects two parallel lines, we know that pairs of same-side interior angles are supplementary. Thus, we know that $x°$ and 45° must add to equal 180°. We can write an algebraic equation and solve for x:

$$x + 45 = 180$$
$$x + 45 - 45 = 180 - 45$$
$$x = 135$$

VIDEO

3.4 PROPERTIES OF INTERSECTING LINES

Watch at http://videos.ssatprep.com

PRACTICE QUESTIONS: LINES AND ANGLES

1. In the figure below, $KM = 5$. If $LM = 3$, what is the length of $\overline{KL}$?

2. In the figure below, G is the midpoint of $\overline{FH}$. If $FG = 4$, what is the length of $\overline{FH}$?

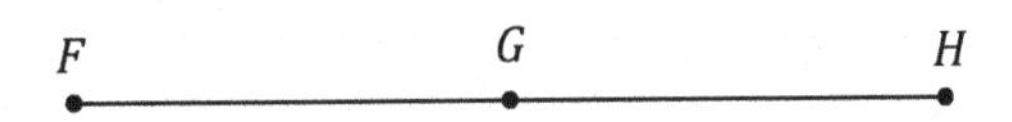

3. In the figure below, R is the midpoint of $\overline{QS}$, and S is the midpoint of $\overline{QT}$. If $QR = 2$, what is the length of $\overline{RT}$?

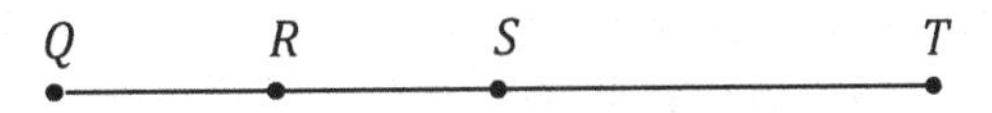

4. How many degrees are in a right angle?

5. Angle A measures 30°. Is Angle A an acute, right, obtuse, or straight angle?

6. Angle B measures 120°. Is Angle B an acute, right, obtuse, or straight angle?

7. How many degrees are in a straight angle?

8. What is the name for two lines that will never intersect?

9. What is the name for two lines that intersect in a right angle?

10. What is the name for two angles that have the same measures?

Questions 11-17 are Middle/Upper Level Only.

11. In the figure below, angles CDE and EDF are complementary. If $\angle CDE$ measures $20°$, what is the measure of $\angle EDF$?

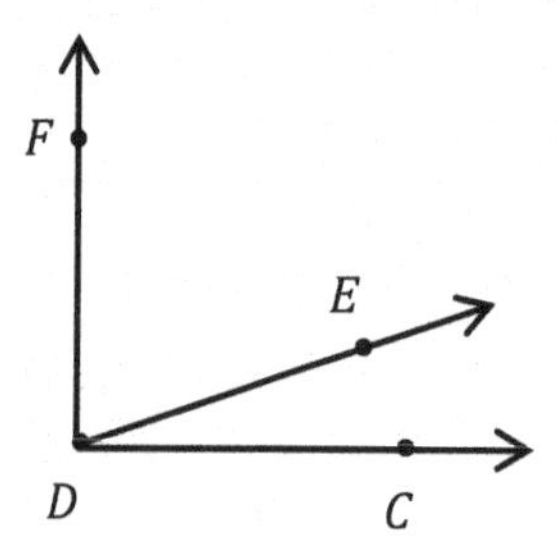

12. In the figure below, angle GHI is a right angle and $b = 50$. If $a = c$, what is the value of c?

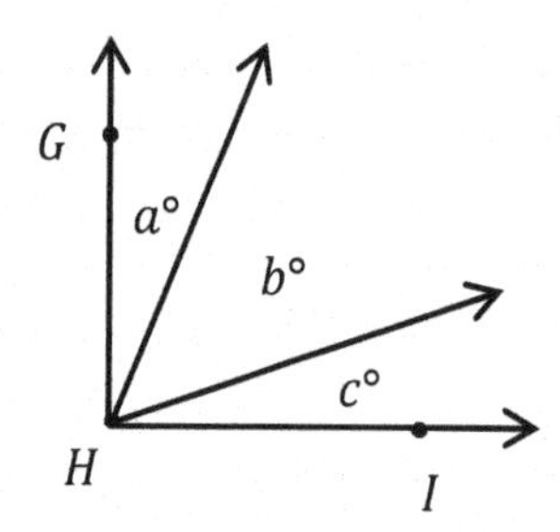

13. In the figure below, line $\overleftrightarrow{NO}$ bisects $\angle MNP$. If $\angle MNO$ measures $60°$, what is the measure of $\angle MNP$?

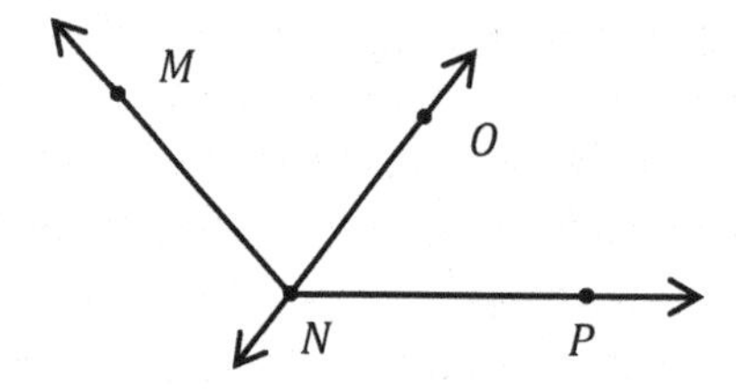

14. In the figure below, $\angle HJK$, $\angle KJL$, and $\angle LJM$ are supplementary. If $\angle LJM$ measures $70°$ and line $\overleftrightarrow{JK}$ bisects $\angle HJL$, what is the measure of $\angle KJL$?

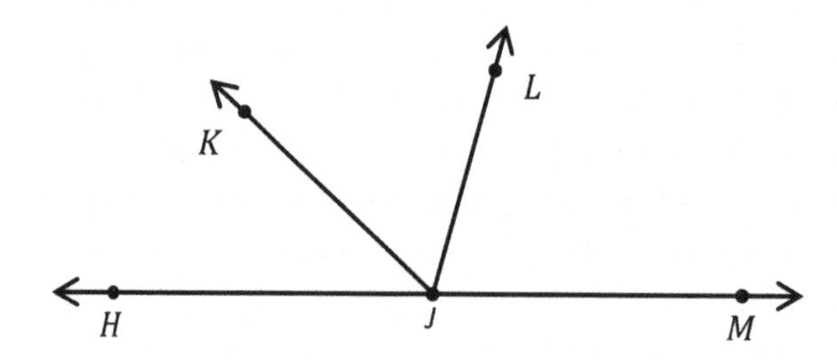

15. The three angles in the figure below form a straight line. If $y = 120$, what is the value of $x + z$?

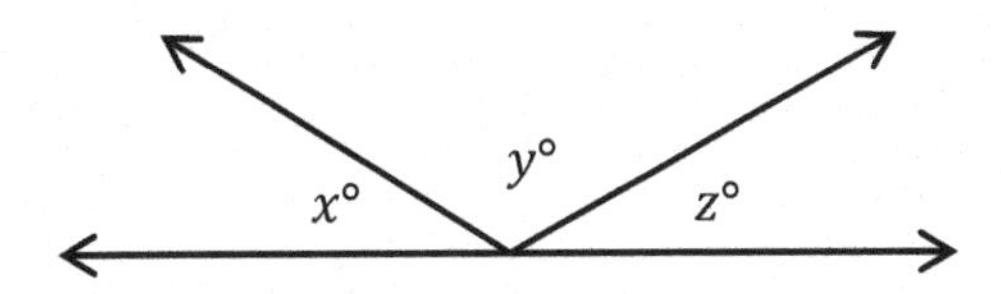

16. In the figure below, four lines intersect at point R to form four angles, and $\angle PRT$ is congruent to $\angle TRS$. If $\angle PRQ$ is a right angle, and $\angle QRT$ measures 150°, what is the value of $\angle TRS$?

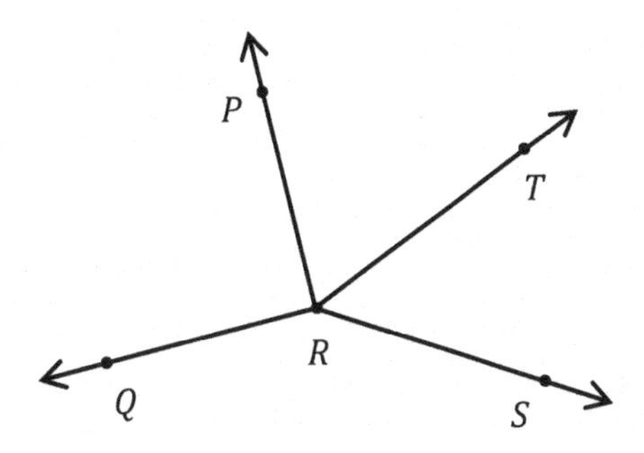

17. In the figure below, five lines intersect at a point to form five angles. If $a = 170$ and $b = 60$, what is the value of $c + d + e$?

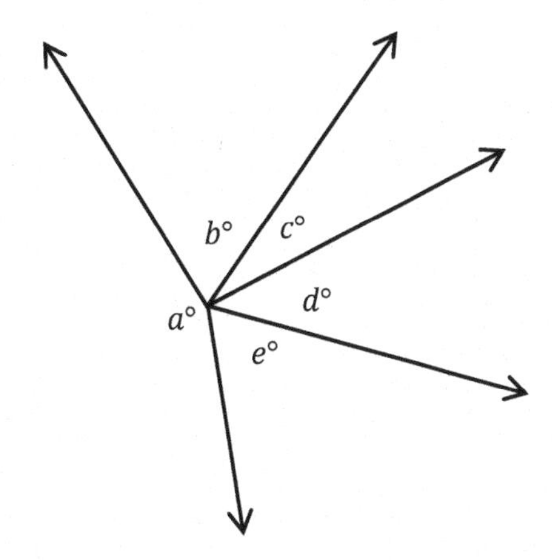

Questions 18-25 are Upper Level only.

18. In the following diagram, two lines intersect to form four angles. If $x = 30$, what is the value of y?

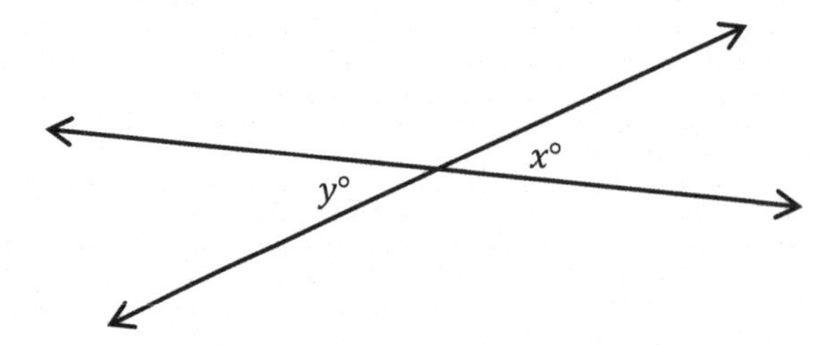

19. In the following diagram, lines m and n are parallel. If $a = 70$, what is the value of b?

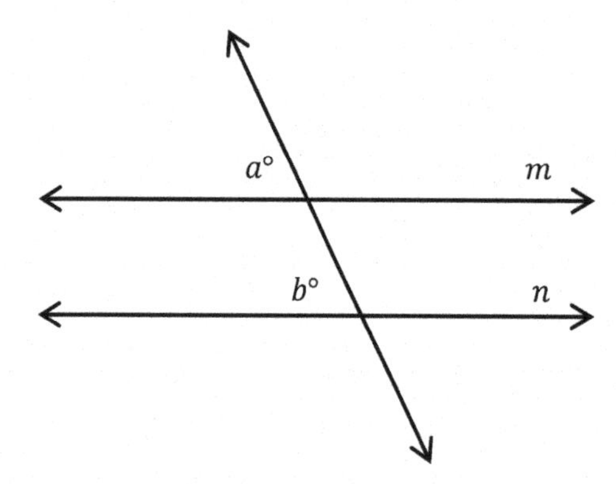

20. In the following diagram, lines g and h are parallel. If $z = 120$, what is the value of y?

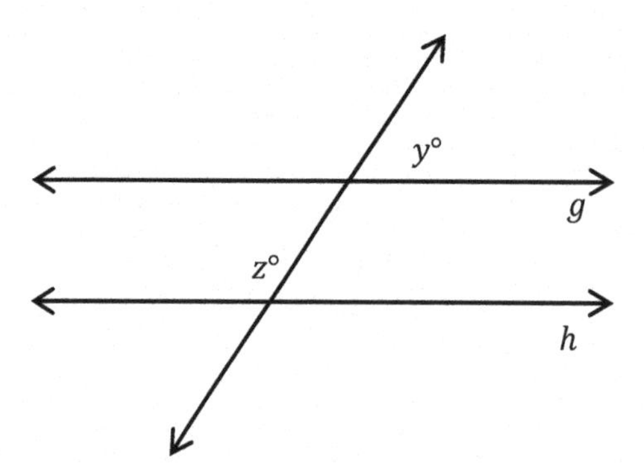

21. In the following diagram, lines j and k are parallel. If $c = 50$, what is the value of d?

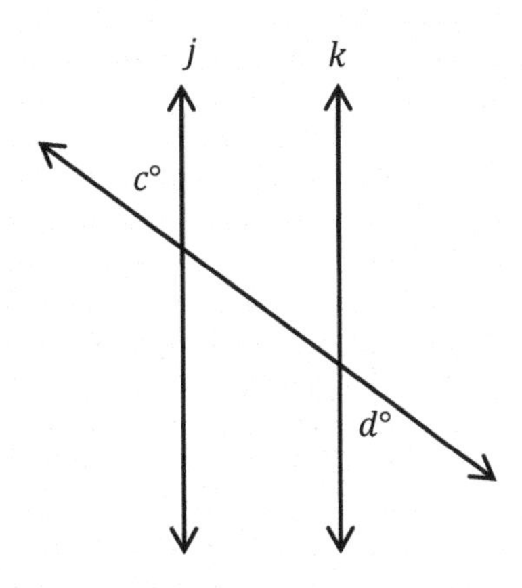

22. In the following diagram, lines d and e are parallel. What is the value of x?

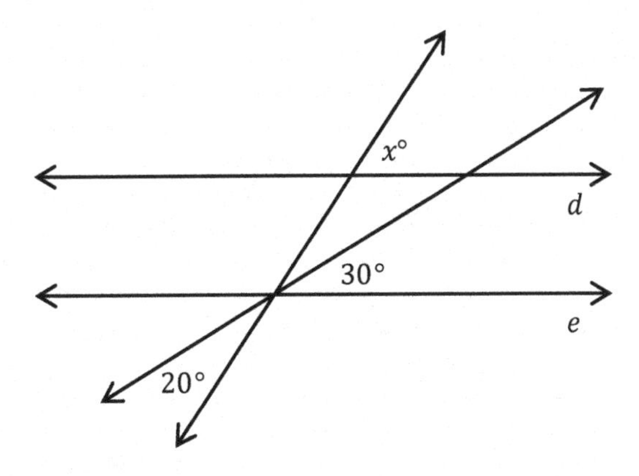

23. In the following diagram, lines p and q are parallel, and lines r and s are parallel. What is the value of $a + b + c + d$?

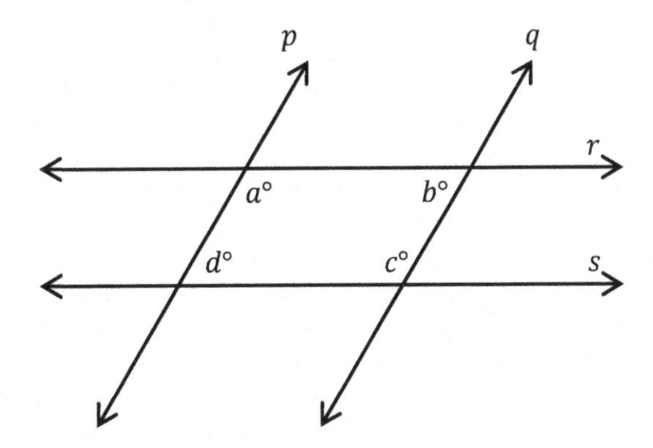

24. In the following diagram, lines l and m are parallel and are both perpendicular to line n. What is the value of y?

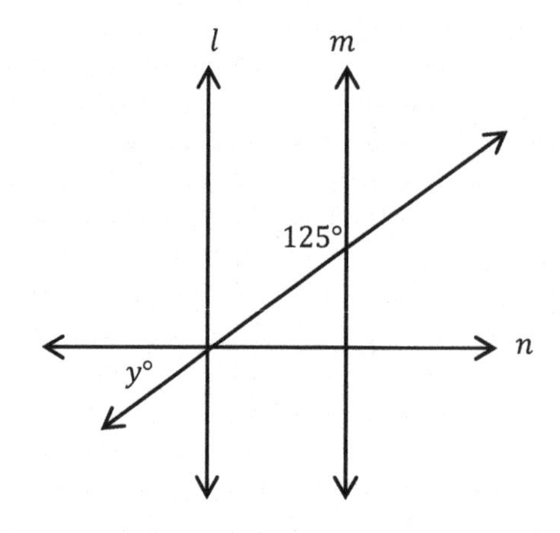

25. In the following diagram, lines u and v are parallel. What is the value of g?

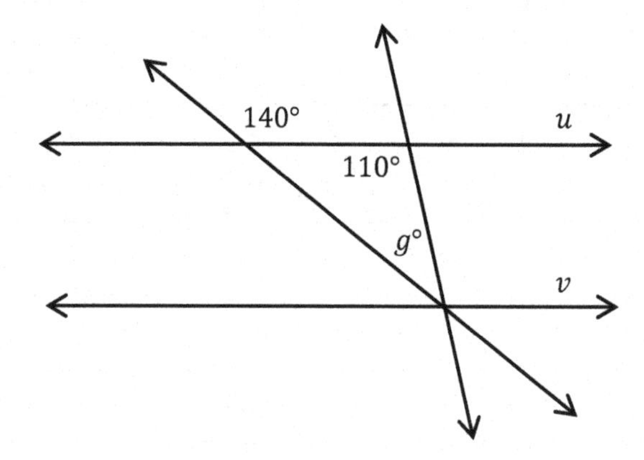

INTRODUCTION TO POLYGONS

ALL LEVELS

SECTION 2

A **polygon** is an enclosed two-dimensional shape with straight edges. "Poly" means "many" and "gon" comes from the Greek word for "angle," so a polygon is literally a "many-angled" shape. An **interior angle** of a polygon is an angle on the inside of the polygon formed by the intersection of two sides. A **vertex** of a polygon is a point where two sides meet.

Polygons can be classified by the number of their sides:

TYPES OF POLYGONS		
Name	**Number of Sides**	**Example**
Triangle	3	△
Quadrilateral	4	□
Pentagon	5	⬠
Hexagon	6	⬡
Heptagon	7	
Octagon	8	

In a polygon, equal sides are often marked with matching dash marks. For example, the diagram below shows a quadrilateral with two pairs of equal sides. The longer sides (with one dash mark) have equal lengths, and the shorter sides (with two dash marks) also have equal lengths.

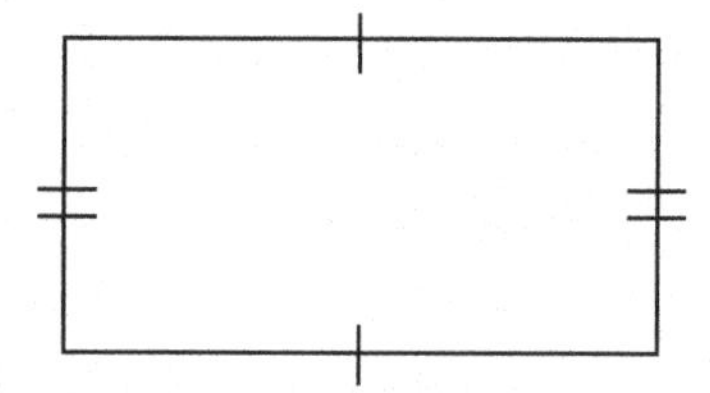

A **regular polygon** has all equal sides and all equal angles. For example, a square is a regular quadrilateral because it has four equal sides and four equal angles.

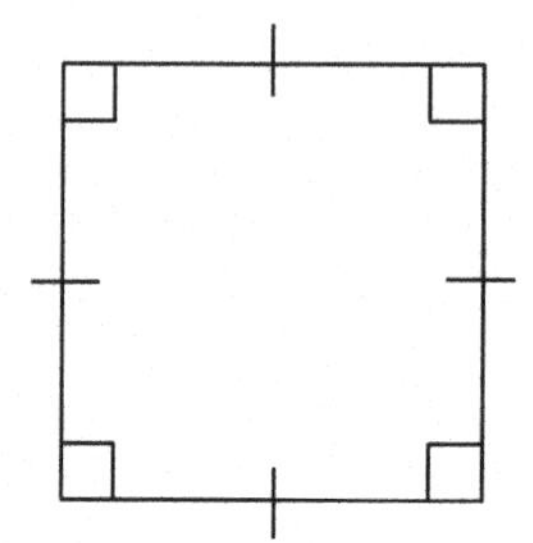

TRIANGLES

A **triangle** has exactly three sides. Four different types of triangles are shown below:

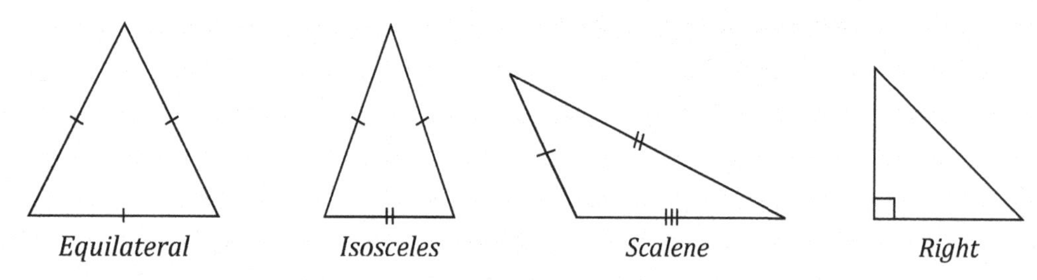

- In an **equilateral** triangle, all three sides are the same length.
- In an **isosceles** triangle, two of the sides are the same length.
- In a **scalene** triangle, all three sides are different lengths.
- In a **right** triangle, two legs of the triangle are perpendicular, creating a right angle.

QUADRILATERALS

A **quadrilateral** has exactly four sides. Six important types of quadrilaterals are shown below:

- A **parallelogram** is a quadrilateral with two sets of parallel sides. The opposite sides of a parallelogram have equal lengths.

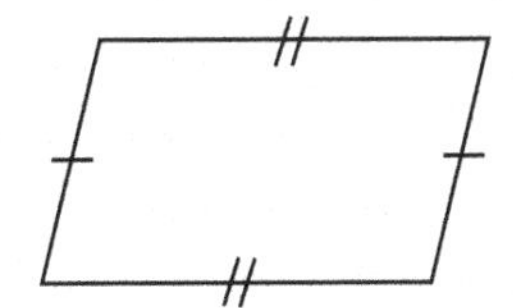

- A **rectangle** is a parallelogram with four right angles. Like all parallelograms, the opposite sides of a rectangle are parallel and have equal lengths.

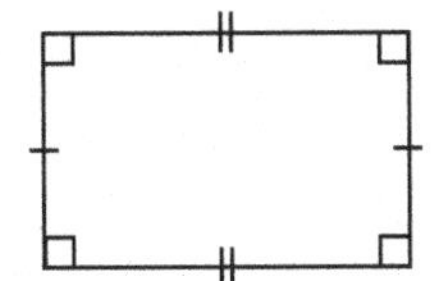

- A **square** is a rectangle with four equal sides. A square is a regular quadrilateral because all sides are the same length and all angles are the same measure (90°).

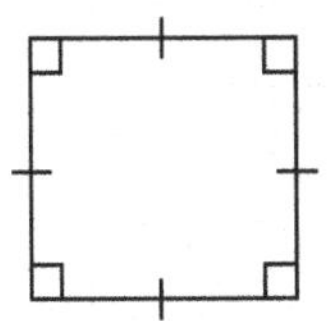

- A **rhombus** is a parallelogram with four equal sides, in the shape of a diamond. A rhombus is like a square, but it does not necessarily have any right angles.

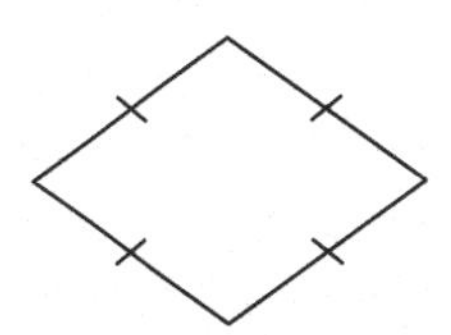

- A **trapezoid** is a quadrilateral with only one set of parallel sides. These parallel sides are called the trapezoid's bases.

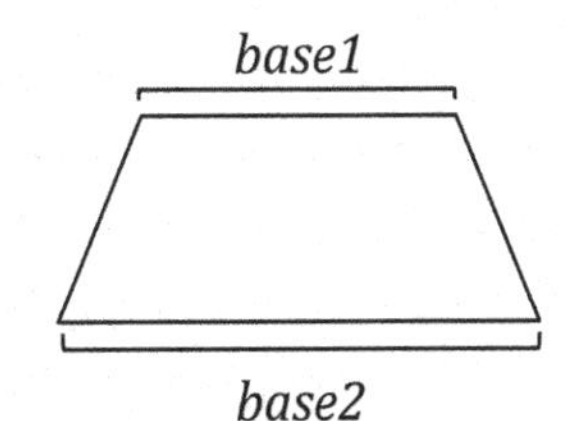

- A **kite** is a quadrilateral whose sides are grouped in two pairs that have the same length. The pairs of equal-length sides are next to each other, unlike the equal-length sides of a parallelogram, which are opposite each other. Unlike a parallelogram, a kite does not have any parallel sides.

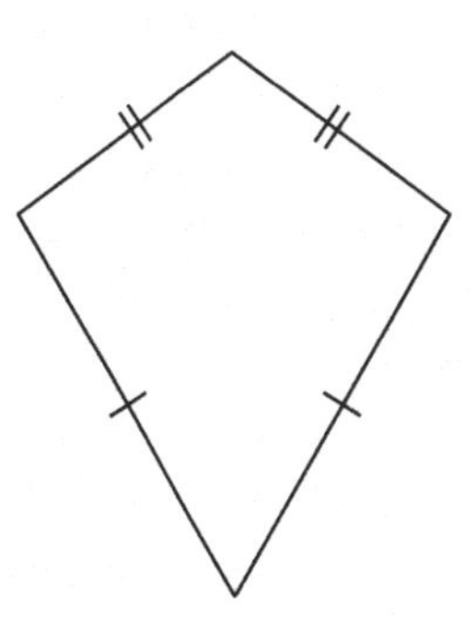

PERIMETER

The **perimeter** of any polygon is the distance around its sides. To find the perimeter of a polygon, add together the lengths of its sides.

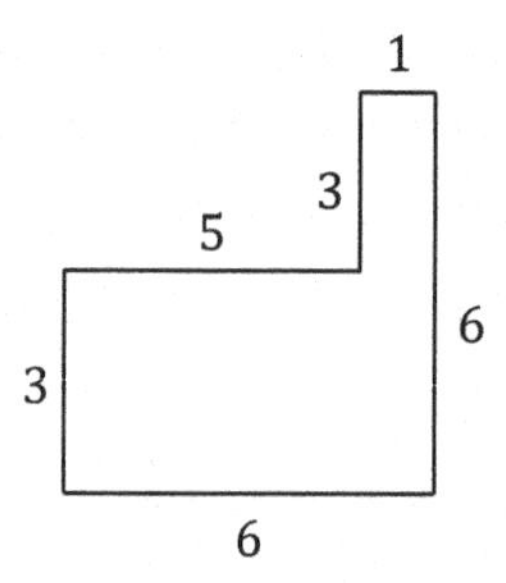

The perimeter of this polygon is equal to $3 + 6 + 6 + 1 + 3 + 5 = 24$.

AREA

The **area** of any polygon is the total space inside a polygon's perimeter. Area is always expressed terms of square units, such as square feet (ft^2) or square centimeters (cm^2).

Because polygons can have different numbers of sides, each type of polygon has its own formula for calculating area. In upcoming sections, we'll discuss the more complicated formulas for area that Middle and Upper Level students will need to know. However, students of all levels will need to know how to calculate the area of rectangles, squares, and triangles using the formulas below.

To find the area of a rectangle, multiply its length by its width:

$$Area\ of\ a\ rectangle = length \times width$$

In the figure to the right, the rectangle has a length of 7 units and a width of 5 units. Its area is:

$$area = 7 \times 5 = 35\ square\ units$$

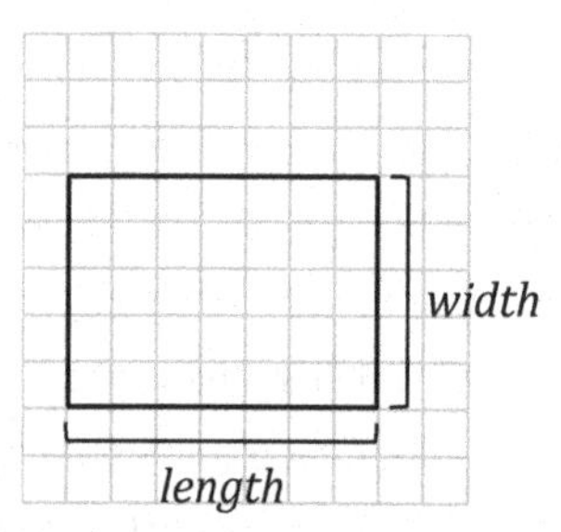

To check this answer, you can count the number of squares inside of the rectangle. There are 35 squares, which is why we say that it has an area of 35 *square* units.

To find the area of a square, multiply the length of one of its sides by itself:

$$Area\ of\ a\ square = side \times side$$

In the figure to the right, the square has a side of 5 units. Its area is:

$$area = 5 \times 5 = 25 \; square \; units$$

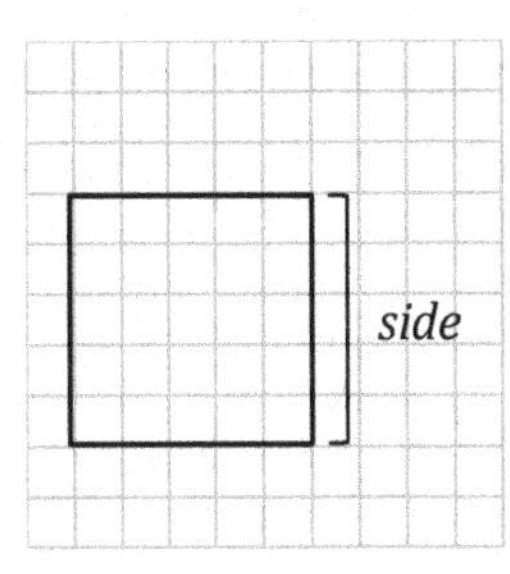

To check this answer, you can count the number of small squares inside of the square.

To find the area of a triangle, multiply its base times its height, and divide by two:

$$Area \; of \; a \; triangle = \frac{base \times height}{2}$$

In the figure to the right, the triangle has a base of 8 units and a height of 6 units. Its area is:

$$area = \frac{8 \times 6}{2} = 24 \; square \; units$$

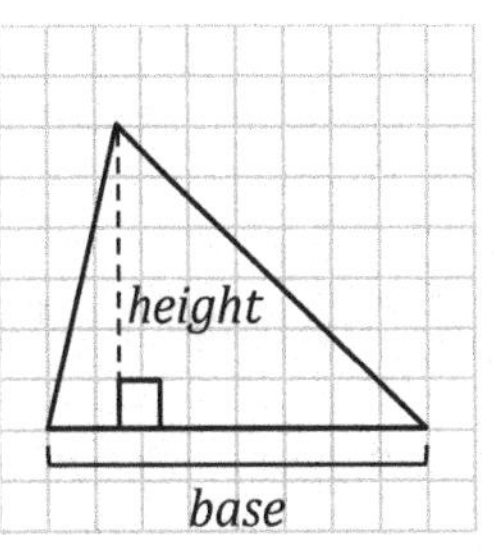

You can check this answer by estimating the number of squares inside of the triangle.

If you're not sure how to find a shape's area, you can try dividing it into simpler shapes whose area you know how to calculate, like rectangles, squares, and triangles. Here is an example:

What is the area of the quadrilateral shown below?

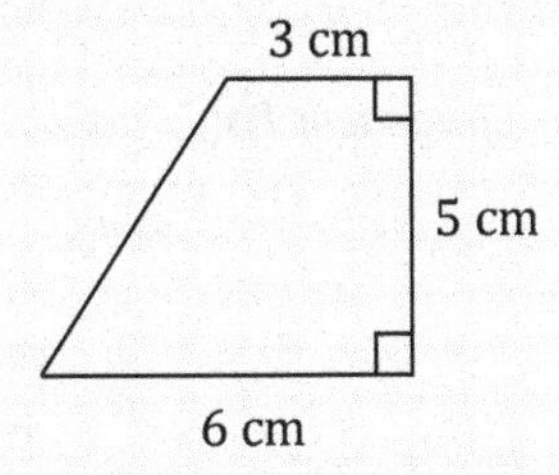

It is easier to find the area of this quadrilateral if we see it as a rectangle attached to a triangle. We can draw a dashed line perpendicular to the quadrilateral's base that divides it into one triangular section and one rectangular section:

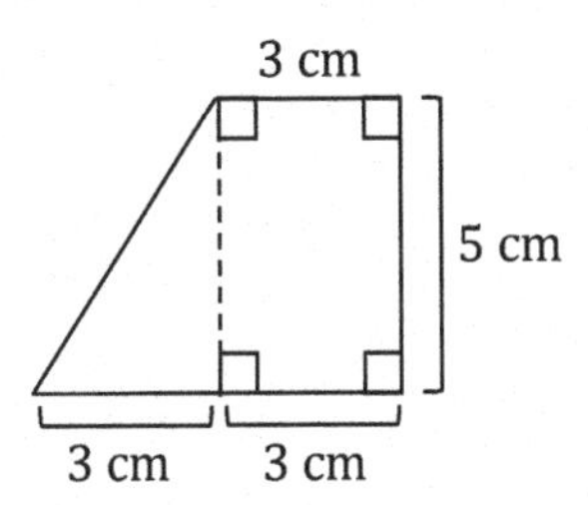

The quadrilateral is now made up of one triangle with a base of 3 cm and a height of 5 cm, plus one rectangle with a length of 3 cm and a width of 5 cm.

Now we can use the triangle and rectangle formulas to find the area of each section:

$$Area\ of\ triangle = \frac{base \times height}{2} = \frac{3\text{ cm} \times 5\text{ cm}}{2} = 7.5\text{ cm}^2$$

$$Area\ of\ rectangle = length \times width = 3\text{ cm} \times 5\text{ cm} = 15\text{ cm}^2$$

Finally, we can add these areas together to find the area of the whole figure:

$$Total\ area\ of\ quadrilateral = 7.5\text{ cm}^2 + 15\text{ cm}^2 = 22.5\text{ cm}^2$$

The quadrilateral's area is 22.5 cm^2.

CONGRUENT POLYGONS

Two polygons are **congruent** if they have the same size and shape. The number of their sides is equal, the lengths of their corresponding sides are equal, and the measures of their corresponding interior angles are equal. For example, the following trapezoids are congruent because they are identical in shape and in size. One just happens to be rotated.

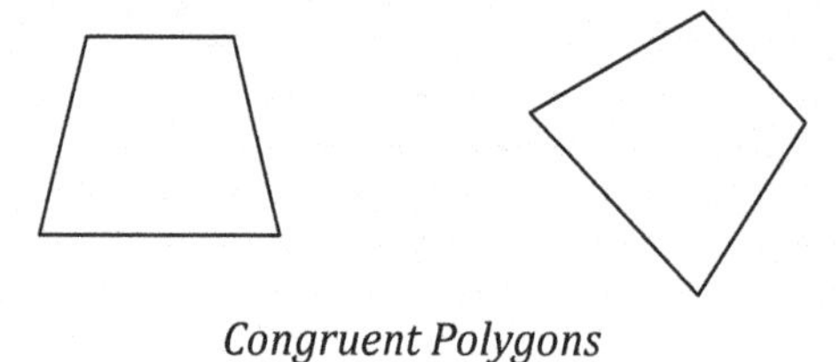

Congruent Polygons

SIMILAR POLYGONS

Two polygons are considered **similar** if they have the same shape, but not the same size. The number of their sides is equal, the measures of their corresponding interior angles are equal, and the lengths of their corresponding sides are proportional—that is, they maintain the same ratio. For example, the two triangles below are similar because their angles are the same and their sides maintain the same ratio of 3:4:5. However, the triangle on the right is twice as large as the triangle on the left.

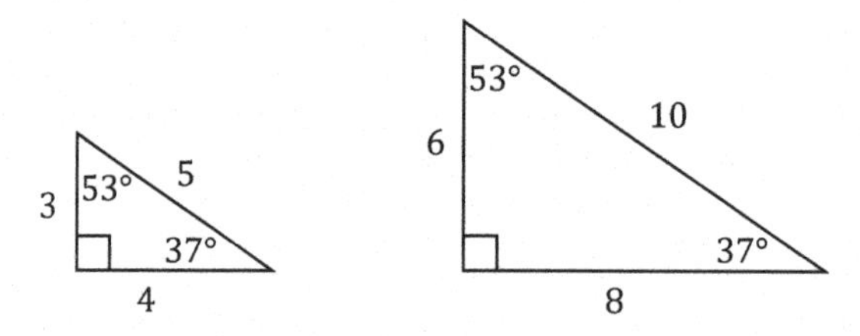

Similar Polygons

PRACTICE QUESTIONS: INTRODUCTION TO POLYGONS

1. What is the name for a polygon with four sides?

2. What is the name for a polygon with six sides?

3. What is the name for a polygon with eight sides?

4. What is the name for a triangle with all equal sides?

5. What type of triangle is shown below?

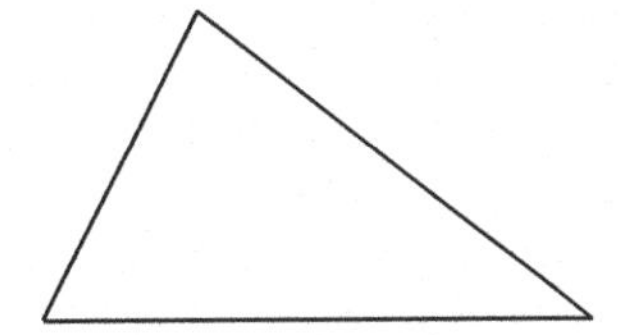

6. What type of quadrilateral is shown below?

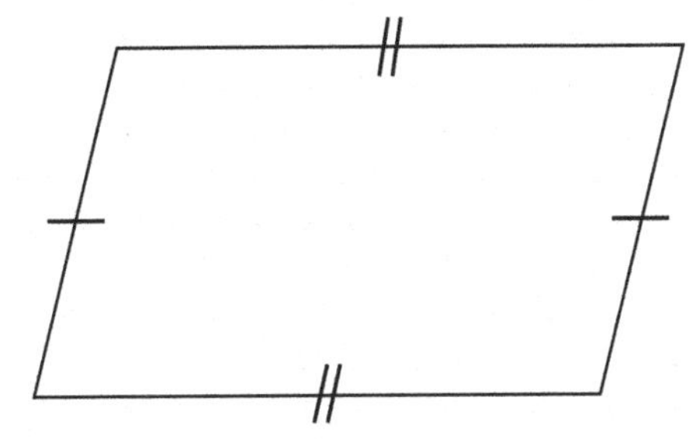

7. What is the name for a regular quadrilateral?

8. What is the name for a quadrilateral with only one set of parallel sides?

9. What type of quadrilateral is shown below?

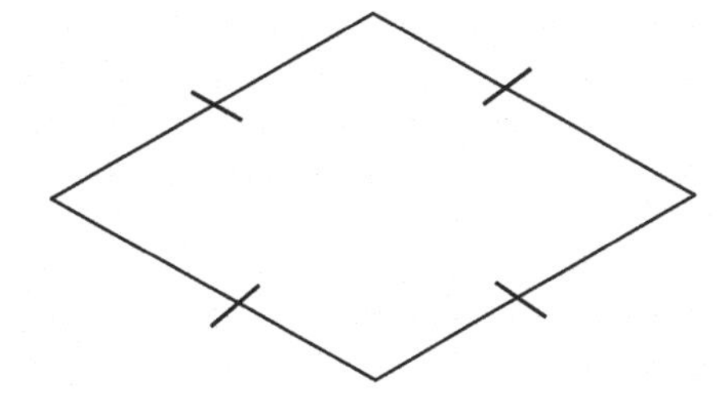

10. What is the name for a quadrilateral with two sets of equal sides, but no parallel sides?

11. What is the perimeter of the triangle below?

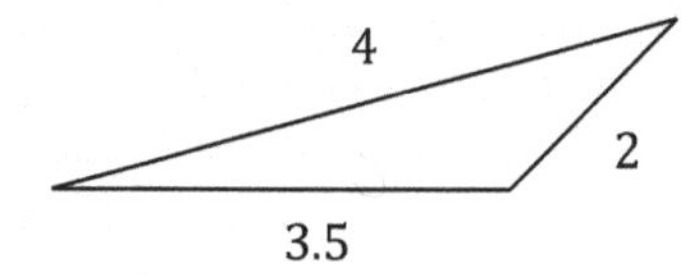

12. What is the perimeter of the rectangle below?

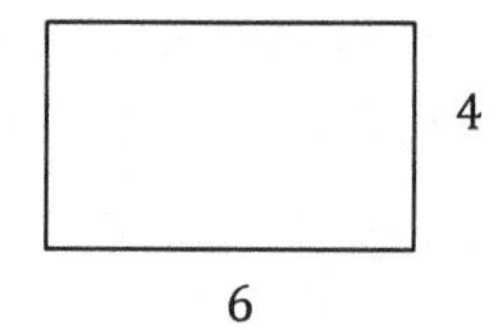

13. What is the perimeter of the square below?

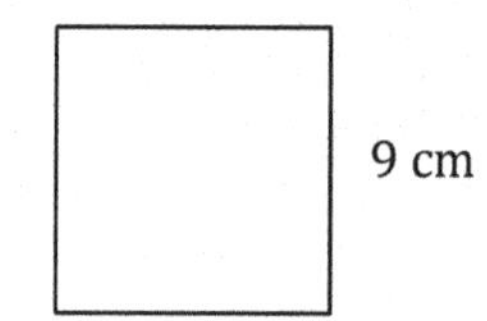

14. What is the perimeter of the polygon below?

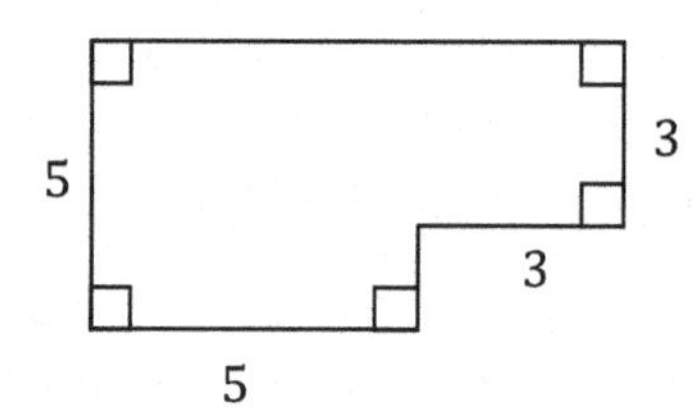

15. If an equilateral octagon has a total perimeter of 48, how long is each side?

16. What is the perimeter of the square shown below?

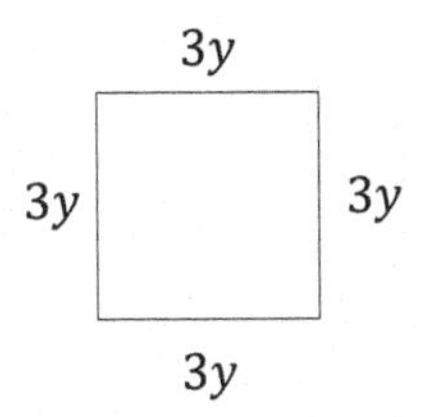

17. If the perimeter of the triangle below is 60, what is the length of side x?

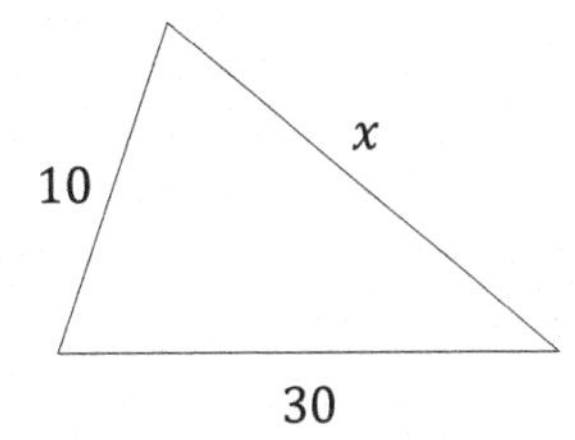

18. If the triangle below is isosceles, what is its perimeter?

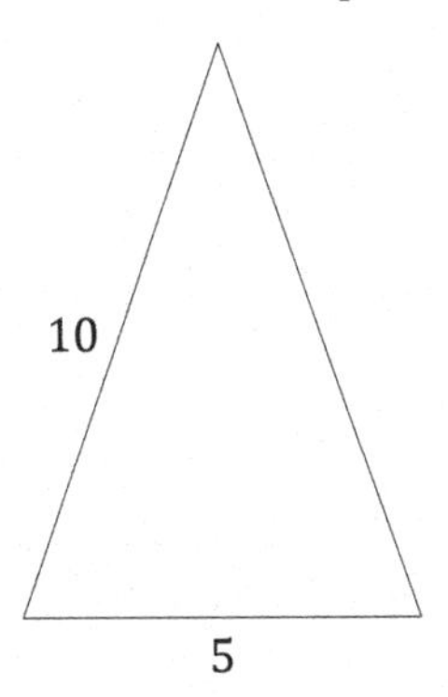

19. What is the area of the rectangle below?

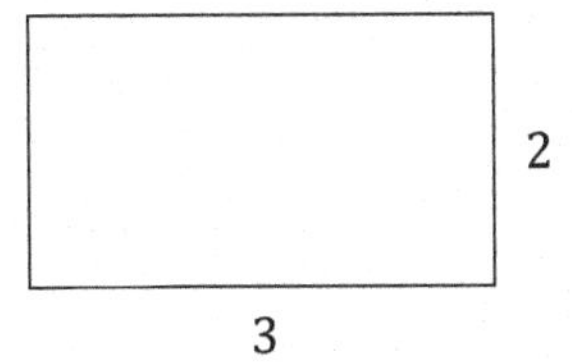

20. What is the area of the triangle below?

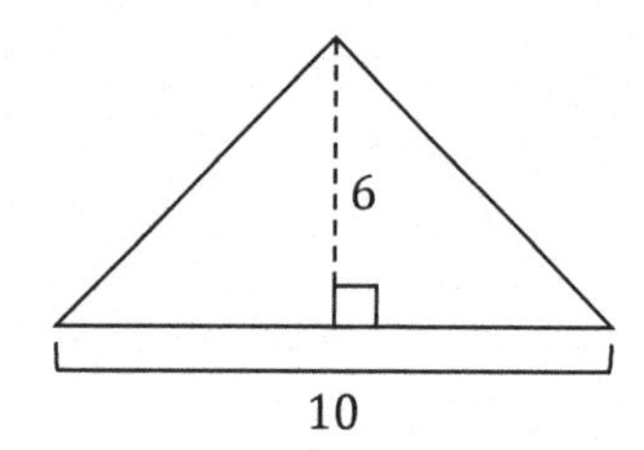

21. What is the area of the rectangle shown below?

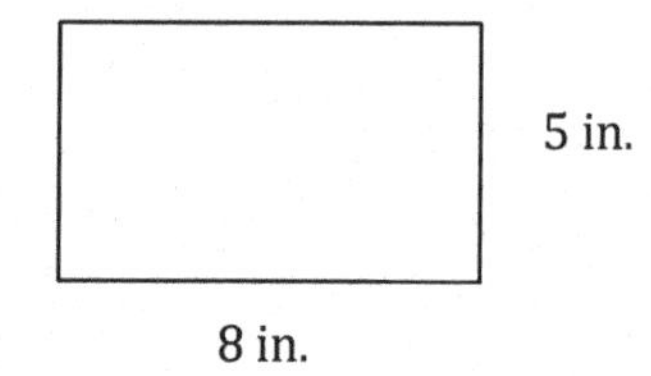

22. What is the area of the square shown below?

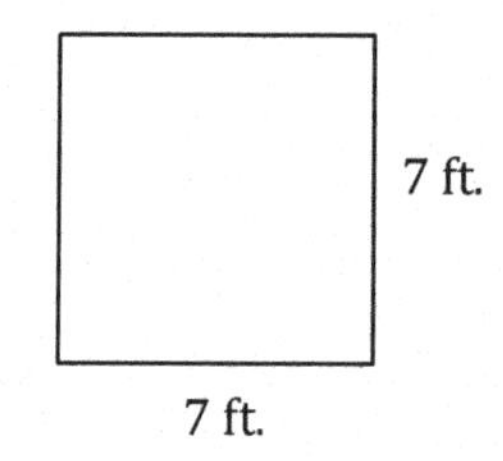

23. What is the area of the triangle shown below?

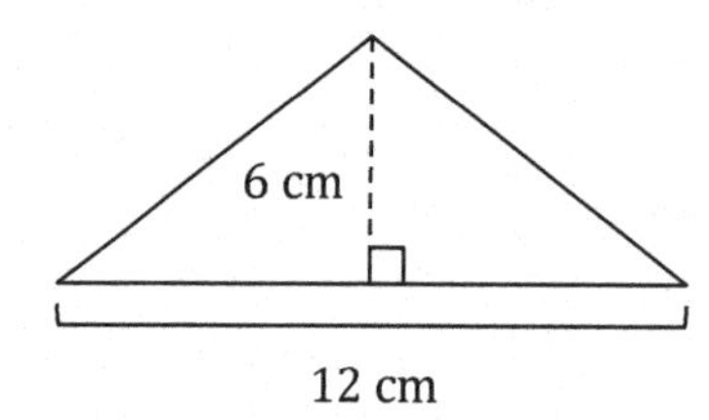

24. What is the area of the square shown below?

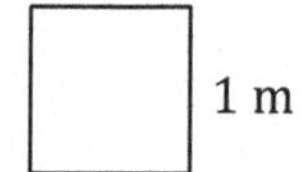

25. If the rectangle below has an area of 50, what is the value of y?

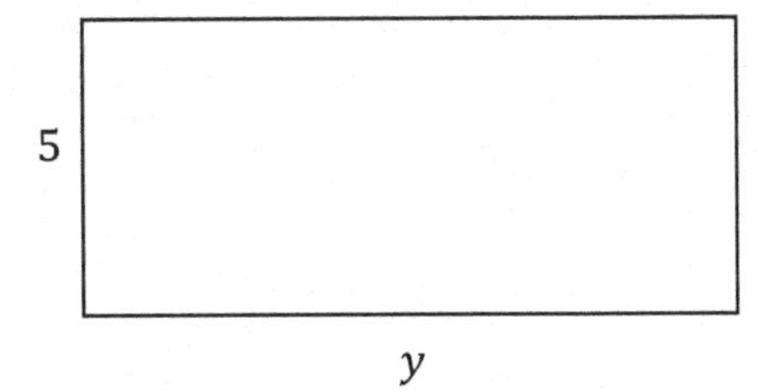

26. If the area of a square is 64 square inches, what is the length of one of the square's sides?

27. What is the area of the quadrilateral shown below?

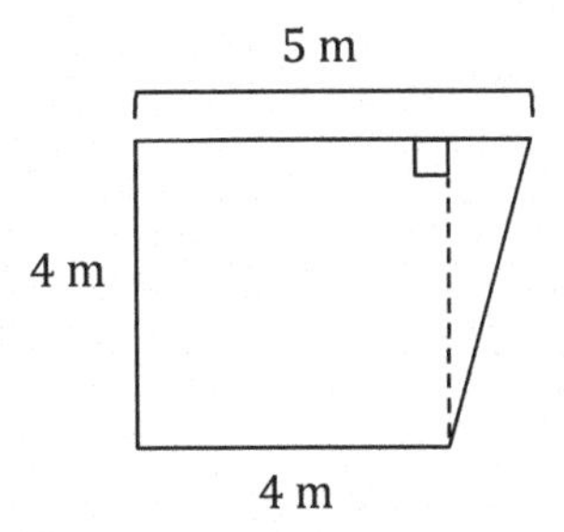

28. What is the area of the polygon shown below?

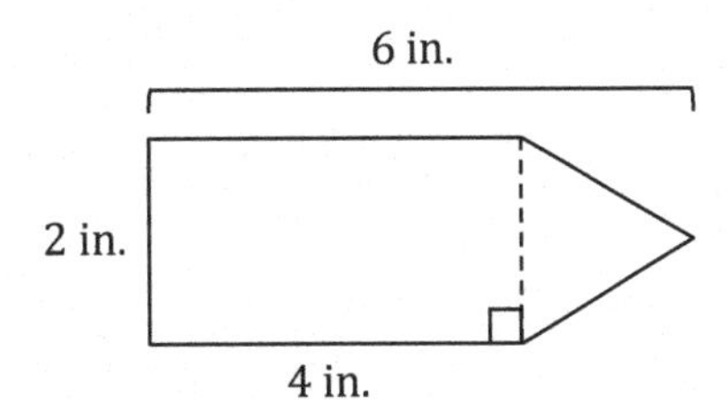

29. Pentagon A is congruent to pentagon B. If pentagon A's perimeter is 40 cm, what is the perimeter of pentagon B?

30. Rectangle D is similar to rectangle E. What is the area of rectangle D?

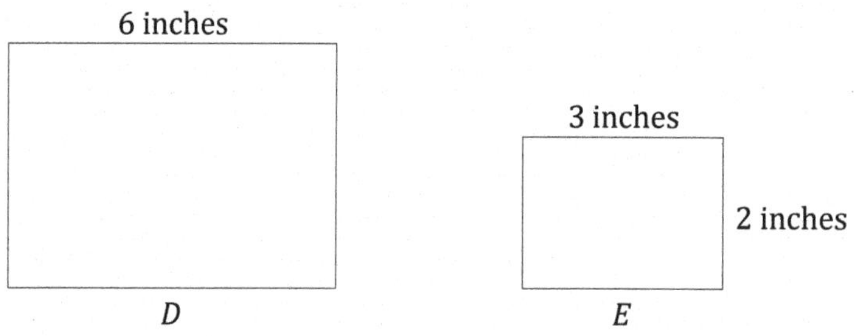

6 inches

3 inches

2 inches

D E

ADVANCED TRIANGLES

MIDDLE/UPPER LEVEL ONLY

SECTION 3

In the last section, we discussed some basic properties of triangles: their side lengths, perimeters, and areas. In this section, we'll discuss some more advanced information about the angles of triangles and right triangles.

ANGLES OF A TRIANGLE

In the previous section, we saw that triangles are classified by the lengths of their sides. Triangles are also classified by the measures of their angles:

- An **equilateral** triangle has three equal sides and three congruent angles. All three of these angles measure 60°.
- An **isosceles** triangle has two equal sides and two congruent angles across from these sides.
- A **scalene** triangle has three sides of different lengths and three angles of different measures.
- A **right** triangle has one angle measuring 90°.
- An **acute** triangle has all acute angles.
- An **obtuse** triangle has one obtuse angle.

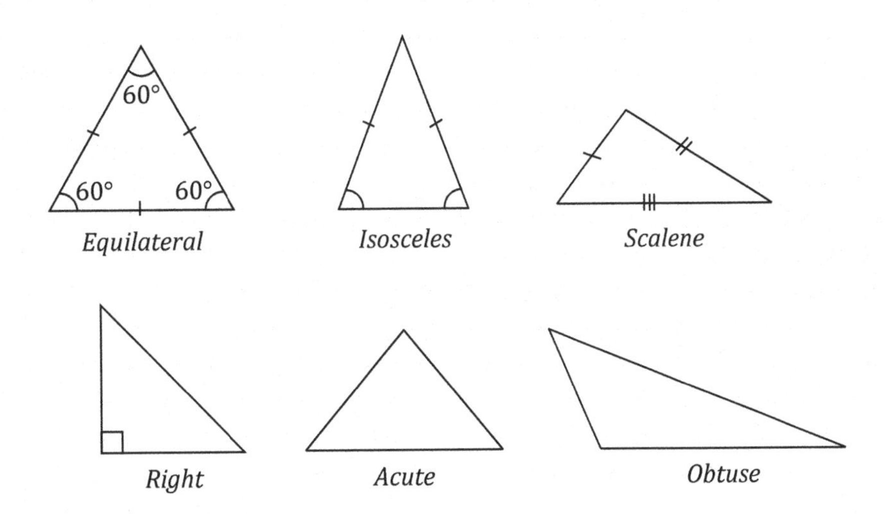

The **sum of the interior angles of a triangle** is always 180°. For example, in the following figure, we can calculate the missing interior angle:

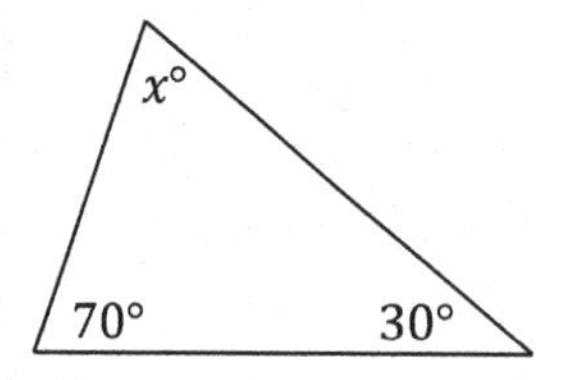

To find x, all we need to do is subtract 70 and 30 from 180:

$$x = 180 - 70 - 30 = 80$$

The missing angle measures 80°.

You can use your knowledge of the types of triangles to solve for missing angles. If you know your triangle is isosceles and you are given one of the angles, you can use this information to solve for the other two angles. For example:

In the triangle below, what is the value of x?

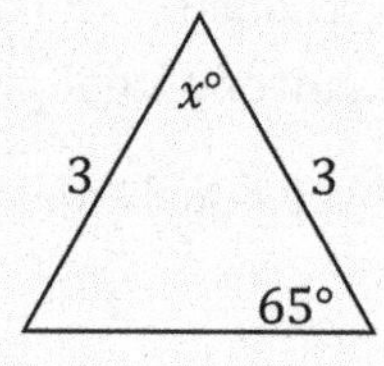

In the example above, we know we have an isosceles triangle because both sides are the same length. We also know the two angles opposite these sides must be the same length.

Because our triangle is isosceles, we know that the other corresponding angle also measures 65°:

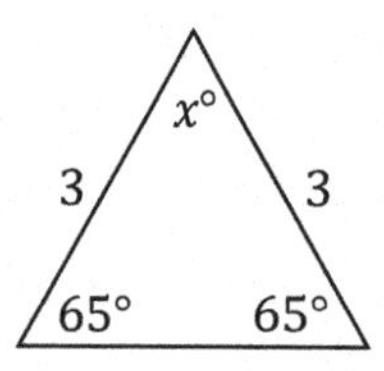

Because the sum of all angles in a triangle is 180°, we can solve for x by subtracting both angles from 180°:

$$x = 180 - 65 - 65 = 50$$

The missing angle measures 50°.

AREA OF OBTUSE AND RIGHT TRIANGLES

In the previous section, we saw how to find the area of an acute triangle. Recall that we found this area by multiplying the length of the triangle's base by its height, which is drawn perpendicular to its base, and then dividing by two:

$$Area = \frac{base \times height}{2}$$

height

base

We can use the same formula to find the area of an obtuse triangle, but an obtuse triangle might have its height located outside of the triangle. For example:

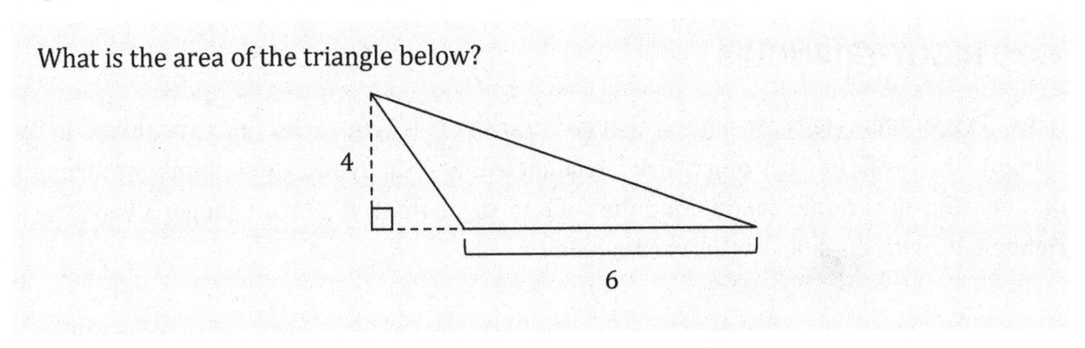

Even though it is located outside of the triangle, 4 is the height of the triangle because it is perpendicular to the base. We can find the area of the triangle by multiplying base times height and dividing by two:

$$Area = \frac{6 \times 4}{2} = 12$$

The area of the triangle is 12 square units.

In a right triangle, the height might be equal to the length of one of the triangle's legs. For example:

What is the area of the triangle below?

6

10

8

The triangle's base is equal to 8, and the line perpendicular to the triangle's base is the same as its other leg—that is, its height and its second leg both have a length of 6. To find its area, we plug these numbers into our formula:

$$Area = \frac{8 \times 6}{2} = 24$$

The triangle has an area of 24 square units.

VIDEO
3.6 INTRO TO TRIANGLES
Watch at http:// videos.ivyglobal.com

3:4:5 RIGHT TRIANGLES

A **3:4:5 right triangle** is considered special because the lengths of its sides are always in the ratio of 3 to 4 to 5. Recognizing a 3: 4: 5 triangle allows you to quickly remember the length of a missing side, rather than taking the time to calculate it. A 3: 4: 5 triangle always has a right angle, with the side lengths shown below:

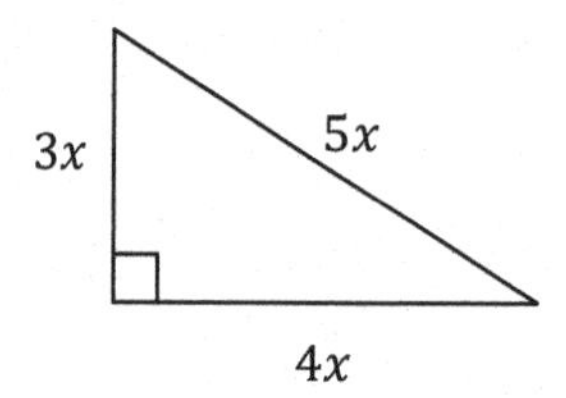

The diagram shows the side lengths written with the variable x because the actual length of the sides can change, as long as they maintain the 3:4:5 ratio. The variable x can be used to change the size of the triangle while maintaining the same shape. If $x = 1$, for example, the triangle has the standard side lengths of 3, 4, and 5.

The **hypotenuse** of a right triangle is the side opposite the right angle. In a 3:4:5 triangle, the hypotenuse always has the length $5x$, and the other two sides have lengths $3x$ and $4x$.

Here is an example:

In the triangle below, what is the value of y?

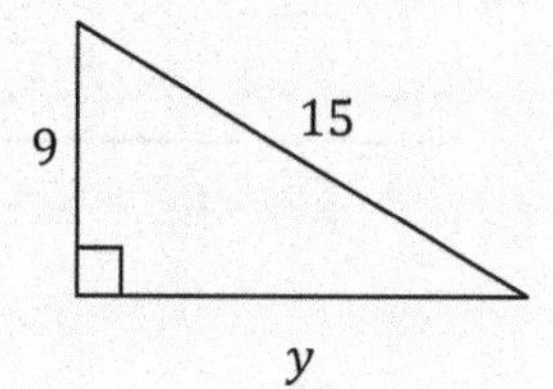

In this question, we have a right triangle with two side lengths given. Both of these side lengths have a common factor of 3. If we re-write these numbers as multiples of 3, we can see that they are in a ratio of 5 to 3:

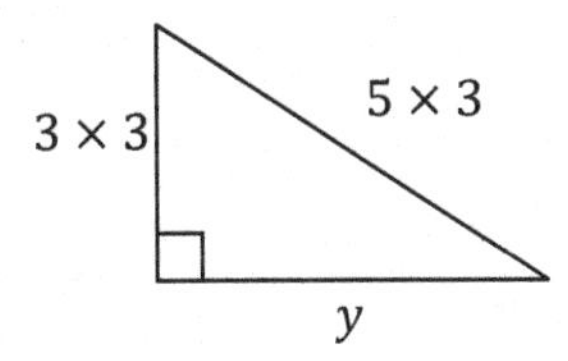

Because the right triangle's hypotenuse and one of its sides are in a ratio of 5 to 3, this is a special $3:4:5$ triangle. The missing side must be a multiple of 4. Because our common factor is 3, we know that $y = 4 \times 3 = 12$. Therefore, $y = 12$.

THE PYTHAGOREAN THEOREM (UPPER LEVEL ONLY)

Not all right triangles will have side lengths in a ratio of 3:4:5. To find the missing side of a right triangle that doesn't have a special side-length ratio, we can use the **Pythagorean Theorem.** If the two legs of a right triangle have lengths a and b and the hypotenuse has a length c, then the Pythagorean Theorem states that:

$$a^2 + b^2 = c^2$$

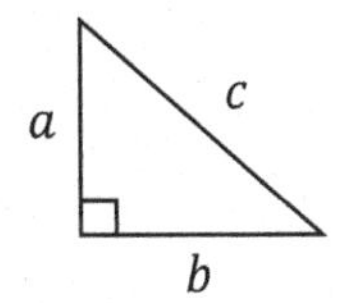

Here is an example:

What is the value of x in the figure below?

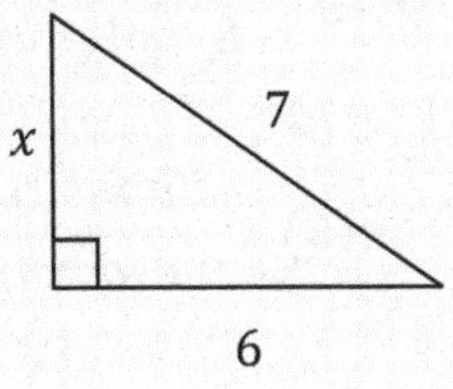

To find the length of the missing side, we plug the lengths of the two sides given into the Pythagorean Theorem and solve for x. The sum of the lengths of our two sides squared ($x^2 + 6^2$) is equal to the length of the hypotenuse squared (7^2):

$$x^2 + 6^2 = 7^2$$

$$x^2 + 36 = 49$$

$$x^2 = 13$$

$$x = \sqrt{13}$$

13 isn't a perfect square, so you can't simplify this expression further. Because you are not allowed a calculator on the ISEE, you can leave your answer as a square root: $x = \sqrt{13}$.

VIDEO
3.7 SOLVING RIGHT TRIANGLES
Watch at http:// videos.ivyglobal.com

TRIGONOMETRY (UPPER LEVEL ONLY)

Trigonometry is a more specialized type of math that deals with relationships between sides and angles in right triangles. In addition to using the Pythagorean Theorem, you can use trigonometry to calculate the length of sides in right triangles. You can also use trigonometry to calculate all of a right triangle's interior angles.

In trigonometry, the relationship between sides and angles of right triangles can be written as ratios with specific names. The three ratios you will find on the ISEE are **sine** (abbreviated sin), **cosine** (abbreviated cos), and **tangent** (abbreviated tan). The sine of an angle is found by dividing the length of the side opposite the angle by the length of the triangle's hypotenuse. The cosine is found by dividing the length of the side adjacent to the angle by the length of the hypotenuse. The tangent is found by dividing the length of the opposite side by the length of the adjacent side. These ratios are summarized in the following formulas, where θ stands for the measure of any angle in the triangle:

$$sin(\theta) = \frac{opposite}{hypotenuse}$$

$$cos(\theta) = \frac{adjacent}{hypotenuse}$$

$$tan(\theta) = \frac{opposite}{adjacent}$$

In order to help you remember these ratios, it can be useful to think of the acronym **SOHCAHTOA**: **S**ine **O**pposite/**H**ypotenuse, **C**osine **A**djacent/**H**ypotenuse, **T**angent **O**pposite/**A**djacent.

Here is an example:

What is the value of x in the figure below?

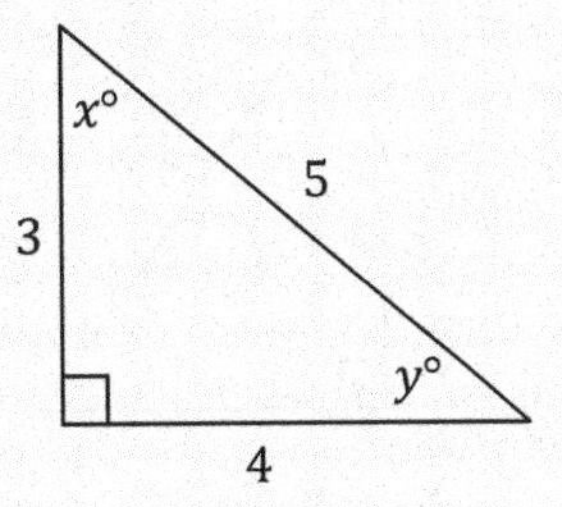

In order to calculate the sine, cosine, and tangent for angle x in this 3:4:5 triangle, we first locate the opposite and adjacent sides to x. The opposite side has a length of 4, and the adjacent side has a length of 3. Then, we plug these lengths into the formulas for sine, cosine, and tangent:

$$sin(x°) = \frac{opposite}{hypotenuse} = \frac{4}{5}$$

$$cos(x°) = \frac{adjacent}{hypotenuse} = \frac{3}{5}$$

$$tan(x°) = \frac{opposite}{adjacent} = \frac{4}{3}$$

The sine of $x°$ is $\frac{4}{5}$, the cosine is $\frac{3}{5}$, and the tangent is $\frac{4}{3}$.

While the hypotenuse of a right angle triangle is always found opposite to the right angle corner, note that the adjacent and opposite sides of the triangle differ according to the angle that you are using in your calculations. For example, if we're calculating these ratios for angle x in our triangle above, the opposite side is 4 units long and the adjacent side is 3 units long. However, if we're calculating these ratios for angle y, the opposite side is 3 units long and the adjacent side is 4 units long.

We can use our knowledge of sine, cosine, and tangent to solve for the length of one of the sides of a triangle. For example, let's look at the following question:

In the triangle below, what is the value of B?

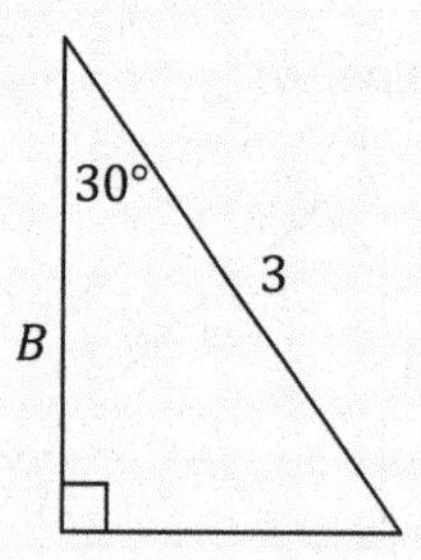

In this triangle, we know the measure of an angle and the length of the hypotenuse. We need to find the length of the side adjacent to the angle. "**SOHCAHTOA**" reminds us that the cosine of an angle compares the adjacent side with the hypotenuse. We can plug the values from our triangle into the cosine ratio formula:

$$cos(\theta) = \frac{adjacent}{hypotenuse}$$

$$cos(30°) = \frac{B}{3}$$

Then, we can solve for B:

$$B = cos(30°) \times 3$$

On the ISEE, the answer will always be in this format. Because you may not use a calculator, you will never be required to calculate the exact sine, cosine, or tangent of an angle.

PRACTICE QUESTIONS: ADVANCED TRIANGLES

1. Triangle ABC is equilateral. What is the measure of angle B?

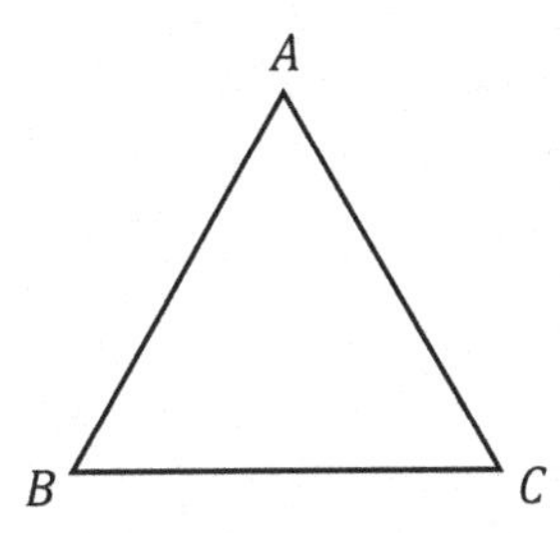

2. The triangle below is isosceles. What is the measure of angle G?

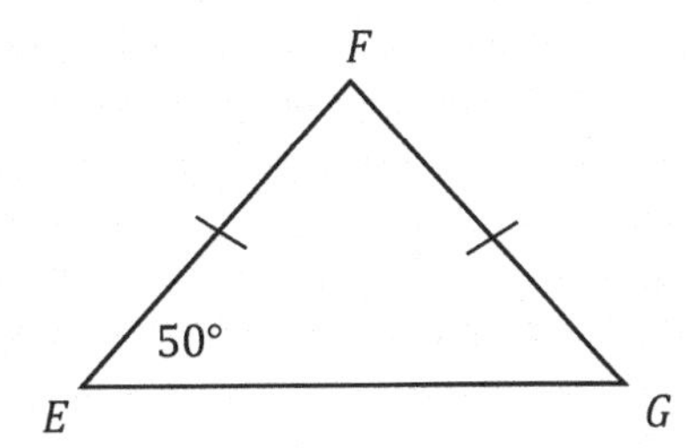

3. What is the value of x in the triangle below?

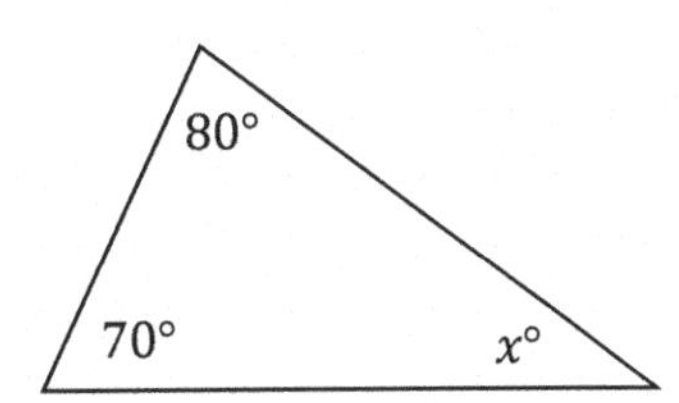

4. What is the value of y in the triangle below?

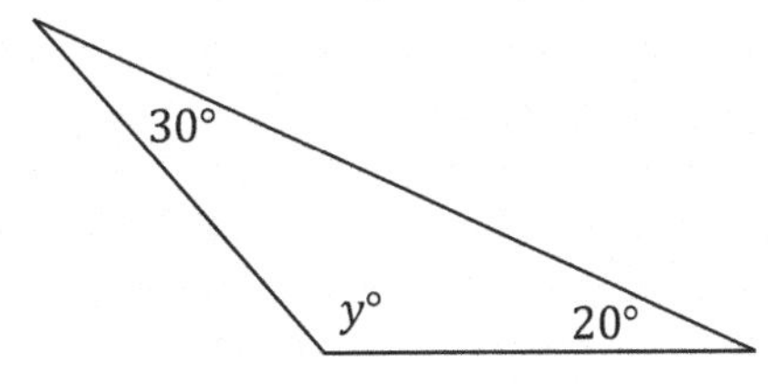

5. In the triangle below, what is the measure of angle K?

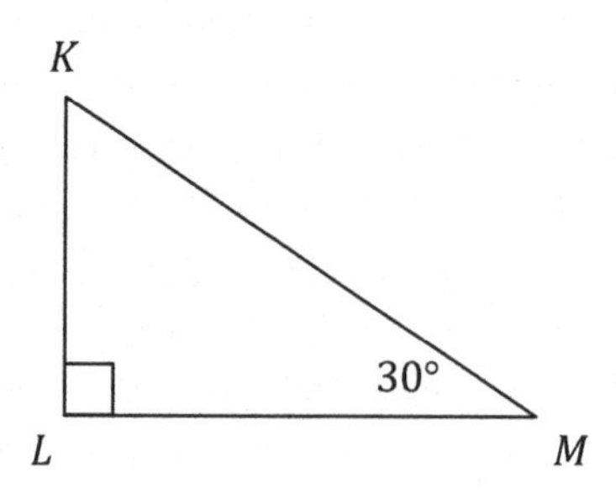

6. In the triangle below, $XY = YZ$. What is the measure of $\angle Z$?

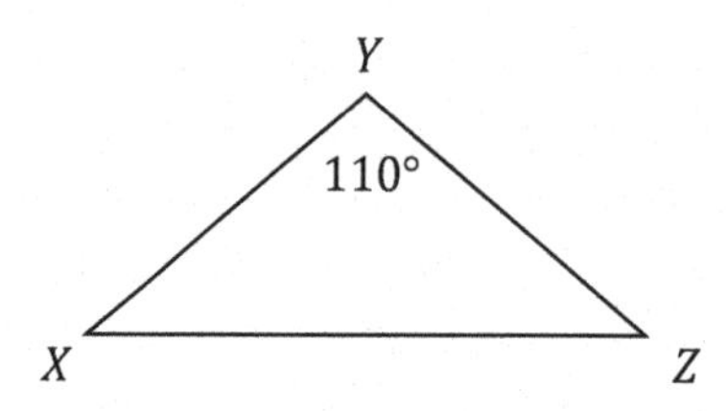

7. Triangle FGH is an isosceles right triangle. What is the measure of angle G?

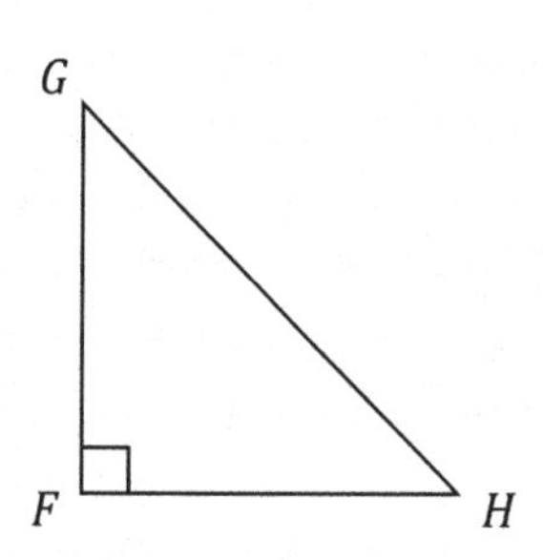

8. What is the area of the right triangle below?

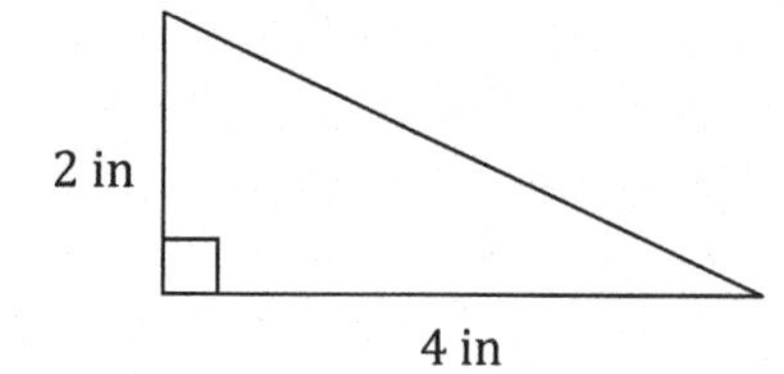

9. If the area of the triangle below is 12, what is the value of x?

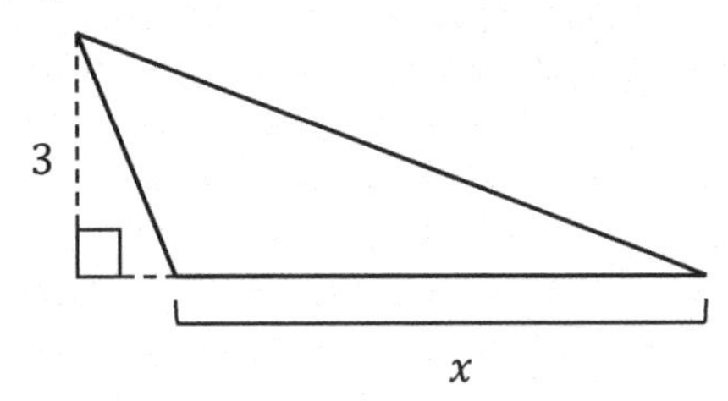

10. In the figure below, triangle LMP is an equilateral triangle, and $MNOP$ is a square. If the area of the entire figure is 22, what is the height h of triangle LMP?

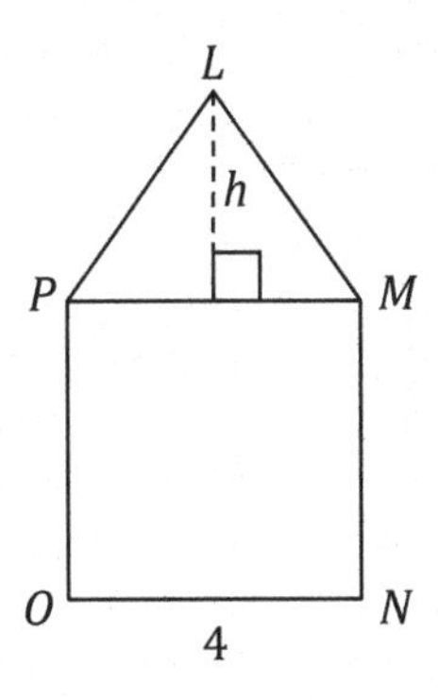

11. Triangle RST is a right triangle. If $RT = 6$ and $ST = 10$, what is the length of $\overline{(RS)}$?

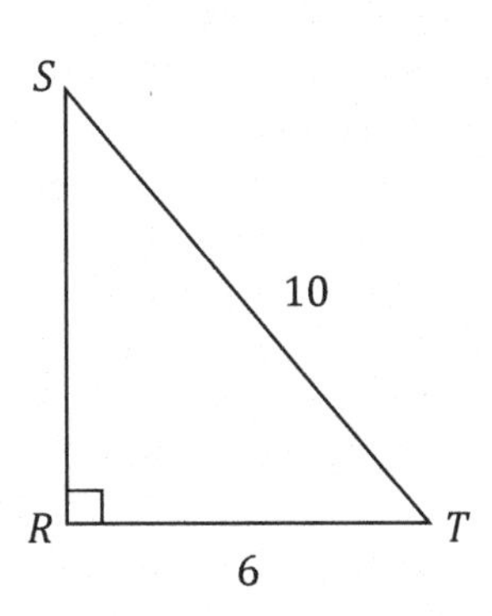

12. What is the area of the right triangle below?

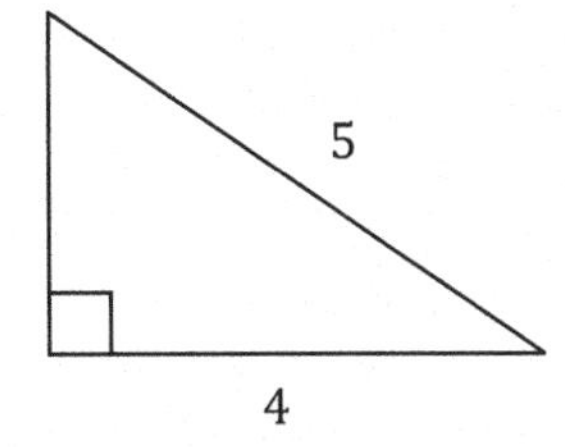

Questions 13-24 are Upper Level only.

13. Triangle CDE is a right triangle. What is the length of $\overline{(DE)}$?

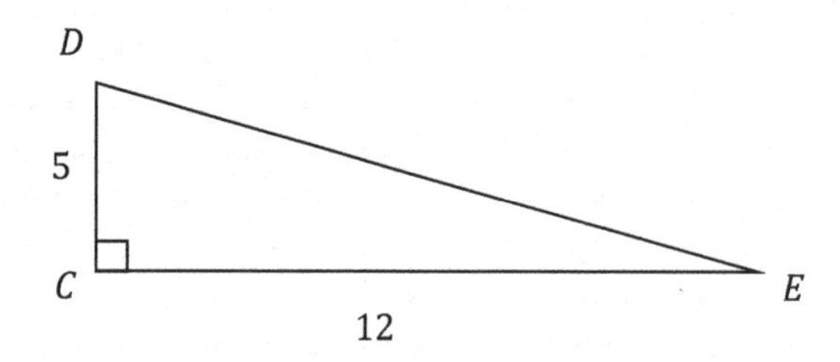

14. What is the value of x in the right triangle below?

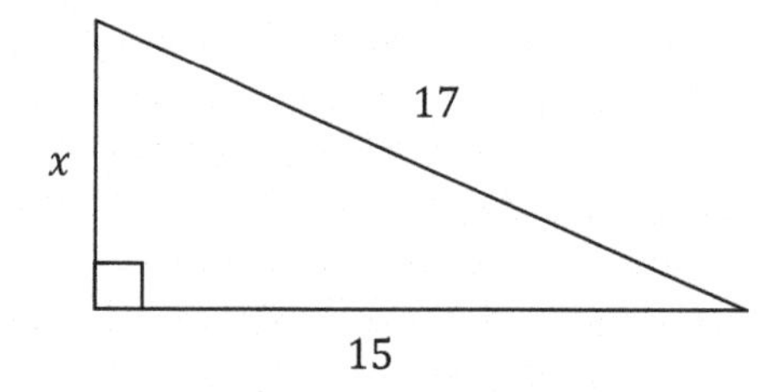

15. What is the length of side AB in the right triangle below?

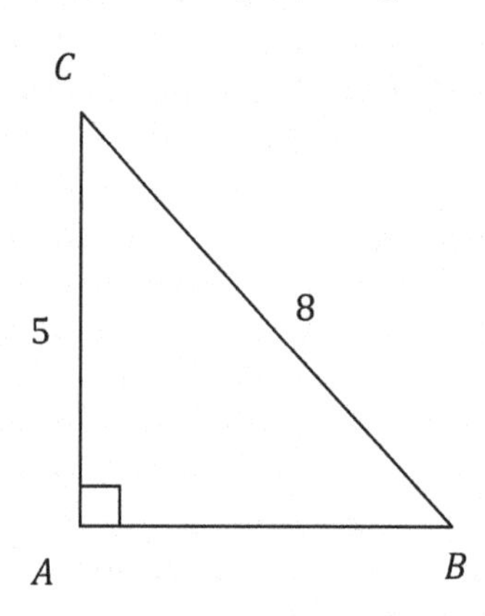

16. TUV is an isosceles right triangle. What is the area of triangle TUV?

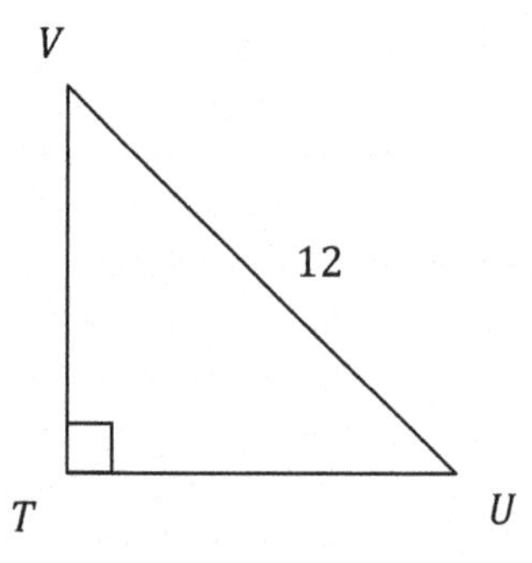

17. If the square below has an area of 50, what is the value of x?

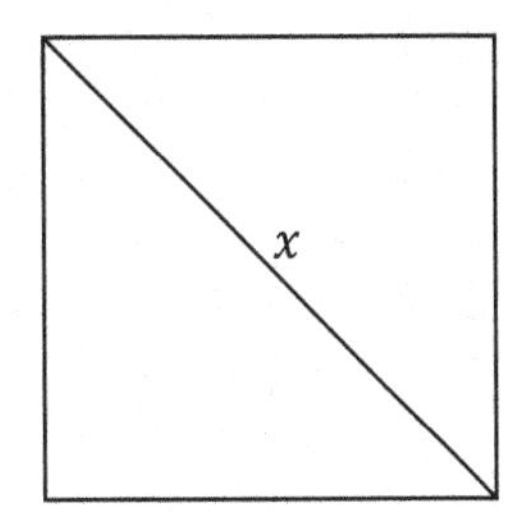

For questions 18-21, refer to the figure below.

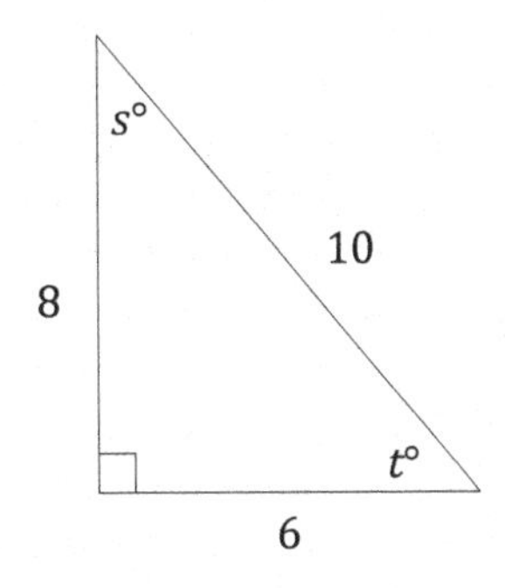

18. What is the sine of $s°$?

19. What is the cosine of $t°$?

20. What is the tangent of $s°$?

21. What is the tangent of $t°$?

22. What is the value of y in the right triangle below? State your answer in terms of sine, cosine, or tangent.

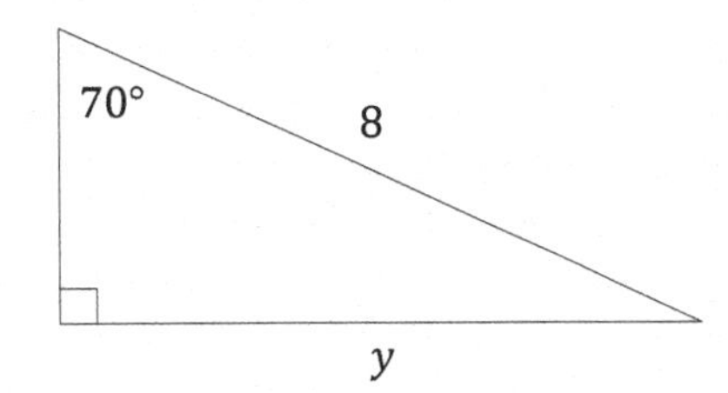

23. If $z = 65$, what is the value of w in the right triangle below? State your answer in terms of sine, cosine, or tangent.

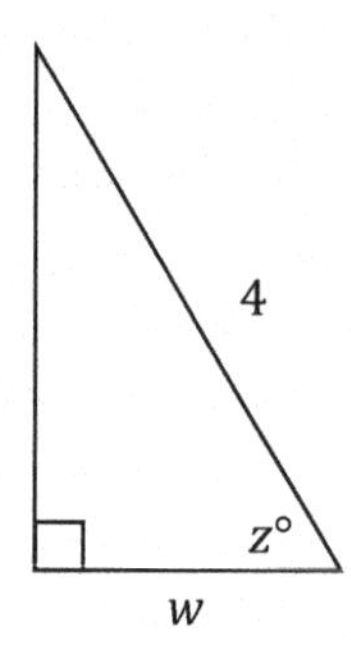

24. If the angle T measures 40°, what is the length of $\overline{(RT)}$ in the right triangle below? State your answer in terms of sine, cosine, or tangent.

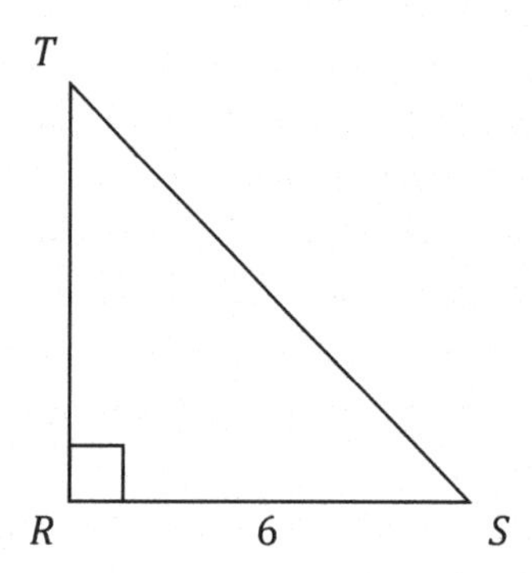

ADVANCED QUADRILATERALS

MIDDLE/UPPER LEVEL ONLY

SECTION 4

In Section 2, we discussed the classifications of quadrilaterals and the areas of rectangles and squares. In this section, we'll discuss some more advanced information about the angles of quadrilaterals and the areas of parallelograms, trapezoids, and kites.

ANGLES OF QUADRILATERALS

The **sum of the interior angles of any quadrilateral** is 360°. For example, in the following figure, we can calculate the missing interior angle:

What is the value of x?

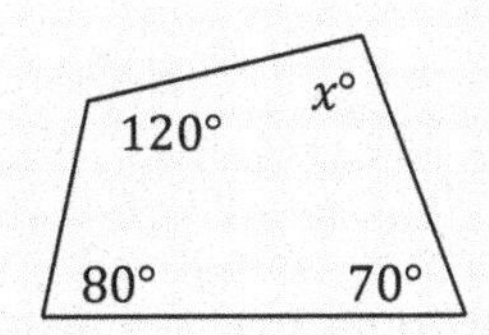

Because the sum of all angles in a quadrilateral is 360°, we can solve for x by subtracting the three given angles from 360°:

$$x = 360 - 120 - 80 - 70 = 90$$

Our missing angle measures 90°.

AREAS OF PARALLELOGRAMS, TRAPEZOIDS, AND KITES

Remember that a **parallelogram** is a quadrilateral with two sets of parallel sides. The opposite sides and opposite angles of a parallelogram are equal. You can find the area of a parallelogram by multiplying the length of its base by its height (a line drawn perpendicular to the base):

$$\text{Area of a parallelogram} = \text{base} \times \text{height}$$

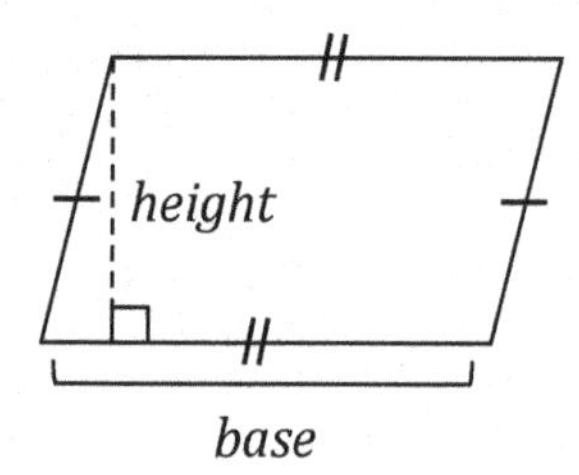

A **rhombus** is a parallelogram whose four sides all have the same length. A rhombus does not necessarily have any right angles, but the opposite angles of a rhombus are equal. You can find the area of a rhombus by multiplying its base times its height, or by finding half the product of its two diagonals.

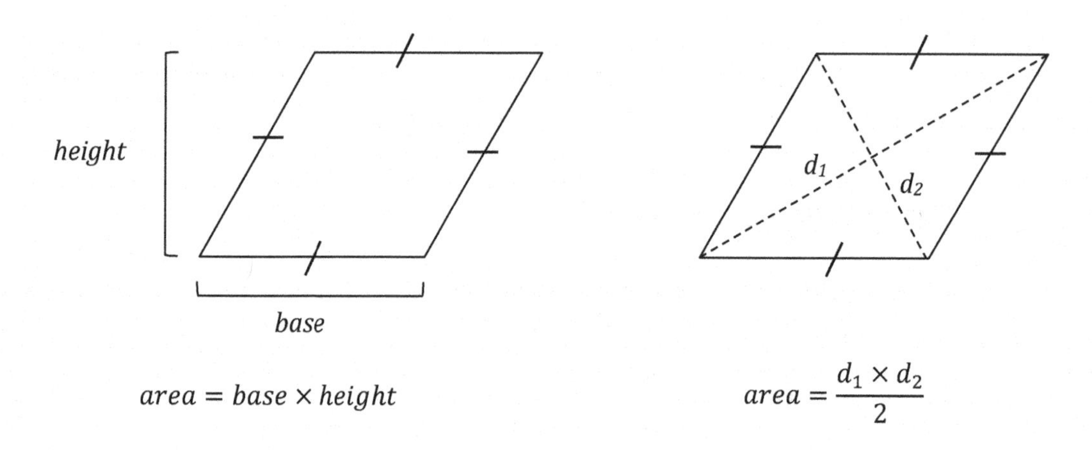

A **trapezoid** is a quadrilateral with only one set of parallel sides, which are called the trapezoid's **bases**. You can find the area of a trapezoid by multiplying one half of the trapezoid's height by the sum of the lengths of its two bases:

$$Area = 1/2 \times height \times (base\ 1 + base\ 2)$$

base1
height
base2

Finally, a **kite** is a quadrilateral whose sides are not parallel, but are grouped in two equal-length pairs. A kite's area is one half the product of its **total height** and its **base**. To find the kite's total height, divide it into two triangles and calculate the height of each of them; the sum of the heights of these triangles (*h1* and *h2*) is the total height of the kite. The kite's base is equal to the horizontal line at the largest section of the kite.

$$Area = (total\ height \times base)/2$$

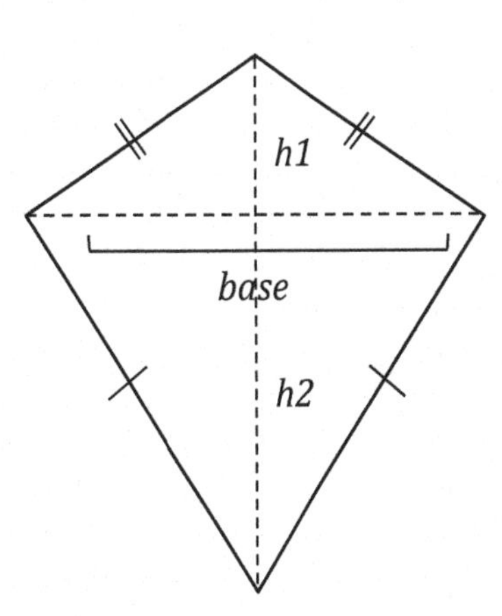

PRACTICE QUESTIONS: ADVANCED QUADRILATERALS

1. What is the value of x in the quadrilateral below?

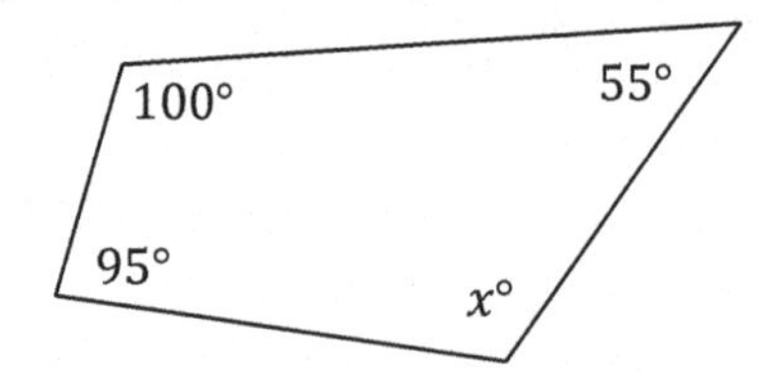

2. What is the value of $a + b$ in the quadrilateral below?

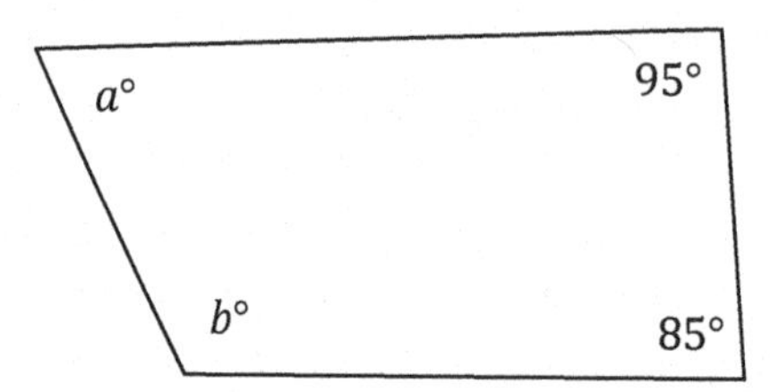

3. In trapezoid $NOPQ$, $\angle N$ and $\angle O$ are right angles, and $\angle P$ measures $130°$. What is the measure of $\angle Q$?

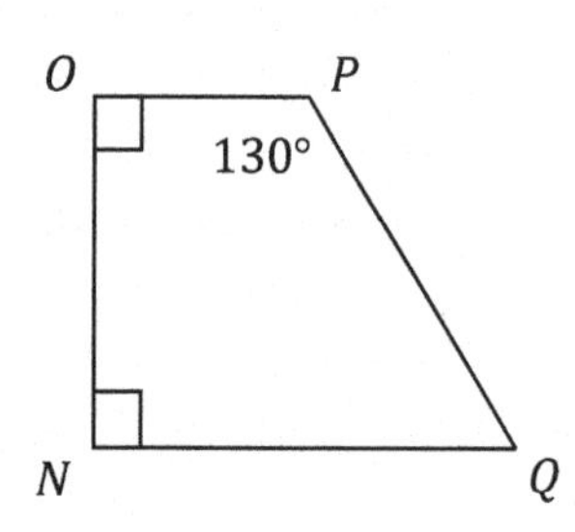

4. What is the area of the parallelogram below?

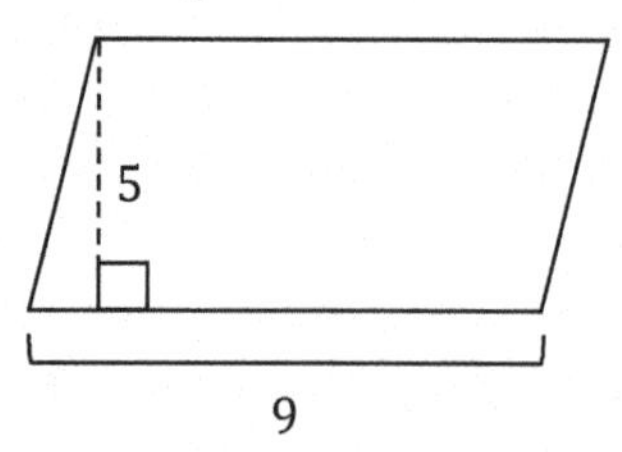

5. What is the area of the rhombus shown below?

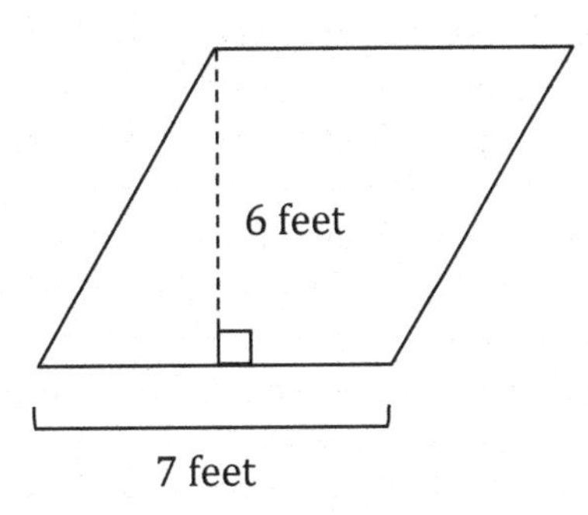

6. What is the area of the trapezoid below?

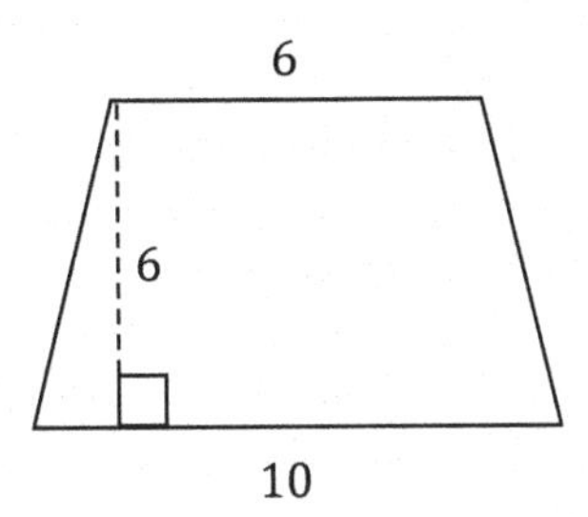

7. If $AC = 4$ and $= 6$, what is the area of rhombus $ABCD$ below?

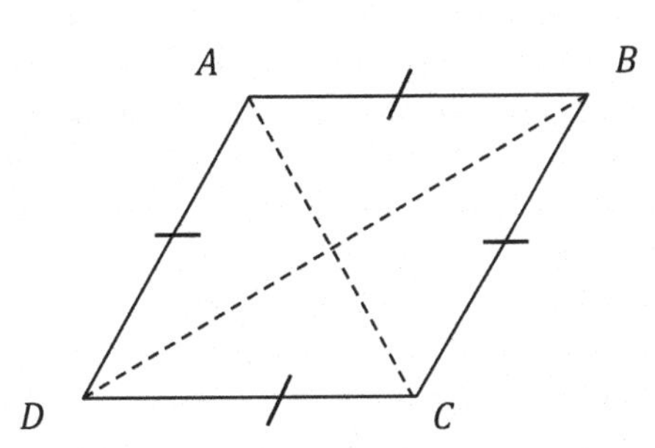

8. What is the area of the figure below?

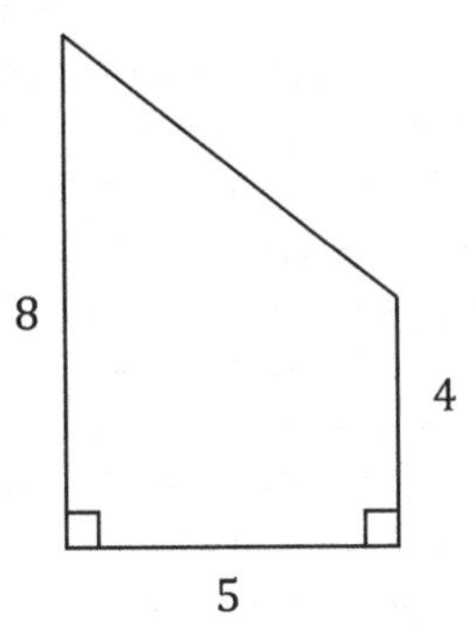

9. What is the area of the shaded region below?

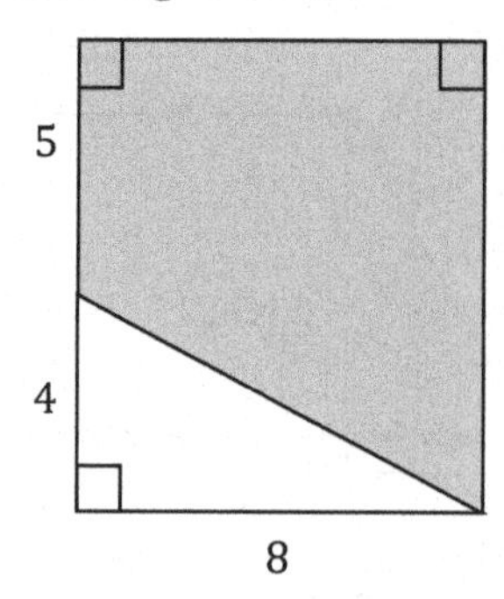

10. Jerome wants to build a kite with a total height of 9 inches and a base measuring 6 inches. How many square inches of material will he need?

11. Mr. and Mrs. Lewis want to pave their irregularly shaped driveway, shown below. How many square meters of cement will they need to use?

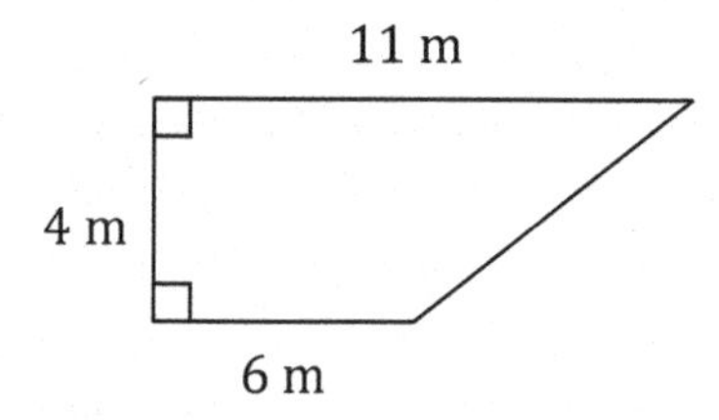

12. The kite below has an area of 48 and a base of 8. What is its total height?

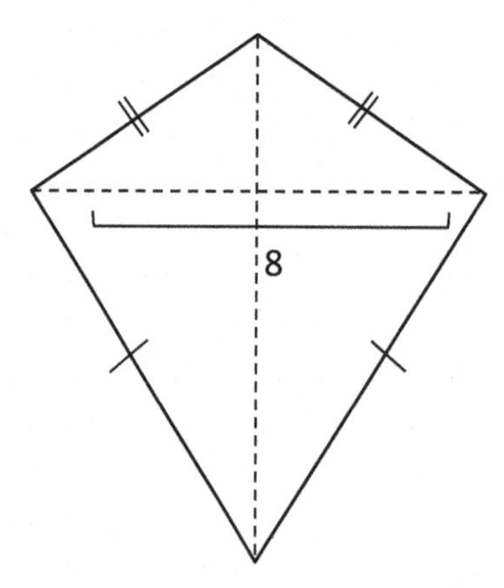

13. Rose wants to paint one wall of her shed, shown in the figure below. How many square feet of paint will she need to paint this wall?

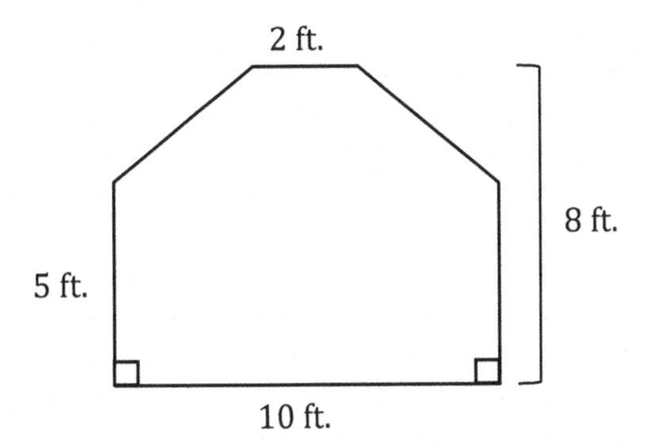

Questions 14-16 are Upper Level only.

14. The rhombus below is inscribed in a rectangle so that it only touches the rectangle at four points. What is the area of the shaded region?

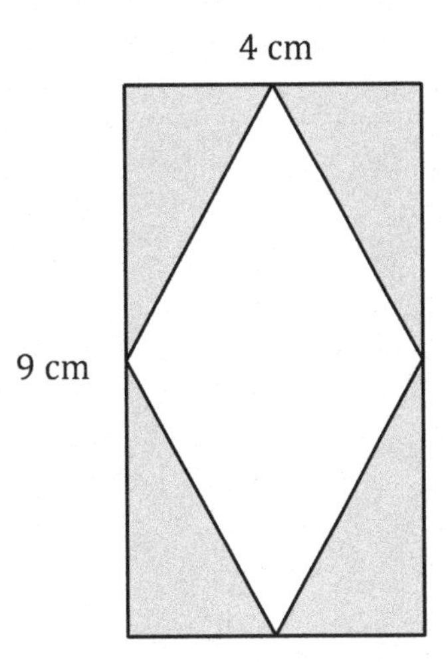

15. The figure below shows a trapezoid that has been placed in a rectangle. The area of the shaded region below is 20 in^2. What is the value of b?

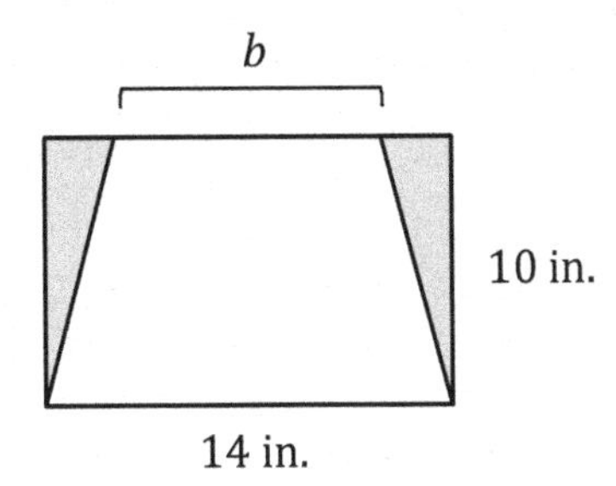

16. A rhombus is shown in the figure below. What is the value of B?

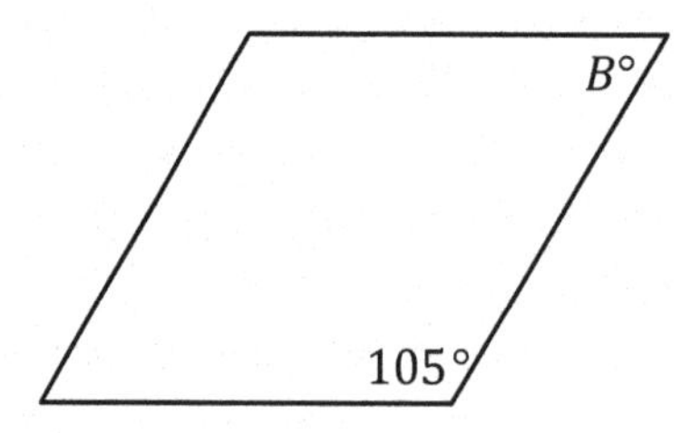

CIRCLES

MIDDLE/UPPER LEVEL ONLY

SECTION 5

A **circle** is a two-dimensional figure made up of points that are all the same distance from its center. The distance from the center of the circle to any point on the edge of the circle is called a **radius** (plural: radii). All possible radii of a circle are the same length.

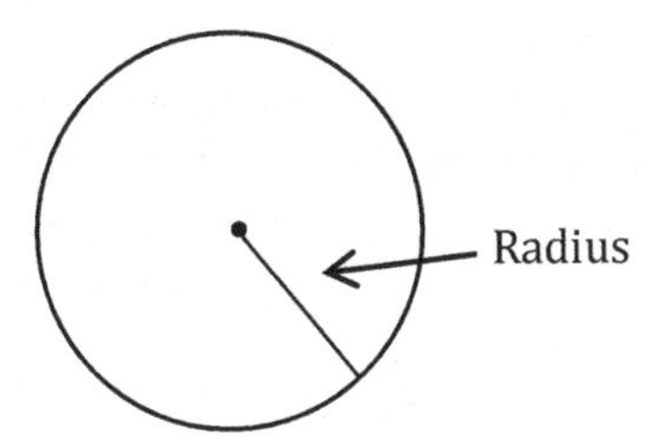

The **diameter** of a circle is a line that connects two points on the circle and passes through its center. The diameter of a circle is equal to twice the length of its radius. All diameters of a circle are the same length.

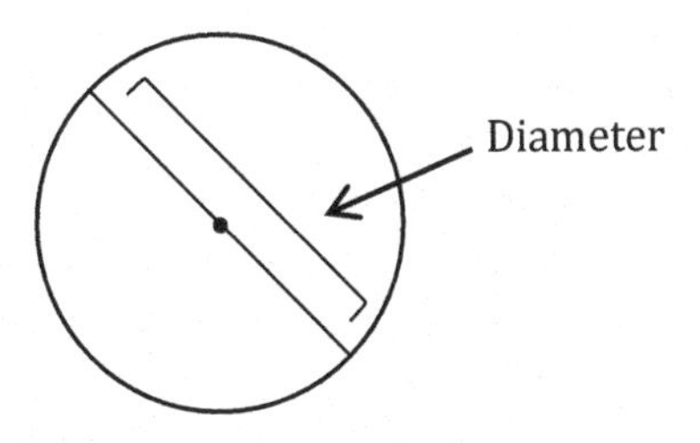

$$diameter = 2 \times radius$$

This is also written as $d = 2r$.

CIRCUMFERENCE OF A CIRCLE

The **circumference** of a circle is the distance around the circle. It can be found by multiplying the diameter by $\boldsymbol{\pi}$ ($\boldsymbol{pi}$), a special number equal to approximately **3.14**:

$$circumference = diameter \times \pi$$

Because π is a non-repeating, non-ending decimal number (3.1415927...), we often leave the symbol π as it is when calculating the circumference or area of a circle. This gives a more accurate answer than rounding a lengthy decimal number.

For example:

Calculate the circumference of the circle below.

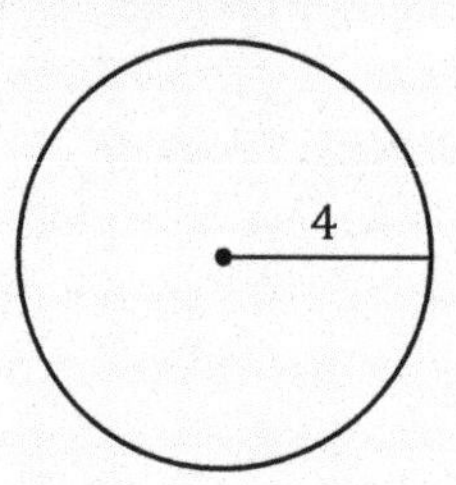

We can use the radius of 4 to find the diameter (remember, $d = 2r$) and then multiply by π:

$$circumference = diameter \times \pi = (2 \times 4) \times \pi = 8\pi$$

The circumference of the circle is 8π. Answers on the ISEE will always be left in terms of π.

AREA OF A CIRCLE

To find the **area** of a circle, multiply π by the radius squared:

$$area = \pi \times radius^2$$

For instance:

Find the area of the circle below.

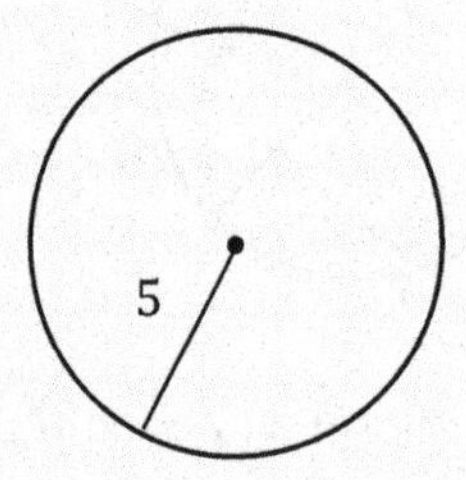

In order to solve this problem, square the radius and multiply by π:

$$area = \pi \times radius^2 = \pi \times 5^2 = 25\pi$$

The area of the circle is 25π units squared.

VIDEO
3.9 CIRCLES
Watch at http:// videos.ivyglobal.com

PRACTICE QUESTIONS: CIRCLES

1. What is the diameter of a circle with a radius of 3 inches?

2. What is the radius of a circle with a diameter of 20 centimeters?

3. What is the radius of the circle below?

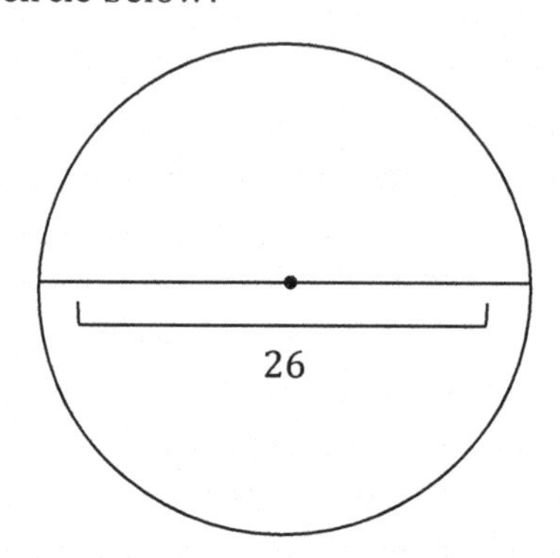

4. What is the diameter of the circle below?

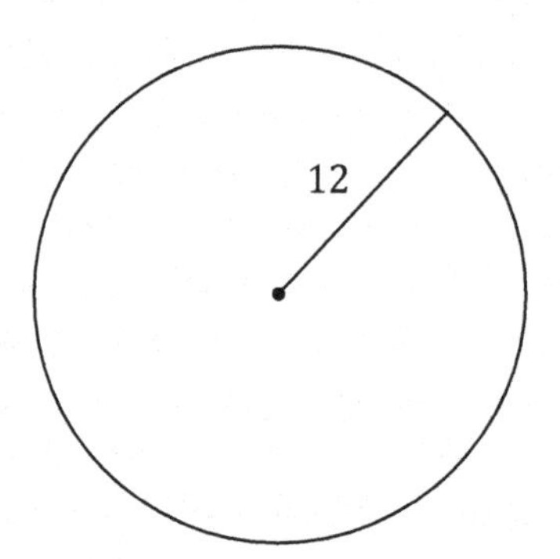

5. Line segment $\overline{AB}$ passes through the centers of both circles in the figure below. If each circle has a radius of 2, what is the distance between point A and point B?

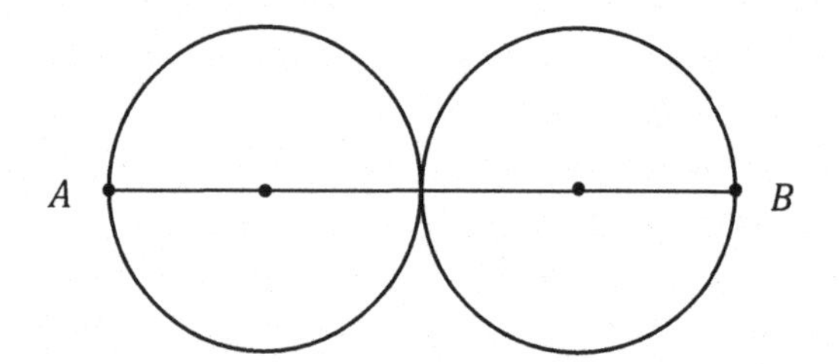

6. Triangle EFG is formed by connecting the centers of circles E, F, and G. Each of these circles touches the other two circles at exactly one point. If each circle has a diameter of 10, what is the perimeter of triangle EFG?

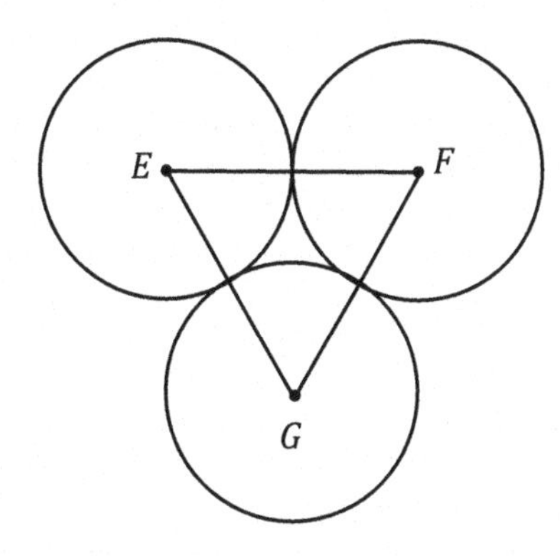

7. Square $RSTU$ touches circle V at exactly one point on each side. If circle V has a radius of 3, what is the area of square $RSTU$?

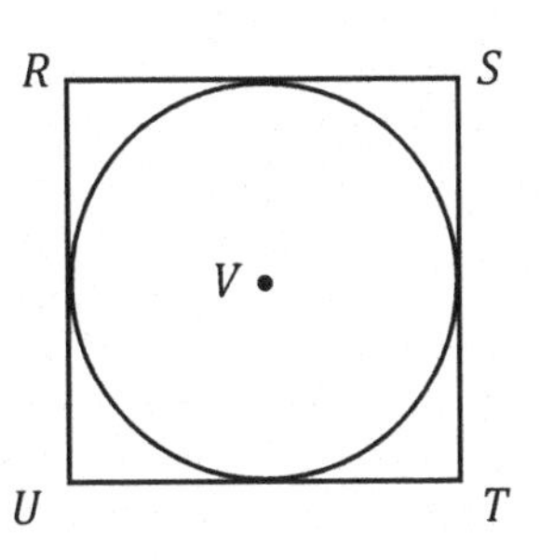

8. How many non-overlapping circles with a 2-inch radius can be drawn inside the rectangle below?

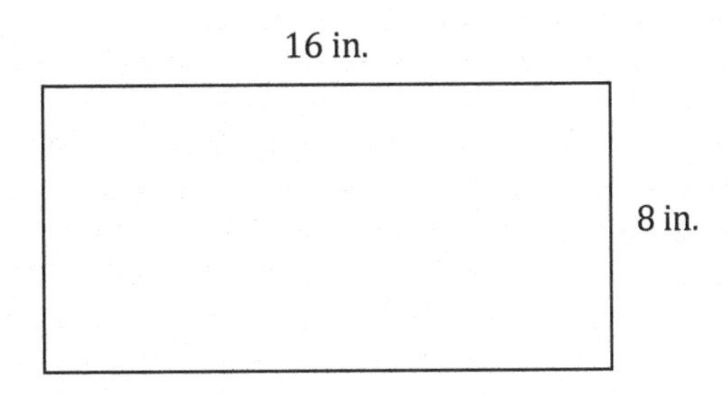

9. What is the area of a circle with a radius of 4 meters?

10. What is the circumference of a circle with a diameter of 10 inches?

11. What is the area of the circle below?

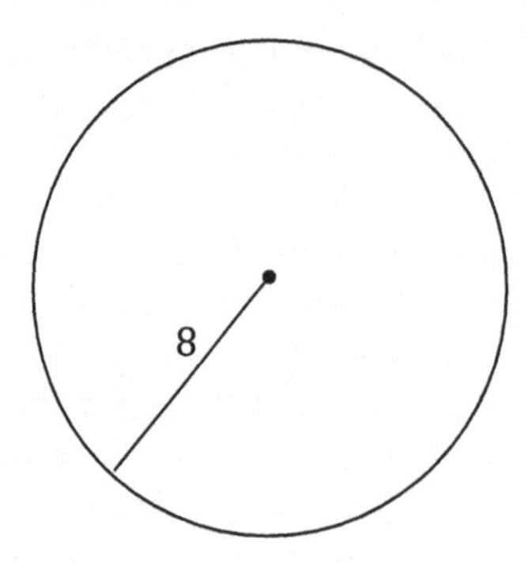

12. If the area of a circle is 49π, what is its diameter?

13. What is the circumference of the circle below?

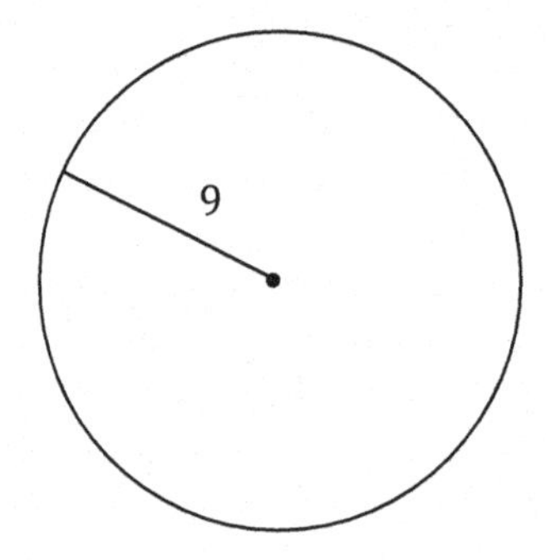

14. If the circumference of a circle is 36π, what is its diameter?

15. If the area of a circle is 100π, what is its circumference?

Questions 16 – 18 are Upper Level Only.

16. A goat is tethered to a fence with a 6-foot long rope. He can move within a semicircular region bounded by the fence, as shown below. What is the area of this region?

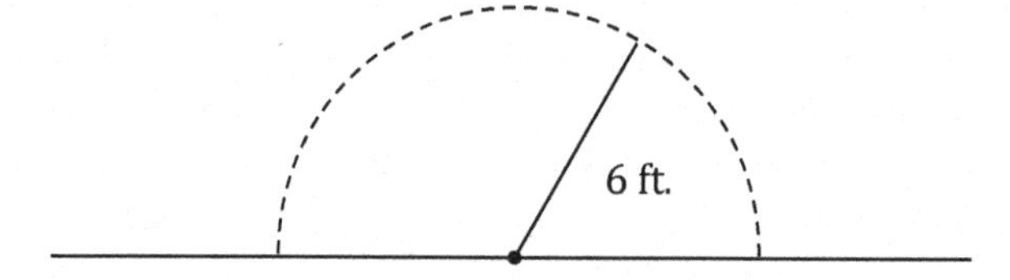

17. In the figure below, a dart board is formed with three circles that share a center, each spaced 2 inches apart. If the area of the smallest circle is 9π inches squared, what is the circumference of the largest circle?

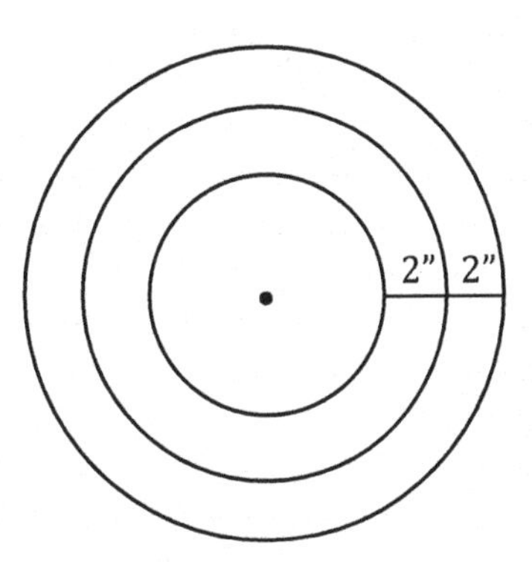

18. In the figure below, square $ABCD$ touches circle E at exactly one point on each side. If the perimeter of the square is 40, what is the area of the shaded region?

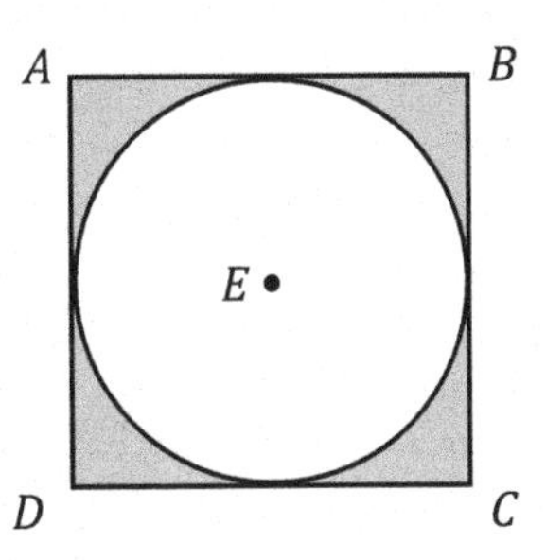

SOLID GEOMETRY

ALL LEVELS

SECTION 6

A **solid** is a three-dimensional object that has a length, width, and height. The **volume** of a solid is the region contained within the solid. The **surface area** of a solid is the area of its outside surfaces.

CUBES

A **cube** is a kind of solid that has squares for all six of its sides. This means that its length, width, and height are all equal.

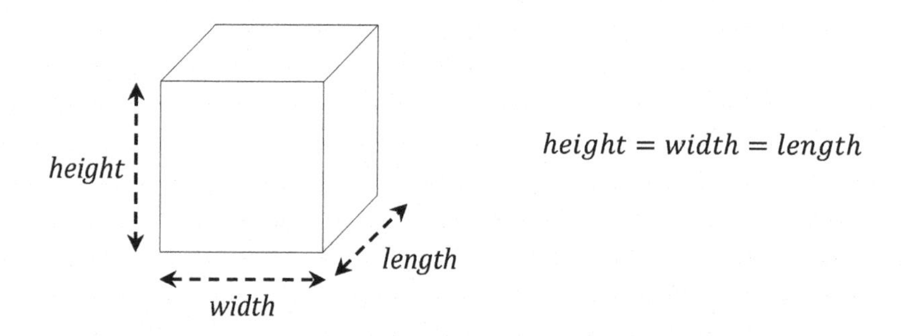

One way to determine the volume of a cube is by using a smaller **unit cube**. A unit cube has a volume of 1:

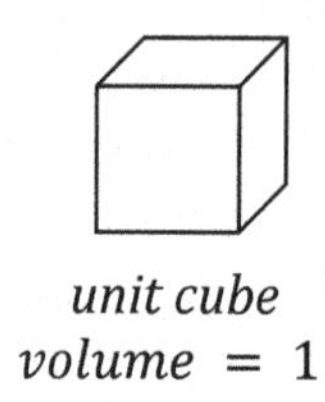

unit cube
$volume = 1$

You can find the volume of a larger cube by imagining that it is built out of many smaller unit cubes. Here is an example:

The volume of Cube A is 1. What is the volume of Cube B?

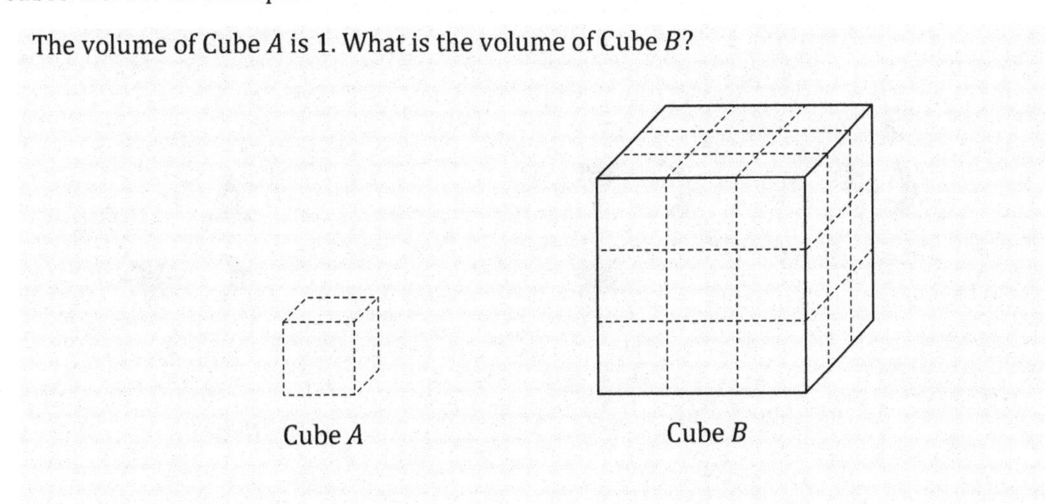

We know that Cube A is a unit cube because it has a volume of 1. We can see by the dashed lines that Cube B has been built out of many of these unit cubes. To know the volume of Cube B, we just need to know how many unit cubes were used to build it.

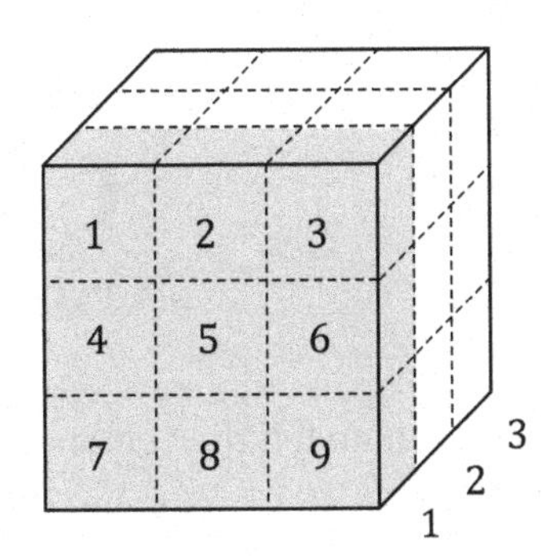

By counting, we see that the front layer of Cube B is made of 9 unit cubes. We can also see on the side of the cube that there are 3 rows of these layers. Therefore, there must be $9 \times 3 = 27$ unit cubes in the large cube. Because 27 unit cubes were used to build Cube B, the volume of Cube B must be $27 \times 1 = 27$.

You can also think of a cube as an empty box that can be disassembled and unfolded. Because a cube has six faces, an unfolded cube should be made up of six squares of equal size. An unfolded three-dimensional shape is called a **net**.

Here is an example of a problem involving a net:

Which of the two nets below could be a net for cube C?

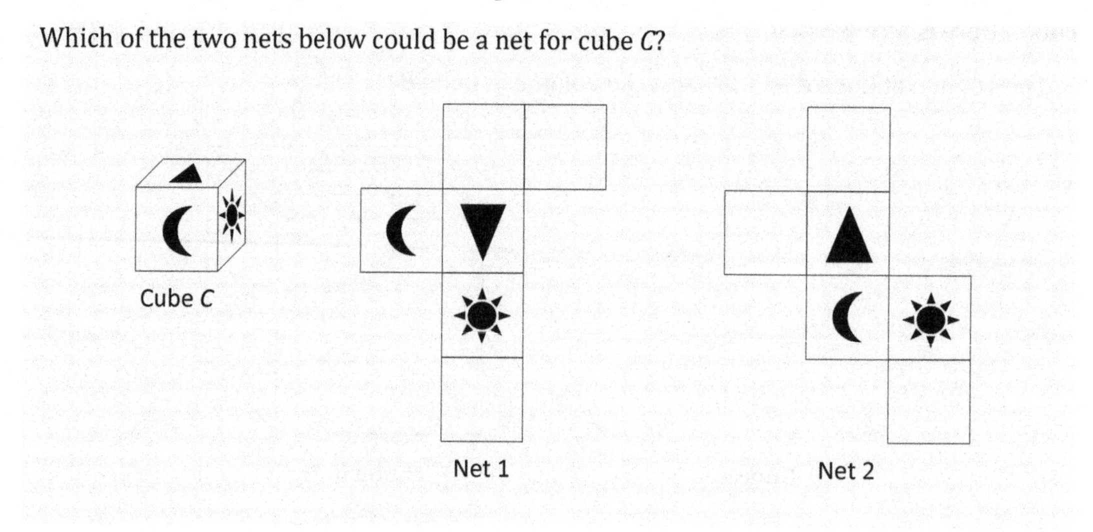

Both of these nets have six equal-sized squares that can be folded into a cube. However, the orientation of the symbols on Cube C helps us know which one truly is the cube's net. We must imagine folding the two nets along their edges and pay attention to which direction the symbols point. If both of these nets were folded into cubes, they would look like:

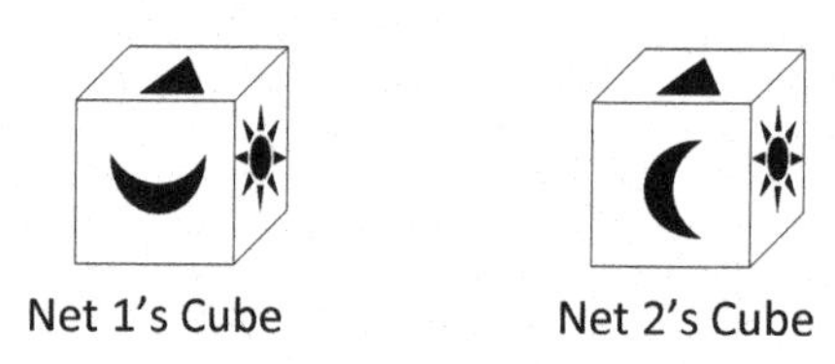

We can see that Net 1 cannot be folded to match the cube because the crescent moon shape faces up, rather than to the right. Therefore, Net 2 must be the answer.

PRISMS (MIDDLE/UPPER LEVEL ONLY)

A **prism** is any solid with two congruent polygons, called **bases**, joined by perpendicular rectangles. Each exterior surface of a prism is called a **face**, the lines where these faces intersect are called **edges**, and the points where these edges intersect are called **vertices** (singular: vertex).

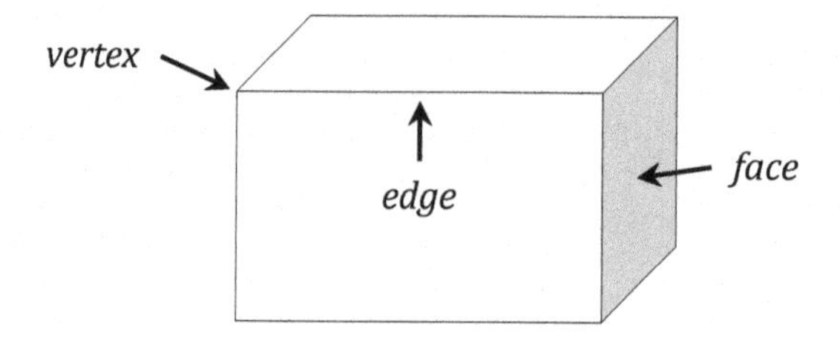

Prisms are classified by the shape of their bases:

TYPES OF PRISMS		
Name	**Shape of Base**	**Example**
Triangular Prism	Triangle	
Rectangular Prism	Rectangle	
Pentagonal Prism	Pentagon	
Hexagonal Prism	Hexagon	

SURFACE AREA OF PRISMS

The surface area of any prism can be found by adding together the areas of its faces. The surface area of a rectangular prism is shown below, where w = width, h = height, and l = length:

$$Area = 2lw + 2lh + 2wh$$

height

width

length

For example, consider the following question:

The figure below shows the dimensions of a cardboard box. If there are no overlapping sides, how many square inches of cardboard are needed to make this box?

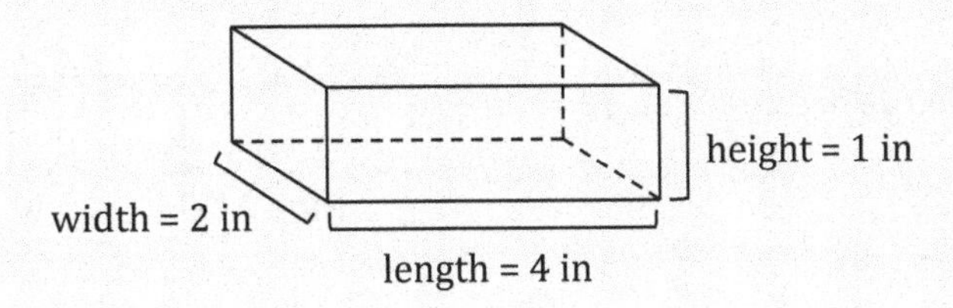

This question is asking us to find the surface area of a rectangular prism with a height of 1 inch, a width of 2 inches, and a length of 4 inches. To find how many square inches of cardboard make up the exterior of the box, we need to find the area of each rectangular face and then add these areas together.

The areas of the top and bottom faces are each $length \times width = 4 \text{ in} \times 2 \text{ in} = 8 \text{ in}^2$. The areas of the front and back faces of the box are each $length \times height = 4 \text{ in} \times 1 \text{ in} = 4 \text{ in}^2$. The areas of the left and right faces are each $width \times height = 2 \text{ in} \times 1 \text{ in} = 2 \text{ in}^2$. To find the total surface area of the box, we'll add together the areas of each of these faces:

$$surface\ area = 2lw + 2lh + 2wh$$
$$= (2 \times 8 \text{ in}^2) + (2 \times 4\text{in}^2) + (2 \times 2\text{in}^2) = 28 \text{ in}^2$$

The total surface area of the box is 28 in^2, which means that it will take 28 in^2 of cardboard to make.

VOLUME OF PRISMS

To find the volume of a rectangular prism, multiply its length by its width by its height:

$$Volume = length \times width \times height$$

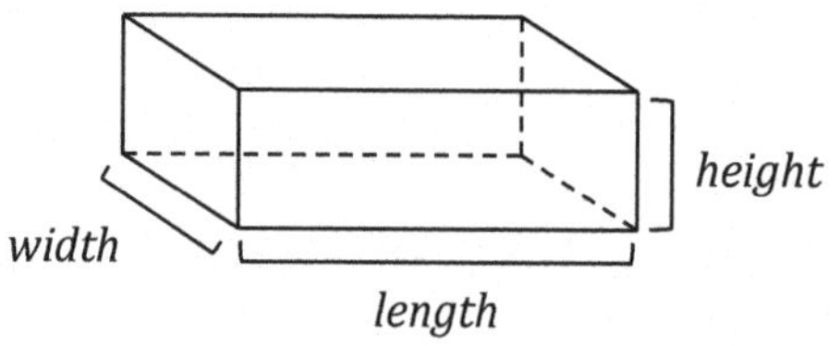

For example:

What is the volume of a box that measures 5 feet by 3 feet by 10 feet?

To find the volume of this box, multiply $5 \text{ ft} \times 3 \text{ ft} \times 10 \text{ ft} = 150 \text{ ft}^3$.

As we saw earlier in this section, a cube is a special type of rectangular prism with squares for all six faces. The length, width, and height of a cube are equal, so the volume can be found by cubing the length of one of its edges:

$$Volume = edge \times edge \times edge = edge^3$$

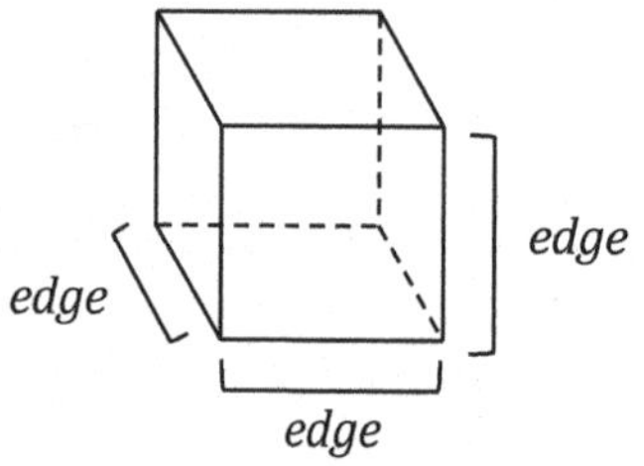

The volume of any other type of prism can be found by multiplying the area of one of its bases by its height, or the length of the edge perpendicular to its bases.

For instance:

Find the volume of the triangular prism below:

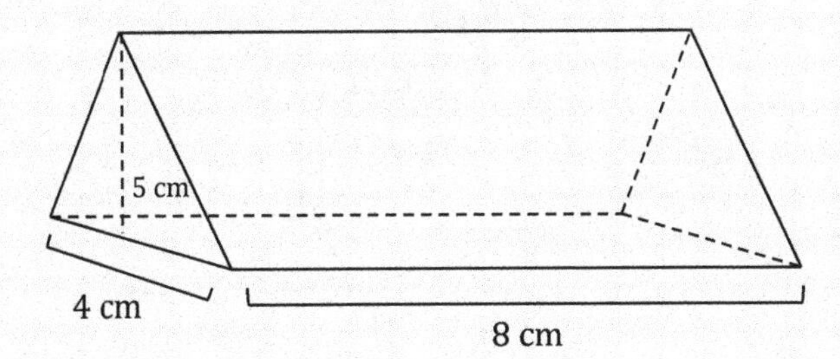

To find the volume, first find the area of its triangular base by multiplying $\frac{1}{2} \times 4$ cm $\times$ 5 cm. Then multiply by its height, 8 cm.

$$\left(\frac{1}{2} \times 4 \text{ cm} \times 5 \text{ cm}\right) \times 8 \text{ cm} = 10\text{cm}^2 \times 8 \text{ cm} = 80 \text{ cm}^3.$$

The volume of the triangular prism is 80 cm^3.

VIDEO

3.10 INTRO TO SOLID GEOMETRY

Watch at http:// videos.ivyglobal.com

ADVANCED NETS (MIDDLE/UPPER LEVEL ONLY)

As we saw before, a **net** is a two-dimensional figure formed by "unfolding" a solid along its edges. Nets can be useful to help you calculate the surface area of a solid. For instance, the following figure is a net of a rectangular pyramid:

Find the total surface area of the pyramid below.

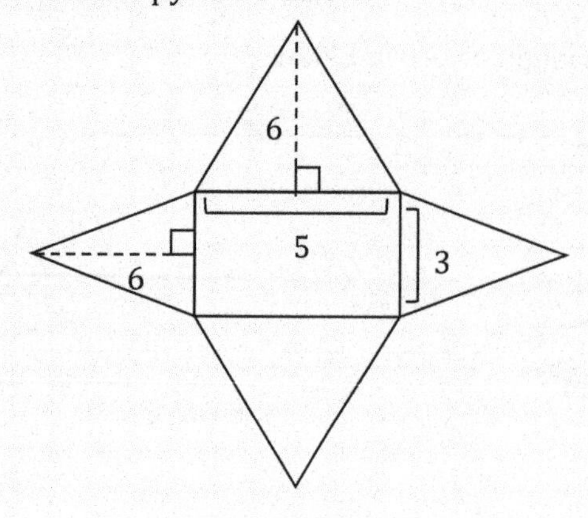

If this net were cut out and folded into a solid, it would form a pyramid with a rectangular base measuring 5×3.

To calculate the surface area of this pyramid, we need to calculate the area of the net above. The area of the rectangular base is $3 \times 5 = 15$. The area of each of the larger triangles is half their base (5) multiplied by their height (6): $\frac{1}{2} \times 5 \times 6 = 15$. The smaller triangles each have a base of 3 and a height of 6, so their area is $\frac{1}{2} \times 3 \times 6 = 9$.

To find the total surface area of the pyramid, we need to add together the area of each of these polygons:

$$Total\ area = 15 + (2 \times 15) + (2 \times 9) = 63$$

The total area of this net, and therefore the surface area of the pyramid, is 63 square units.

CYLINDERS (UPPER LEVEL ONLY)

A **cylinder** is like a prism, but its base is a circle instead of a polygon. A cylinder is formed by two circular bases connected by a perpendicular curved surface:

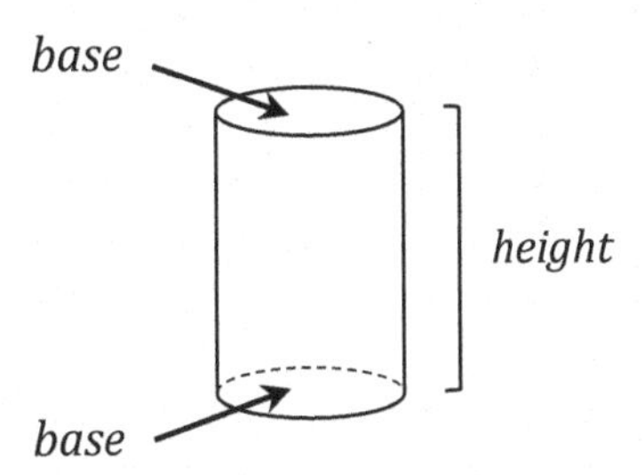

SURFACE AREA OF CYLINDERS

To find the surface area of a cylinder, imagine that the cylinder was sliced along its height and "unfolded" on a flat surface. You would then have two circular bases and one rectangle that normally wraps around the bases. To find the surface area of the cylinder, you need to add up the areas of the bases and the area of this rectangle.

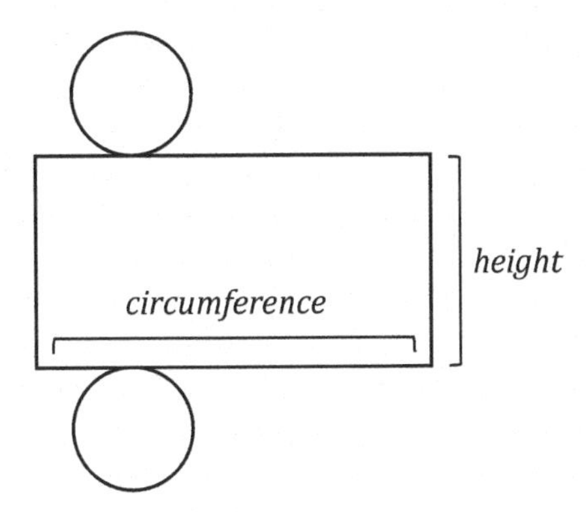

This rectangle has a length that is equal to the circumference of one of the bases, and a width that is equal to the height of the cylinder. Thus, to find the area of this rectangle, you would multiply the cylinder's circumference by its height. You would then add this number to the area of the two bases to find the total surface area of the cylinder:

$$Surface\ area = (area\ of bases) + (circumference \times height)$$

For instance:

Find the surface area of the cylinder below.

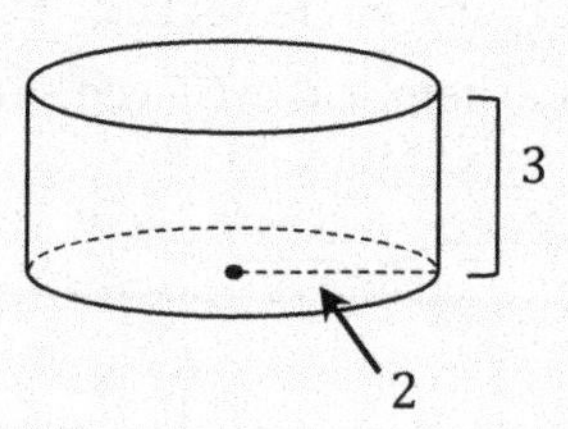

To solve this problem, first find the area of the bases. Each base has an area equal to π times 2 squared:

$$Area\ of\ each\ base = \pi \times 2^2 = 4\pi$$
$$Area\ of\ both\ bases = 4\pi + 4\pi = 8\pi$$

Then, find the circumference by multiplying 2 times π times the radius:

$$Circumference = 2 \times \pi \times 2 = 4\pi$$

Finally, find the area of the curved rectangular surface by multiplying the circumference by the height (3), and add this value to the area of the bases to find the total surface area of the cylinder:

$$\begin{aligned} Surface\ area &= (area\ of\ bases) + (circumference \times height) \\ &= (8\pi) + (4\pi \times 3) \\ &= 8\pi + 12\pi = 20\pi \end{aligned}$$

The total surface area of the cylinder is 20π.

VOLUME OF CYLINDERS

The volume of a cylinder is equal to the area of its base multiplied by its height:

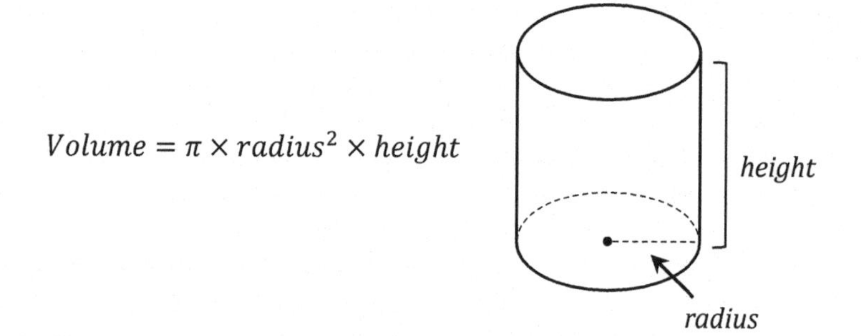

For example:

What is the volume of the cylinder below?

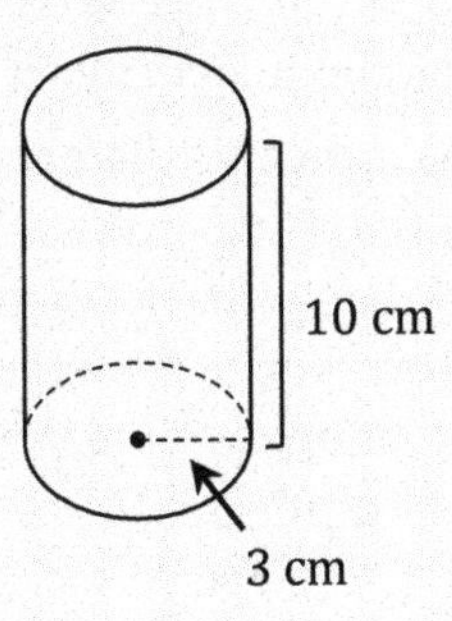

First, find the area of the cylinder's base and then multiply by its height:

$$\begin{aligned} Volume &= (\pi \times radius^2) \times height \\ &= \pi \times 3^2 \times 10 \\ &= \pi \times 9 \times 10 = 90\pi \end{aligned}$$

The volume of the cylinder is 90π cubic centimeters.

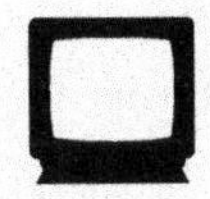

VIDEO

3.11 CYLINDERS

Watch at http:// videos.ivyglobal.com

SPHERES, PYRAMIDS, AND CONES (UPPER LEVEL ONLY)

A **sphere** is like a three-dimensional circle: it is a collection of points in space all the same distance away from the center. As in a circle, this distance is called the sphere's radius, and all radii of a sphere are equal.

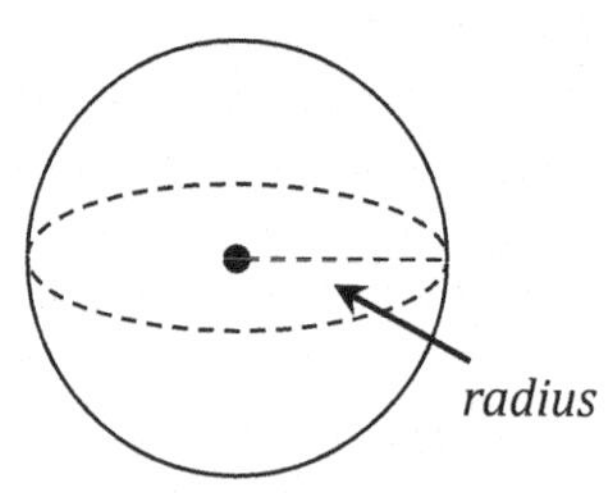

A **pyramid** has a polygon for a base and triangular faces that join in a point, called the **vertex** of the pyramid. The distance between a pyramid's base and its vertex is called its height. Like prisms, pyramids are named after the shape of their bases. For instance, a triangular pyramid has a triangle for its base, a rectangular pyramid has a rectangle for its base, and so on.

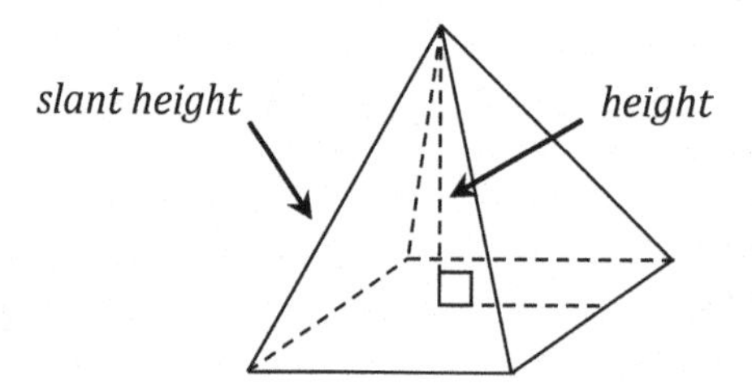

A **cone** is like a pyramid, but it has a circle for a base and a curved surface that tapers to a point, which is also called its vertex. The height of a cone is the distance between its base and its vertex.

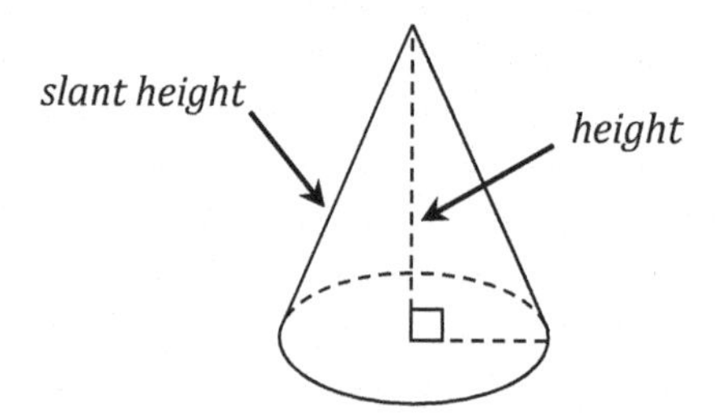

On the ISEE, you will not need to memorize formulas for volume and surface area for these solids. However, you may need to calculate volume and surface area from a given formula on the exam. Here are some formulas you might see:

Solid	Volume	Surface Area
Sphere	$\frac{4}{3}\pi r^3$	$4\pi r^2$
Pyramid	$\frac{1}{3}$ $(base\ area) \times height$	$base\ area + \frac{P \times l}{2}$ $P = base\ perimeter$ $l = slant\ height$
Cone	$\frac{1}{3}(\ base\ area)\ \times height$	$\pi \times r^2 + \pi \times r \times l$ $l = slant\ height$

PRACTICE QUESTIONS: SOLID GEOMETRY

For Questions 1-3, refer to the figures below.

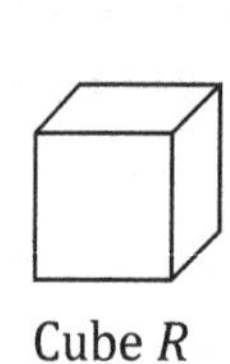
Cube R

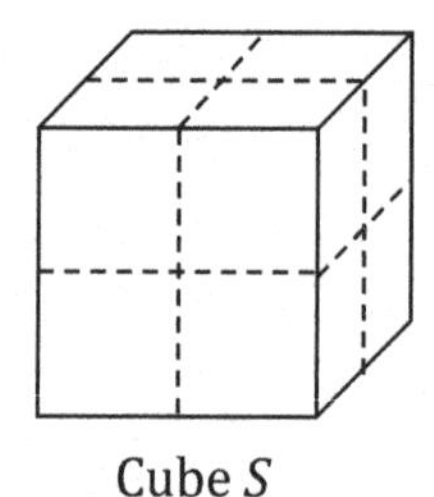
Cube S

1. How many times would Cube R fit into Cube S?

2. If Cube R has a volume of 1, what is the volume of Cube S?

3. Amanda built a third cube, called Cube T, that has twice the volume of Cube S. How many times would Cube R fit into Cube T?

4. James has a large crate he wants to fill with as many moving boxes as possible. Both the crate and the moving boxes, shown in the figure below, are cubes. How many moving boxes can he fit in the crate?

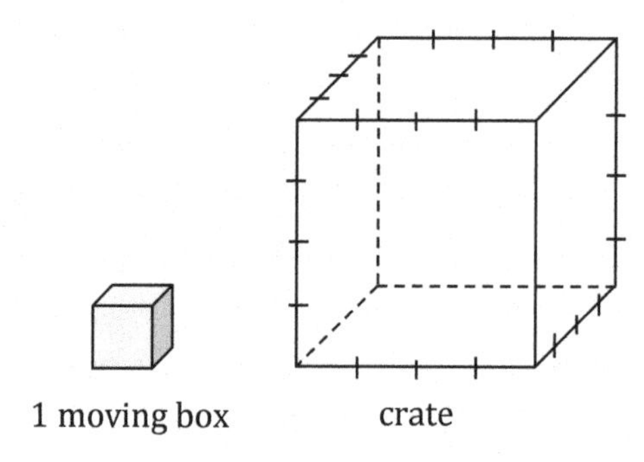

5. Which of the nets shown below (A, B, or C) could be a net for Cube W?

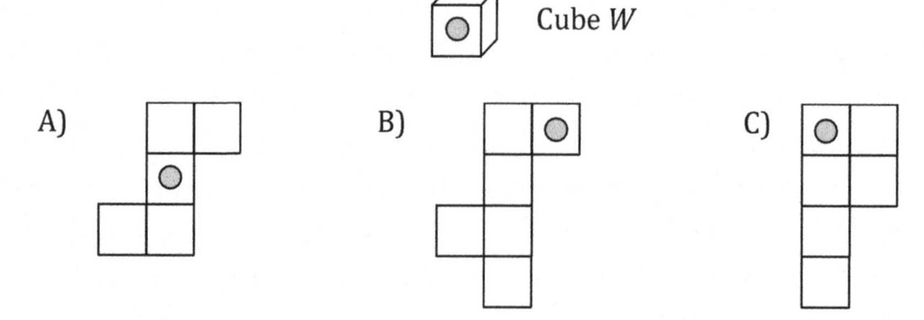

Questions 6 – 23 are Middle/Upper Level Only.

6. What is the volume of the three-dimensional object represented by this net? (Key: 1 grid square $= 1\ \text{cm}^2$).

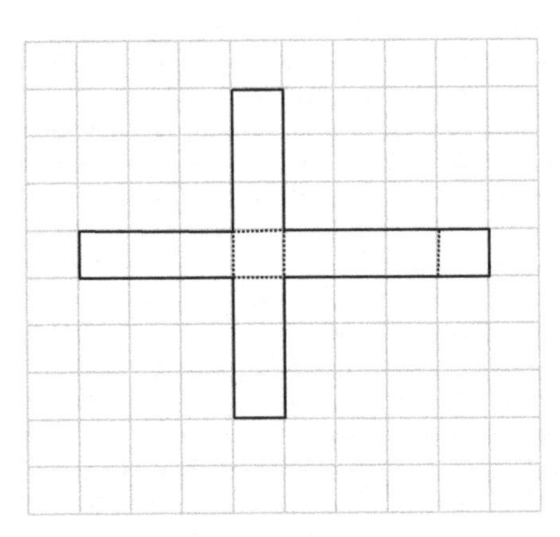

7. What is the volume of the box below?

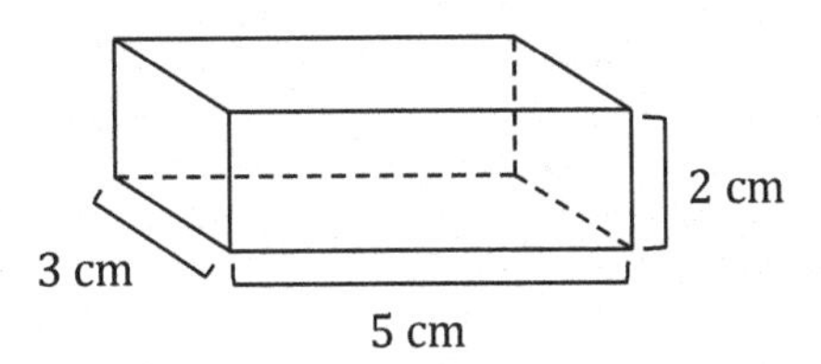

8. What is the volume of the cube below?

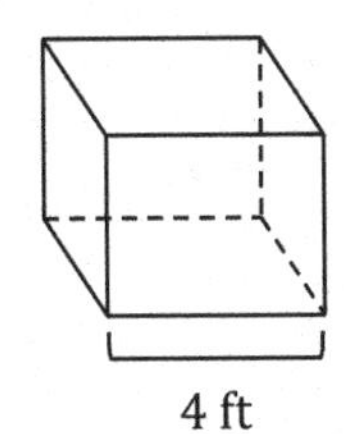

9. If a box has a volume of 48 cubic feet, and its length and width each measure 4 feet, what is its height?

10. In the figure below, the cube 2 has a side length that is twice that of the cube 1. What is the ratio of the volume of cube 1 to the volume of cube 2?

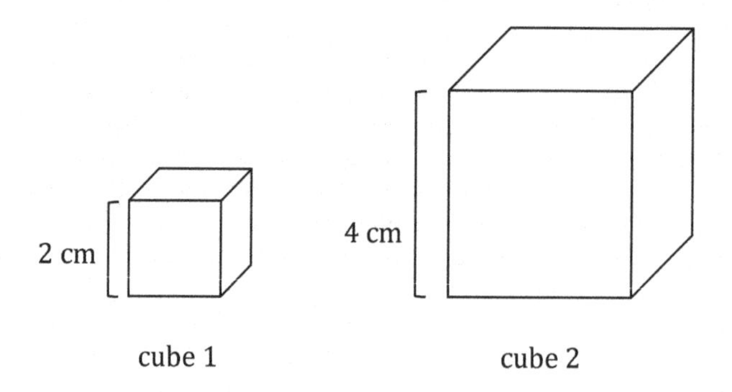

11. If a cube has a volume of 27 cubic meters, what is the length of one of its edges?

12. Jake is painting the outside of a cube that measures 6 inches on each edge. How many square inches of paint will he need?

13. How many edges does a pentagonal prism have?

14. How many vertices does a square pyramid have?

15. What is the surface area of a rectangular prism with a height of 7 mm, a width of 5 mm, and a length of 4 mm?

16. Amy is ordering wallpaper for her bedroom, which is 10 feet long by 12 feet wide by 9 feet high. If she wants to completely cover all four walls of her room with wallpaper, how many square feet of wallpaper will she need?

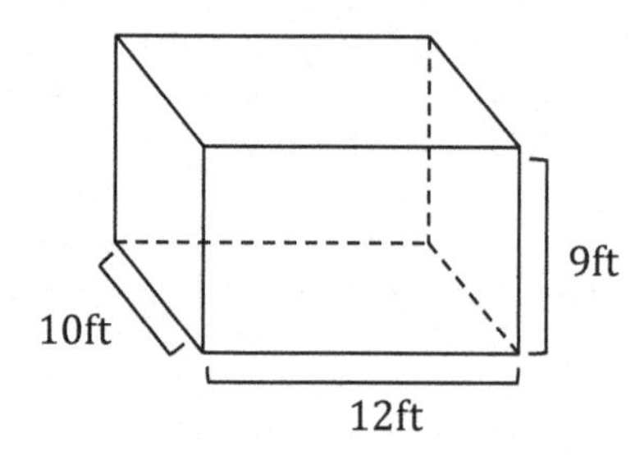

17. What is the volume of the triangular prism below?

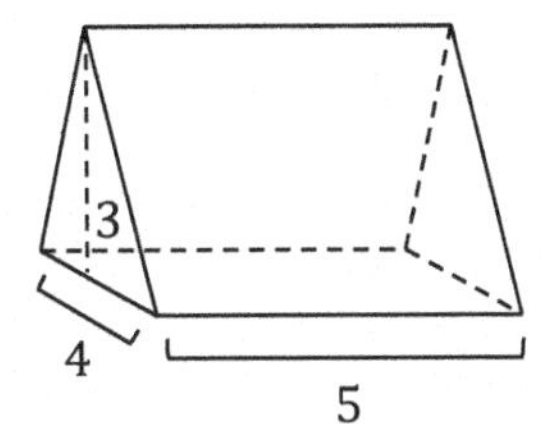

18. If the triangular prism below has a volume of 24, what is the value of x?

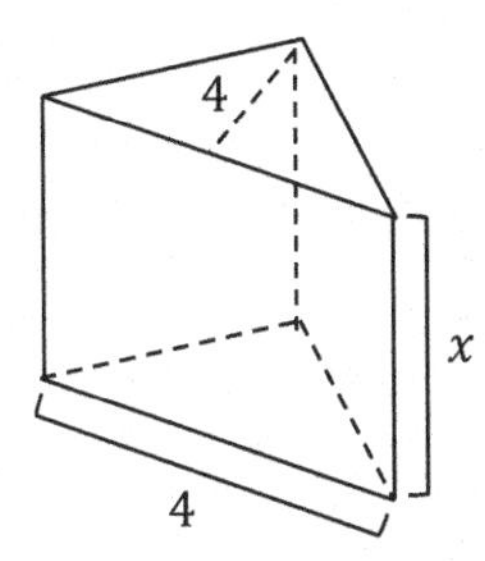

19. A tent manufacturer makes outdoor tents that are 6 meters wide, 4 meters tall, and 12 meters long, as shown below. The walls and the front and back of the tent are made out of canvas held up by a frame, and the bottom of the tent is open. How many square meters of canvas are needed to construct one tent?

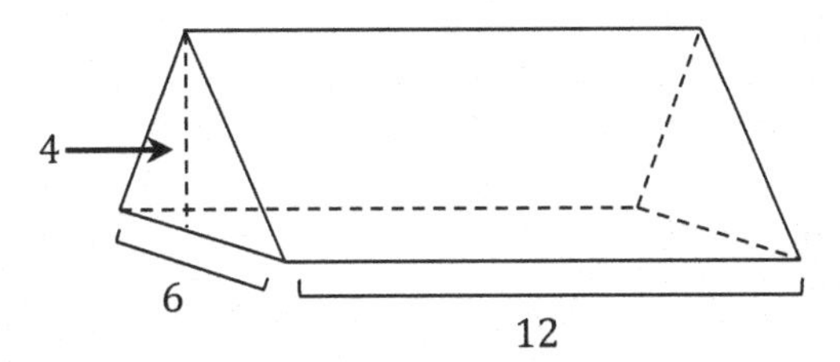

20. A cereal manufacturer ships its cereal boxes in plastic bins that measure 1 meter long, 1 meter wide, and 1.8 meters high. If each cereal box is 30 centimeters long, 5 centimeters wide, and 40 centimeters tall, how many boxes will fit into one plastic bin?

21. All of the edges of the net below are 4 cm. If this net is cut out and folded along its edges to make a solid, what will its volume be?

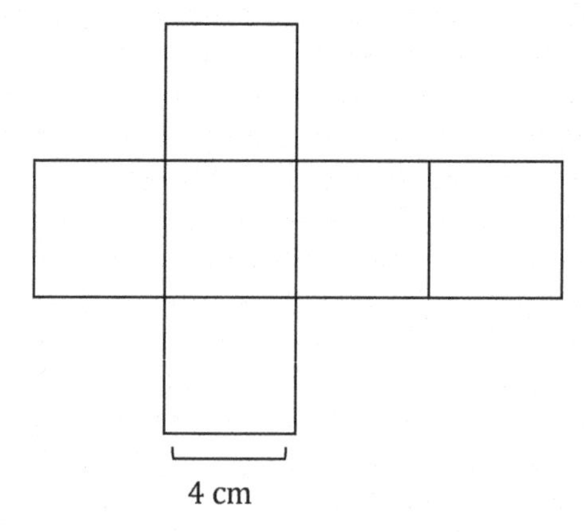

22. If the total surface area of a cube is 150 cm^2, what is its volume?

Questions 23-30 are Upper Level Only.

23. What is the volume of the cylinder below?

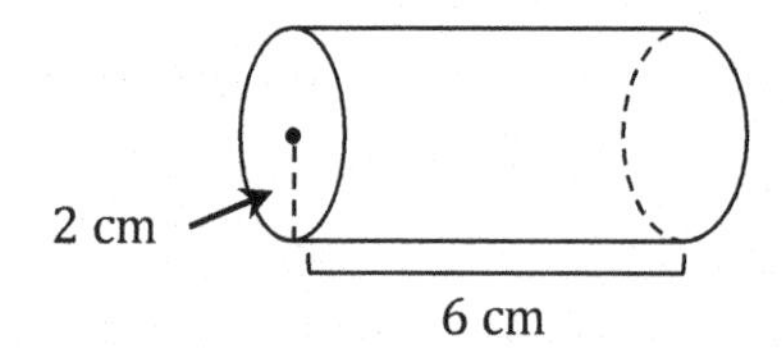

24. What is the surface area of a cylinder with a radius of 5 cm and a height of 8 cm?

25. For a school project, Jerry needs to construct an open tube out of paper with a length of 20 centimeters and a diameter of 5 centimeters. How many square centimeters of paper will he need to construct this tube?

26. A manufacturer of tennis balls wants to package them in rectangular boxes that will fit 40 tennis balls each. If each tennis ball has a diameter of 3 inches, what is the smallest possible volume, in inches cubed, for each box?

27. A golf ball manufacturer packages golf balls in clear cylindrical containers, as shown below. If each golf ball has a diameter of 2 inches, what is the volume of the smallest possible cylindrical container that will fit 4 golf balls?

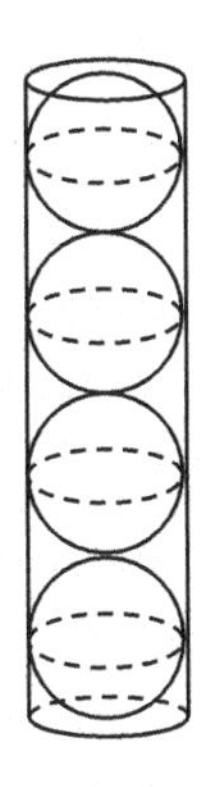

28. Company A and B both sell soda in aluminum cans. Company A's cans have a diameter of 3 inches and a height of 5 inches, and Company B's cans have diameter of 2 inches and a height of 4 inches. How many more square inches of aluminum per can are used by Company A than by Company B?

29. The formula for the volume of a sphere is $V = \frac{4}{3}\pi r^3$. Louis wants to use helium to inflate a perfectly spherical balloon so it has a diameter of 6 inches. How many cubic inches of helium will he need in order to fill the balloon?

30. Given the formula $SA = \pi \times r^2 + \pi \times r \times l$ where $l = \textit{slant height}$, what is the surface area of the cone below?

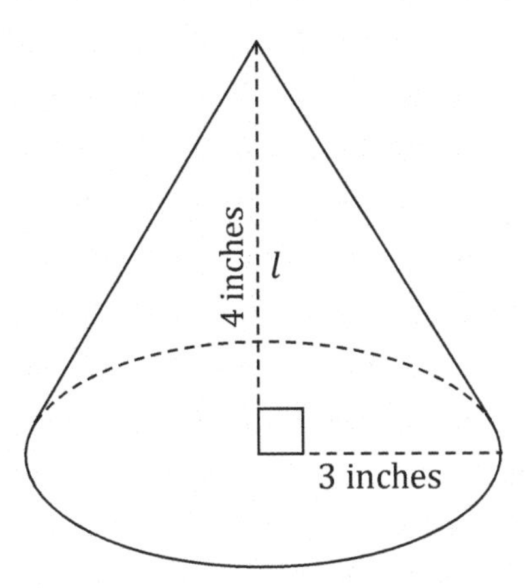

COORDINATE GEOMETRY

ALL LEVELS

SECTION 7

Coordinate geometry is the study of points, lines, and shapes in the coordinate plane. A **plane** is a flat, 2-dimensional surface that has no defined width or length—it stretches forever in both directions.

The coordinate plane is formed by two perpendicular number lines called **axes** (singular: axis). The horizontal number line is called the x-axis because it is marked with the letter x. The vertical number line is called the y-axis because it is marked with the letter y. The point where the two axes intersect is called the **origin**, where both axes have the value of zero:

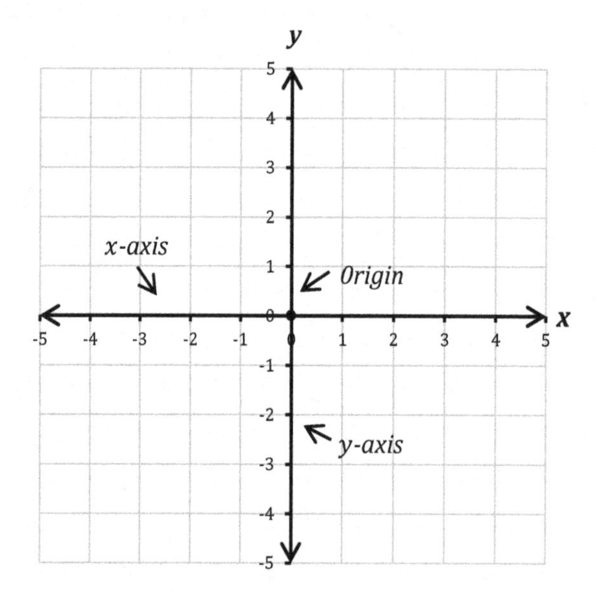

As the diagram shows, values on the x-axis are positive (above zero) to the right of the origin and negative (below zero) to the left of the origin. Values on the y-axis are positive above the origin and negative below the origin:

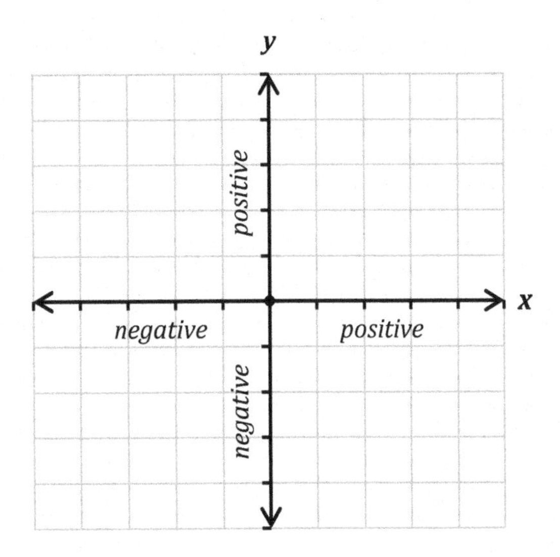

POINTS IN THE COORDINATE PLANE

As you saw in the previous diagram, the x- and y-axes intersect to form a grid. You can find the location of any point on this grid if you know two numbers: the point's horizontal and vertical distance away from the origin. These two numbers are called its **coordinates**. The **x-coordinate** tells you the point's horizontal location along the x-axis, and the **y-coordinate** tells you the point's vertical location along the y-axis.

The coordinates for a point are normally written in parentheses, with the x-coordinate first and the y-coordinate second. This standard way of writing coordinates is called an **ordered pair**. If your point's coordinates were given by the ordered pair $(3, 2)$, this means that 3 is your point's x-coordinate and 2 is your point's y-coordinate. Therefore, your point is a distance of 3 units to the right of the origin and 2 units above it. You would plot this point by finding the intersection of 3 on the x-axis and 2 on the y-axis:

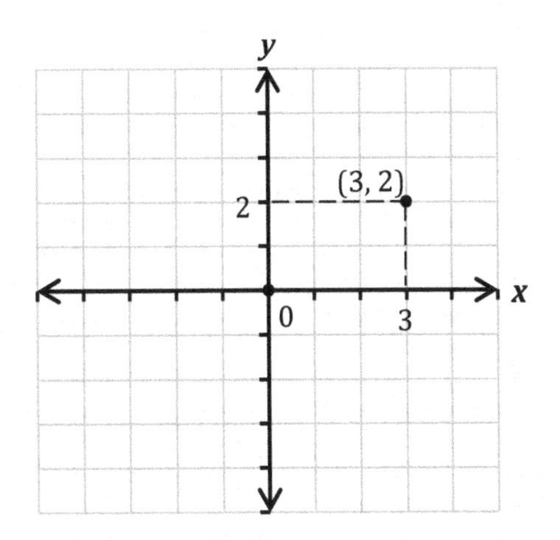

Remember that negative values along the x-axis are found to the left of the origin, and negative values along the y-axis are found below the origin. Therefore, if your point has the coordinates $(-1, -4)$, you would plot this point 1 unit to the left of the origin and 4 units below the origin:

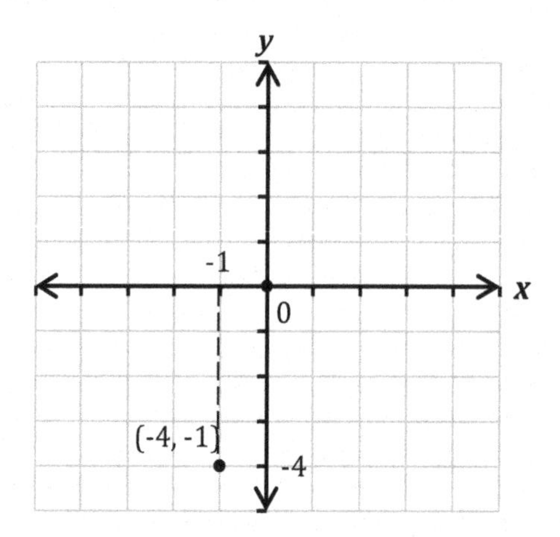

SHAPES IN THE COORDINATE PLANE

If you connect points in the coordinate plane, you can graph a line or shape. For example, in the figure below, we've connected four points to form a parallelogram:

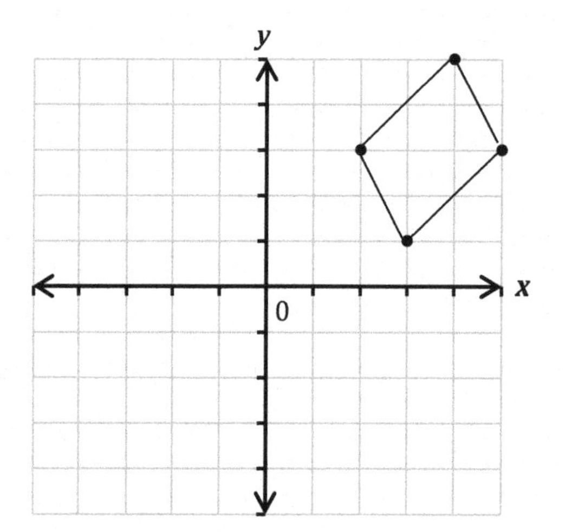

Shapes can also be moved around on the coordinate plane. A translation moves an object horizontally and/or vertically along the coordinate plane without changing its size or shape. A translation basically "slides" an object into another position without changing the direction it faces. An object can be translated a certain number of units horizontally, vertically, or both. The following diagrams show what happens when a triangle is translated horizontally 6 units to the left or vertically 6 units down:

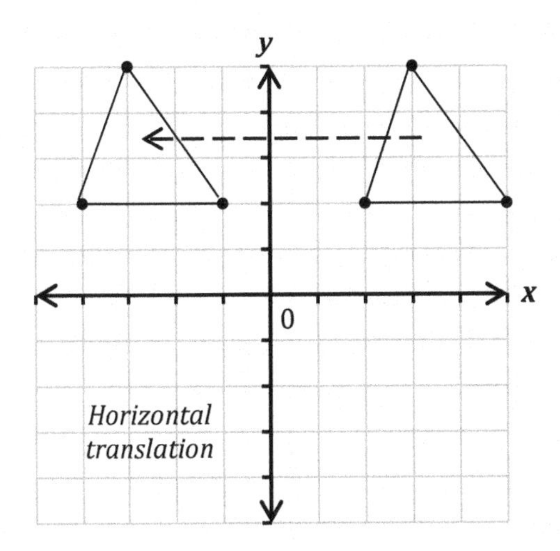

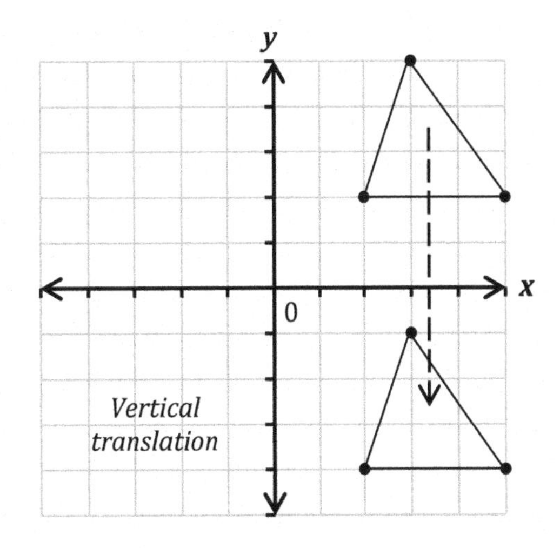

What if you need to translate an object both horizontally and vertically? Move each one of its points the same vertical and horizontal distance. In the diagram below, we can translate parallelogram $EFGH$ six units to the right and five units up by moving each point the same distance:

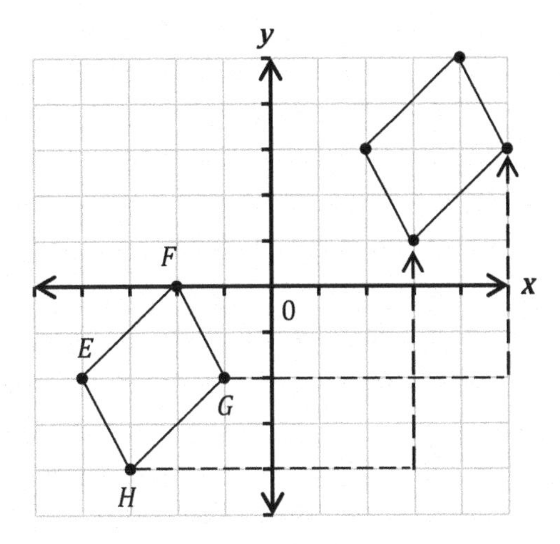

The dotted arrows show how points G and H are each moved horizontally 6 units and vertically 5 units. To complete the parallelogram, points E and F are moved in the same way.

A **rotation** occurs when an object is "turned" around a point called the **center of rotation**. If an object is rotated 90°, it appears to be on its side. If it is rotated 180°, it appears to be upside-down. If an object is rotated 360°, it comes "full circle" back to its original position because there are a total of 360 degrees in a circle.

Look at what happens when the triangle below is rotated 90° and 180° around the origin:

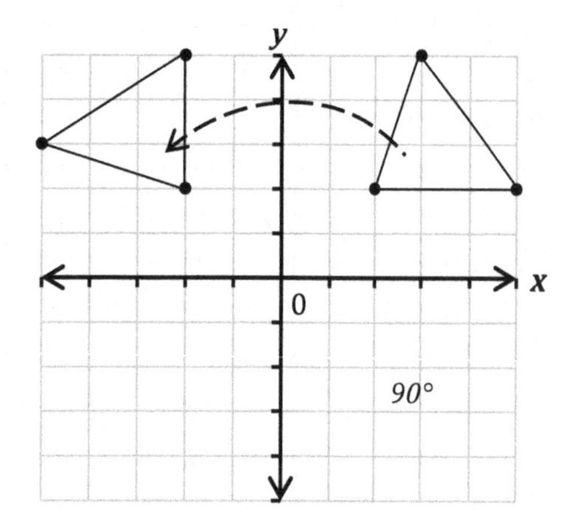

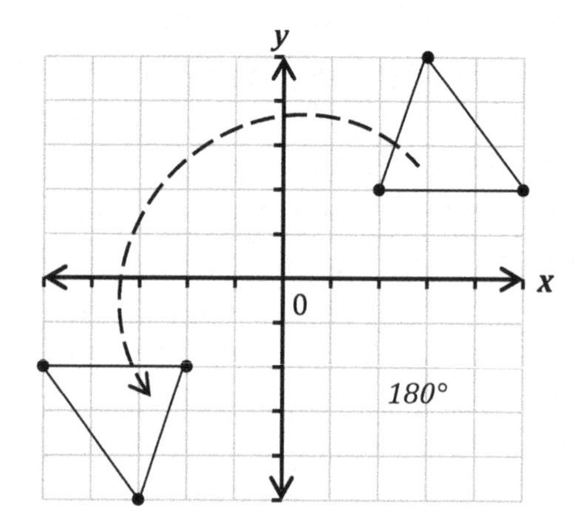

A **reflection** of an object takes place when an object is "flipped" over a line called the **line of reflection**. The new object will be facing the opposite direction, like a mirror image of the original object. In the coordinate plane, a line or shape can be reflected over any line or axis. In the diagrams below, look what happens when a triangle is reflected horizontally over the y-axis or reflected vertically over the x-axis:

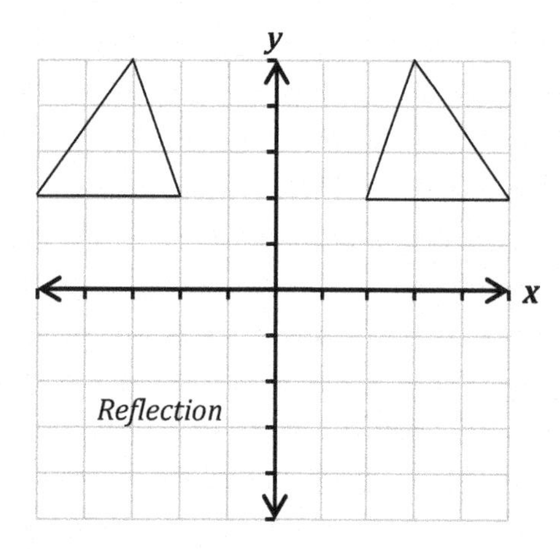

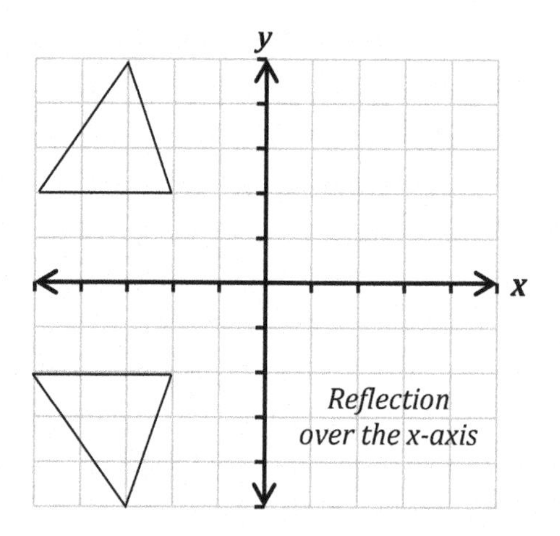

A figure has **reflectional symmetry** if it could be folded along an imaginary line so that its two halves match up perfectly. In other words, the two halves on either side of this line must be "reflections" or mirror images of each other. This line is called a **line of symmetry**. A figure may have multiple lines of symmetry or none at all. Here are some examples:

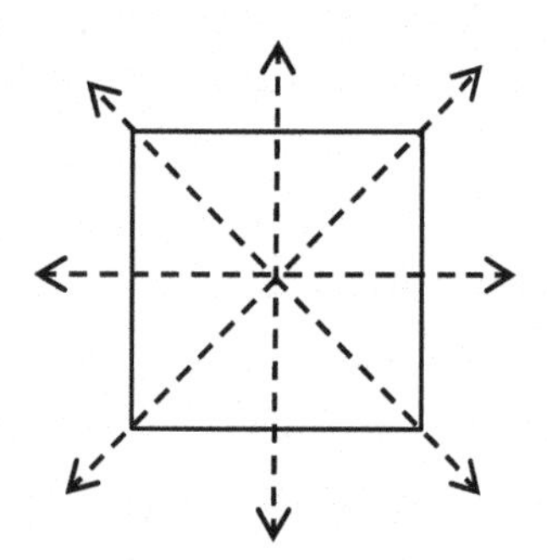

4 lines of symmetry

1 line of symmetry

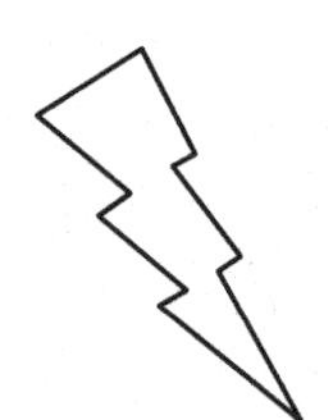

0 lines of symmetry

VIDEO
3.15 REFLECTIONS, ROTATIONS, AND TRANSLATIONS
Watch at http:// videos.ivyglobal.com

QUADRANTS (MIDDLE/UPPER LEVEL ONLY)

The axes of the coordinate plane divide it into four areas called **quadrants**. These are numbered counter-clockwise beginning with the top right quadrant:

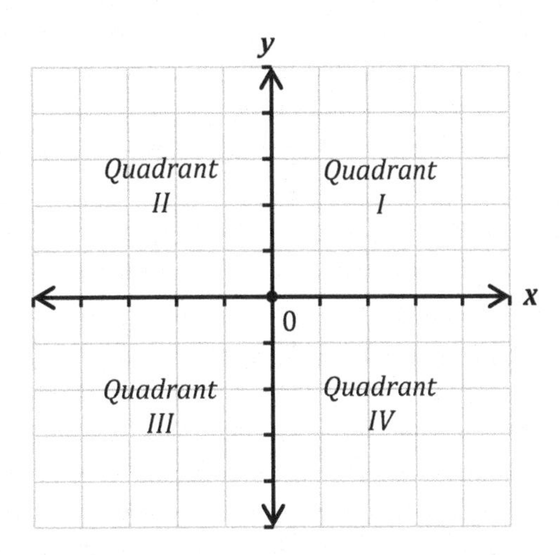

If you know what quadrant a point is in, you know whether its coordinates are positive or negative. For example, both the x- and y-coordinates of any point in Quadrant I are positive, and both the x-and y-coordinates of any point in Quadrant III are negative. The chart below summarizes this information:

TYPES OF POLYGONS		
	x-coordinates	y-coordinates
Quadrant I	+	+
Quadrant II	−	+
Quadrant III	−	−
Quadrant IV	+	−

With this information, you can find the coordinates of any point as long as you know its quadrant and its horizontal and vertical distance away from the origin.

For example:

> A point in Quadrant IV is 2 horizontal units and 5 vertical units away from the origin. Plot this point on a graph on a separate piece of paper.

If you were just told that the point is 2 horizontal units and 5 vertical units away from the origin, you wouldn't know whether these coordinates should be positive or negative. But since you were told that the point is in Quadrant IV, you know its x-coordinate will be positive and its y-coordinate will be negative, so its coordinates must be $(2, -5)$:

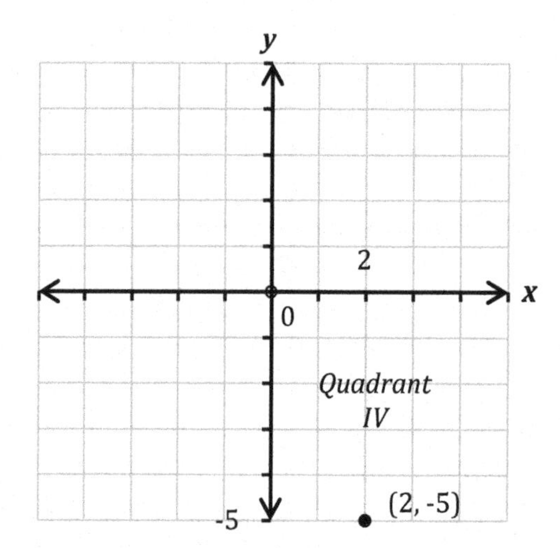

LENGTH AND AREA IN THE COORDINATE PLANE (MIDDLE/UPPER LEVEL ONLY)

You may be asked to find the length of a line segment drawn in the coordinate plane. To find the length of a horizontal line segment, calculate the difference between its two x-coordinates. To find the length of a vertical line segment, calculate the difference between its y-coordinates.

For example:

Find the length of the line segments $\overline{AB}$ and $\overline{AC}$:

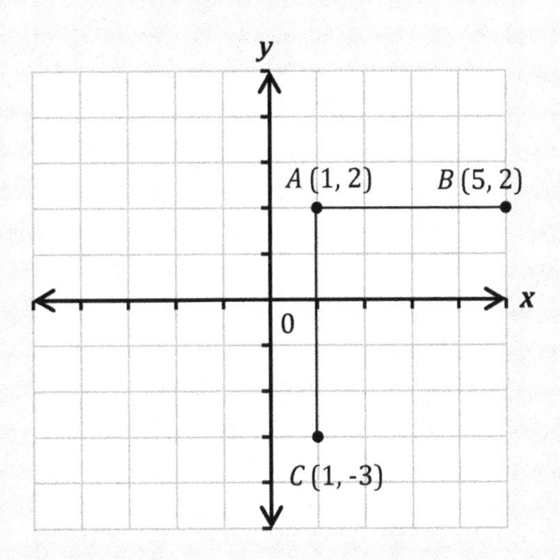

The x-coordinates of the horizontal line segment $\overline{AB}$ are 1 and 5, so the length of $\overline{AB}$ is $5 - 1 = 4$ units. The y-coordinates of the vertical line segment $\overline{AC}$ are 2 and -3, so the length of $\overline{AC}$ is $2 - (-3) = 5$ units.

It doesn't matter in which order you choose to subtract, but remember that the length of a segment is always positive. If you end up with a negative number, just reverse the sign. And if this sounds too complicated, remember that you're only dealing with number lines—you can always double-check your work by counting the spaces between two points!

You can use your knowledge of distances in the coordinate plane in order to calculate the areas of polygons.

For example:

Find the area of triangle JKL below.

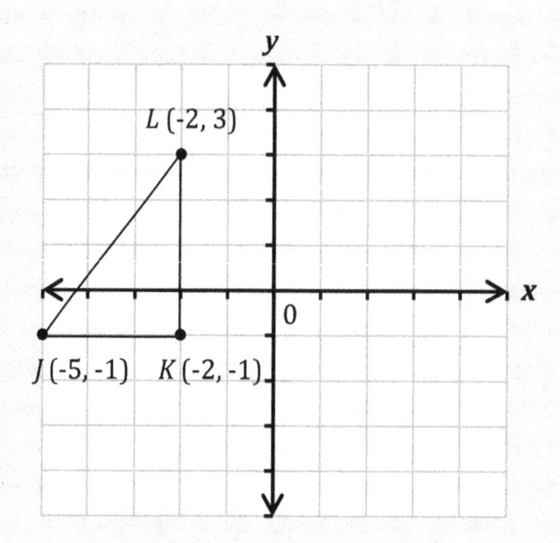

To find the area of triangle JKL, we need to find the length of its base and height. Its base is the horizontal line segment $\overline{JK}$, and we can find the length of $\overline{JK}$ by subtracting the x-coordinates of points J and K:

$$JK = -2 - (-5) = 3$$

The height of the triangle is the vertical line segment $\overline{KL}$, and we can find the length of $\overline{KL}$ by subtracting the y-coordinates of points K and L:

$$KL = 3 - (-1) = 4$$

Now that we know that the base of the triangle is 3 and the height is 4, we can use our formula for finding the area of a triangle:

$$Area = \frac{1}{2} \times 3 \times 4 = 6$$

The area of triangle JKL is 6 square units.

VIDEO

3.12 INTRO TO COORDINATE GEOMETRY

Watch at http:// videos.ivyglobal.com

DISTANCE USING THE PYTHAGOREAN THEOREM (UPPER LEVEL ONLY)

What if you were asked the following question about the previous figure?

What is the length of line segment $\overline{JL}$ in triangle JKL?

This is not a horizontal or vertical line segment, so you can't simply take the difference of the x- or y-coordinates.

However, $\overline{JL}$ is the hypotenuse of a right triangle, so you can use the Pythagorean Theorem:

$$a^2 + b^2 = c^2$$

In the section above, we determined that the two legs of the triangle, $\overline{JK}$ and $\overline{KL}$, had lengths of 3 and 4, respectively. We can square these lengths and add them together to get the square of the hypotenuse, then solve for the missing length:

$$JK^2 + KL^2 = JL^2$$
$$3^2 + 4^2 = JL^2$$
$$25 = JL^2$$
$$JL = \sqrt{25} = 5$$

Therefore, the line segment $\overline{JL}$ is 5 units long. (*For a review on solving right triangles with the Pythagorean Theorem, see Part 3, Section 4 in this math review*).

This method can be used to find the length of any line segment in the coordinate plane. Even if the line segment is not the hypotenuse of a right triangle, you can draw an imaginary right triangle and use these imaginary sides to solve for the length of your segment.

For example:

What is the length of the line segment $\overline{MN}$ in the diagram below?

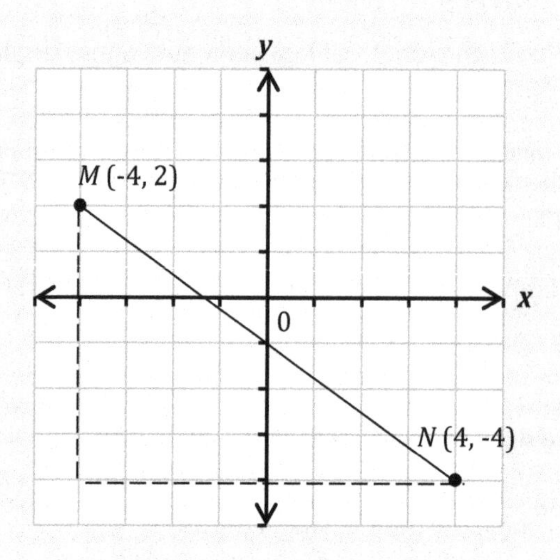

The dotted lines above show the legs of the imaginary right triangle that we have drawn with $\overline{MN}$ as its hypotenuse. To find the length of the horizontal leg, we can just subtract the x-coordinates of M and N: $4 - (-4) = 8$ units. To find the length of the vertical leg, we subtract the y-coordinates of M and N: $2 - (-4) = 6$ units.

We can then use the Pythagorean Theorem to solve for the length of $\overline{MN}$:

$$8^2 + 6^2 = MN^2$$

$$100 = MN^2$$

$$MN = \sqrt{100} = 10$$

$\overline{MN}$ is 10 units long.

VIDEO

3.14 DISTANCE USING THE PYTHAGOREAN THEOREM

Watch at http:// videos.ivyglobal.com

PRACTICE QUESTIONS: COORDINATE GEOMETRY

For questions 1-5, refer to the diagram to the right.

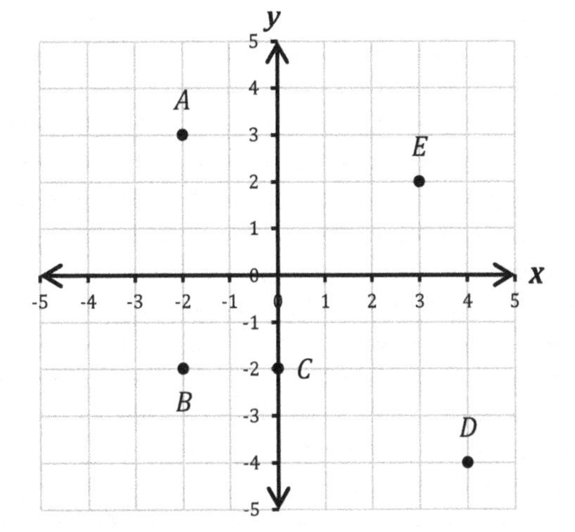

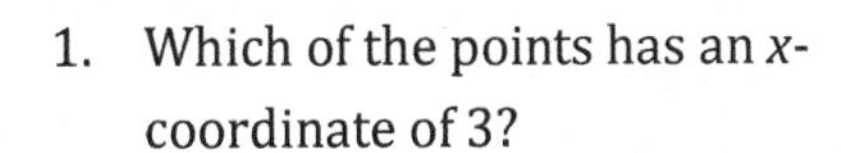

1. Which of the points has an x-coordinate of 3?

2. Which two points have y-coordinates of -2?

3. Which point has the coordinates $(4, -4)$?

4. What are the coordinates of point A?

5. Erin wants to plot a point three units to the right of point B and five units above. What will be the coordinates of her point?

6. Consider the letters below. Which letter has more than one line of symmetry?

(A) **M**

(B) **H**

(C) **P**

(D) **D**

7. Which of the following figures shows triangle ABC and its 90° rotation about the origin?

(A)

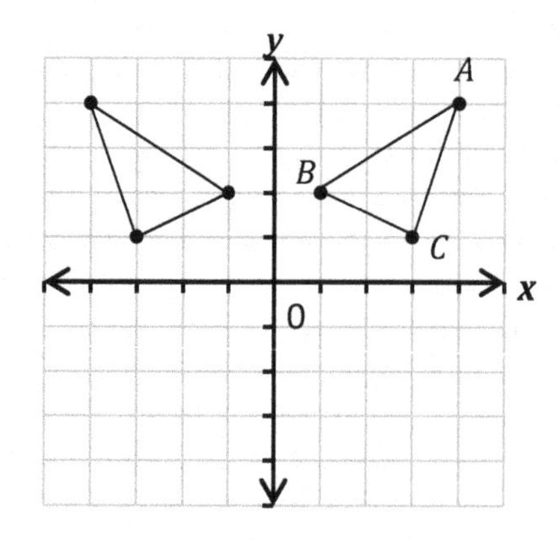

(C)

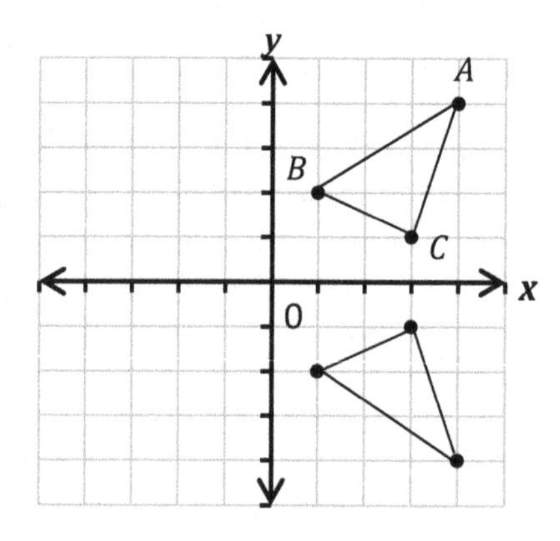

(B)

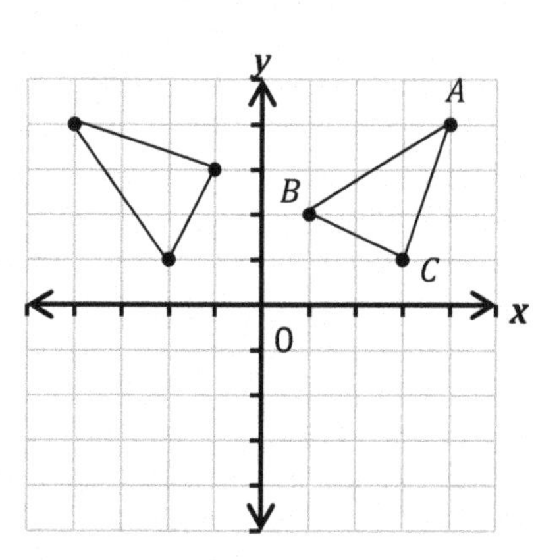

(D)

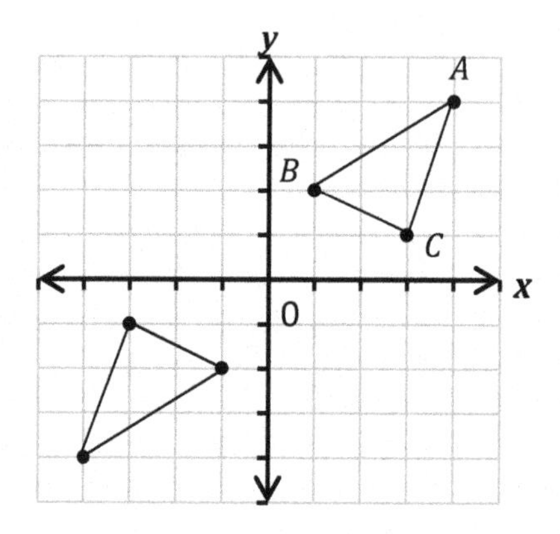

For questions 8-12, refer to the diagram to the right.

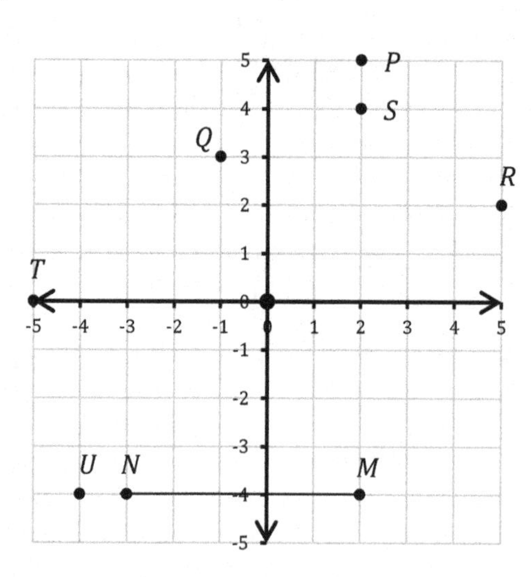

8. Which point has coordinates $(2, 5)$?

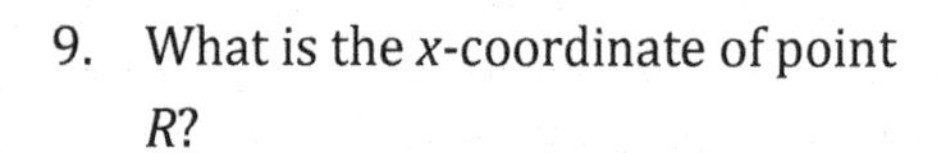

9. What is the x-coordinate of point R?

10. Georgios starts at point Q, and plots a new point 5 units to the right and 3 units down. What is the coordinate of his new point?

Questions 11-18 are Middle/Upper Level Only.

11. In which quadrant is point M located?

12. What is the length of line segment $\overline{MN}$?

13. Mike has plotted a point located four vertical units and five horizontal units away from the origin. If this point is located in Quadrant II, what are its coordinates?

14. What is the length of line segment $\overline{GH}$ in the diagram below?

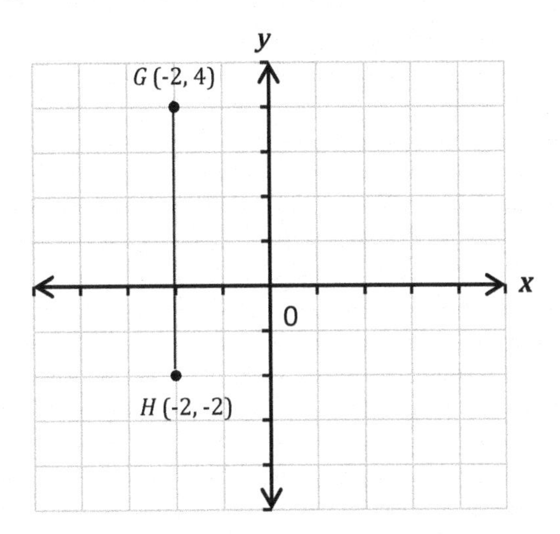

15. Sarah has drawn a line segment whose endpoints have the coordinates $(2, 4)$ and $(-2, 4)$. What is the length of this line segment?

16. What is the perimeter of rectangle *KLMN* in the diagram below?

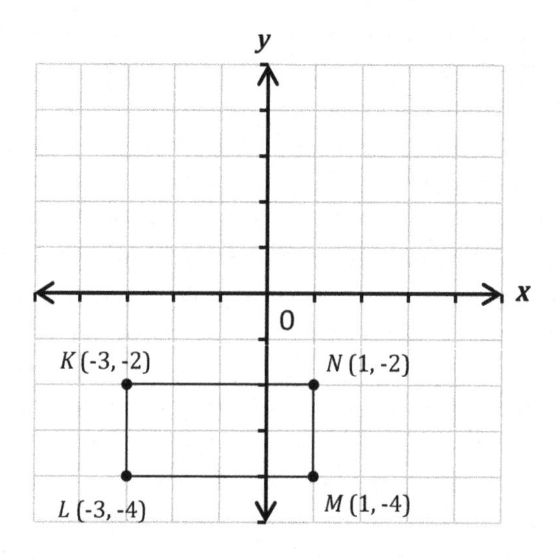

17. What is the area of the shaded triangle in the figure below?

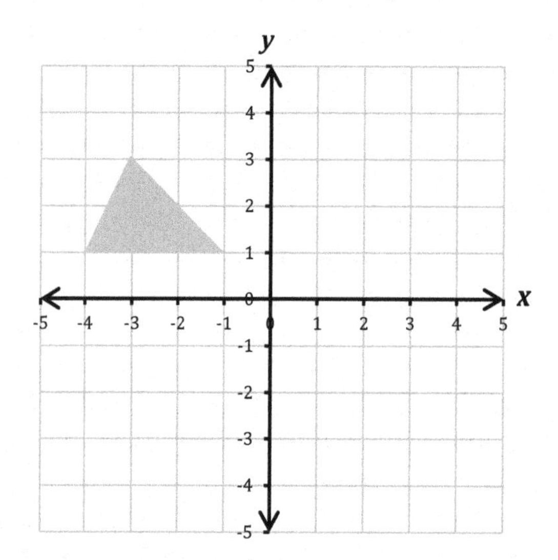

18. One vertex of the parallelogram *HIJK* was accidentally erased from the figure below. What were the coordinates of the missing vertex?

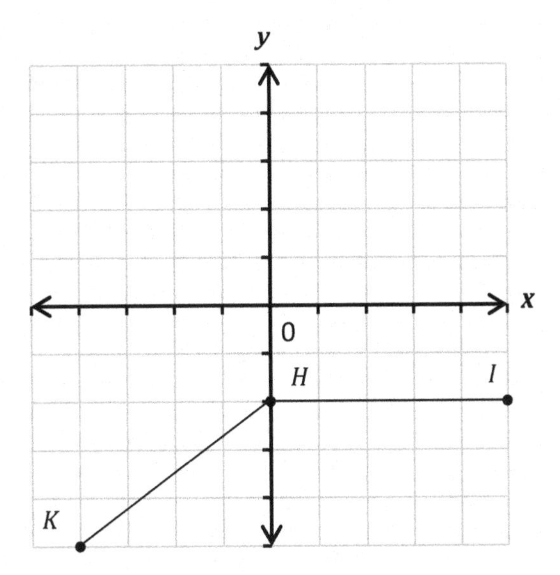

19. What is the length of line segment $\overline{RS}$ in the diagram below?

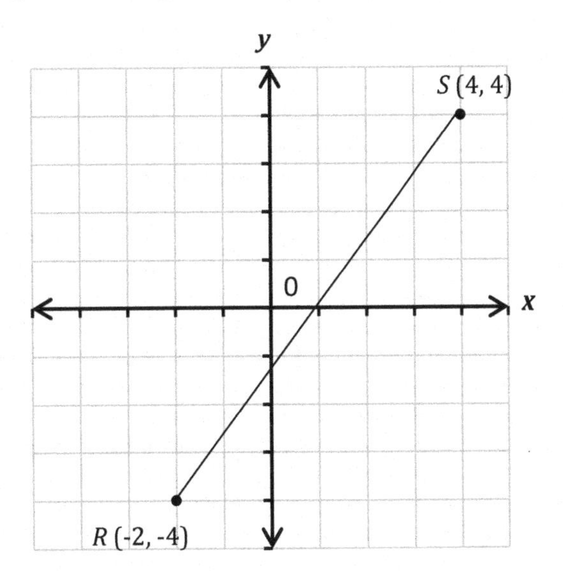

20. What is the perimeter of parallelogram $HIJK$ in the diagram below?

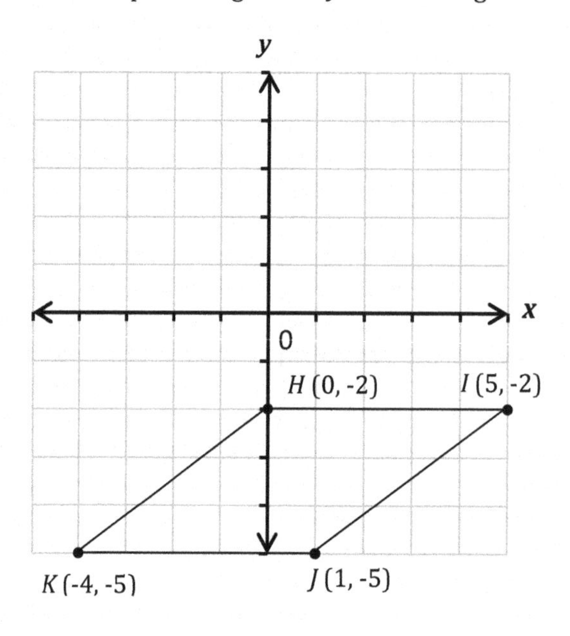

21. What is the perimeter of the triangle shown below?

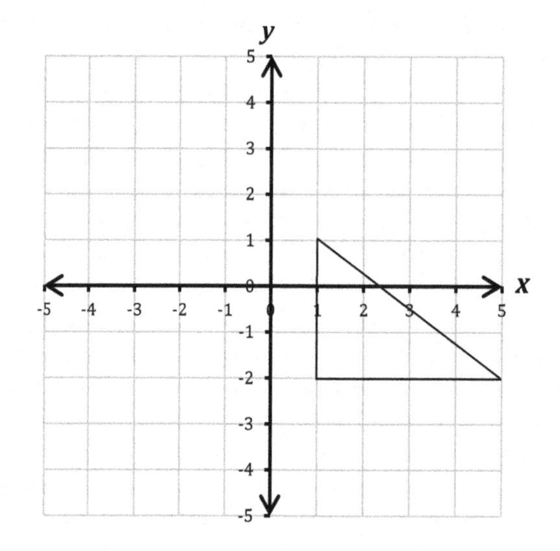

GRAPHS OF FUNCTIONS

MIDDLE/UPPER LEVEL ONLY

SECTION 8

A **function** is a relationship between two sets of data. In Part 2, we briefly talked about functions as "input" and "output" rules. A function shows how an "input" value is transformed into an "output" value. In other words, every value from the first set of data is associated with exactly one value from the set of second set of data.

To graph a function, we represent the first set of data points along the x axis and the second set of data points along the y axis. Each x-value of the function (the input value) is graphed with its corresponding y-value (its output value). These two values are written as an **ordered pair**, which is graphed as a point in the coordinate plane. Graphing a function means graphing all of the ordered pairs that result from that function. Here is an example:

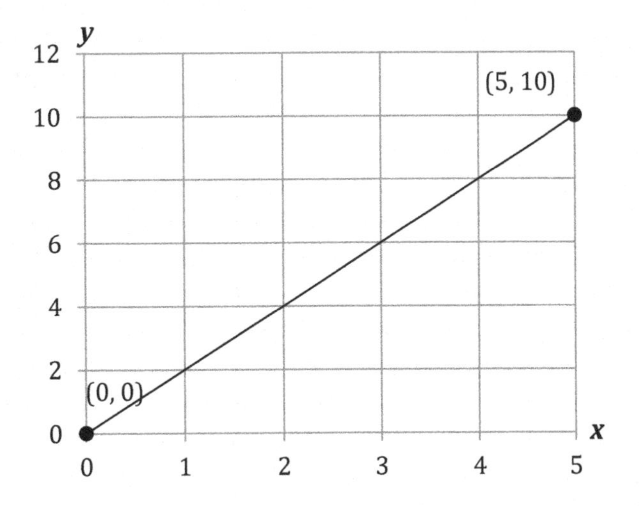

This function shows a set of ordered pairs, where each x-value corresponds to exactly one y-value. For example, the point (5, 10) is an ordered pair in this function, which tells us that an input of 5 gives an output of 10. The point (0, 0) is another ordered pair in this function, which tells us that an input of 0 gives an output of 0. Not every point is labelled on this function. However, we can assume that all of the points that the line passes through are points that belong to the function.

GRAPHS OF LINEAR FUNCTIONS

A **linear function** is a function that has a constant rate of change. This means that every time the x value changes by one, the y value will increase or decrease by a set amount. This type of function is called "linear" because its graph looks like a straight line. The graph on the previous page is an example of a linear function. Every time the x value increases by one, the y value increases by 2.

Any linear function can be written as an equation in the form:

$$y = mx + b$$

In this equation, every value of x is multiplied by m and added to b in order to generate a value for y. The constant b represents the **y-intercept**, which is the point where the line crosses the y-axis. If the equation of a line does not have a value for b, then $b = 0$. This means that the line intersects the y-axis where y equals 0.

The equations of the two lines below differ only in their values of b. You can see that the two lines intersect the y-axis at different points corresponding to the values of b in their equations:

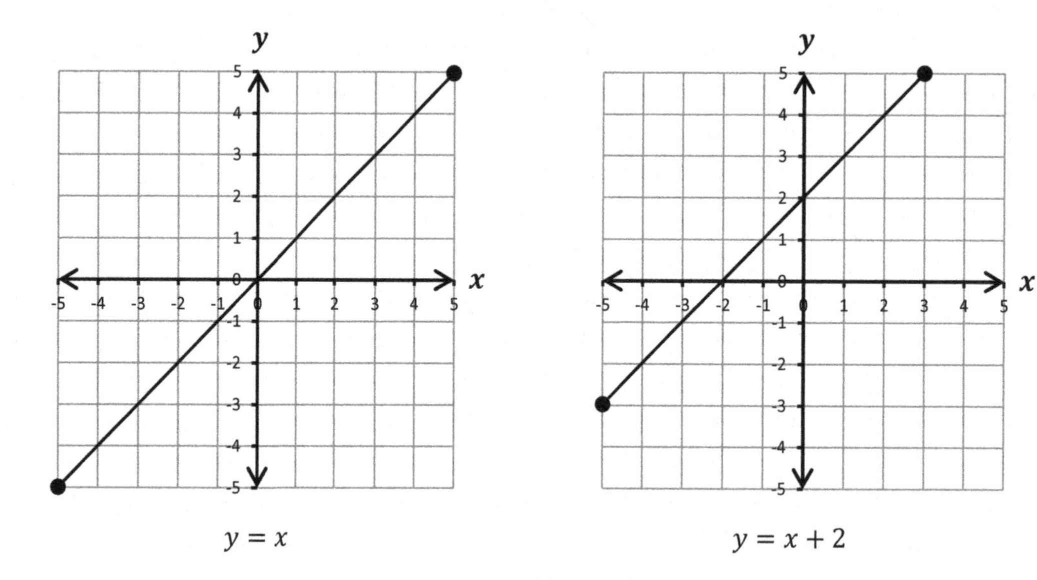

$y = x$ $\qquad$ $y = x + 2$

In the equation $y = x$, there is no value for b, which means that the line intersects the y-axis at 0. In the equation $y = x + 2$, b has a value of 2. This means that the line intersects the y-axis at 2.

The constant m is the slope of the line. The **slope** of a line segment tells us how steeply it is going upwards or downwards. This "steepness" can also be described as the **rate of change** between two points.

In order to determine the slope of a line, divide **rise over run**. In other words, subtract the y-values of any two points (the rise), subtract the x-values of the same two points (the run), and divide the result:

$$m = \frac{rise}{run} = \frac{y_2 - y_1}{x_2 - x_1}$$

Here is what rise and run look like on a graph:

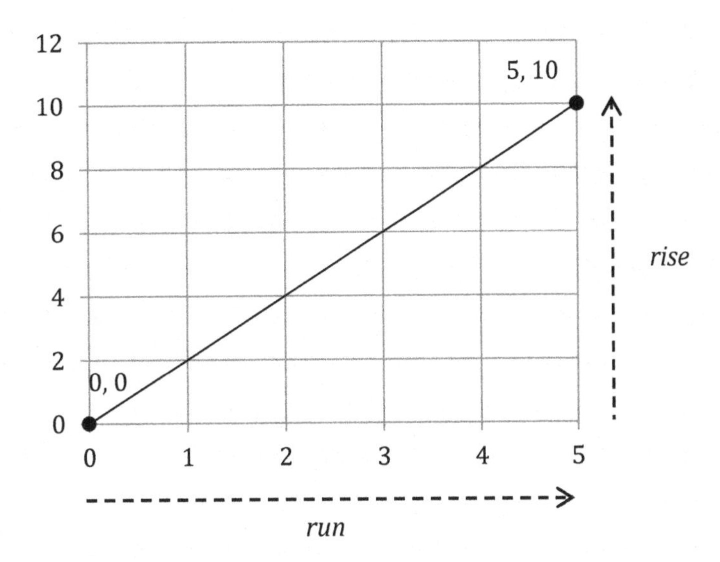

To calculate the slope of the line above, we need to calculate the rise and run between any two points that we know are on the line. We could use any points on the line, but let's use the two points that are labelled: (5, 10) and (0, 0). To find the slope of the line, we find the difference between the two y-values of these points (the rise), and we divide by the difference between the two x-values (the run):

$$m = \frac{rise}{run} = \frac{y_2 - y_1}{x_2 - x_1} = \frac{10 - 0}{5 - 0} = \frac{10}{5} = 2$$

The slope of the line is 2. This means that when x increases by 1, y increases by 2.

For example:

What is the slope of a line connecting the two points (5, 5) and (-5, 7)?

Using the formula above, we can find the rise by subtracting the y-values and then find the run by subtracting the x-values. Then, we'll divide these two differences:

$$m = \frac{rise}{run} = \frac{7 - 5}{-5 - 5} = \frac{2}{-10} = -\frac{1}{5}$$

The slope of this line is $-\frac{1}{5}$. This means that every time x increases by 1, y decreases by $\frac{1}{5}$.

WRITING A LINEAR EQUATION

Now that we know all of the components of a linear equation, we can use the formula $y = mx + b$ to write a linear equation connecting any two points in the coordinate plane.

Here is an example:

What is the equation of the line that passes through the two points (5, 5) and (-5, 7)?

In order to create an equation in the form $y = mx + b$, we need to find the values of m and of b. In the previous example, we saw that the slope of the line connecting these two points is $-\frac{1}{5}$. Therefore, we can plug in $-\frac{1}{5}$ for m in our formula:

$$y = -\frac{1}{5}x + b$$

In order to finish this equation, we need to find the value of b, the y-intercept. We can determine this value by plugging in the x and y values of one point on the line into our formula. Let's use our point at (-5, 7). We can plug in -5 for x and 7 for y into our formula and then solve for b:

$$y = -\frac{1}{5}x + b$$

$$7 = \left(-\frac{1}{5}\right)(-5) + b$$

$$7 = 1 + b$$

$$6 = b$$

The y-intercept of our line is 6. When we plug in 6 for b in our formula, we have the full equation for our line:

$$y = -\frac{1}{5}x + 6$$

A simple way to check this result is by using the second point we are given for our line: (5, 5). If we plug the x value (5) into our equation, we should get a y value of 5 as well:

$$y = -\frac{1}{5} \times 5 + 6$$

$$y = -1 + 6$$

$$y = 5$$

For an x value of 5, we have calculated 5 as the y value. This corresponds with our point (5, 5), so we know that we have found the correct equation for this line.

KEY FACTS ABOUT SLOPE

A line pointing upwards from left to right means that as x increases, y increases as well, so its slope is positive. A line pointing downwards from left to right means that as x increases, y decreases, so its slope is negative. The steeper a line is, the faster y is changing as x changes, so the slope will be more positive or more negative.

A **horizontal line** has a slope of zero. For example:

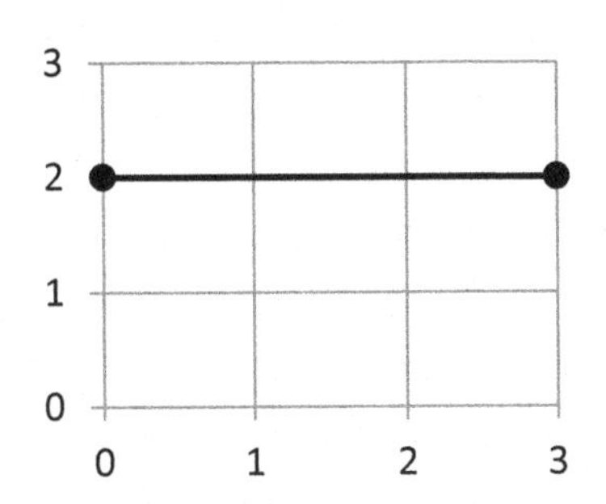

$$m = \frac{rise}{run} = \frac{0}{3} = 0$$

For this line, the slope is zero because when x changes, y does not change at all. No matter what value is plugged in for x, y will always stay the same.

A **vertical line** has an undefined slope. For example:

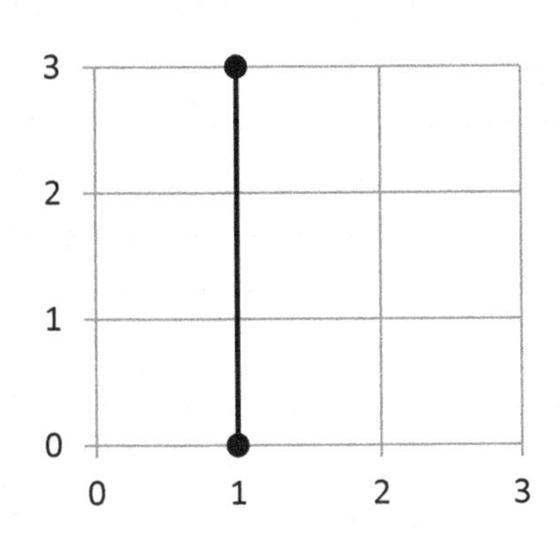

$$m = \frac{rise}{run} = \frac{3}{0} = undefined$$

The slope of this line is undefined because it is impossible to divide by zero. The purpose of a linear function is to tell us what the value of y will be for a given value of x. In this graph, an x value of 1 could give a y value of 0, 1, 2, or 3. Since we cannot determine one value of y for one value of x, this graph cannot be a linear function with the equation of $y = mx + b$.

Non-vertical **parallel lines** have equal slopes.

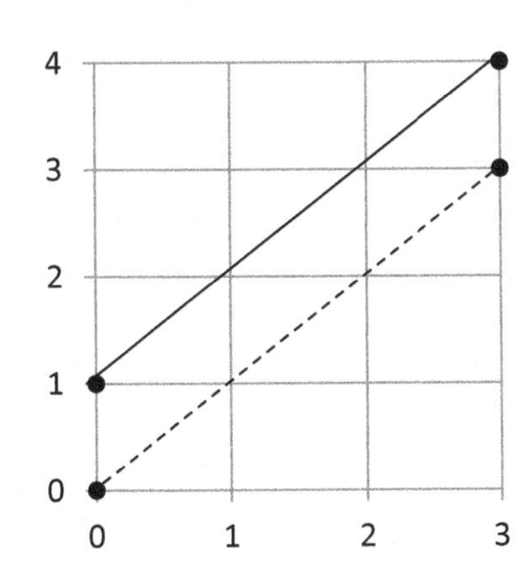

Parallel lines never intersect. Therefore, two lines that are parallel must always have the exact same steepness. They both need to be changing at the same rate.

In the graph on the left, both lines have a slope of $m = 1$. However, the solid line has a y-intercept of $b = 1$, while the dashed line has a y-intercept of $b = 0$.

Non-vertical **perpendicular** lines have slopes whose product is -1.

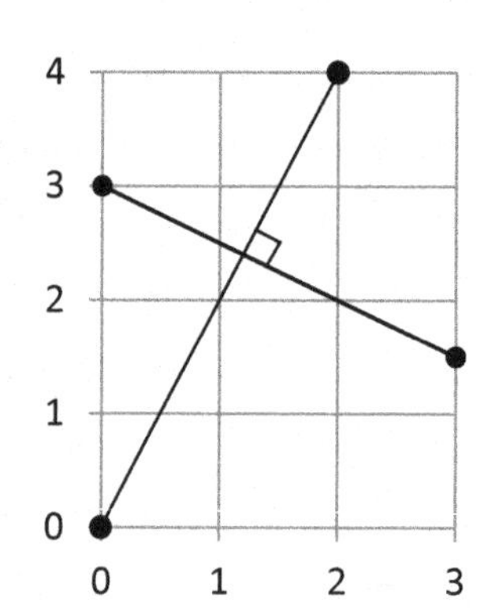

The slope of the dashed line is: $\frac{rise}{run} = \frac{-1.5}{3} = -\frac{1}{2}$.

The slope of the solid line is: $\frac{rise}{run} = \frac{4}{2} = 2$.

The product of these two slopes is: $-\frac{1}{2} \times 2 = -1$.

If the slope of a line is m, the slope of the line perpendicular to it will be $\frac{-1}{m}$.

Here is an example of a question involving slope:

Line P has a slope of $-\frac{1}{5}$. Line Q passes through the points $(k, 7)$ and $(-1, -3)$. If Line P and Line Q are perpendicular, what is the value of k?

First, we need to figure out the slope of Line Q. We know that Line P has a slope of $-\frac{1}{5}$, and that Line Q is perpendicular to Line P. Therefore, we know that the product of Line P's slope and Line Q's slope is -1. Let's write this product with m standing for Line Q's slope:

$$-\frac{1}{5}\, m = -1$$

Now, we can solve for m:

$$-\frac{1}{5}m = -1$$
$$m = 5$$

We've found that Line Q has a slope of 5. We can now plug this into our formula for slope to find the value of k:

$$m = \frac{rise}{run} = \frac{y_2 - y_1}{x_2 - x_1}$$
$$5 = \frac{y_2 - y_1}{x_2 - x_1}$$

Using the coordinates in the two points given, we can plug in 7 for y_1, -3 for y_2, k for x_1, and -1 for x_2:

$$5 = \frac{y_2 - y_1}{x_2 - x_1}$$
$$5 = \frac{-3 - 7}{-1 - k}$$

$$5(-1-k) = -10$$
$$-1-k = -2$$
$$k = 1$$

The value of k is 1.

PRACTICE QUESTIONS: GRAPHS OF FUNCTIONS

For questions 1-7, calculate the slope of the line connecting the two points given.

1. $(0,0)$ and $(2,2)$

2. $(2,3)$ and $(4,6)$

3. $(-2,3)$ and $(2,7)$

4. $(-5,2)$ and $(0,1)$

5. $(-5,2)$ and $(1,-1)$

6. $(5,2)$ and $(0,-1)$

7. $(-5,-2)$ and $(-7,-1)$

For questions 8-10, refer to the graph below.

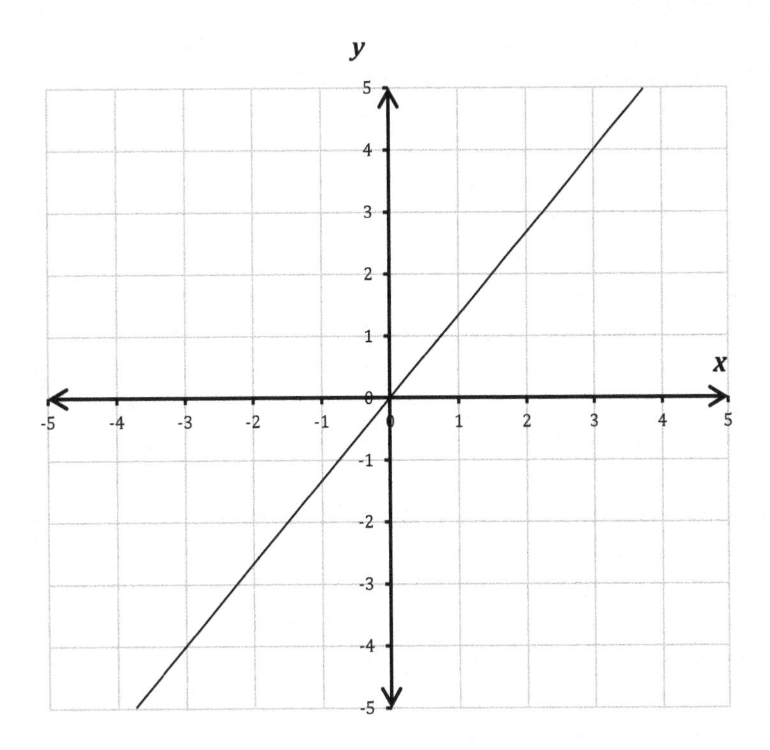

8. What is the y-intercept of this line?

9. What is the slope of this line?

10. What is the equation for this line, in the form $y = mx + b$?

For questions 11-13, refer to the graph below.

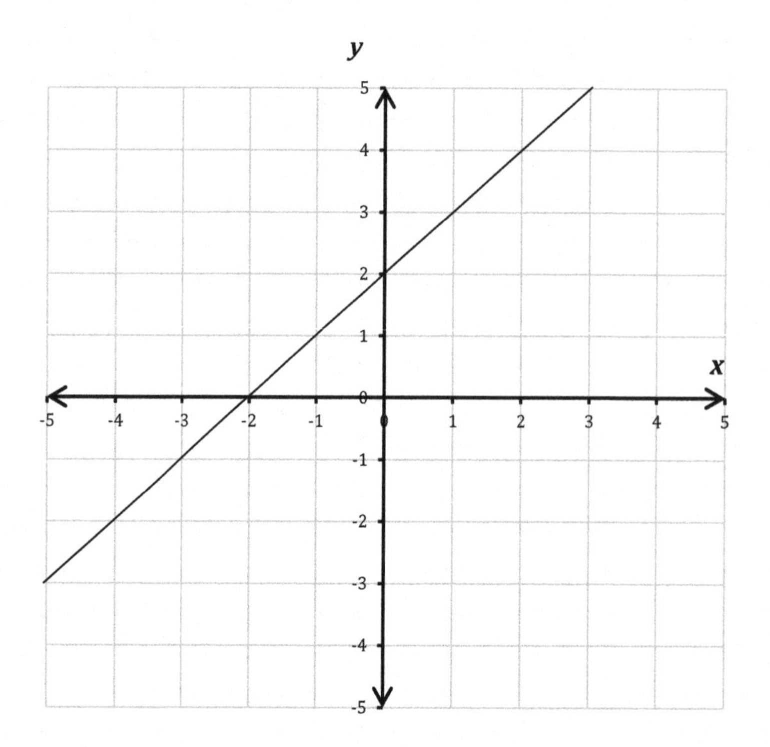

11. What is the y-intercept of this line?

12. What is the slope of this line?

13. What is the equation for this line, in the form $y = mx + b$?

14. What is the equation for the line below, in the form $y = mx + b$?

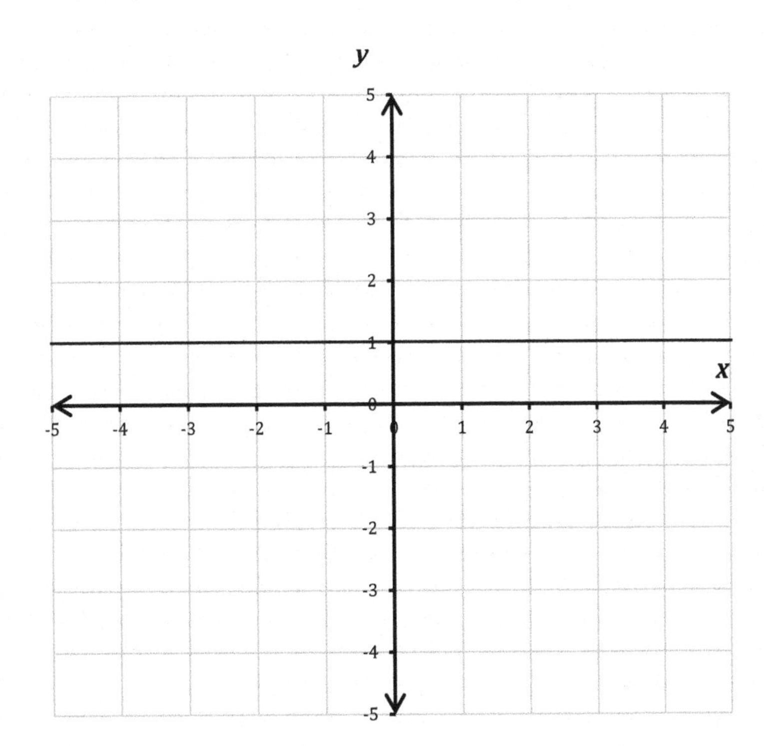

For questions 15-18, calculate the slope of a line perpendicular to the function given.

15. $y = x + 5$

16. $y = -2x$

17. $y = -\frac{1}{3}x + 30$

18. $y = \frac{1}{5}x - 25$

For questions 19-20, refer to the graph below.

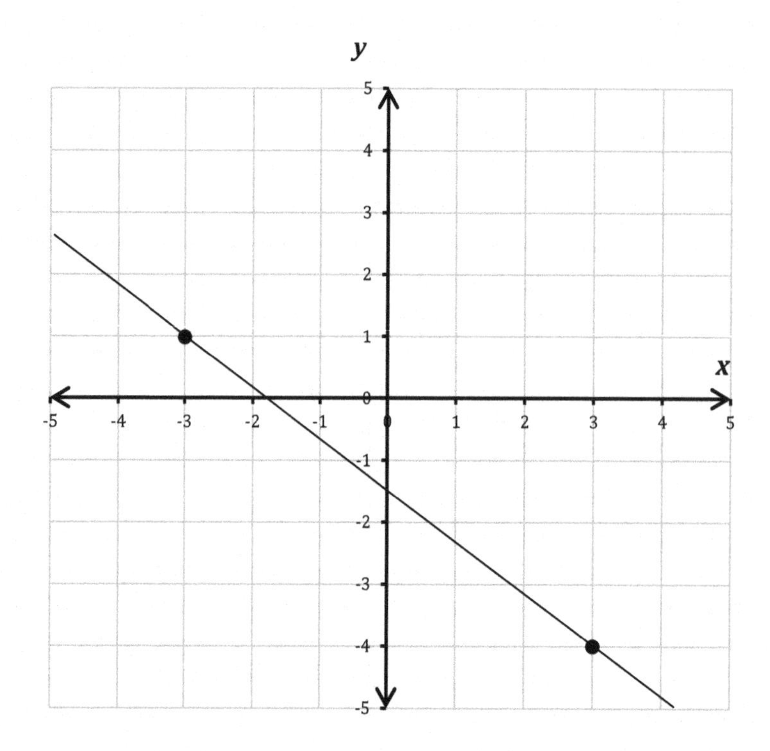

19. What is the equation for the line perpendicular to the line above at $(0, -1.5)$?

20. What is the slope of a line parallel to the line above?

PART 3 REVIEW

GEOMETRY

In this section, you will find 50 practice questions to review the geometry content tested on the ISEE's Math Achievement section. The Lower Level questions cover the geometry content that you will find on the Lower Level section, as well as the easier geometry content on the Middle and Upper Level sections. The Middle Level questions cover content that you will only find on the Middle and Upper Level sections. The Upper Level questions cover content that you will only find on the Upper Level section.

Each question is followed by four suggested answers. Read each question and then decide which one of the four suggested answers is best.

LOWER LEVEL QUESTIONS

Use these questions to practice the geometry content that you will see on the Lower Level Math Achievement section, as well as the easier geometry content that you will see on the Middle and Upper Levels. Lower, Middle, and Upper Level students should attempt these questions.

1. What is the name of a polygon with eight sides?

   (A) square
   (B) pentagon
   (C) hexagon
   (D) octagon

2. A 24-kilometer race is divided into three separate segments. If the first segment is 9 kilometers long and the second segment is 4 kilometers long, how long is the third segment?

   (A) 11 kilometers
   (B) 12 kilometers
   (C) 13 kilometers
   (D) 15 kilometers

3. The shape below has sides of equal length. What is its perimeter?

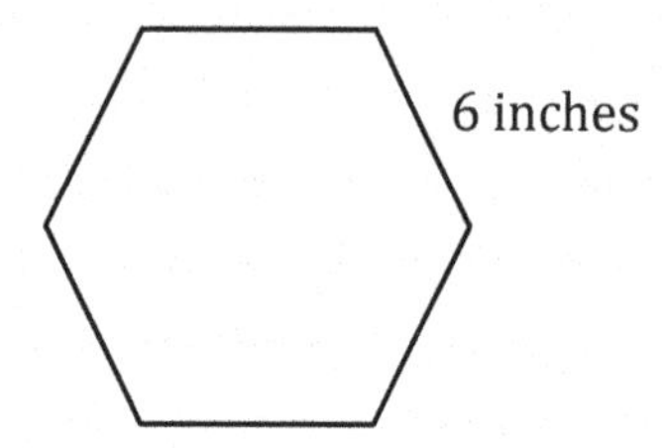

   (A) 6 inches
   (B) 18 inches
   (C) 36 inches
   (D) 72 inches

4. A rectangular grid is 5 centimeters long and 4 centimeters wide. If each square magnet is 1 square centimeter, how many magnets can be placed on the grid?

   (A) 9
   (B) 10
   (C) 15
   (D) 20

5. What is the area of a triangle that has a base of 10 cm and a height of 8 cm?

   (A) 18 cm^2
   (B) 20 cm^2
   (C) 40 cm^2
   (D) 80 cm^2

6. A ranch is building a cattle corral in the shape of a regular pentagon. If each side of the corral uses 15 feet of fence, how many feet of fence will it take to build the entire corral?

   (A) 3
   (B) 60
   (C) 75
   (D) 90

7. Joe painted a wall that measured 8 feet tall and 20 feet wide. How many square feet did he paint?

   (A) 28
   (B) 84
   (C) 130
   (D) 160

For questions 8 – 10, refer to the figure below.

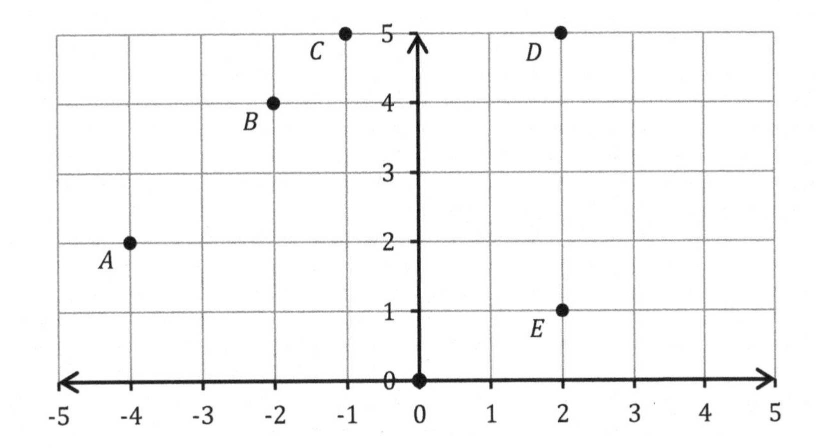

8. Which point is located at coordinates $(-2, 4)$?

   (A) Point A
   (B) Point B
   (C) Point C
   (D) Point D

9. What are the coordinates of point E?

(A) $(2, 1)$
(B) $(1, 2)$
(C) $(-1, -2)$
(D) $(2, -1)$

10. Which point is located the shortest distance away from point D?

(A) Point A
(B) Point B
(C) Point C
(D) Point E

11. A rectangular carpet is 12 feet wide and has an area of 84 square feet. What is the length of the carpet?

(A) 4 ft.
(B) 6 ft.
(C) 7 ft.
(D) 12 ft.

12. Chase reflected triangle ABC across the y-axis to make triangle DEF, but point F accidentally got erased. Where should Chase draw point F to complete the triangle?

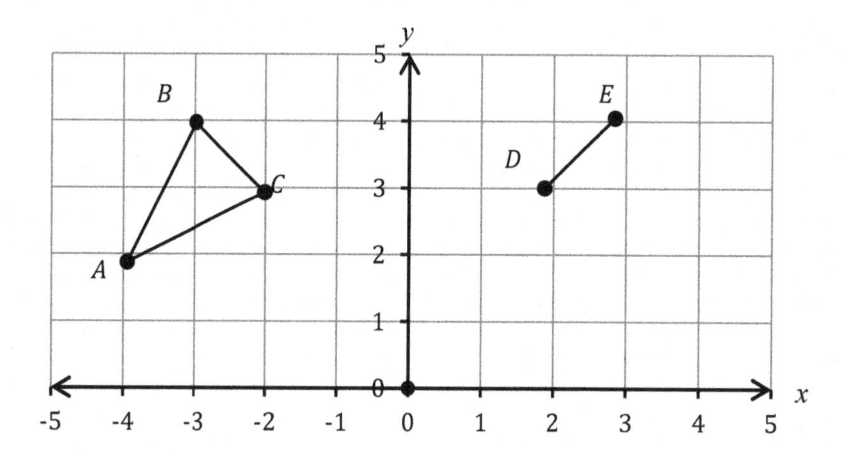

(A) (-4, 2)
(B) (1, 4)
(C) (3, 2)
(D) (4, 2)

13. The shape below has a total perimeter of 45 cm.

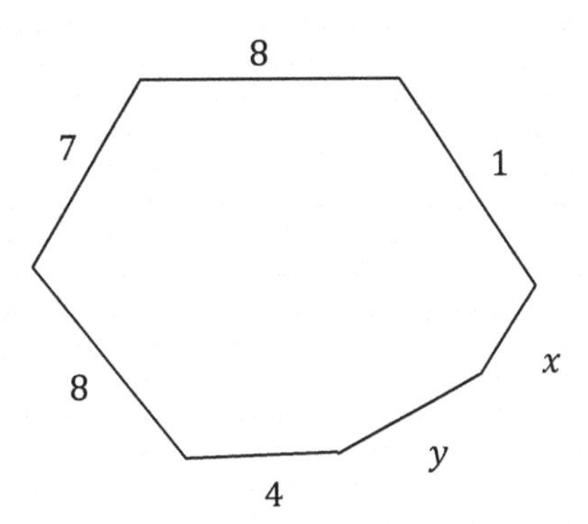

What is the value of $x + y$?

(A) 45
(B) 10
(C) 8
(D) 5

14. Line segment $\overline{KL}$ has a length of 2 inches, and $\overline{KM}$ has a length of 5 inches. What is the length of $\overline{LM}$?

(A) 3 in
(B) 4 in
(C) 5 in
(D) 7 in

15. The diagram below shows a small cube box and a large rectangular box. Amy wants to pack as many of the small boxes as she can fit into the large box. How many small boxes can she fit?

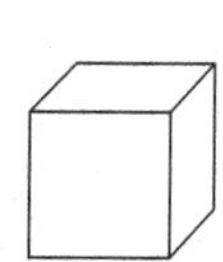
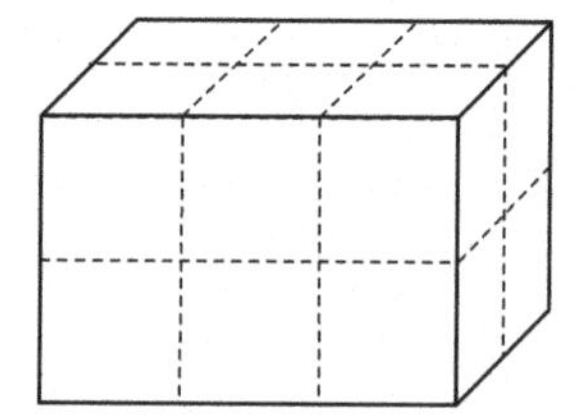

(A) 6
(B) 8
(C) 12
(D) 16

16. Georgia is building a deck with the dimensions shown below. What is the area of her deck, in square feet?

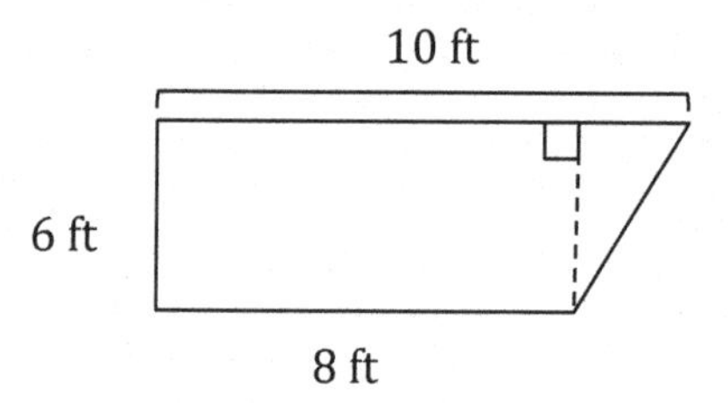

(A) 48
(B) 54
(C) 60
(D) 80

17. The rectangular ceiling of a room measures 16 feet by 10 feet. Emil decides to install a wooden border along the perimeter of the ceiling. Each wooden plank is 2 feet long. How many wooden planks will Emil need?

(A) 26
(B) 16
(C) 13
(D) 10

18. Kadesh has a box in the shape of a cube, and each side of the box is 6 units long. He also has many small unit cubes, and each unit cube has a side length of 1 unit. How many unit cubes can he fit in the box?

(A) 6
(B) 12
(C) 24
(D) 36

MIDDLE LEVEL QUESTIONS

Use these questions to practice the content that you will only see on the Middle Level and Upper Level ISEE. Only Middle and Upper Level students should attempt these questions.

1. Kolten's fish tank holds 1200 cubic inches of water. If the tank's height is 24 inches and its width is 10 inches, what is its length?

   (A) 5 inches
   (B) 40 inches
   (C) 120 inches
   (D) 240 inches

2. The figure below shows three complementary angles. If angle A measures 15° and angle B measures 25°, what is the measure of the third angle?

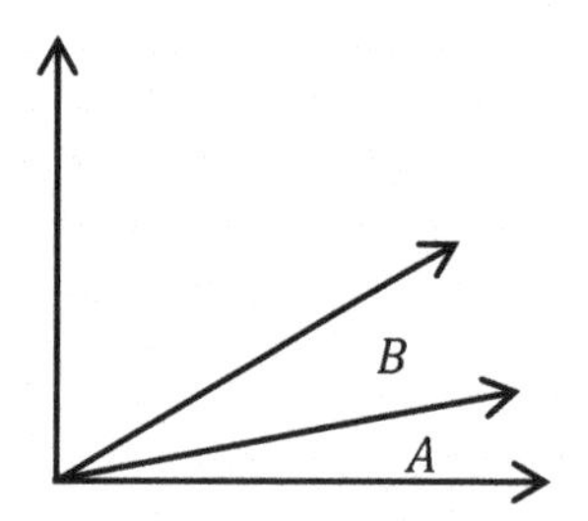

   (A) 15°
   (B) 40°
   (C) 50°
   (D) 90°

3. Alessandria is wallpapering the walls of her living room. There are four walls in her living room and each wall is 2 meters wide by 3 meters tall. The wallpaper costs $4.00 per square meter. How much will Alessandria need to spend on wallpaper?

   (A) $192.00
   (B) $96.00
   (C) $48.00
   (D) $24.00

4. Angela wants to make trapezoid out of construction paper in the dimensions below. How many square inches of paper will she need?

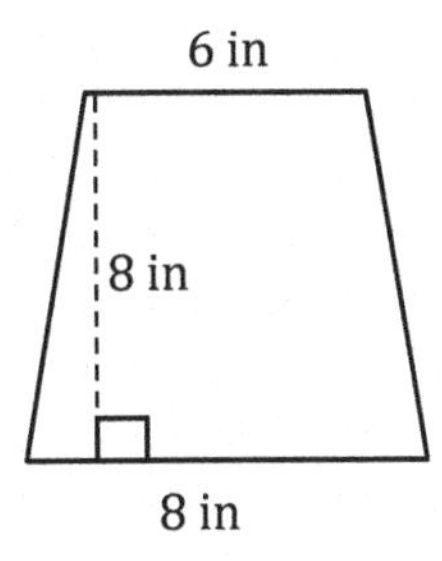

(A) 56
(B) 64
(C) 80
(D) 192

5. The grid shows three coordinates of a rhombus. Which could be the fourth coordinate?

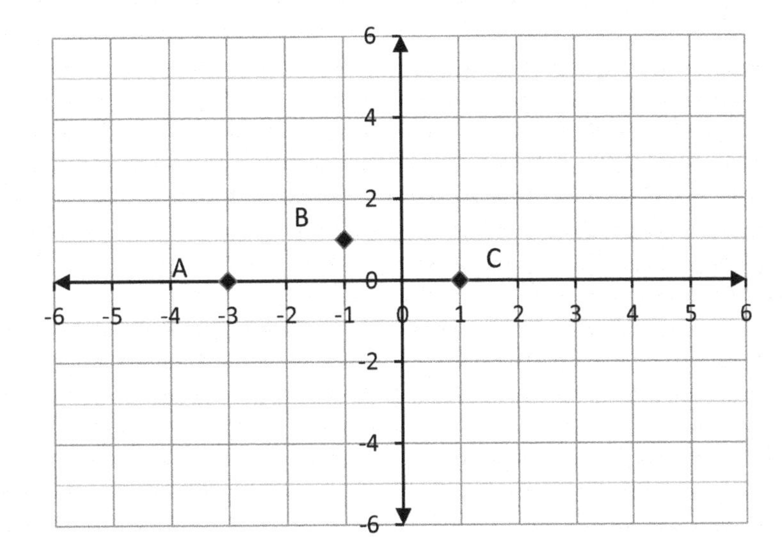

(A) $-1, -1$
(B) $1, -1$
(C) 2,2
(D) Impossible to determine

6. A tank in the shape of a cube, with sides of 4 feet, is being filled with water by a hose. If the hose carries 2 cubic feet of water into the tank every second, how long will it take for the tank to be full?

(A) 16 seconds
(B) 32 seconds
(C) 64 seconds
(D) 128 seconds

7. What is the area of the parallelogram below?

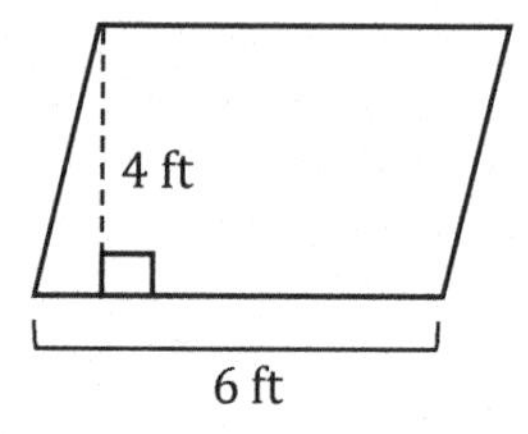

(A) 10 ft^2
(B) 12 ft^2
(C) 18 ft^2
(D) 24 ft^2

8. The triangular prism to the right is 4 units tall and 8 units long. If the total volume of the prism is 96 cubic units, what is the value of x?

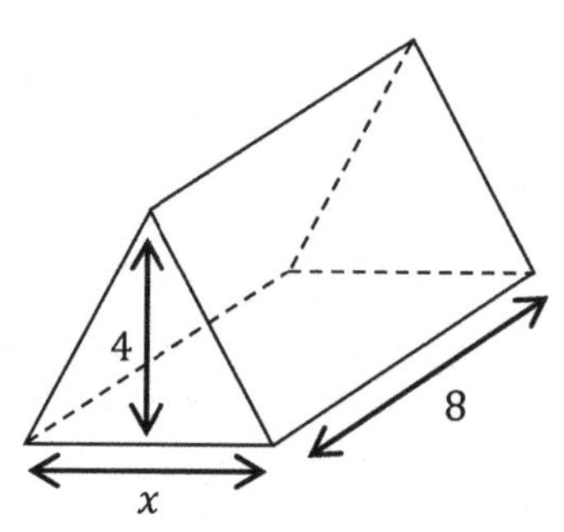

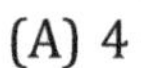

(A) 4
(B) 6
(C) 12
(D) 24

9. A cargo ship is being loaded with rectangular crates. Each crate measures 2 meters by 3 meters by 5 meters. If the ship's cargo area is 10 meters long, 30 meters wide, and 50 meters tall, how many crates will fit into the ship's cargo area?

(A) 30
(B) 150
(C) 500
(D) 15000

10. The triangle below is isosceles. What is the value of x?

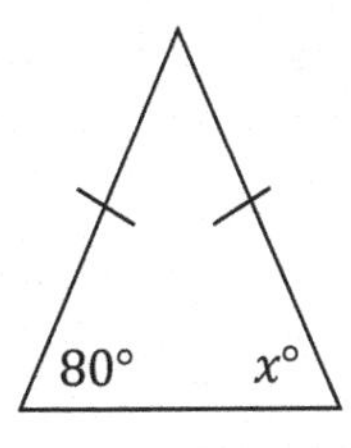

(A) 20°
(B) 80°
(C) 100°
(D) 120°

11. The figure below shows a rotating sprinkler spraying water 4 meters in each direction in order to water a circular area of grass. What is the area of the watered grass? (Area of a circle = πr^2)

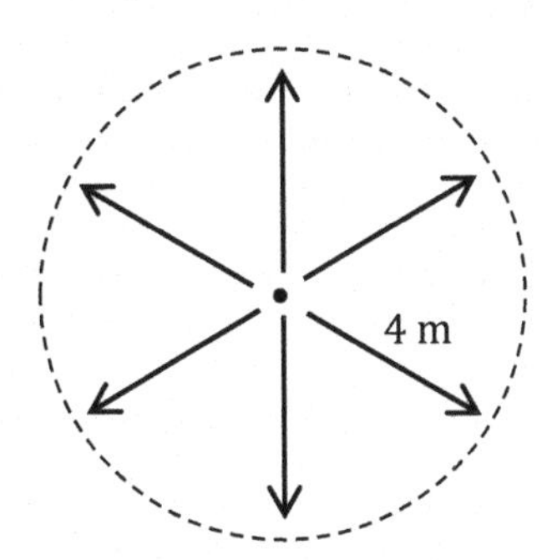

(A) 4π m^2
(B) 8π m^2
(C) 16π m^2
(D) 32π m^2

12. If three angles are supplementary, which of the following could NOT be the measure of one of these angles?

(A) 61°
(B) 93°
(C) 179°
(D) 180°

13. A rectangular block of metal is 5 inches long, 8 inches wide, and 2 inches tall. If each cubic inch of metal weighs 5 pounds, what is the total weight of the block?

(A) 40 pounds
(B) 80 pounds
(C) 200 pounds
(D) 400 pounds

14. The two right triangles below are similar. What is the area of triangle *DEF*?

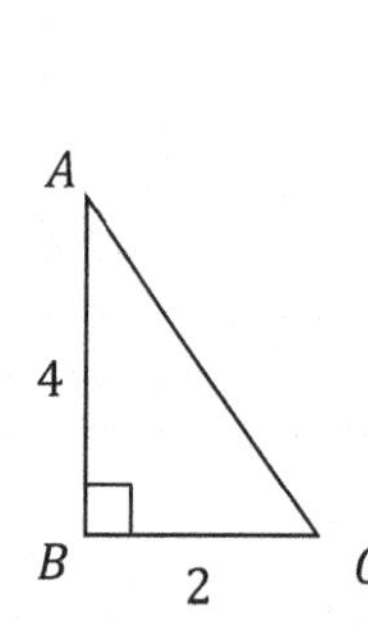

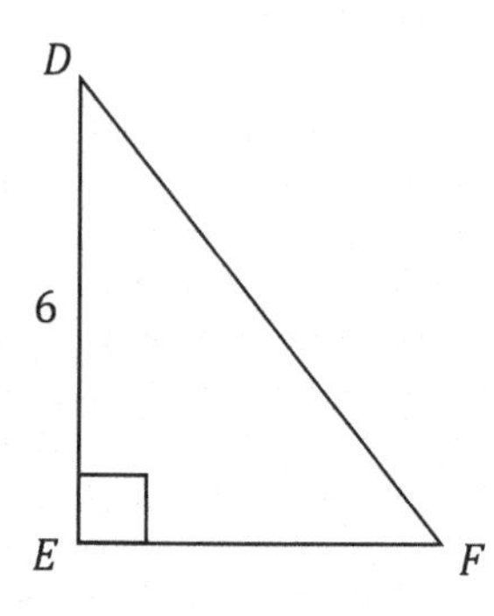

(A) 4
(B) 8
(C) 9
(D) 12

15. In the figure to the right, angles *H* and *K* are complementary. If angle *H* is twice as large as angle *K*, what is the measure of angle *K*?

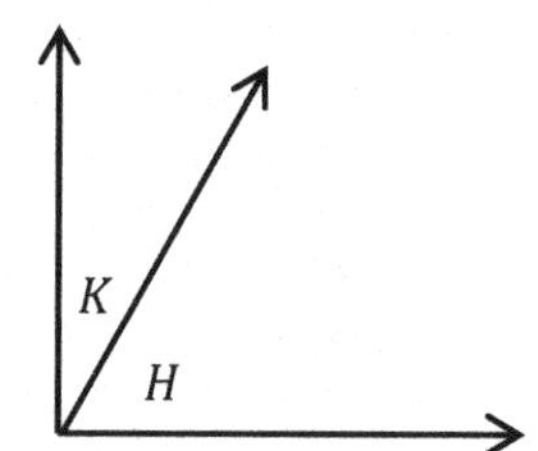

(A) 30
(B) 40
(C) 60
(D) 90

16. The top of a standard hockey puck is a circle with a diameter of 6 inches. What is the surface area of the top of the puck, in square inches?

(A) 3π
(B) 6π
(C) 9π
(D) 18π

17. What is the equation for a line that passes through the points $(-2,2)$ and $(-4,0)$?

(A) $y = -x$
(B) $y = x + 2$
(C) $y = x + 4$
(D) $y = -2x + 2$

18. What is the perimeter of the shaded triangle in the figure to the right?

(A) 5
(B) 7
(C) 12
(D) 14

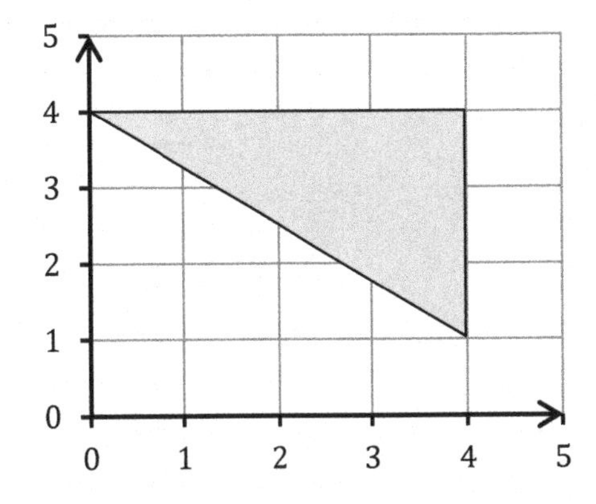

19. In the figure to the right, what is the value of n?

(A) 20
(B) 40
(C) 50
(D) 140

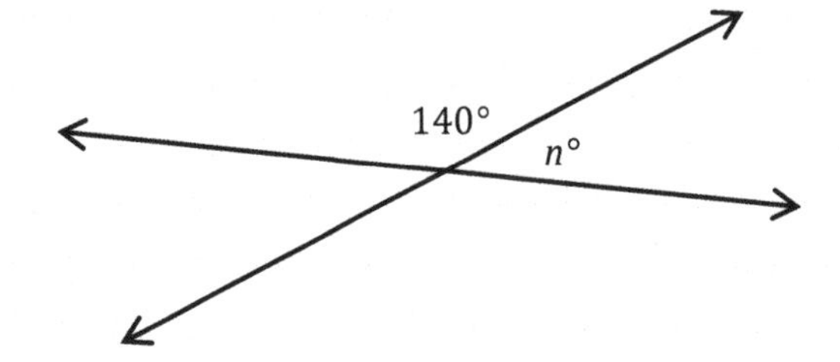

20. The graph below shows Line R.

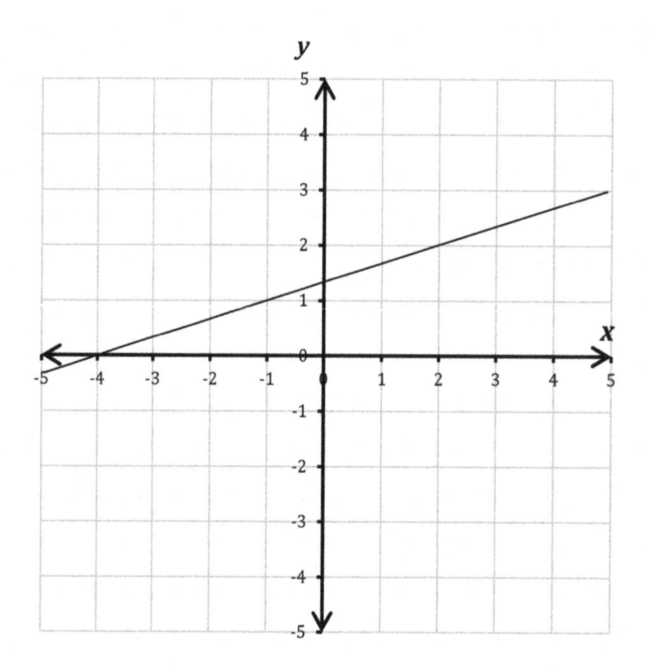

What could be an equation for a line perpendicular to Line R?

(A) $y = 3x + 1\frac{1}{2}$

(B) $y = -3x + 1\frac{1}{2}$

(C) $y = \frac{1}{2}x + 1\frac{1}{2}$

(D) $y = -\frac{1}{2}x + 1\frac{1}{2}$

21. In the figure below, $ABDC$ is a rectangle. If angle AEF measures 120° and angle DBF measures 50°, what is the value of x?

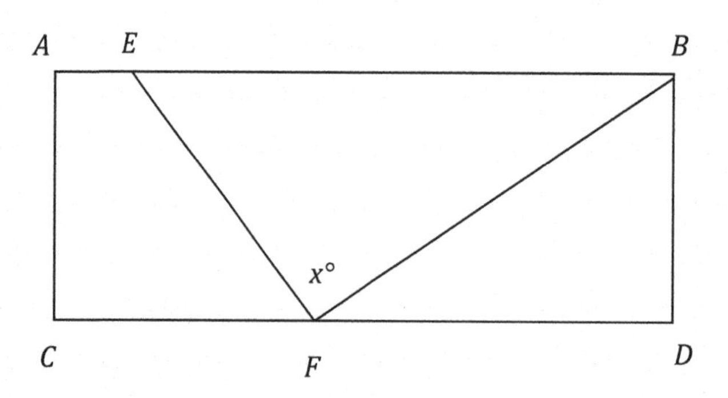

(A) 30
(B) 50
(C) 60
(D) 80

22. The right triangle in the figure below has a base of 8 and a hypotenuse of 10. What is the area of this triangle?

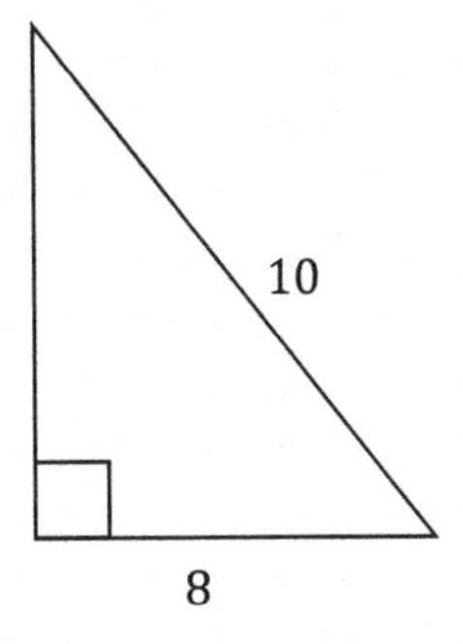

(A) 6
(B) 24
(C) 48
(D) 80

UPPER LEVEL QUESTIONS

Use these questions to practice the most challenging difficulty level you will see on the Upper Level ISEE. Only Upper Level students should attempt these questions.

1. In the figure below, lines r and s are parallel. What is the value of y?

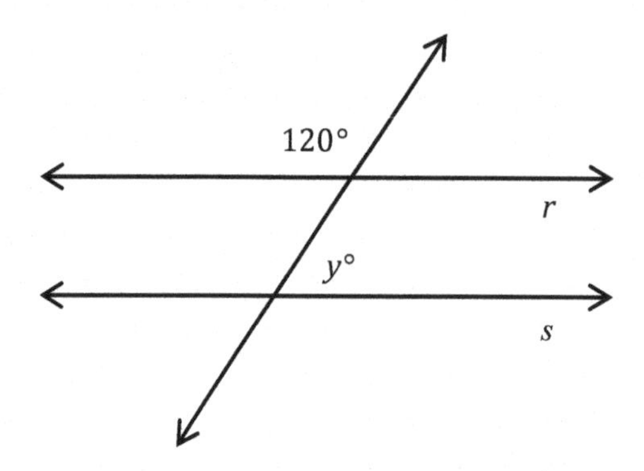

(A) 60°
(B) 70°
(C) 80°
(D) 120°

2. What is the volume, in cubic centimeters, of a cylinder with a diameter of 10 centimeters and a height of 8 centimeters?

(A) 80 π
(B) 160π
(C) 200π
(D) 800π

3. The figure below shows a circular disk rotating around its center. A point on the outside edge of this disk travels at a rate of 2π inches per second and takes 6 seconds to make a complete rotation. What is the radius of the disk, in inches?

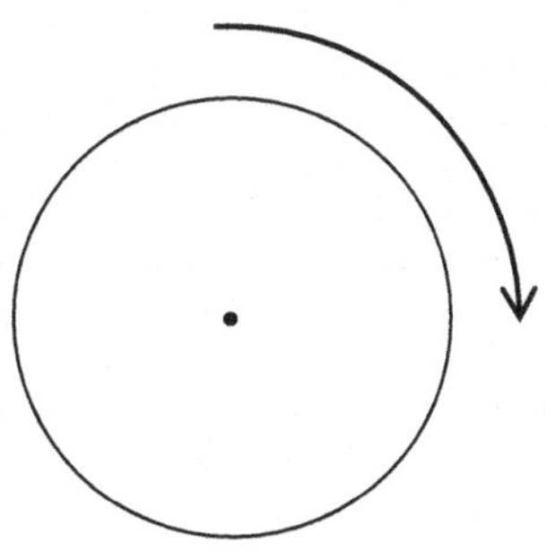

(A) 6
(B) 12
(C) 6π
(D) It cannot be determined from the information given.

4. The right triangle in the figure below has a base of 12 and a hypotenuse of 13. What is the area of this triangle?

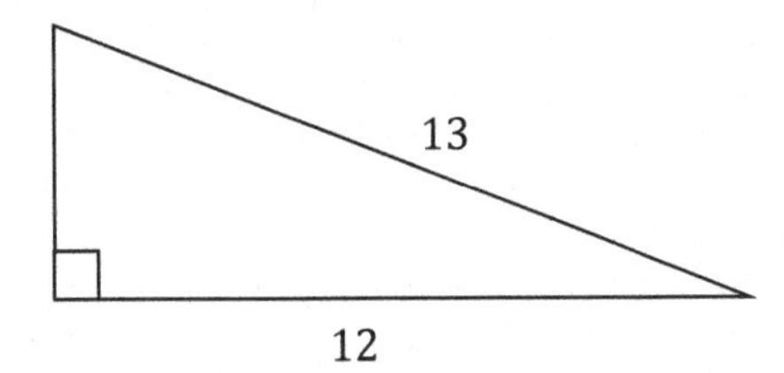

(A) 5
(B) 30
(C) 55
(D) 60

5. The formula for the surface area of a sphere is $SA = 4\pi r^2$, where r is the radius of the sphere. A sphere with a surface area of 36π cm^2 is placed into a cubic box that completely contains it. How tall must the box be?

(A) 2 cm
(B) 6 cm
(C) 8 cm
(D) 13 cm

6. In the figure below, $v = 82$ and $w = 56$. What is the value of u?

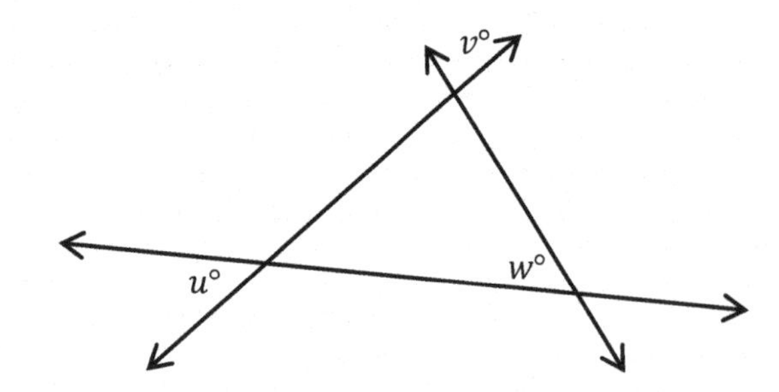

(A) 34
(B) 42
(C) 56
(D) 64

7. If the volume of a cylinder is 400π cubic feet and its height is 25 feet, what is its radius?

(A) 4 ft.
(B) 5 ft.
(C) 8 ft.
(D) 40 ft.

For questions 8-9, refer to the information below.

Triangle ABC is shown below. Angle ABC is equal to 33° and the length of $\overline{BC}$ is 4 cm.

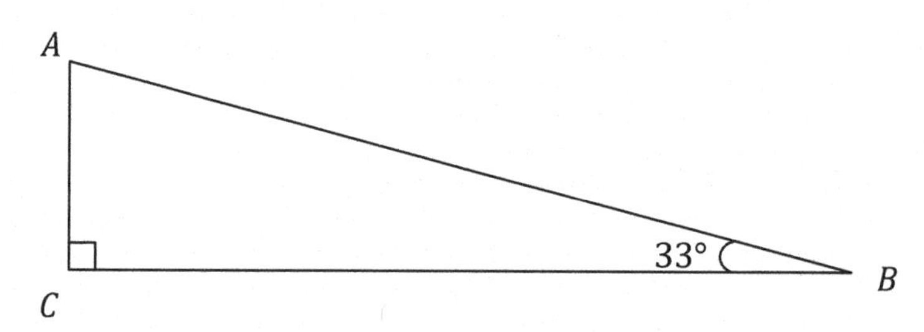

8. Which expression is equal to the length of side $\overline{AC}$?

(A) $\sin(33°) \times 4$
(B) $\frac{\sin(33°)}{4}$
(C) $\frac{4}{\cos(33°)}$
(D) $\tan(33°) \times 4$

9. Which expression is equal to the length of side $\overline{BC}$?

(A) $\sin(33°) \times 4$

(B) $\frac{\sin(33°)}{4}$

(C) $\frac{4}{\cos(33°)}$

(D) $\tan(33°) \times 4$

10. The square in the figure below has a diagonal of 8 cm. What is the area of the square?

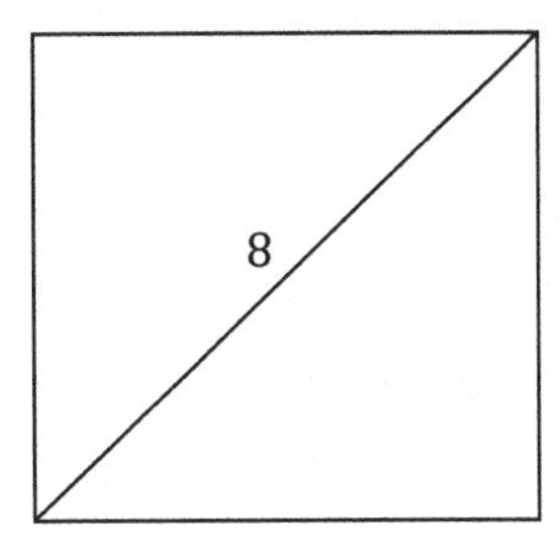

(A) 4 cm^2
(B) 16 cm^2
(C) 32 cm^2
(D) 48 cm^2

DATA INTERPRETATION

PART 4

CHARTS AND GRAPHS

ALL LEVELS

SECTION 1

The ISEE will test your ability to analyze information presented in many different formats. When you see a diagram in the form of a chart or graph, examine it carefully to make sure you understand it. Ask yourself the following questions:

- What is the **main purpose** of this chart or graph?
- What is being measured?
- What is the **scale**, or what **units** are being used?

Let's use these questions to analyze the chart below:

POPULATION BY TOWN, 1960-2000			
	Population (in thousands)		
Town	**1960**	**1980**	**2000**
Cedarville	72	83	104
Franklin	80	82	73
Pine Ridge	121	136	143

What is the **main purpose** of this chart or graph?

To answer this question, always look at the title of the chart or graph. From its title, we can tell that the chart above is meant to show the population of several towns from 1960 to 2000.

What is being measured?

Charts and graphs often measure things like population, distance, or height. To figure out what is being measured, look closely at the data labels found on each column, row, or axis. The labels in the chart above tell us that this chart measures population. Population is measured over time and is split into three towns. The chart is comparing the population of these three different towns (Cedarville, Franklin, and Pine Ridge) at three different dates (1960, 1980, and 2000).

What is the **scale**, or what **units** are being used?

Read very carefully any information given about scale or units in order to understand how numbers on a chart or graph are being represented. In the chart above, we are told that the population data is being represented "in thousands." This information is very important—without this information, we would think that the population of Cedarville in 1960 was only 72 people instead of 72,000 people!

Now that we understand this data in chart format, let's take a look at how it might be represented in different types of graphs. The most common types of graphs include pictographs, bar graphs, line graphs, and pie charts.

PICTOGRAPHS

Pictographs use pictures to represent and compare pieces of data. A picture might represent one single item of data, or it might represent a group of data. For example, the picture might represent one single person, or it might represent a group of people. The title of the pictograph will tell you what data is being compared, and the legend will tell you what the pictures in the graph represent.

The following pictograph shows the approximate number of people in Cedarville, Franklin, and Pine Ridge in 1960.

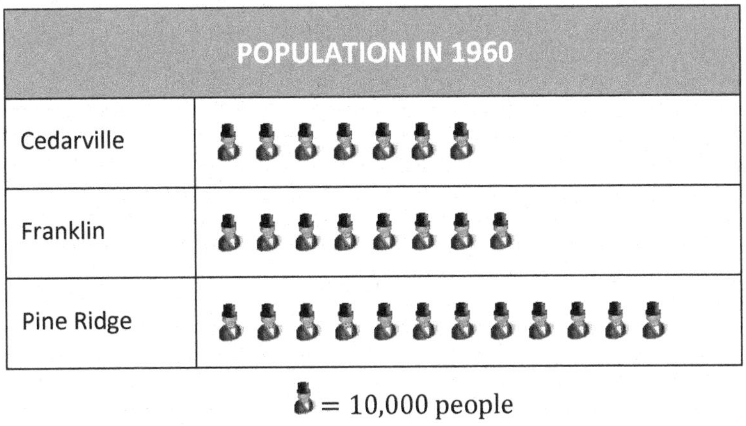

POPULATION IN 1960	
Cedarville	
Franklin	
Pine Ridge	

= 10,000 people

This graph uses the picture to compare the populations of Cedarville, Franklin, and Pine Ridge in 1960. By looking at how many pictures show up next to each city, we can tell that there were fewer people in Cedarville than in Franklin or Pine Ridge. We can also see that there were approximately two times more people in Pine Ridge than in Cedarville.

We can also use the pictograph to calculate the approximate number of people in one of the cities. To do this, we need to multiply the number of pictures for that city by the number of people that each picture stands for. For example, there are 7 pictures for Cedarville. Because the legend tells us that each picture stands for 10,000 people, we multiply 7 by 10,000: $7 \times 10{,}000 = 70{,}000$. The population in Cedarville was approximately 70,000 in 1960.

PIE CHARTS

A **pie chart** compares different sections of data as fractions out of a whole. A circle represents the total amount, and differently sized sections of that circle represent parts out of the whole. These sections look like pieces of pie, which is why this type of graph is called a "pie chart." A legend or labels on the chart explain what data each section represents.

Let's look again at the populations of Cedarville, Franklin, and Pine Ridge in 1960. Here is what these populations would look like as a pie chart:

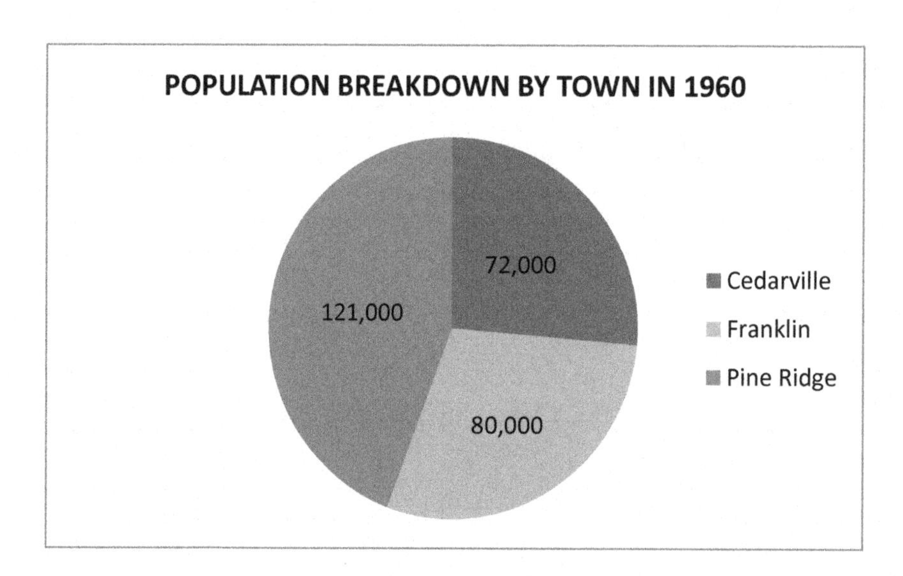

The title of this graph tells us that we are looking at population in 1960, and the legend tells us that each of the slices in this pie chart represents a town. The entire pie chart represents the total population of all three towns. The data labels for each slice also tell us exactly how many people lived in each town. This information is not always given in a pie chart, but we can use these numbers to find the total population of all three towns. To do this, we add together the individual populations of each town: $72{,}000 + 80{,}000 + 121{,}000 = 273{,}000$. All three towns had a total population of 273,000 in 1960.

By comparing the size of these slices, we can tell that a little more than a quarter of the people lived in Cedarville, a little more than a quarter lived in Franklin, and a little less than a half lived in Pine Ridge.

BAR GRAPHS

A **bar graph** uses bars of different lengths to visually compare different sizes of data. Like the coordinate plane, bar graphs represent data along two axes. The x-axis is horizontal and usually tells us how the data was measured. The y-axis is vertical and usually displays the measurements. However, sometimes a bar graph might be displayed "sideways," so the y-axis tells us how the data was gathered and the x-axis gives the measurements. Pay close attention to the labels on each axis so you can determine how the information is being displayed. If a bar graph uses differently colored or patterned bars, a legend explains what other variables these colors or patterns represent.

Bar graphs are useful for comparing data in different groups over different time periods. Because it compares the population of different groups (towns) over different time periods, the data from the chart we saw earlier can be represented in the following bar graph:

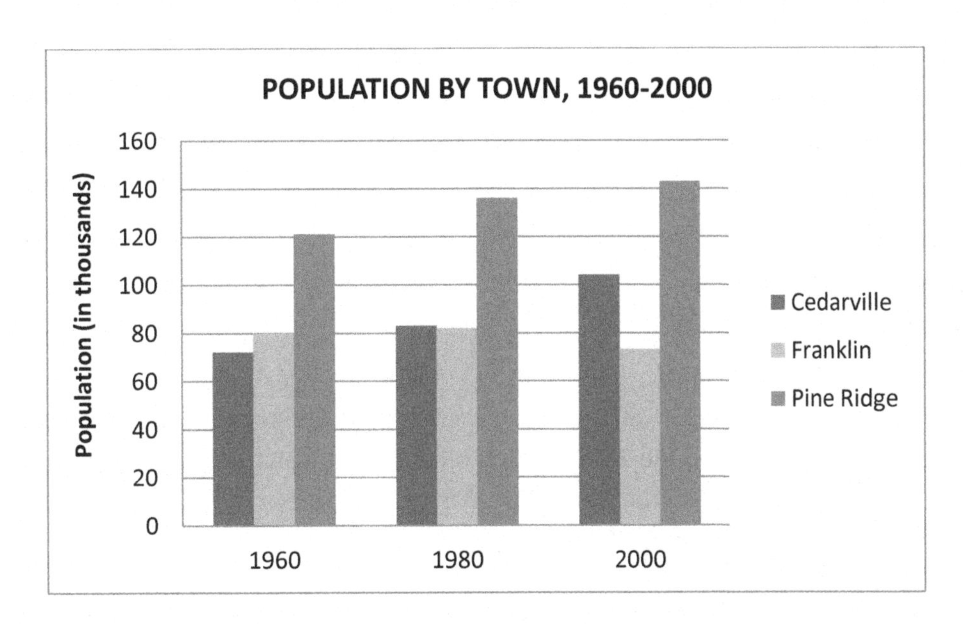

In this graph, the legend tells us that the different-colored bars represent different towns. These are grouped together at each date along the x-axis. The y-axis displays what is being measured: population. Again, we are told that the units are in thousands of people.

We can use this information to interpret the scale of the y-axis and make conclusions about data. Because numbers are given in thousands, each tick mark along the y-axis represents 20,000 people. With these tick marks, we can tell that the population of Pine Ridge in 1960 was about 120,000, and by 1980 it had grown by about 15,000. We can also tell that the populations of Cedarville and Franklin were relatively similar in 1960 and 1980, but they differed by about 30,000 people in 2000.

LINE GRAPHS (MIDDLE/UPPER LEVEL ONLY)

A **line graph** uses a line or several lines to visually represent changes in amounts, usually over time. Like bar graphs, line graphs also represent data along two axes. The horizontal x-axis displays different dates or time periods, and the vertical y-axis displays the amounts being measured. If a line graph uses differently colored or patterned lines, a legend explains what variables these colors or patterns represent.

Here is how the population data for Cedarville, Franklin, and Pine Ridge would be represented on a line graph:

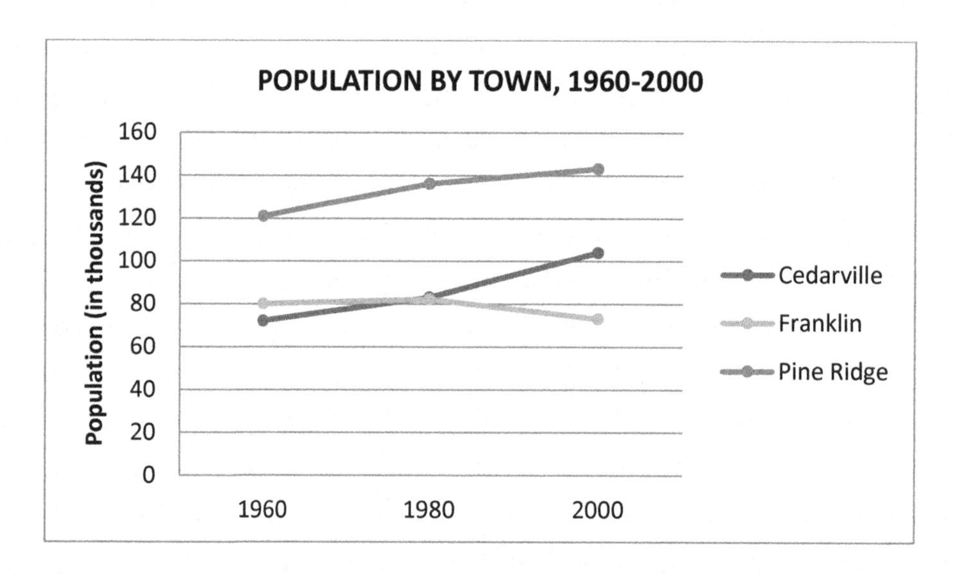

The legend tells us that each line on this graph represents the population of a different town. The three dates (1960, 1980, and 2000) are spaced out evenly along the x-axis of the graph, and population is measured on the y-axis. Just like our bar graph, the scale of the y-axis tells us that each tick mark represents 20,000 people.

Because this graph displays a line across the whole time period we are examining, we can use the graph to make estimates about population at specific years that are not listed in the chart we saw before. For example, we don't know the exact population of Pine Ridge in 1970, but by looking at the middle of the line drawn from 1960 to 1980, we can estimate that the population was around 130,000.

We can also use a line graph to determine how quickly amounts are changing over a particular time period. The **slope** of a line segment, or how steeply it is going upwards or downwards, tells us the rate of change between two points. A line going upwards means amounts are increasing, and a line going downwards means amounts are decreasing. A steep slope means amounts are increasing or decreasing quickly, and a less steep slope means amounts are changing slowly. An entirely flat (horizontal) line segment means there is no change in amount at all between the two data points.

In our graph, the line segment representing the population of Franklin between 1960 and 1980 looks pretty flat because the population of Franklin didn't change very much between 1960 and 1980. However, the line segment between 1980 and 2000 has a much steeper downward slope because the population of Franklin between those two dates changed a lot more, and it decreased. The line for Pine Ridge has an upward slope over the whole time period because the population of Pine Ridge kept increasing. However, the line is steeper from 1960 to 1980 than it is from 1980 to 2000. This means that the population of Pine Ridge increased more quickly from 1960 to 1980 than it did from 1980 to 2000.

VIDEO

4.1 CHARTS AND GRAPHS

Watch at http:// videos.ivyglobal.com

DATA SAMPLING (MIDDLE/UPPER LEVEL ONLY)

So far, we have looked at how data is displayed, but not at how it is collected. Data can be collected in an experiment, in which an experimenter records different measurements that he or she observes. Data can also be collected through surveys of people's preferences or behaviors. In this case, the experimenter gives a survey to a **sample** of the population being investigated. For example, if it's too difficult to give a survey to every student at a school, an experimenter might give a survey to a sample of just a few students. The experimenter can then try to use the responses from this sample of students to predict the responses for the school as a whole.

When collecting data through a survey, it is very important to avoid **sampling bias**. Sampling bias occurs when the group of people taking part in a survey is not a good representation of the population under study. For example, suppose an elementary school wanted to find out whether students prefer to play basketball or soccer at recess. If they only hand out surveys to students in the first and second grade, the responses that they receive might not reflect what the older children prefer. The way to avoid sampling bias is to survey a random sample of the population. If the school hands out surveys to a sample of randomly selected students, each grade level, gender, and other group within the school has an equal chance of being represented.

PRACTICE QUESTIONS: CHARTS AND GRAPHS

For questions 1-3, refer to the information below.

The following pictograph demonstrates the amount of apples found in a store, sorted by variety.

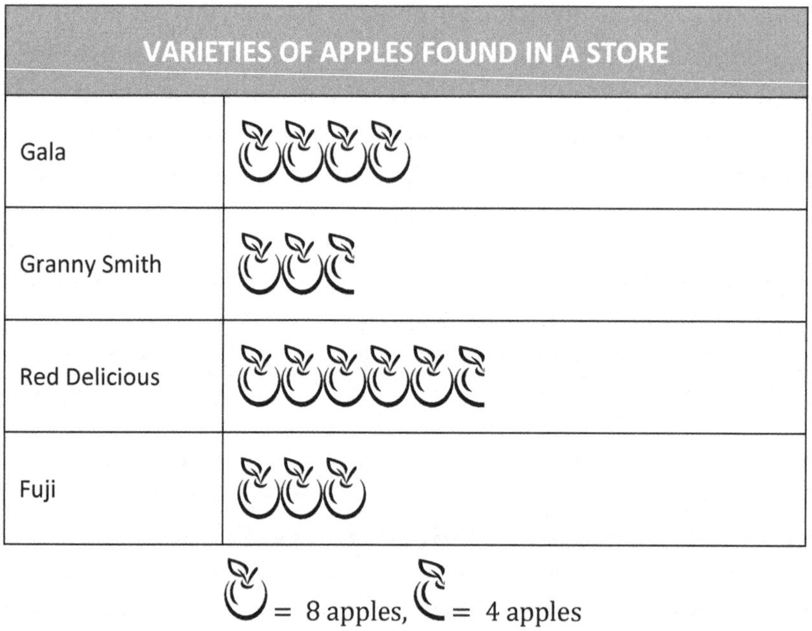

VARIETIES OF APPLES FOUND IN A STORE	
Gala	
Granny Smith	
Red Delicious	
Fuji	

= 8 apples, = 4 apples

1. How many Gala apples are found in the store?

2. How many Red Delicious apples are found in the store?

3. How many fewer Fuji apples are there than Red Delicious apples in the store?

For questions 4-5, refer to the graph below.

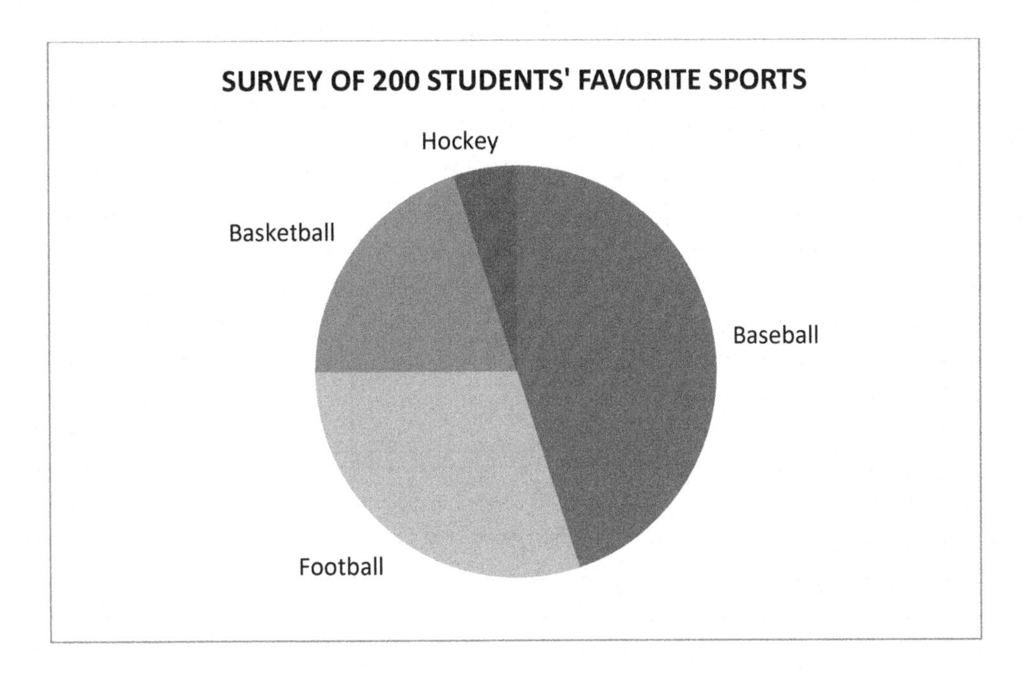

4. According to the chart, about 1/4 of the total group of students liked which two sports combined?

5. Approximately how many students liked either baseball or football?

For questions 6-9, refer to the chart below.

JENNIFER'S COOKIES FOR THE BAND FUNDRAISER		
Type of Cookie	**Price per Box**	**Number of Boxes Sold**
Chocolate Chip	$2.40	10
Peanut Butter	$2.50	8
Oatmeal Raisin	$3.00	8
Shortbread	$3.20	6

6. How many total boxes of cookies did Jennifer sell?

7. How much money did Jennifer make by selling shortbread cookies?

8. How much more money did Jennifer make by selling oatmeal raisin cookies than by selling peanut butter cookies?

9. Jennifer made exactly the same amount of money by selling which two types of cookies?

For questions 10-13, refer to the graph below.

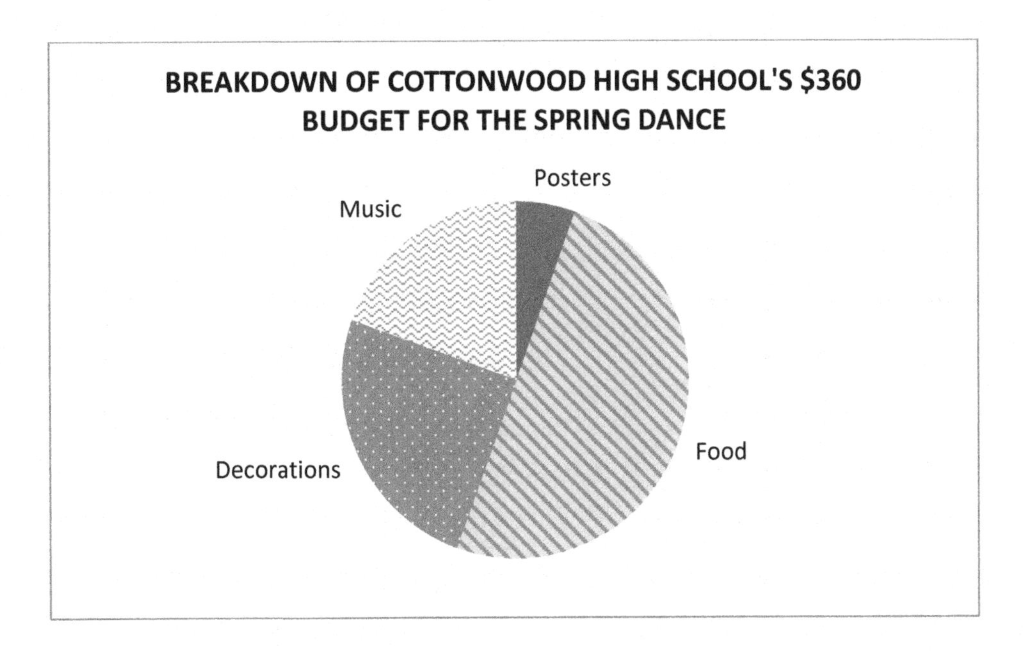

10. About what fraction of the budget is devoted to decorations for the Spring Dance?

11. About how much money is Cottonwood High School spending on food for the Spring Dance?

12. Cottonwood High School has budgeted the same amount for decorations as for what other two categories combined?

13. If Cottonwood High School decided to eliminate funding for posters and divide its total budget evenly among food, music, and decorations, approximately how much more money would it spend on decorations?

For questions 14-17, refer to the graph below.

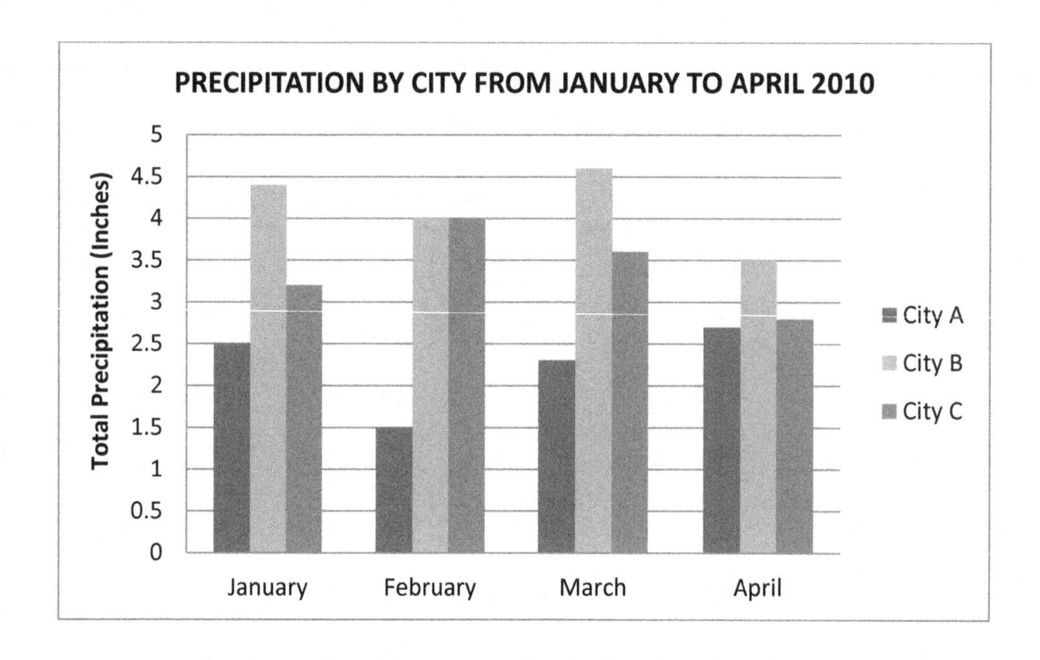

14. In which month did City B and City C experience the same amount of precipitation?

15. Which city's precipitation increased between January and February?

16. In which month did City B experience about twice as much precipitation as City A?

17. Over all four months, about how much greater was the total precipitation of City C than the total precipitation of City A?

For questions 18-20, refer to the chart below.

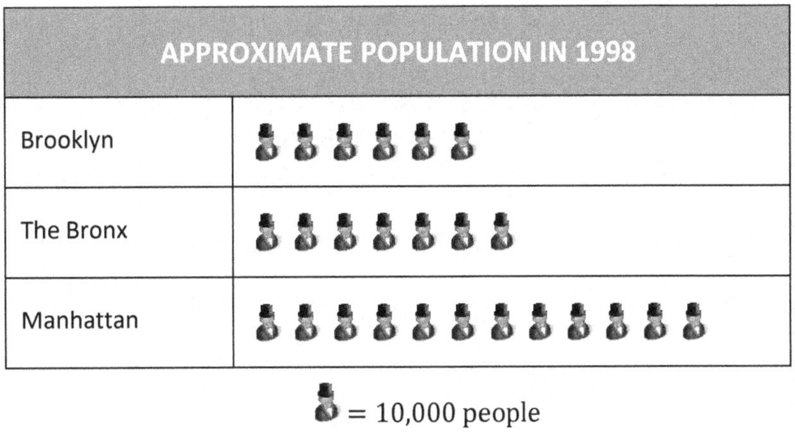

APPROXIMATE POPULATION IN 1998	
Brooklyn	👤👤👤👤👤👤
The Bronx	👤👤👤👤👤👤👤
Manhattan	👤👤👤👤👤👤👤👤👤👤👤👤

👤 = 10,000 people

18. Approximately how many people lived in Brooklyn in 1998?

19. Approximately what was the total population across Brooklyn, the Bronx and Manhattan in 1998?

20. About how many more people lived in the Bronx than in Brooklyn in 1998?

Questions 21-29 are Middle/Upper Level Only.

For questions 21-24, refer to the graph below.

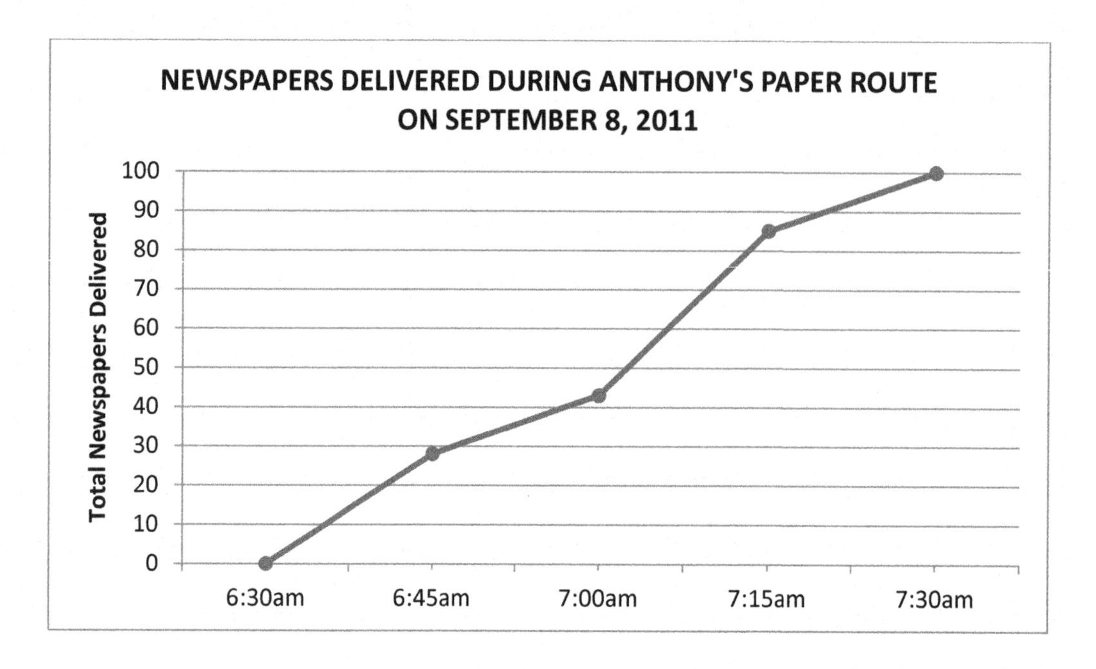

21. About how many newspapers did Anthony deliver between 7:15 and 7:30am?

22. Over what 15-minute time period did Anthony deliver newspapers at the fastest rate?

23. How many total newspapers did Anthony deliver on the morning of September 8, 2011?

24. Was Anthony's overall delivery rate faster during the first half or the second half of his paper route?

For questions 25-26, refer to the chart below.

HIGHWAY REPAIR COSTS BY COUNTY IN 2011		
County	**Highway Repair Costs**	**Miles of Highway in County**
Pinellas	$45,000	300
Hillsborough	$169,000	1,300
Glendale	$81,000	450

25. According to the chart above, which county had the highest repair costs per mile of highway in 2011?

26. Pinellas County wants to reduce the amount of money it spends repairing each mile of highway. If Pinellas County could have repaired its highways at the same repair cost per mile as Hillsborough County, how much money would Pinellas County have saved in 2011?

27. A news agency is conducting a telephone poll about a national issue. If the news agency only calls people during the hours of 12:00pm and 2:00pm, why might this introduce sampling bias?

28. Jessica wants to know the relative number of birds of each species present at her local park. She only counts birds that are roosting on oak trees. Why does this cause sampling bias?

29. Votetown had a low turnout in its last municipal election. In response, Votetown's mayor set up an online poll to ask residents what they believed the factors were that led to the low turnout. What sampling bias is present?

RANGE, MEAN, MEDIAN, AND MODE

ALL LEVELS

SECTION 2

In order to draw conclusions about sets of data, you will need to know how to determine the range, mean, median, and mode. Let's look at the definitions for these concepts and how to use them.

RANGE

The **range** of a set of data is the difference between the biggest and smallest values. The range tells you the interval where all of the data occur. To find the range of any set of data, put the data in numerical order and subtract the smallest from the biggest value.

For example:

Find the range of Adam's quiz scores in the chart below.

ADAM'S HISTORY QUIZ SCORES				
Quiz 1	**Quiz 2**	**Quiz 3**	**Quiz 4**	**Quiz 5**
83	87	90	87	94

This chart shows a student's scores on five history quizzes. To find the range of these scores, let's first put them in numerical order:

$$83, 87, 87, 90, 94$$

Adam's lowest score was 83 and his highest was 94, so his range is the difference between these two:

$$Range = 94 - 83 = 11$$

Adam's scores fall within a range of 11 points.

MEAN (AVERAGE)

The **mean** of a set of data is the same thing as its **average**. We often hear the word "average" in phrases like "the average student" or "the average family," when we want to talk about characteristics typical of a lot of different students or families. It is important to remember that an average is just a way of summarizing a lot of different points of data, but it might not actually exist in real life. For example, we might be told that the average family in a country has 2.5 people. Of course this is impossible—there is no such thing as a half of a person! This probably means that most of the families surveyed had either 2 or 3 people, and the best way of summarizing the data is to say that the "average" family is halfway in between 2 and 3 people.

To calculate the mean or average of a set of data, add up all of the data and divide by the total number of data pointss:

$$Average = \frac{Sum\ of\ data}{Total\ number\ of\ values}$$

For example, let's answer another question about Adam's quiz scores using the previous chart:

What is the average of Adam's quiz scores?

To calculate the average, we would find the sum of all of his quiz scores and then divide by the total number of scores (5):

$$Average = \frac{83 + 87 + 90 + 87 + 94}{5} = \frac{441}{5} = 88.2$$

According to this formula, Adam's average quiz score was 88.2. Adam didn't actually score 88.2 on any quiz, but his scores center around this number.

MEDIAN

The **median** refers to the value that is exactly in the middle of a set of data. The median is another way of summarizing your data, but it is often a different number than the average. To find the median, put all of the data in numerical order and locate the middle number.

Here is another question about the chart of Adam's quiz scores:

What is the median of Adam's quiz scores?

To solve the problem, we would put Adam's quiz scores in numerical order:

$$83, 87, 87, 90, 94$$

The middle number in this data set is 87, so Adam's median history quiz score is 87.

What if your data set has an even number of values, so there is no middle number? In this case, the median is the average of the two numbers closest to the middle. Go through the same process to put the data in numerical order and find the two numbers closest to the middle. Then, take their average by adding them together and dividing by two.

For example:

If Adam is able to score a 99 on his sixth history quiz, what will his new median score be?

If Adam manages to score a 99, the data for his scores will be as follows:

$$83, 87, 87, 90, 94, 99$$

There is no number in the middle of this set of data, but the two numbers closest to the middle are 87 and 90. To find the median of this set of data, take the average of these two numbers:

$$\frac{87 + 90}{2} = 88.5$$

The average of 87 and 90 is 88.5, so 88.5 would be the median of Adam's six history quiz scores.

MODE

The **mode** of a set of data refers to the value that occurs most frequently. A set of data may have one or more modes if there are one or more numbers that occur more frequently than any other number. A set of data may have no mode if all values occur the same number of times.

For example, consider the chart of Adam's quiz scores again:

ADAM'S HISTORY QUIZ SCORES				
Quiz 1	**Quiz 2**	**Quiz 3**	**Quiz 4**	**Quiz 5**
83	87	90	87	94

What is the mode of Adam's history quiz scores?

In Adam's history quiz scores, the number 87 occurs twice. There is no other number that occurs more than once in this set of data, so 87 is the mode.

Here is another example:

Here are all of the scores that Adam and his classmates received on their last history quiz: 91, 88, 94, 90, 82, 79, 84, 94, 85, 88, 93, 97, 92, 80, 96. Does this set of data have a mode or modes? If so, identify the mode or modes.

The answer to this question is easiest to find out if we put the data in numerical order:

$$79, 80, 82, 84, 85, \boxed{88, 88} 90, 91, 92, 93, \boxed{94, 94} 96, 97$$

Both 88 and 94 occur two times, and the rest of the values only occur once. Therefore, 88 and 94 are the two modes of these quiz scores.

ADVANCED STRATEGIES FOR MEAN (MIDDLE/UPPER LEVEL ONLY)

Some questions may ask you to work backwards and find a certain piece of information based on an average that is provided. For these types of questions, you will need to use a little bit of algebra to solve for a missing number.

For example, let's look at Adam's quiz scores one more time:

ADAM'S HISTORY QUIZ SCORES				
Quiz 1	**Quiz 2**	**Quiz 3**	**Quiz 4**	**Quiz 5**
83	87	90	87	94

Adam has one more history quiz coming up, and he would like to raise his average to 90. What would need to score on the next quiz in order to raise his average from 88.2?

We know that his average is equal to the sum of all of his scores divided by the total number of scores, and with one extra quiz, the total number would be 6. For his average to equal 90, the sum of his scores would have to be equal to 90 multiplied by 6:

$$\frac{Sum\ of\ scores}{6} = 90$$

$$Sum\ of\ scores = 90 \times 6 = 540$$

The sum of Adam's scores after he takes his sixth quiz needs to be 540. Therefore, we can subtract all of his other scores from 540 to find what his sixth score needs to be:

$$Sixth\ score = 540 - (83 + 87 + 90 + 87 + 94) = 99$$

Adam would need to score a 99 on his sixth history quiz in order to raise his average from 88.2 to 90.

VIDEO

4.2 RANGE, MEAN, MEDIAN AND MODE

Watch at http:// videos.ivyglobal.com

STEM AND LEAF PLOTS (MIDDLE/UPPER LEVEL ONLY)

Stem and leaf plots are a method for organizing numbers into intervals. They are a kind of shorthand for representing a set of numbers, making it quick to determine the range, mean, median, and mode of the data. In a stem-and-leaf plot, each number in the left-hand column is a **stem**, which represents the tens place of a number. Each number next to a stem is a **leaf**, which represents the ones place of a number.

For example, let's take a look at the following question:

The following ages are reported in a stem and leaf plot:

Stem	Leaf
1	1 2 6
2	0 2
3	1
4	5 6
6	1 2

What are the individual ages represented by this plot?

To find the ages represented by this plot, we glue the stems together with their leaves, row by row. The stem in the first row is 1, and the leaves are 1, 2, and 6. Putting the stem in the tens place and each leaf in the ones place of a number, we get the ages 11, 12, and 16.

Once we have completed the first row of numbers, we move to the rest of the rows in the plot until we are finished. Our final set of ages are 11, 12, 16, 20, 22, 31, 45, 46, 61, and 62.

We have a total of 10 numbers because there are 10 leaves in the plot.

Using stem and leaf plots, we can quickly identify information about the entire data set. Here is another question about the previous stem and leaf plot:

What is the median age in the stem and leaf plot?

Recall that the median is the middle number within an ordered data set. Because we have ten numbers in our stem and leaf plot, the median will be between the fifth and sixth numbers. Counting the leaves on the plot, we can see that the fifth number is 22 and the sixth number is 31. The median is the average of these two numbers:

$$\frac{22+31}{2}=\frac{53}{2}=26.5$$

The median age is 26.5.

HISTOGRAMS (UPPER LEVEL ONLY)

A **histogram** is a specialized graph that is frequently used in data analysis. It represents a graphical distribution of data, grouped together by values or ranges of values. By grouping the data together, a histogram displays the **frequency** of those groupings, which is the number of times those values or ranges occurred in the data set. A histogram is another tool that allows us to graphically calculate specific statistical information such as range, mean, median, and mode. Furthermore, the graphical representation of data often allows us to quickly find or estimate some of this information without calculation.

Here is an example of a histogram:

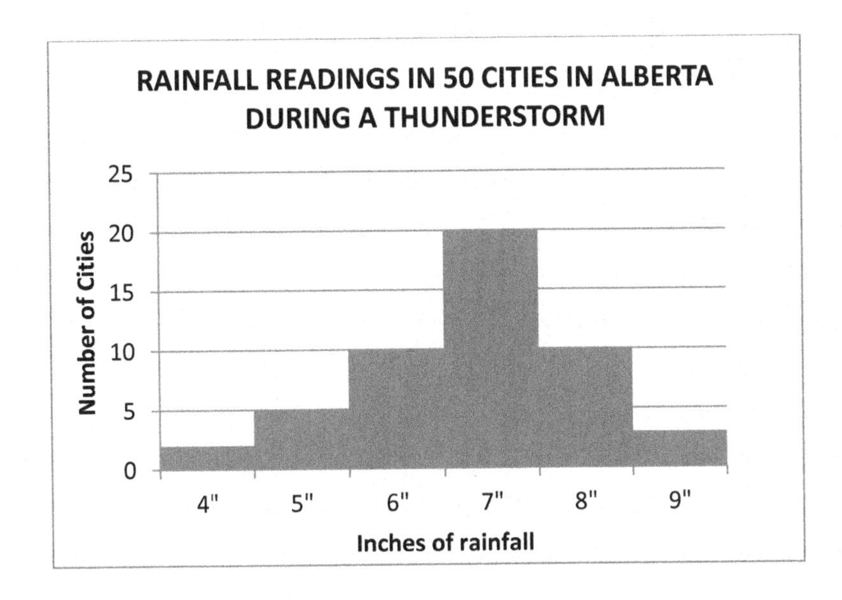

What does this histogram tell us? Most obviously, we can see how much it rained in Alberta during a thunderstorm. The x-axis displays the different rainfall readings (in inches) that were recorded. The y-axis displays the number of cities that recorded each reading. This information tells us the frequency with which each reading occurred. For example, the graph shows that 20 cities recorded 7" of rainfall, but only about 2 cities recorded 4" of rainfall.

Looking at this histogram, it is easy to estimate the mode and the range of the data. Recall that the mode of the data is the most frequently occurring value. Therefore, to find the mode of the data above, all we need to do is see which rainfall reading occurred the most frequently. 7" was the most frequent value recorded, so 7 is the mode of this data. To find the range of this data, we simply subtract the smallest rainfall reading (4") from the largest (9"): $9 - 4 = 5$. The range of the data is 5.

We can also use the histogram to calculate other statistical information. Here is an example:

What is the mean rainfall in the histogram above?

The find the mean in a histogram, we first need to multiply each grouping by its frequency and add those products together. This will tell us the sum of all of the data in the graph. In this case, we multiply each rainfall amount by its frequency, and then add those products together to get the total rainfall reported in the graph:

$$(4 \times 2) + (5 \times 5) + (6 \times 10) + (7 \times 20) + (8 \times 10) + (9 \times 3) = 340$$

The sum of all of the data is 340.

Then, we need to divide this sum by the total number of data points in the graph. If we add together all of the frequencies for each rainfall reading, we can find the total number of readings in the graph:

$$2 + 5 + 10 + 20 + 10 + 3 = 50$$

There are 50 rainfall readings in the graph, which makes sense because the title says there are 50 cities reporting rainfall.

Finally, we divide the sum of all of the data by the number of values:

$$\frac{340}{50} = 6.8$$

The mean rainfall reading in this data is 6.8". On the graph, this would lie between 6" and 7".

Here is one more example question:

What is the median rainfall in the histogram on the previous page?

Because the median is the middle number in a data set, we need to find which rainfall reading would represent the middle number if all 50 readings were arranged in order from least to greatest. Because we have 50 readings, the middle number would be the 25th reading.

Which group on the histogram would contain the 25th reading? To find this, we can start adding up the frequencies of each grouping, from left to right, and stop when we get above 25. There were 2 readings of 4", 5 readings of 5", and 10 readings of 6". This is 17 readings total, which is still less than 25. However, there were 20 readings of 7", which brings us to 37 readings total. Therefore, the 25th reading must be in the 7" group. We can conclude that the median rainfall reading is 7".

BOX AND WHISKER GRAPHS (UPPER LEVEL ONLY)

A **box and whisker graph** is a graphical way of showing the range, median, and quartiles of a set of data. Each data set has three **quartiles**, which divide the data evenly into four groups. One quarter (25%) of the data is below the first quartile, half (50%) of the data is below the second quartile, and three quarters (75%) of the data is below the third quartile. Because the second quartile is right in the middle of the data set, it is also the median of the data.

A box and whisker graph uses "boxes" and "whiskers" to show this information. The box part of the graph shows the first quartile, the median, and the third quartile. The whisker parts of the graph are lines extending from the box to the smallest and largest data points:

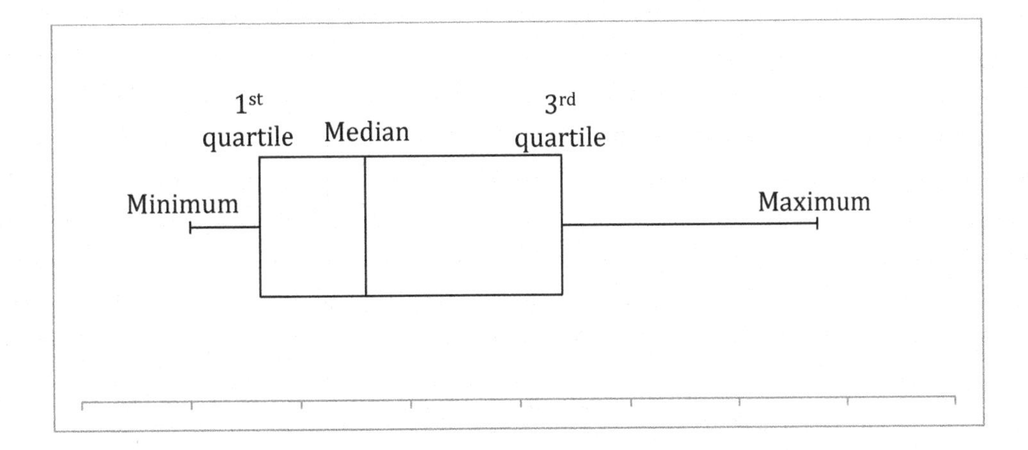

Let's take a look at the following question:

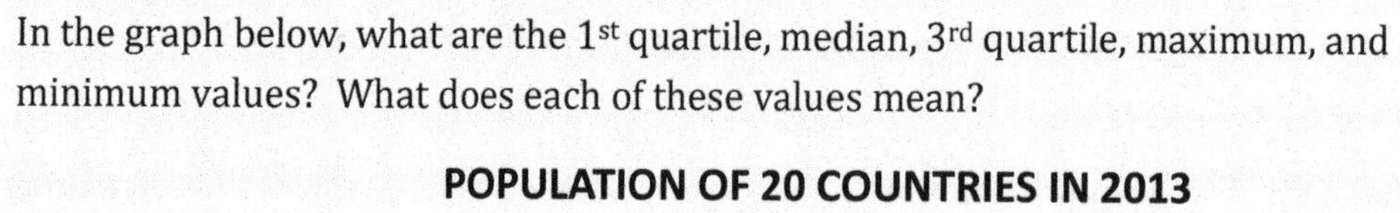

In the graph below, what are the 1st quartile, median, 3rd quartile, maximum, and minimum values? What does each of these values mean?

POPULATION OF 20 COUNTRIES IN 2013

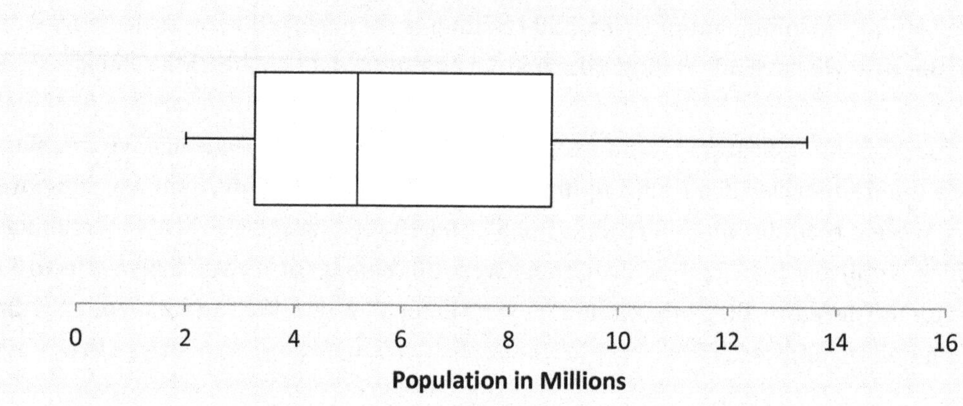

By looking at the lines in the box of this graph, we can estimate that the median (the middle line) is about 5.5 million, the 1st quartile (the left line) is about 3 million, and the 3rd quartile (the right line) is about 9 million. By looking at the endpoints of the whiskers, we can estimate that the minimum value is about 2 million and the maximum value is about 13.5 million.

What does this mean? Remember that the median is the middle value of the data; half (50%) of the data is found above the median, and half (50%) of the data is found below the median. Because the median for the data in this graph is about 5.5 million, we know that the middle population size of these 20 countries was about 5.5 million in 2013. For 10 of those countries, the population was greater than 5.5 million, and for the other 10 of those countries, the population was less than 5.5 million.

We know that 25% of the data lies below the 1st quartile, which also means that 75% of the data lies above the 1st quartile. Because the 1st quartile in the graph is about 3 million, we know that 5 countries (25%) had populations less than 3 million, and 15 countries (75%) had populations greater than 3 million.

We also know that 75% of the data lies below the 3rd quartile, and therefore 25% of the data lies above the 3rd quartile. Because the 3rd quartile in the graph is about 9 million, we know that 15 countries (75%) had populations less than 9 million, and 5 countries (25%) had populations greater than 9 million.

Finally, we know that the minimum value of this data is about 2 million and the maximum value is about 13.5 million. This means that 2 million is the population of the smallest country on this graph, and 13.5 million is the population of the largest country.

PRACTICE QUESTIONS: RANGE, MEAN, MEDIAN, AND MODE

For questions 1-4, refer to the chart below.

SARAH'S SNACKS AND COFFEE PURCHASES				
Monday	**Tuesday**	**Wednesday**	**Thursday**	**Friday**
\$2.50	\$1.20	\$4.00	\$1.20	\$3.10

1. What is the range of this set of data?

2. What is the median of this set of data?

3. On average, how much did Sarah spend per day on snacks and coffee?

4. Does this set of data have a mode or modes? If so, identify the mode or modes:

For questions 5-9, refer to the data below.

To train for a race, Marion is timing herself during her 10-kilometer practice runs. Here are her times (in minutes) for her last 6 runs:

$$53, 51, 52.5, 50, 49.5, 50$$

5. What is the range of Marion's practice times?

6. What was her average time?

7. What was her median time?

8. Does this set of data have a mode or modes? If so, identify the mode or modes:

For questions 9-12, refer to the graph below.

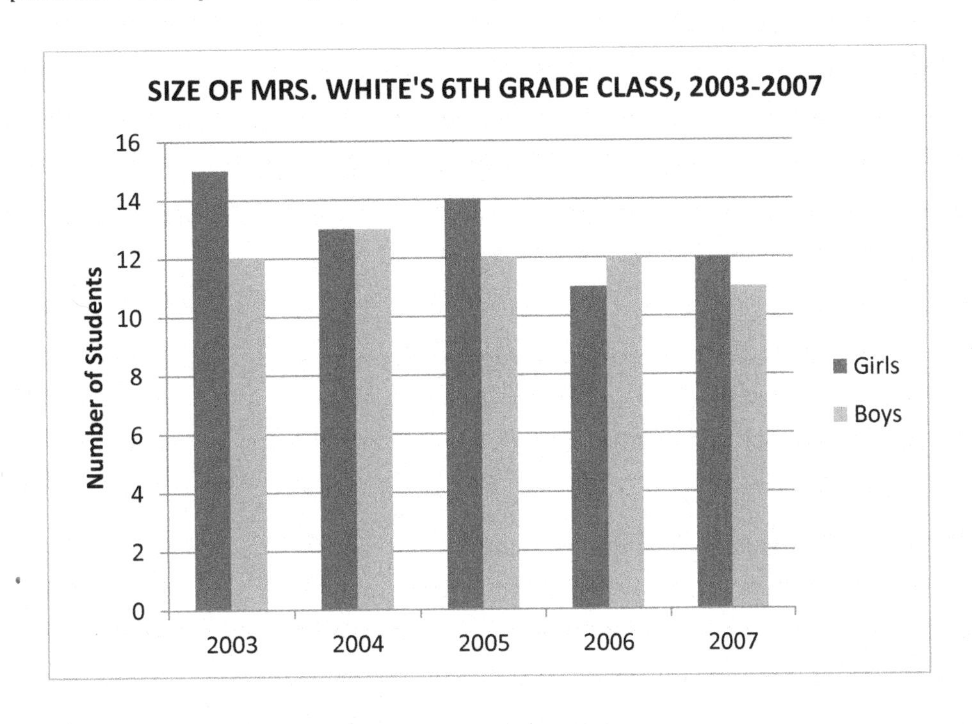

9. What was the median number of boys in Mrs. White's class from 2003 to 2007?

10. What was the average number of students in Mrs. White's class from 2003 to 2007?

11. What was the range of Mrs. White's total class size from 2003 to 2007?

12. On average, how many more girls than boys were in Mrs. White's class each year?

Questions 13-25 are Middle/Upper Level Only.

13. If the average of four numbers is 12, what is the sum of these four numbers?

14. Jordan's class can win a pizza party if each student reads an average of 5 books over the period of a month. So far, the 24 students in Jordan's class have read a total of 96 books. How many more books, on average, does each student need to read in order for the class to win a pizza party?

15. Allen scored an average of 91 on five algebra tests. If his first four test scores were 92, 90, 86, and 88, what did he score on his fifth test?

16. The sum of three consecutive even integers is 18. What is the median of these three integers?

17. Elisa has a summer job at a bicycle store. In June and July, she sold an average of $680 per month in bicycles and equipment. If she would like to bring her monthly average up to $700 by the end of the summer, how many dollars of bicycles and equipment does she need to sell in August?

18. A set of five numbers had an average of 14. When two of these numbers were removed, the remaining three numbers had an average of 13. What was the sum of the two numbers that were removed?

19. Jenny's family has 4 children, and Jenny is the second youngest. Each child in Jenny's family was born at least two years apart from any other child. If the median age of Jenny and her siblings is exactly 12, and her oldest sibling is 15 years old, how old is Jenny?

For questions 20-22, refer to the information below.

An experiment was performed. The following laboratory results were reported in degrees Fahrenheit.

Stem	Leaf
5	0 1 3 4
6	0 0 0 1
8	1 5

9 | 1 *represents 91 degrees Fahrenheit*

20. What is the average temperature?

21. What is the mode of temperatures?

22. How many temperatures were recorded?

For questions 23-25, refer to the information below.

Snowfall was recorded for the city of Nanaimo twice per week for six weeks. The results in centimeters are summarized in the following stem and leaf graph.

Stem	Leaf
0	0 1 2 5 7 8
1	1 1 2 2 2
2	1

1 | 1 represents 11 centimeters of snowfall

23. What is the range of snowfall reported for the six weeks in Nanaimo?

24. What was the most frequent amount of snowfall recorded?

25. Is a snowfall of 11 centimeters above or below the average snowfall for the period?

Questions 26-38 are Upper Level Only.

For questions 26-29, refer to the information below.

The histogram below shows the test scores of students in a writing class.

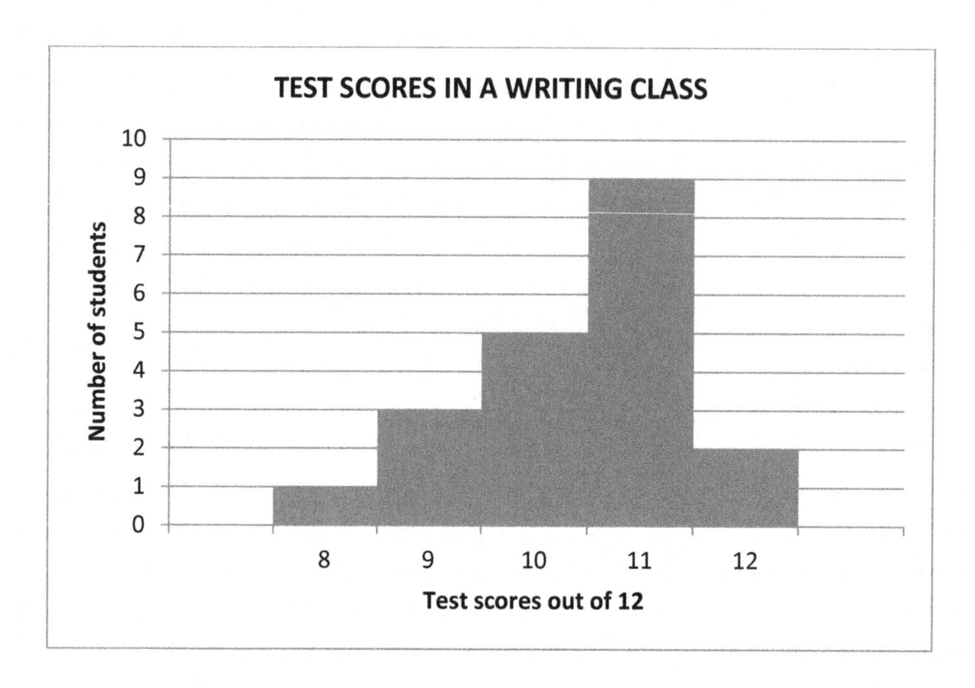

26. How many students are there in the class?

27. What is the mode of the test scores in this histogram?

28. What is the mean test score?

29. What is the median test score?

For questions 30-32, refer to the information below.

The diagram below summarizes the weights of fish caught by a commercial fishery during the first week of April 2010.

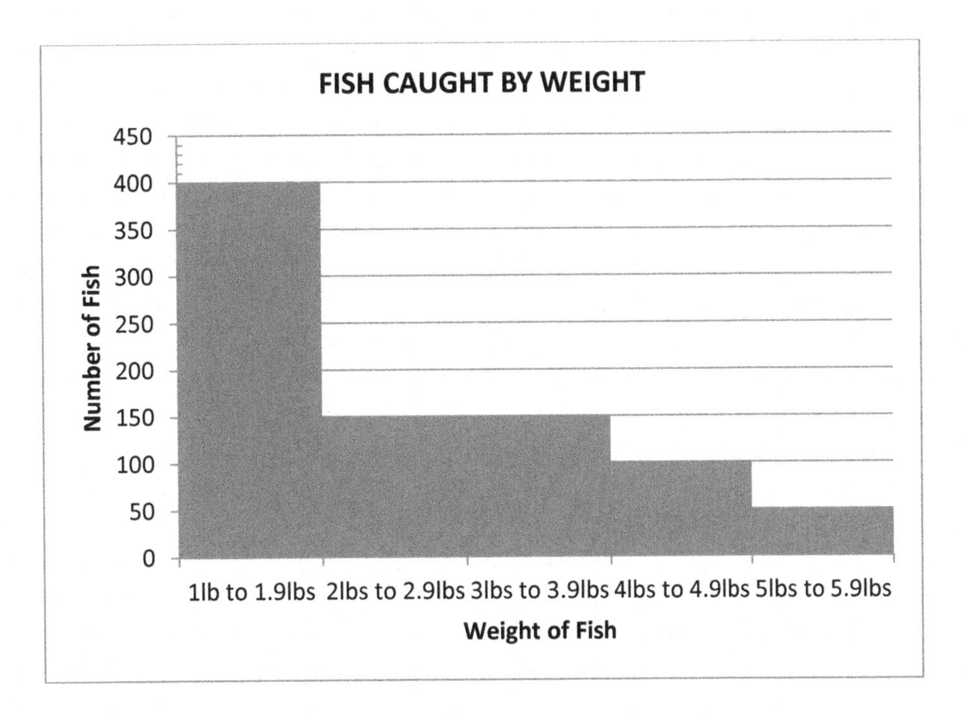

30. What is the range of fish weights in this histogram?

31. Is the range less than or greater than the average weight?

32. The median weight in this data is between which two numbers, in pounds?

For questions 33-35, refer to the information below.

The box-and-whisker plot below represents wind gust speeds in miles per hour at a certain location. Wind gust speeds were measured once per day over 20 days.

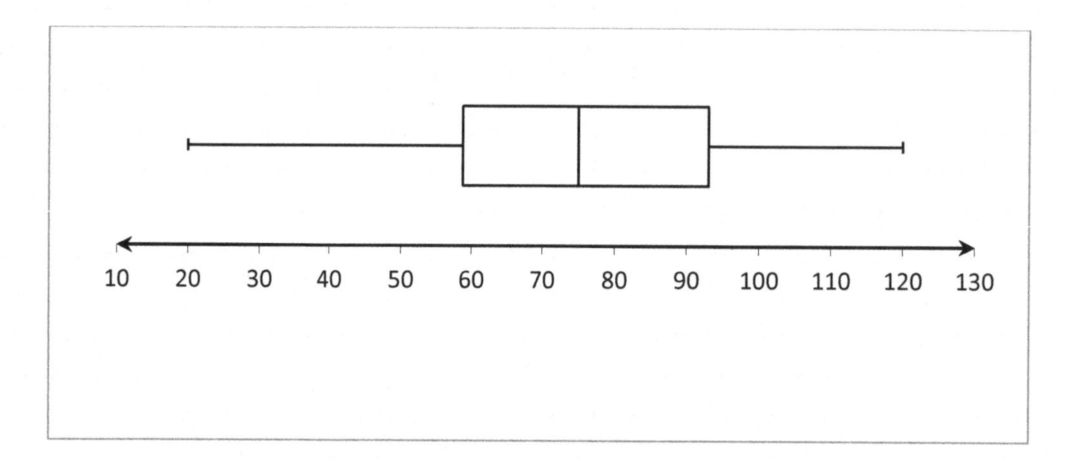

33. What is the range of the data?

34. The median of the data is found between which two wind gust speeds on the graph?

35. A wind gust speed of 90 miles per hour is found between which quartiles of the graph?

ORGANIZED COUNTING

ALL LEVELS

SECTION 3

In this section, we discuss methods of organized counting using Venn diagrams, the counting principle, permutations, and combinations. These are important concepts to master before working on probability, which we will discuss in Section 4.

VENN DIAGRAMS

A **Venn diagram** uses overlapping circles that demonstrate relationships between different groups. An **intersection** is where the circles overlap. The intersection is where the groups in the overlapping circles have something in common.

For example, let's look at the question below:

The following Venn diagram shows children who do the dishes and children who mow the grass. According to this diagram, how many children both do the dishes and mow the grass?

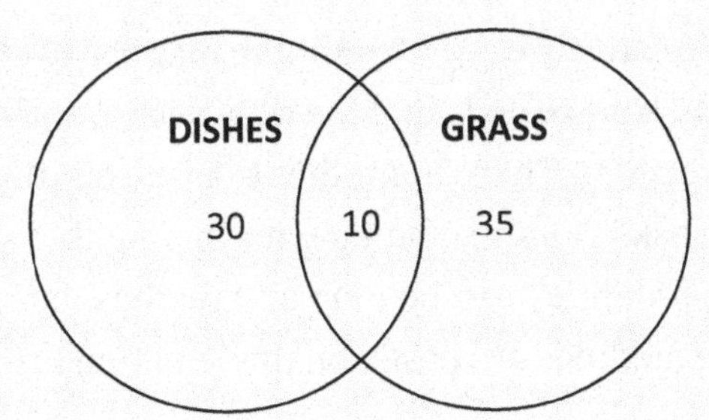

The Venn diagram above has two circles: one labeled "DISHES" and one labeled "GRASS." Based on the information in the question, we can conclude that the circle labeled "DISHES" shows children who do the dishes, and the circle labeled "GRASS" shows children who mow the grass. The intersection of the two circles shows children who both do the dishes and mow the grass, and the number 10 in this intersecting area tells us that there are 10 children who do both of these tasks. This is the answer to our question: 10 children both do the dishes and mow the grass.

Let's look at another question:

In the previous Venn diagram, how many children mow the grass but do not do the dishes?

The "GRASS" circle has two areas, each with a different number. We've already identified that the area with the number 10 is the intersection between the two circles; this area tells us how many children both do the dishes and mow the grass. The other area does not overlap with the "DISHES" circle, so it represents all of the children who mow the grass but do not do the dishes. Because this area has the number 35, we can conclude that 35 children only mow the grass.

Let's look at one more question:

How many total children are represented in the previous Venn diagram?

To find out how many children are represented in the Venn diagram, all we have to do is count up all of the children represented in each group. Reading left to right, there are 30 children who only do the dishes, 10 children who both do the dishes and mow the grass, and 35 children who only mow the grass:

$$30 + 10 + 35 = 75$$

There are 75 total children represented in this Venn diagram.

THE COUNTING PRINCIPLE

As we have just seen, it is relatively easy to count the number of elements in a certain group of a Venn diagram— all you have to do is find the right sections of the Venn diagram and add up the numbers in those sections. There is another type of counting question, however. This type of counting question asks you to come up with the number of possibilities for a given situation. Listing these possibilities can be long and tedious, but luckily there are ways to count them quickly. These methods are based on the Counting Principle.

The **Counting Principle** tells us how to find the number of possibilities for completing two or more tasks at the same time. To find the number of ways you can complete these tasks together, multiply together the number of ways you can complete each task individually.

Here is an example:

Christy has two scarves and three hats. She wants to pick one scarf and one hat to wear. How many different combinations of one scarf and one hat could she pick?

Let's think about this problem using the Counting Principle. Christy is trying to complete two tasks: her first task is to pick a scarf, and her second task is to pick a hat. Christy has 2 ways to complete her first task because she has two scarves she could pick. She has 3 ways to complete her second task because there are three hats she could pick.

To find the number of ways to complete both task, we multiply the number of ways Christy could complete the first task (2) by the number of ways she could complete the second task (3):

$$hats \times scarves = 2 \times 3 = 6$$

There are 6 different combinations of hats and scarves Christy could choose.

Why does this work? You could diagram this by showing that Christy has two scarves, and for each scarf, she could choose 3 different hats:

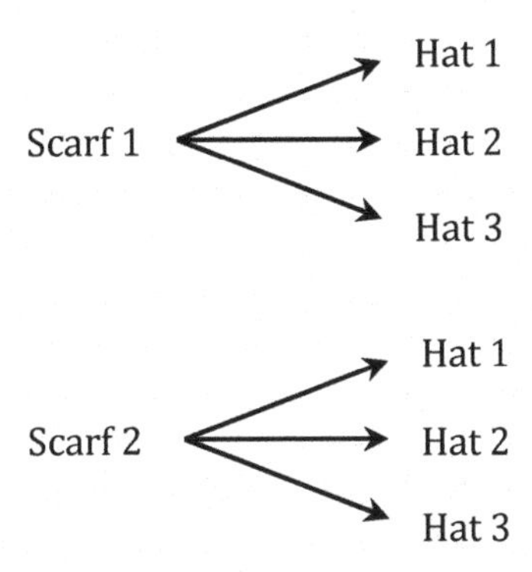

Because there are two scarves and three hat choices for each scarf, there are $2 \times 3 = 6$ combinations in total.

COMBINATIONS AND PERMUTATIONS (UPPER LEVEL ONLY)

In addition to the Counting Principle, some ISEE questions require you to think about **order.** In some cases, the order of the tasks matters. For example, order certainly matters in the result of a race. A combination of tasks where order matters is technically called a **permutation**.

In other cases, order doesn't matter because the result is the same regardless of when you make your choice or how objects are arranged. For instance, if you are picking fruit to go in a basket, it doesn't matter whether you pick an apple first and an orange second, or an orange first and an apple second—the contents of your basket will remain the same. In mathematics, the term **combination** is technically used only for situations like this, where order does not matter.

On the Upper Level ISEE, it is important to be able to tell the difference between a combination and a permutation. Think of your lock on your school locker. You have a group of numbers on a dial and the order in which you select them matters. If you get the order wrong, your lock won't open. These kinds of locks are often called "combination locks," but in fact they should be *permutation* locks!

CALCULATING PERMUTATIONS

Let's look at how you would calculate the number of permutations possible for a specific set of tasks. Here is an example:

> How many different three-digit numbers can you write using the digits 1, 2, and 3, without repeating any digits?

This question involves permutations because the order in which the digits are arranged matters. The number 123 is not the same as 213 or 231. Here are all of the permutations involving these three digits:

123	213	312
132	231	321

There are 6 different numbers possible. We could have calculated this result faster using the Counting Principle, multiplying the number of choices we have for the first digit by our choices for the second digit and our choices for third digit. We would have 3 choices for the first digit. Because we can't repeat any digits, we'd only have 2 choices left for the second digit, and we'd only be left with one choice for the third digit.

To visualize this process, it can be helpful to draw slots for each task we are considering, then multiply together the number of items that could go in each slot. In our permutaiton problem, each number must have three digits, so we write down three slots:

$$\_\_ \times \_\_ \times \_\_$$

There are 3 possible digits that can go into the first slot, so we put a 3 into that slot:

$$\underline{\ 3\ } \times \_\_ \times \_\_$$

Because one digit gets used up in the first slot, that leaves 2 possible digits for the second slot:

$$\underline{\ 3\ } \times \underline{\ 2\ } \times \_\_$$

Finally, there is 1 possible digit for the third slot:

$$\underline{\ 3\ } \times \underline{\ 2\ } \times \underline{\ 1\ }$$

We can now find the product of the numbers in the slots: $3 \times 2 \times 1 = 6$.

This pattern of multiplication, where we multiply an integer by all of the postive integers below it, is called a **factorial**. Factorials are written with an exclamation point:

$$3! = 3 \times 2 \times 1 = 6$$

Therefore, we could also say that the number of permutations possible for these three digits is $3!$, or 3 factorial. If we wanted to calculate permutations for 4, 5, or more digits, we would find a similar pattern in our results. For 4 digits, we would have $4! = 4 \times 3 \times 2 \times 1 = 24$ permutations. For 5 digits, we would have $5! = 5 \times 4 \times 3 \times 2 \times 1 = 120$ permutations. Therefore, to find all of the possible permutations of a certain number of tasks, we only need to take the factorial of that number.

Some questions will ask for permutations that are smaller than the number of elements in the set. In other words, the number of slots may be smaller than the number of objects to arrange. The number of elements in each permutation is called its **size**.

For instance, consider the following question:

> To determine the 1st, 2nd, and 3rd prize of a lottery drawing, three tickets are selected one at a time from a pool of 50 total tickets, with no repeats allowed. In how many ways can the 3 tickets be selected?

This is a permutation question because the order matters: selecting one person for 1st place and a second person for 3rd place is different than selecting one person for 3rd place and the second person for 1st place. However, we don't need to find the number of permutations for *all* places in the lottery drawing, only for these first three places. Therefore, we only have three tasks to complete: selecting a 1st, 2nd, and 3rd place ticket.

There are 50 tickets we could select for 1st place. We would then have 49 tickets left for 2nd place and 48 tickets left for 3rd place. Therefore, the number of unique groups of tickets is $50 \times 49 \times 48 = 117{,}600$.

We can also use a formula involving factorials to calculate permutations of a certain size. In general, the number of permutations of n items taken r at a time is:

$$\frac{n!}{(n-r)!}$$

In our lottery example, we have 50 items (tickets), and we're calculating a permutation of 3 of those tickets at a time. When we plug these numbers into the formula above, we get:

$$\frac{50!}{(50-3)!} = \frac{50!}{47!}$$

We can simplify this expression by identifying a common factor in the numerator and denominator. Remember that $47!$ is equal to $47 \times 46 \times 45 \times 44 \times 43 \ldots$ and so on, multiplying 47 by all of the positive integers below it. Because $50!$ is 50 multiplied by all of the positive integers below it, these integers include all of the integers in $47!$:

$$50! = 50 \times 49 \times 48 \times 47 \times 46 \times 45 \ldots = 50 \times 49 \times 48 \times 47!$$

Therefore, we can simplify our fraction by dividing both our numerator and denominator by the common factor of $47!$:

$$\frac{50 \times 49 \times 48 \times 47!}{47!} = 50 \times 49 \times 48 = 117{,}600$$

This is the same result we calculated earlier.

CALCULATING COMBINATIONS

Let's take a look at how we would calculate the number of combinations possible for a specific set of tasks, where order does not matter. For example:

> John, Sue, Marie, and Tom are members of a soccer team. In how many ways can their coach choose two of them to be midfielders?

If we cared about the order that the players were chosen, then we would have the following 12 possibilities:

John and Sue	John and Marie	John and Tom
Sue and John	Sue and Marie	Sue and Tom
Marie and John	Marie and Sue	Marie and Tom
Tom and John	Tom and Sue	Tom and Marie

However, we don't care about the order in which the players are chosen. If John and Sue are chosen as midfielders, this is the same is saying that Sue and John are chosen as midfielders. Therefore, we have to cross out all of the duplicate possibilities on our table:

John and Sue	John and Marie	John and Tom
~~Sue and John~~	Sue and Marie	Sue and Tom
~~Marie and John~~	~~Marie and Sue~~	Marie and Tom
~~Tom and John~~	~~Tom and Sue~~	~~Tom and Marie~~

Because order doesn't matter, there are only 6 ways that the coach could choose two players to be midfielders. When we treated this combination problem as a permutation problem, we overcounted by a factor of 2.

In general, when we treat a combination problem as a permutation problem, we overcount the number of combinations by a factor of $r!$, where r is the size of each combination. Therefore, when we are calculating a combination, we have to "scale down" the permutation formula by a factor of $r!$. The number of combinations of n items taken r at a time is

$$\frac{n!}{r!\,(n-r)!}$$

In the soccer example above, we had 4 items (soccer players), and we were calculating combinations of two players at a time. When we plug these numbers into our formula, we get:

$$\frac{4!}{2!\,(4-2)!} = \frac{4!}{2! \times 2!}$$

Then, we simplify by dividing by a common factor:

$$\frac{4!}{2! \times 2!} = \frac{4 \times 3 \times 2!}{2! \times 2!} = \frac{4 \times 3}{2!} = \frac{12}{2 \times 1} = 6$$

We have 6 possible combinations, which is the same answer we got above.

Here is another example to illustrate this concept:

Michael has 10 friends that he wishes to invite to his birthday party, but his parents have told him that he can only invite 6. In how many ways can Michael choose 6 friends to invite?

Michael has 6 friends to invite, so we might start by drawing 6 slots:

$$\_\_ \times \_\_ \times \_\_ \times \_\_ \times \_\_ \times \_\_$$

Assuming that order matters, Michael would have 10 friends possible for his first choice, 9 for his second, 8 for his third, and so on. We would fill out the slots like this:

$$\underline{10} \times \underline{9} \times \underline{8} \times \underline{6} \times \underline{5}$$

There would be $10 \times 9 \times 8 \times 7 \times 6 \times 5$ ways for Michael to choose 6 friends from 10 friends, if order mattered.

However, in the question above, order does not matter. It doesn't matter which friend Michael chooses first, second, or third—what matters is how many different combinations of friends he can invite. Remember that when we treat a combination problem as a permutation problem, we overcount the number of combinations by a factor of $r!$, where r is the size of each combination. The size of each combination in this problem is 6, so we have to divide our total by 6! in order to avoid overcounting:

$$\frac{10 \times 9 \times 8 \times 7 \times 6 \times 5}{6!} = \frac{10 \times 9 \times 8 \times 7 \times 6 \times 5}{6 \times 5 \times 4 \times 3 \times 2 \times 1} = \frac{10 \times 9 \times 8 \times 7}{4 \times 3 \times 2 \times 1} = \frac{5040}{24} = 210$$

Because order doesn't matter, Michael only has 210 combinations of 6 friends he could choose. You can also try calculating this using our formula for combinations, and you'll get the same result!

PRACTICE QUESTIONS: ORGANIZED COUNTING

For questions 1-4, refer to the chart below.

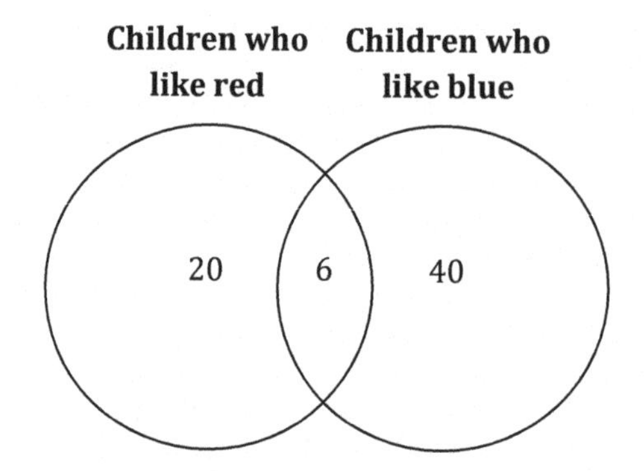

1. How many children like red, in total?

2. How many children like both red and blue?

3. How many children like blue but not red?

4. In this chart, how many children do not like blue?

For questions 5-7, refer to the chart below.

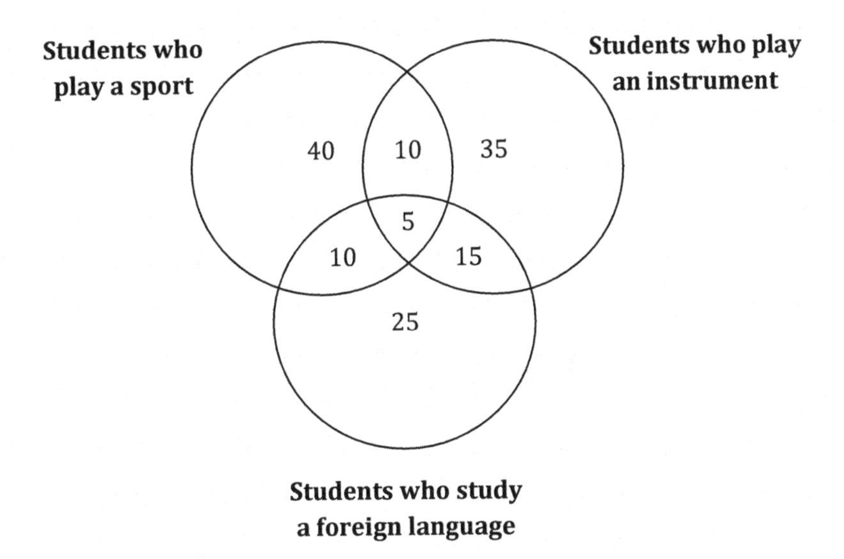

5. How many total students study a foreign language?

6. How many students only play an instrument, but do not play a sport or study a foreign language?

7. How many students both play a sport and play an instrument, but do not study a foreign language?

8. At a restaurant, Emily can choose one of two appetizers and one of four main dishes. How many combinations of one appetizer and one main dish can Emily choose?

9. A phone company gives customers the option to choose the colors of their phones. They can choose a green, blue, pink, or yellow keyboard, and they can choose a black, white, or silver background. How many different color combinations can a customer choose for his or her phone keyboard and background?

10. Fifth grade students at Billings Elementary School choose one elective to take during first period and one elective to take during second period. During first period, they can choose to take dance or gym. During second period, they can choose to take art, music, or theater. How many different combinations of electives are possible for a student to choose?

Questions 12-16 are Upper Level Only.

11. Jorje is a newspaper boy. He has 5 houses on his route. If he can deliver his newspapers to the houses in any order he chooses, how many different combinations of routes does Jorje have?

12. In a lottery, you can choose any three-digit number. If you pick the correct three-digit number, you will win the lottery. How many different numbers can you choose from?

13. A store sells 10 different flavors of cookies. Jaymon wants to buy two cookies, each one a different flavor. How many different pairs of cookies could he buy?

14. A gymnastic team has 12 players. The coach will pick one player to be the captain and one player to be the assistant captain of the team. How many different pairs of students could the coach pick for these positions?

15. Susan is buying groceries. She needs to buy 4 different fruits to fill her basket. There are 10 different types of fruit available. How different ways are possible for her to fill her basket?

16. New Valley High has 8 students in its chess club. It will select three students for the regional championship team. How many different combinations of students can be selected for the team?

17. Raphael wants to prepare a soup with 10 ingredients. He has 12 ingredients on hand, and knows that the order with which he throws his ingredients into the soup pot does not matter. How many different soups could he make?

18. David is trying to remember the code that goes with his combination lock. His lock has 10 numbers. His code has three numbers, and any of the numbers in the code may be the same. How many codes are possible for his lock?

PROBABILITY

ALL LEVELS

SECTION 4

Probability refers to the likelihood that something will happen. Scientists and mathematicians can make educated predictions about the future by analyzing a lot of data and using the principles of probability. For example, weather forecasters use probability to predict the chance of rain tomorrow, and medical researchers use probability to predict people's chances of developing heart disease or lung cancer.

To calculate probability, use the formula below:

$$Probability = \frac{Number\ of\ ways\ to\ get\ a\ certain\ outcome}{Number\ of\ possible\ outcomes}$$

For example:

> What is the probability of rolling an even number on a six-sided number cube, which has the numbers 1 through 6?

Unless the number cube or the surface we are rolling on has been tampered with, there is an equal chance that we will roll any of the numbers from 1 through 6. Therefore, there are six possible outcomes. However, if want to roll an even number, there are only three even numbers that we can roll: 2, 4, and 6. To find the probability of rolling an even number, we divide the number of even-number outcomes (3) by the number of possible outcomes (6):

$$Probability\ of\ rolling\ an\ even\ number = \frac{3}{6} = \frac{1}{2}$$

The probability of rolling an even number is $\frac{1}{2}$. We can also state this as a decimal (0.5) or as a percent (50%). We can say that there is a "50 percent chance" of rolling an even number.

Our predicted probabilities do not always exactly match up with reality, particularly if we only have a small amount of data. For example, suppose you wanted to test out the probability of rolling an even number by doing an experiment. You get an evenly weighted six-sided number cube with numbers 1 through 6 and begin rolling the cube on a flat, even surface. Based on your calculations, you would expect to roll an even number half of the time. At the beginning of your experiment, you might find that this is not true; after four rolls of the cube, maybe only one of them gave you an even number, or maybe three of them did. However, as you continue rolling the cube and accumulating more data, you should find that the fraction of even numbers showing up begins to get closer and closer to $\frac{1}{2}$. It might never reach exactly $\frac{1}{2}$, but as long as it is close, you know your prediction worked for this experiment. If it doesn't get close to $\frac{1}{2}$, you know there was something wrong with either your prediction or the way you conducted the experiment.

If we assume that our predictions are accurate, then we can use probability to find information about a set of data. Here is an example:

A jar contains 40 jellybeans. The probability of choosing a red jellybean is $\frac{1}{4}$. How many red jellybeans are in the jar?

The question tells us that there is a $\frac{1}{4}$ probability of choosing a red jellybean. If we calculated this probability using our formula, we would divide the number of ways we can pick a red jellybean by the number of total jellybeans we could pick, and we would get $\frac{1}{4}$. We're told that the number of total jellybeans is 40, and the number of ways we could pick a red jellybean is the same thing as the number of red jellybeans in the jar. Therefore, we can write:

$$Probability\ of\ choosing\ a\ red\ jellybean = \frac{Number\ of\ red\ jellybeans}{40} = \frac{1}{4}$$

How would we work backwards to find the number of red jellybeans? We need re-write $\frac{1}{4}$ as a fraction with a denominator of 40:

$$\frac{1}{4} = \frac{?}{40}$$

To do this, we multiply the numerator and denominator by 10:

$$\frac{1 \times 10}{4 \times 10} = \frac{10}{40}$$

The number of red jellybeans in the jar is equal to 10.

PROBABILITIES OF ZERO OR ONE

Most probabilities will be fractions or decimals between 0 and 1, or a percent between 0% and 100%. The lower the probability, the less likely an event is to occur. The higher the probability, the more likely an event is to occur.

A probability of 0 means an event is impossible and will absolutely never occur. For instance:

What is the probability of rolling the number 7 on a six-sided number cube, with numbers 1 through 6?

There are six possible outcomes, but the number cube does not have the number 7. Therefore, there are zero ways to roll an outcome of 7. If we plug this into our formula, we get:

$$Probability\ of\ rolling\ the\ number\ 7 = \frac{0}{6} = 0$$

The probability of rolling the number 7 is 0, so there is a no chance that we will roll a 7. This event is impossible.

On the other hand, a probability of 1 or 100 percent means that an event is absolutely certain to happen. For instance:

What is the probability of rolling a whole number on a six-sided number cube, with numbers 1 through 6?

There are six possible outcomes, and all six of these numbers are whole numbers. Therefore, there are also six ways to get a whole number outcome:

$$Probability\ of\ rolling\ a\ positive\ number = \frac{6}{6} = 1$$

The probability of rolling a positive number is 1, so this event is absolutely certain to happen.

Because a probability of 1 means an event is absolutely certain, you will never get a probability greater than 1 or 100%. You might hear someone say that they are "200% certain" that something is going to happen, but this is just an exaggeration—in the language of mathematics, 100% certain is the most you can be!

If you know the probability of getting a certain outcome, you can also calculate the probability of *not* getting that outcome. These two possibilities are called **complementary events**.

Here is an example:

> What is the probability of not rolling in the number 4 on a six-sided number cube?

Rolling the number 4 and not rolling the number 4 are complementary events. When you roll a number cube, you are absolutely certain to either roll a 4 or not roll a 4. In other words, if you were to calculate the probability of either rolling a 4 or not rolling a 4, you would get a probability of 1.

Therefore, the probability of not rolling a 4 is 1 minus the probability that you will roll a 4. You have a $\frac{1}{6}$ chance of rolling the number 4 on a six-sided number cube. To find your chance of not rolling the number 4, subtract $\frac{1}{6}$ from 1:

$$Probability\ of\ not\ rolling\ 4 = 1 - \frac{1}{6} = \frac{5}{6}$$

You have a $\frac{5}{6}$ chance of not rolling the number 4, but rolling any of the other possible numbers (1, 2, 3, 5, or 6).

Finding the probability that something will not happen is 1 minus the probability that it *will* happen.

VIDEO

4.3 INTRO TO PROBABILITY

Watch at http:// videos.ivyglobal.com

ADDITION AND SUBTRACTION WITH PROBABILITY (MIDDLE/UPPER LEVEL ONLY)

Two events are **mutually exclusive** if it is impossible for both of them to happen at the same time. For example, if you roll one number cube, it is impossible to roll both the number 5 and the number 3. You can either roll one number or the other.

You can find the chance of one event *or* another event occurring by adding together their individual probabilities. For example:

> What is the probability of rolling either the number 5 or the number 3 on a six-sided number cube, with numbers 1 through 6?

The probability of rolling the number 5 on a six-sided number cube is $\frac{1}{6}$ and the probability of rolling the number 3 is also $\frac{1}{6}$. To find your chances of rolling the number 5 *or* the number 3, add their probabilities together:

$$Probability\ of\ rolling\ 5\ or\ 3 = \frac{1}{6} + \frac{1}{6} = \frac{1}{3}$$

There is a $\frac{1}{3}$ chance that you will roll either the number 5 or the number 3.

As we learned in the section above, 1 is the biggest possible probability. If you add together the probabilities of all of the different outcomes of an event, you will get the number 1. For example:

What is the probability of rolling the numbers 1, 2, 3, 4, 5, or 6 on a six-sided number cube?

If you roll a six-sided number cube, you have six possible outcomes: the numbers 1, 2, 3, 4, 5, and 6. You have a $\frac{1}{6}$ chance of rolling any one of these numbers. If you add all their probabilities together, you will get the number 1:

$$Probability\ of\ rolling\ 1, 2, 3, 4, 5, or\ 6 = \frac{1}{6} + \frac{1}{6} + \frac{1}{6} + \frac{1}{6} + \frac{1}{6} + \frac{1}{6} = 1$$

You are certain to roll the number 1, 2, 3, 4, 5 or 6 because there are no other options!

MULTIPLICATION WITH PROBABILITY (MIDDLE/UPPER LEVEL ONLY)

If two events are **independent**, the first event does not affect the probability of the second event. For instance, if you were to roll two 6-sided number cubes, your chance of rolling an even number on one cube does not affect your chance of rolling an even number on the second cube. For each cube, you still have a $\frac{1}{2}$ probability of rolling an even number.

If two events are independent, you can find the chance of *both* occurring by multiplying together their individual probabilities. For example:

What is the probability of rolling two even numbers on one roll of two 6-sided number cubes?

The probability of rolling an even number for the first cube is ½, and the probability of rolling an even number on the second cube is also $\frac{1}{2}$. Simply multiply these together:

$$Probability\ of\ rolling\ an\ even\ number\ on\ both\ number\ cubes = \frac{1}{2} \times \frac{1}{2} = \frac{1}{4}$$

You have a ¼ or 25% chance of rolling an even number on both number cubes.

Why does this work? Let's try diagramming all of the possible outcomes on an **outcome table.** In this table, we show all of the different pairs of numbers that you could roll on the two number cubes:

1 and 1	1 and 2	1 and 3	1 and 4	1 and 5	1 and 6
2 and 1	2 and 2	2 and 3	2 and 4	2 and 5	2 and 6
3 and 1	3 and 2	3 and 3	3 and 4	3 and 5	3 and 6
4 and 1	4 and 2	4 and 3	4 and 4	4 and 5	4 and 6
5 and 1	5 and 2	5 and 3	5 and 4	5 and 5	5 and 6
6 and 1	6 and 2	6 and 3	6 and 4	6 and 5	6 and 6

There are 36 possible outcomes. Now, we'll shade all of the outcomes that show two even numbers:

1 and 1	1 and 2	1 and 3	1 and 4	1 and 5	1 and 6
2 and 1	2 and 2	2 and 3	2 and 4	2 and 5	2 and 6
3 and 1	3 and 2	3 and 3	3 and 4	3 and 5	3 and 6
4 and 1	4 and 2	4 and 3	4 and 4	4 and 5	4 and 6
5 and 1	5 and 2	5 and 3	5 and 4	5 and 5	5 and 6
6 and 1	6 and 2	6 and 3	6 and 4	6 and 5	6 and 6

There are 9 possible outcomes that give us two even numbers. 9 possible outcomes divided by 36 total outcomes is equal to $\frac{1}{4}$:

$$\frac{9}{36} = \frac{1}{4}$$

This is the same answer we got before: you have a $\frac{1}{4}$ chance of rolling two even numbers.

VIDEO

4.4 OPERATIONS WITH PROBABILITIES

Watch at http:// videos.ivyglobal.com

Two events are **dependent** if one event affects the probability of the other event occurring. If two events are dependent, we need to figure out what happens to the probability of the second event after the first one has taken place. For example:

> Janice picked cards randomly from a standard 52-card deck. She picked her first card and then set it aside, without replacing it, before drawing her second card. What is the probability that both cards were kings?

The probability for the first card is easy: there are 52 cards in the deck and 4 of them are kings, so Janice has a $\frac{4}{52}$ or $\frac{1}{13}$ chance of picking a king for her first card.

However, now that she has removed one card, the number of cards in the deck has changed. She now has only 51 cards in her deck. If her first card was a king, there are only 3 kings left. Therefore, the probability that her second card will also be a king is only $\frac{3}{51}$.

You've figured out the probability of the first event, and how the probability of the second event will be affected if the first event takes place. You can now multiply these probabilities together to find the probability of both events occurring:

$$Probability\ of\ picking\ two\ kings = \frac{1}{13} \times \frac{3}{51} = \frac{3}{663} = \frac{1}{221}$$

If Janice is drawing two cards one at a time, without putting her first card back in the deck, the probability that she will pick two kings is 1 out of 221.

VIDEO

4.5 PROBABILITY OF DEPENDENT EVENTS

Watch at http:// videos.ivyglobal.com

PROBABILITY AND GEOMETRY (MIDDLE/UPPER LEVEL ONLY)

You may need to use your knowledge of geometry to calculate the probability of something randomly occurring in a specific region of a geometric figure. In this case, the "number of ways to get a certain outcome" is equal to the area of the specific region, and the "number of possible outcomes" is equal to the area of the whole figure:

$$Probability\ of\ something\ happening\ in\ a\ region = \frac{Area\ of\ specific\ region}{Area\ of\ whole\ figure}$$

This type of question often involves randomly throwing an object, such as a dart, at a surface, such as a dartboard. Intuitively, the larger the target, the more likely it is that a dart will hit it. For example:

The following diagram shows a square board with a shaded square in the middle. The board has a side length of 10 inches, and the square in the middle has a side length of 5 inches. What is the chance that a small coin thrown completely at random onto the board will land in the shaded region?

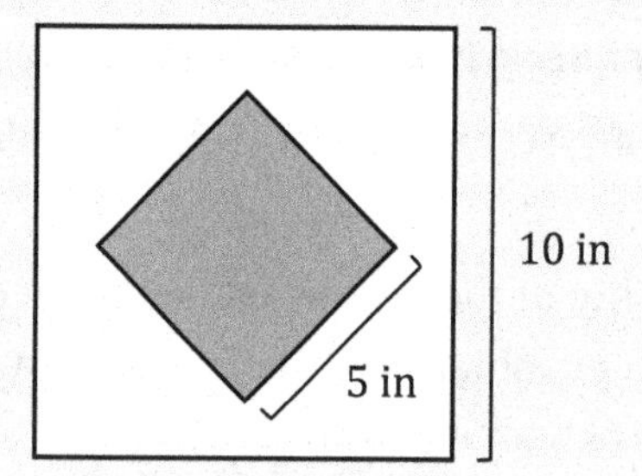

To find the probability that a randomly thrown coin will land in the shaded square, we need to find the area of the shaded square and then divide by the area of the whole figure. The shaded square has a side length of 5 inches, so its area is 25 square inches. The whole board is a square with a side length of 10 inches, so its area is 100 square inches. Therefore, the probability of our coin landing in the shaded region is

$$Probability\ of\ landing\ in\ the\ shaded\ region = \frac{25}{100} = \frac{1}{4}$$

There is ¼ or 25% chance that our coin, thrown truly at random, will land in the shaded square.

VIDEO
4.6 PROBABILITY AND GEOMETRY
Watch at http:// videos.ivyglobal.com

PRACTICE QUESTIONS: PROBABILITY

Unless the instructions say otherwise, write all probabilities as fractions in lowest terms.

1. Mr. Johnson's class has 12 boys and 14 girls. If Mr. Johnson picks one student at random from the class, what is the probability that he will pick a boy?

2. Lisa has 2 black headbands, 1 red headband, and 1 silver headband. If she picks a headband at random, what is the probability that it will be red?

3. Shannon picks one day randomly out of the days of the week. What is the probability that she will pick a day that ends in the letter "y"?

4. The local pet store has 6 black fish and 9 red fish. If Manuel randomly chooses one fish from the pet store, what is the probability that he will choose a red fish?

5. A bakery sells chocolate, cinnamon, maple, honey, and jelly donuts. It currently has 48 total donuts in stock. If Xiwen picks one donut from the bakery at random, she has a 1/4 chance of picking a chocolate donut. How many chocolate donuts does the bakery have in stock?

6. If Mr. Maron picks one student randomly from his class, he has a 1/3 probability of picking a student with blonde hair. There are 27 students in Mr. Maron's class. How many students have blonde hair?

7. A box of paperclips has 4 blue, 5 red, 3 green, and 3 white paperclips. If Adam chooses a paperclip randomly from the box, what is the probability that it will not be red?

8. A jar has 30 red candies, 20 blue candies, 40 green candies, and 10 yellow candies. Of the green candies, half are apple-flavored and half are lime-flavored. If Anisha picks one candy randomly from the jar, what is the probability that she will not pick a green lime-flavored candy?

9. At Wilson Elementary School, there is a 1/5 probability of randomly choosing a 5th-grade student who plays the flute. If there are 80 students in the 5th grade, how many of them are not learning the flute?

For questions 10-12, refer to the figure below. The figure shows the spinner of a board game, which has four equally sized sections in the colors red, orange, pink, and yellow.

10. If the spinner is spun at random, what is the probability that it will land on red?

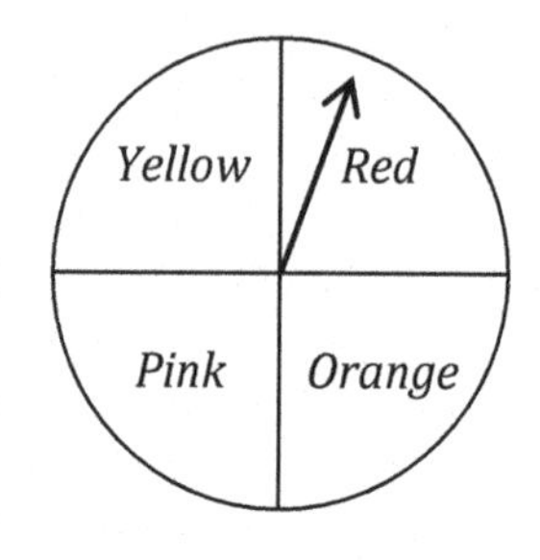

11. What is the probability that the spinner will not land on orange?

12. What is the probability that the spinner will land on green?

Questions 13-20 are Middle/Upper Level Only.

13. Ariel and Trevor are entering a raffle to raise money for the school library. Ariel buys three tickets and Trevor buys five tickets. At the end of the raffle, 240 tickets have been sold, and one ticket is randomly chosen as the winner. What is the probability that either Ariel or Trevor has bought the winning ticket?

14. A standard deck of cards has 4 kings, 4 queens, 4 jacks, and 40 other cards. If Carol picks a card at random from this standard deck, what is the probability that she will pick a king, queen, or jack?

15. Jake has a six-sided die with numbers 1 through 6. If he rolls the die twice, what is the probability that he will roll two numbers whose sum is 12?

16. In the United States, about 40% of people will be diagnosed with some type of cancer at some point in their lifetime. If two people are randomly chosen, what is the probability that both of them will be diagnosed with cancer at some point in their lifetime? Write your answer as a percent.

17. Jonas has four blue socks, ten black socks, and six white socks. If he picks two socks randomly, one at a time, without putting either sock back, what is the probability that he will pick two blue socks?

18. Kimberly has 4 six-sided number cubes, each with numbers 1 through 6. If she rolls all 4 number cubes at the same time, what is the probability that she will roll either a 1 or a 2 with each die?

19. Mrs. Chang's soccer team has 9 girls and 9 boys. In order to determine which two players will bring snacks to the first practice, Mrs. Chang picks one person randomly from the team and then picks a second person from the remaining players. What is the probability that she will pick two girls?

20. In the figure below, a rectangular game board 50 centimeters long and 40 centimeters tall has two square holes, each with a side length of 10 centimeters. If a player tosses a small bean bag randomly at the board, the beanbag will either hit the game board or go through one of the holes. What is the probability that it will go through one of the holes?

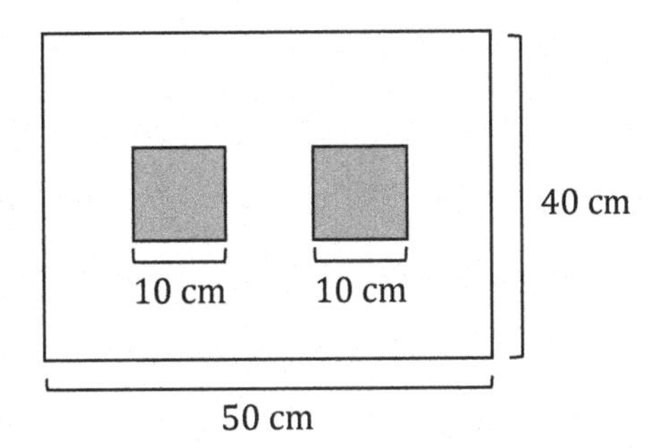

Questions 21-24 are Upper Level Only.

21. In the figure below, a circular target is made up of three concentric circles: one large circle, one medium circle, and one "bull's-eye" in the center. The radius of each concentric circle is twice as large as the radius of the next smallest circle, and the total diameter of the target is 16 inches. An arrow was shot at random and landed somewhere on the target. What is the probability that it landed on the shaded "bull's-eye" in the center?

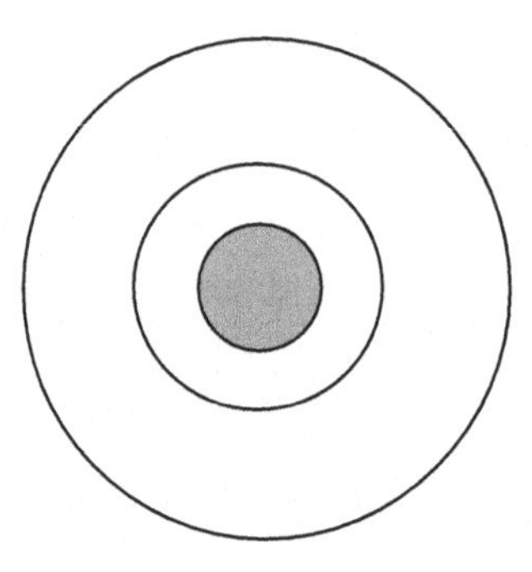

22. Andrew and Lucia are two of 6 people who have signed up for a flower show. The show will award a 1st prize and a 2nd prize. If prizes are given out at random, what is the probability that both Andrew and Lucia will be awarded a prize?

23. In a lottery, Nathan can pick three different numbers out of 10. If he picks the right numbers in the right order, he wins. What are the chances that he wins the lottery?

PART 4 REVIEW

DATA INTERPRETATION

In this section, you will find 50 practice questions to review the data interpretation content tested on the ISEE's Math Achievement section. The Lower Level questions cover the data interpretation content that you will find on the Lower Level section, as well as the easier data interpretation content on the Middle and Upper Level sections. The Middle Level questions cover content that you will only find on the Middle and Upper Level sections. The Upper Level questions cover content that you will only find on the Upper Level section.

Each question is followed by four suggested answers. Read each question and then decide which one of the four suggested answers is best.

LOWER LEVEL QUESTIONS

Use these questions to practice the data interpretation content that you will see on the Lower Level Math Achievement section, as well as the easier data interpretation content that you will see on the Middle and Upper Levels. Lower, Middle, and Upper Level students should attempt these questions.

For questions 1-2, refer to the graph below.

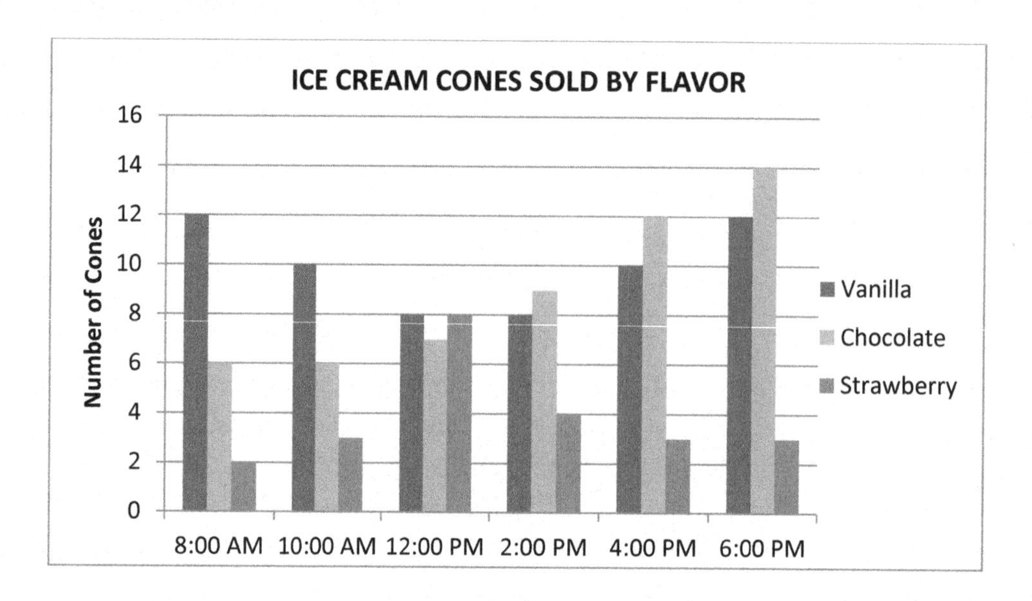

1. How many more total ice cream cones were sold at 6PM than at 12PM?

   (A) 3
   (B) 5
   (C) 6
   (D) 7

2. How many more vanilla ice cream cones than chocolate ice cream cones were sold throughout the entire day?

   (A) 5
   (B) 6
   (C) 7
   (D) 9

Use the diagram to answer the question.

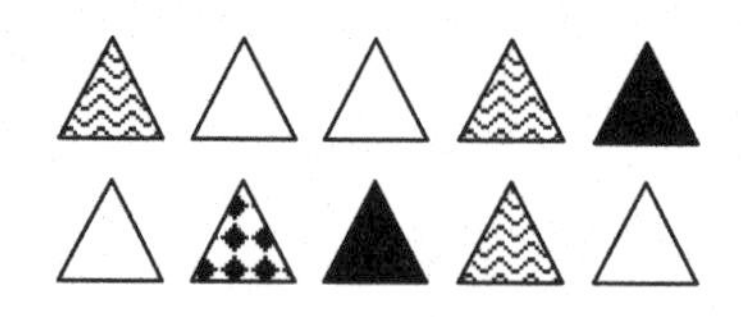

3. If one of the triangles is picked at random, what is the chance that it will be a ?

   (A) 1 out of 10
   (B) 1 out of 5
   (C) 3 out of 10
   (D) 1 out of 3

For questions 4-6, refer to the graph below.

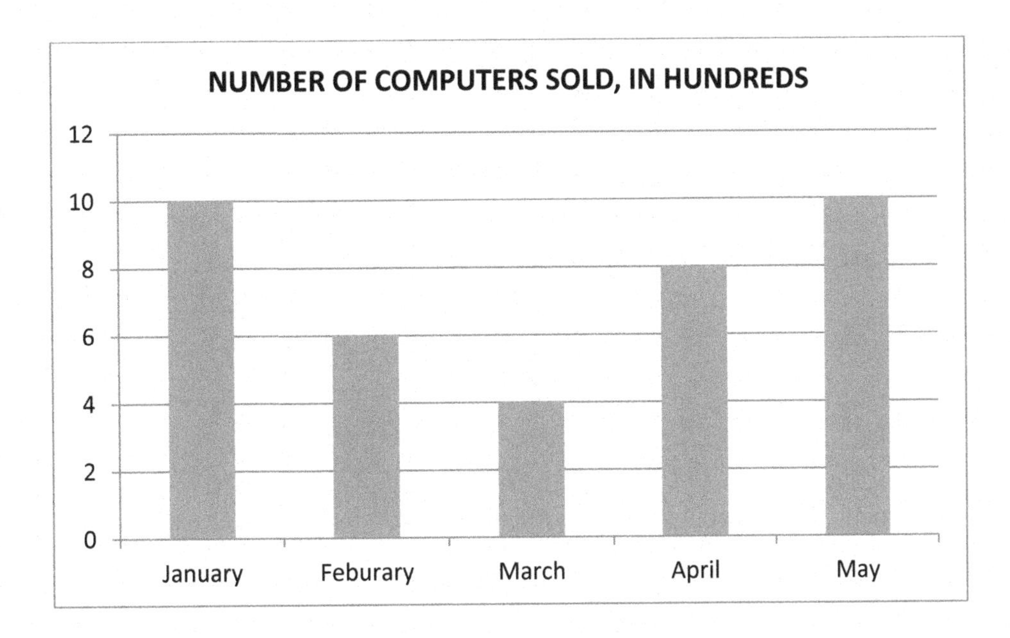

4. How many fewer computers were sold in March than in January?

    (A) 6
    (B) 10
    (C) 400
    (D) 600

5. The number of computers sold in May was how many times the number of computers sold in March?

    (A) 2.5
    (B) 4
    (C) 10
    (D) 600

6. From January through May, what was the average number of computers sold per month?

    (A) 400
    (B) 760
    (C) 940
    (D) 3800

For questions 7-8, refer to the graph below.

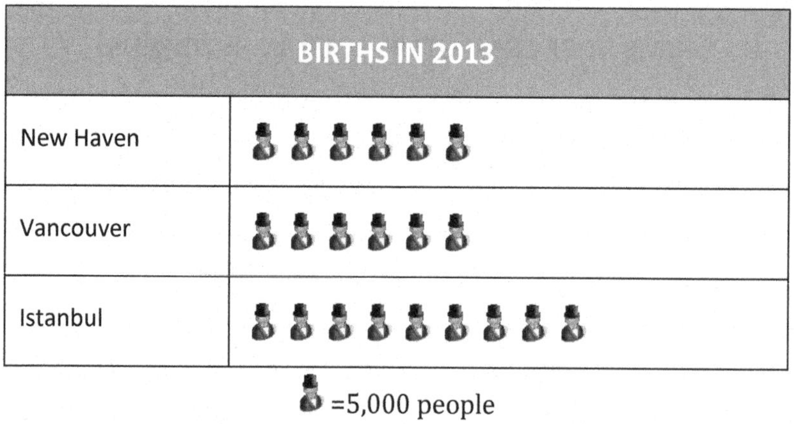

BIRTHS IN 2013	
New Haven	👤👤👤👤👤👤
Vancouver	👤👤👤👤👤👤
Istanbul	👤👤👤👤👤👤👤👤👤

👤 =5,000 people

7. How many more people were born in Istanbul than in Vancouver in 2013?

   (A) 3
   (B) 15
   (C) 3,000
   (D) 15,000

8. What is the mode for the number of births in 2013?

   (A) 30,000
   (B) 5,000
   (C) 9
   (D) 6

9. On three math tests, Raoul scored 8, 9, and 10. What was his average score?

   (A) 8
   (B) 8.5
   (C) 9
   (D) 9.5

For questions 10-11, refer to the chart below.

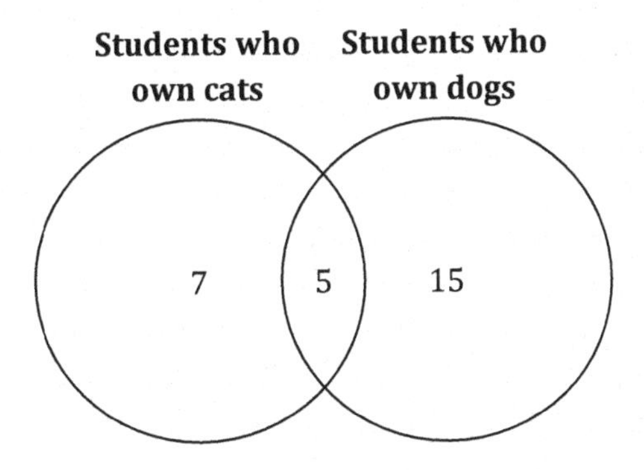

10. How many students own both cats and dogs?

    (A) 5
    (B) 7
    (C) 10
    (D) 15

11. How many students own dogs, in total?

    (A) 15
    (B) 20
    (C) 22
    (D) 27

12. Amelie has three green scarves, two red scarves, and one blue scarf. If she picks a scarf at random, what is the probability that she will pick a red scarf?

    (A) $\frac{1}{6}$
    (B) $\frac{1}{3}$
    (C) $\frac{1}{2}$
    (D) $\frac{2}{3}$

13. In English class, Julia has received scores of 87, 84, 75, and 90 on her first four quizzes. What is the median of Julia's quiz scores?

(A) 75
(B) 84
(C) 85.5
(D) 87.5

14. If Jack rolls one six-sided number cube, he has an equal chance of rolling any number from 1 through 6. What is the probability that he will roll a number less than 3?

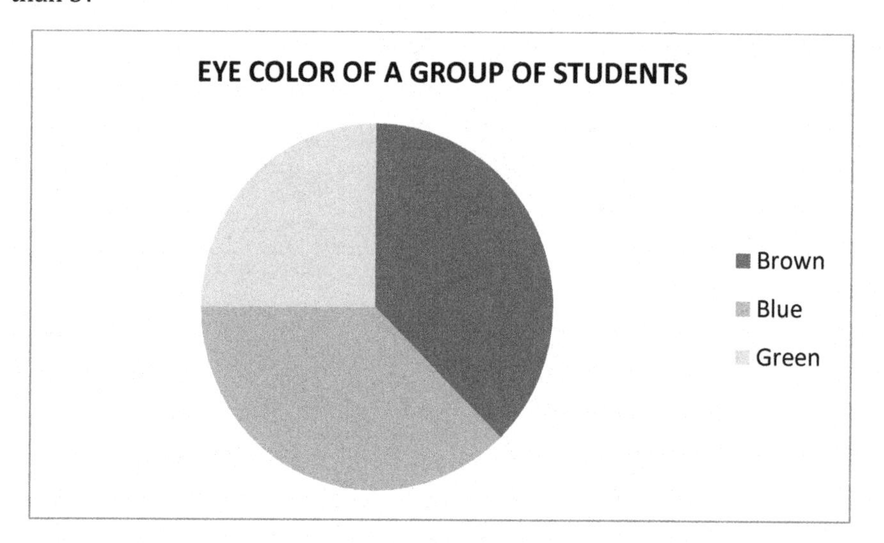

15. If there were 900 students in the group depicted in the graph above, about how many had green eyes?

(A) 225
(B) 300
(C) 350
(D) 450

16. Brian has two nieces and three nephews. He wants to choose one niece and one nephew to come ice skating with him. How many different pairs can he choose from?

(A) 2
(B) 3
(C) 5
(D) 6

17. In Ms. Emerson's class, there is a $\frac{1}{3}$ probability of randomly picking a student who walks to school. What is the probability of picking a student who doesn't walk to school?

(A) $\frac{1}{3}$
(B) $\frac{2}{3}$
(C) 1
(D) 3

18. Alana has eight dogs. If she picks one at random, she has a $\frac{3}{4}$ probability of picking a dog that is older than 6 years old. Of Alana's dogs, how many are younger than 6 years old?

(A) 2
(B) 3
(C) 4
(D) 6

MIDDLE LEVEL QUESTIONS

Use these questions to practice the content that you will only see on the Middle Level and Upper Level ISEE. Only Middle and Upper Level students should attempt these questions.

For questions 1-2, refer to the chart below.

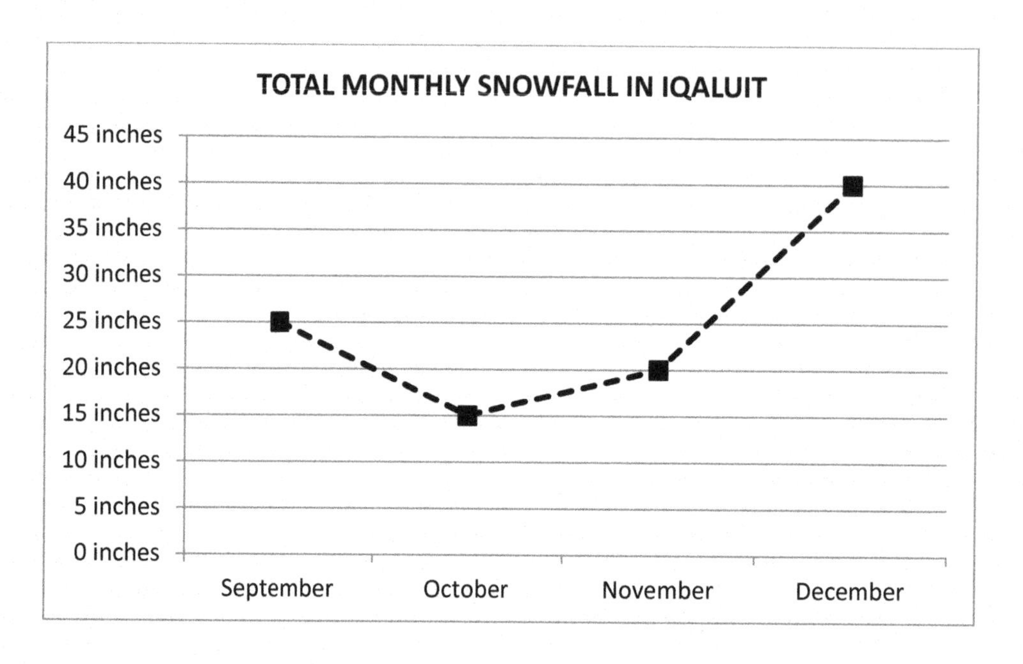

1. What was the average snowfall for Iqaluit from September to November?

   (A) 40 inches
   (B) 25 inches
   (C) 20 inches
   (D) 15 inches

2. How much more snow fell in December than in November?

   (A) 4 inches
   (B) 15 inches
   (C) 20 inches
   (D) 25 inches

3. If Kyle chooses at random one month from the calendar year, what is the probability that he will choose a month whose spelling ends in the letter "y"?

(A) $\frac{1}{6}$
(B) $\frac{1}{4}$
(C) $\frac{1}{3}$
(D) $\frac{1}{2}$

4. The diagram below shows the results of a survey asking people if they owned at least one dog, at least one cat, or both.

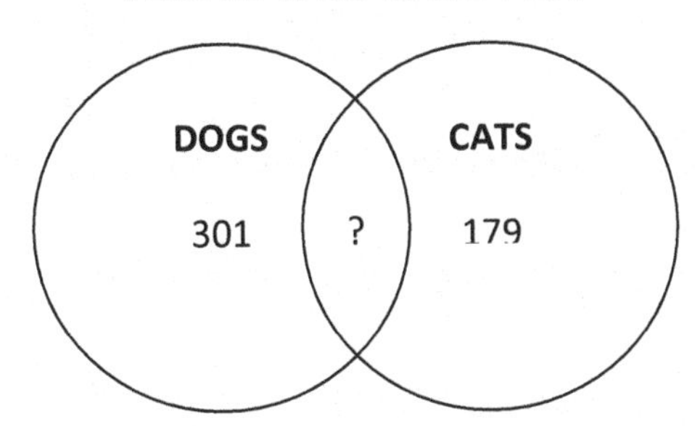

If 500 people were included in this survey, how many people said they owned both a dog and a cat?

(A) 480
(B) 400
(C) 42
(D) 20

5. John and Susan went apple picking four times in September. During these four trips, John picked a total of 144 apples. If Susan picked more apples than John, what is the lowest average number of apples that Susan could have picked on each trip?

(A) 5
(B) 35
(C) 37
(D) 145

For questions 6-7, refer to the graph below.

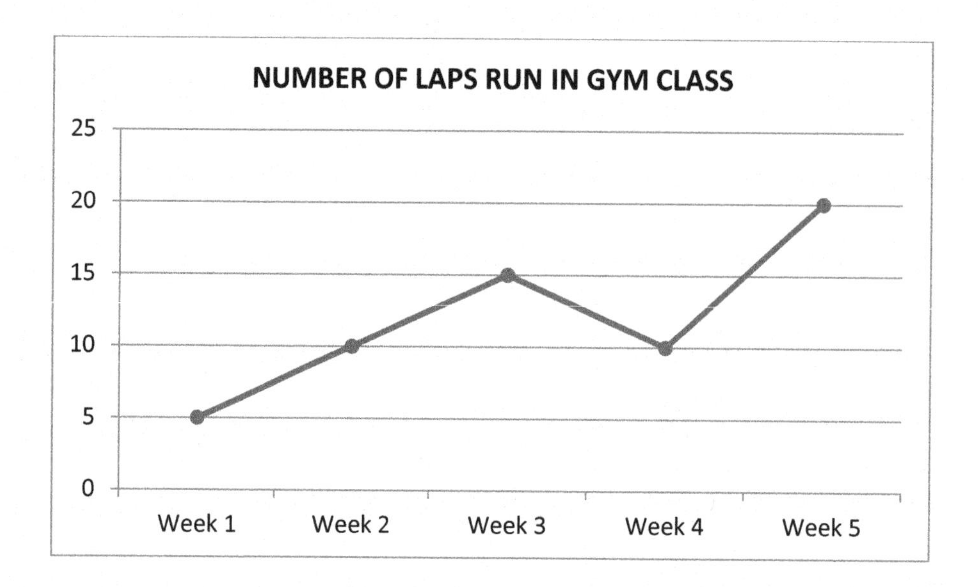

6. During the time period in the graph above, what was the average number of laps run in gym class each week?

   (A) 8
   (B) 10
   (C) 12
   (D) 15

7. What was the mode of laps run in gym class during the time period in the graph above?

   (A) 10
   (B) 12
   (C) 12.5
   (D) 15

8. A standard deck of 52 cards has 4 aces and 4 kings. If Jerome randomly chooses one card from a standard deck, what is the probability that he will choose either an ace or a king?

   (A) 152
   (B) 18
   (C) 213
   (D) 413

For questions 9-10, use the information below.

The following test scores were reported in a stem and leaf plot:

Stem	Leaf
0	1 2 5
2	0 1 3
4	0

9 | 1 = 91

9. What is the average score?

   (A) 11.5
   (B) 16
   (C) 18.25
   (D) 26

10. What is the range of the scores?

    (A) 4
    (B) 11.4
    (C) 40
    (D) 41

11. When Kristine rolls a six-sided number cube, she has an equal chance of rolling any number from 1 through 6. If Kristine rolls the same number cube 100 times, about how many times is she likely to roll a number greater than 4?

    (A) 17 times
    (B) 33 times
    (C) 50 times
    (D) 66 times

12. In her first four basketball games, Jane scored 22, 26, 18, and 12 points. By the end of her fifth game, Jane's average score across all five games was 21 points per game. How many points did Jane score in her fifth basketball game?

    (A) 21
    (B) 22
    (C) 27
    (D) 33

For questions 13-14, refer to the graph below.

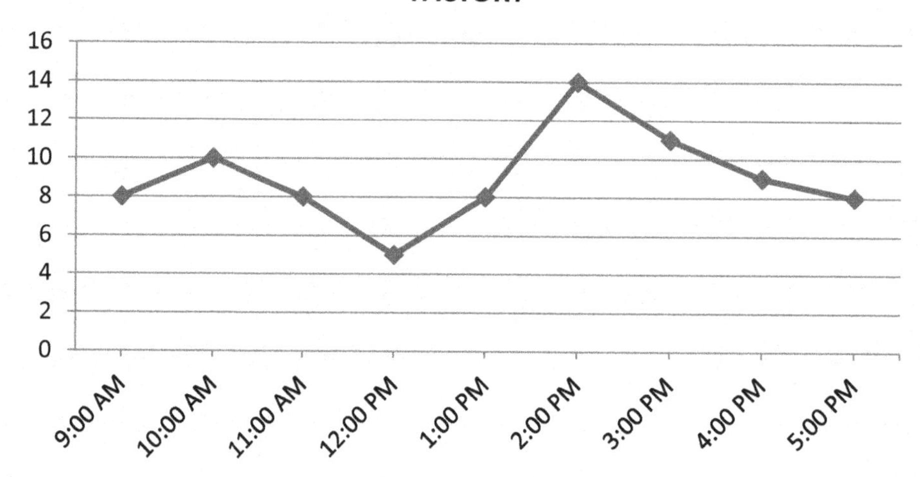

13. Over which time period did the rate of car production increase the most?

    (A) between 9:00 AM and 10:00 AM
    (B) between 12:00 PM and 1:00 PM
    (C) between 1:00 PM and 2:00 PM
    (D) between 2:00 PM and 3:00 PM

14. If the factory had been able to produce cars all day at its highest hourly rate, how many cars would the factory have been able to produce from 8:00 AM to 5:00 PM?

    (A) 45
    (B) 72
    (C) 84
    (D) 126

15. A bookshelf has 3 adventure books, 2 history books, and 3 science fiction books. Out of these books, Brianna has one favorite adventure book, one favorite history book, and one favorite science fiction book. If she randomly chooses one book of each type from the shelf, what is the probability that she will choose all three of her favorite books?

    (A) 118
    (B) 19
    (C) 16
    (D) 13

16. On a certain math exam, the 15 students in Mr. Donaldson's class scored an average of 80. On the same exam, the 10 students in Ms. Smith's class scored an average of 90. What was the combined average score for all of the students in Mr. Donaldson's and Ms. Smith's classes?

    (A) 80
    (B) 84
    (C) 85
    (D) 89

For questions 17-18, refer to the chart below.

VOTER SURVEY BY TOWN			
	Number of Voters		
Town	**Political Party A**	**Political Party B**	**Political Party C**
Fallsburg	121	211	80
Hillcrest	165	95	35
Railroad Junction	75	85	95

17. For the three towns in the chart above, the average number of voters for Political Party C is
    (A) 55
    (B) 60
    (C) 70
    (D) 90

18. How many more Political Party B voters live in Fallsburg than Political Party A voters who live in Hillcrest?
    (A) 46
    (B) 90
    (C) 165
    (D) 211

19. Across all three towns, how many more total voters would Political Party A need in order to have the same number of total voters as Political Party B?
    (A) 20
    (B) 30
    (C) 35
    (D) 45

20. Kim scored an average grade of 82 on her first four science quizzes. She wants to raise her average to a grade of 84. What is the lowest grade she can receive on her fifth science quiz in order to achieve this goal?

(A) 82
(B) 88
(C) 90
(D) 92

UPPER LEVEL QUESTIONS

Use these questions to practice the most challenging difficulty level you will see on the Upper Level ISEE. Only Upper Level students should attempt these questions.

1. When Susan rolls a six-sided number cube, she has an equal chance of rolling any number from 1 through 6. If she rolls two six-sided number cubes, what is the probability that she will roll two numbers with a sum of 7?

   (A) $\frac{1}{9}$
   (B) $\frac{1}{6}$
   (C) $\frac{7}{36}$
   (D) $\frac{1}{4}$

2. The histogram below shows Mrs. Hamilton's students' reading homework.

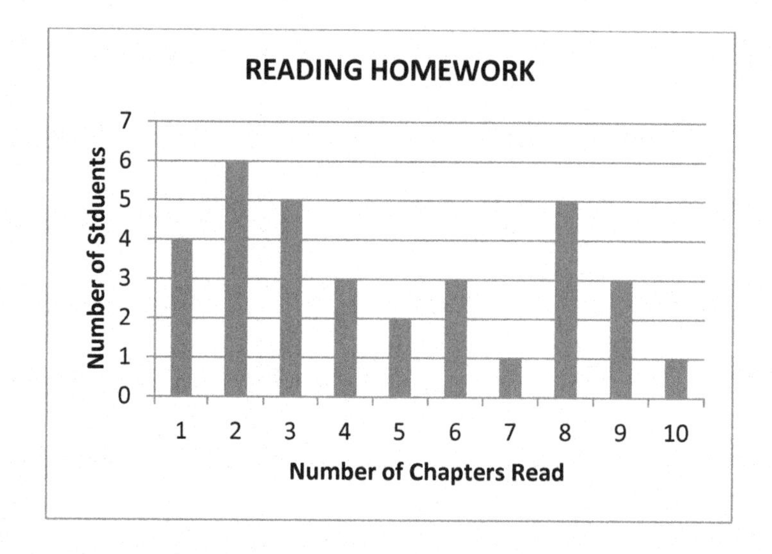

   Three students forgot to report their reading homework. When their information is added to the data, the median number of chapters read increases by 0.5 chapters. What is the smallest whole number of chapters that each student must have read?

   (A) 3
   (B) 4
   (C) 5
   (D) 8

For questions 3-4, refer to the chart below.

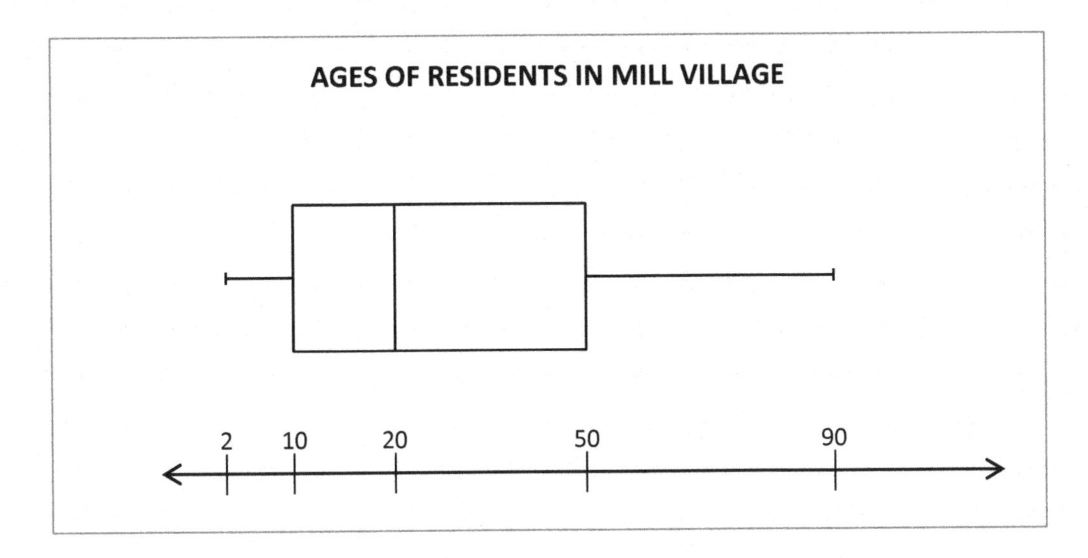

3. 50% of the residents in Mill Village are at least how old?

   (A) 2
   (B) 10
   (C) 20
   (D) 50

4. 25% of the residents in Mill Village are between which two ages?

   (A) 2 and 20
   (B) 10 and 50
   (C) 20 and 150
   (D) 50 and 90

5. The table below shows the result of a survey of 180 students.

FAVORITE SCHOOL LUNCH	
School Lunch	**Number of Students**
pizza	75
hamburger	40
salad	15
soup	5
sandwiches	45

A circle graph is made using the data. What is the central angle of the portion representing pizza?

(A) 15°
(B) 75°
(C) 150°
(D) 180°

6. Ms. Wei's class has 12 boys and 10 girls. Ms. Wei wants to pick one boy and one girl from her class to participate in the school assembly. How many different pairs could she choose from?

(A) 12
(B) 32
(C) 60
(D) 120

7. A bag contains marbles in 5 different colors. The table below shows the 5 different colors and the probability of randomly choosing 1 marble of that color out of the bag.

Color	Probability
red	$\frac{1}{8}$
green	$\frac{1}{8}$
purple	$\frac{1}{6}$
colorless	$\frac{1}{2}$
blue	$\frac{1}{12}$

How many total marbles might be in the bag?

(A) 8
(B) 12
(C) 24
(D) 36

8. There are 19 soccer balls in the team's bag. 13 of the balls are blue, and the rest are other colors. Carol takes one ball out of the bag. Two of her teammates then line up and each teammate selects a ball at random, one at a time. If Carol's ball was blue, what are the chances that both of her teammates' balls are NOT blue?

(A) 2/3
(B) 1/3
(C) 2/17
(D) 5/51

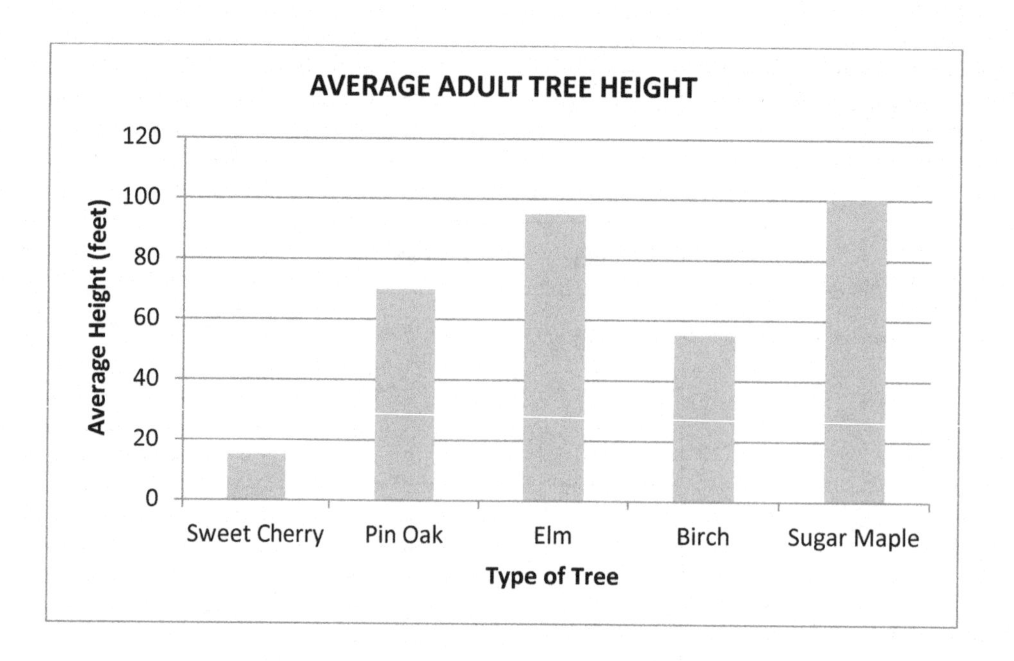

9. Louise planted a tree in her backyard that has grown 10 feet over the last 2 years. The tree will continue growing at this rate for the next 12 years until it reaches its adult height. Which type of tree did she most likely plant?

   (A) Sweet Cherry
   (B) Pin Oak
   (C) Elm
   (D) Birch

10. A game is played with a deck of 10 cards. To start the game, the first player is dealt a hand of 3 cards from the deck. How many different hands of cards could the first player be dealt?

    (A) 30
    (B) 120
    (C) 720
    (D) 1000

11. The table below shows the population density and the total population of three different towns.

Town	Total Population	Population Density (per square mile)
A	100,000	800
B	250,000	500
C	50,000	50

What is the range of the area of these three towns in square miles?

(A) 875
(B) 600
(C) 550
(D) 125

12. The figure below shows a circular board with a painted circle in the middle. The board has a total diameter of 8 inches, and the painted circle has a diameter of 4 inches. A dart was thrown at random and landed somewhere on the board. What is the probability that it landed in the painted circle?

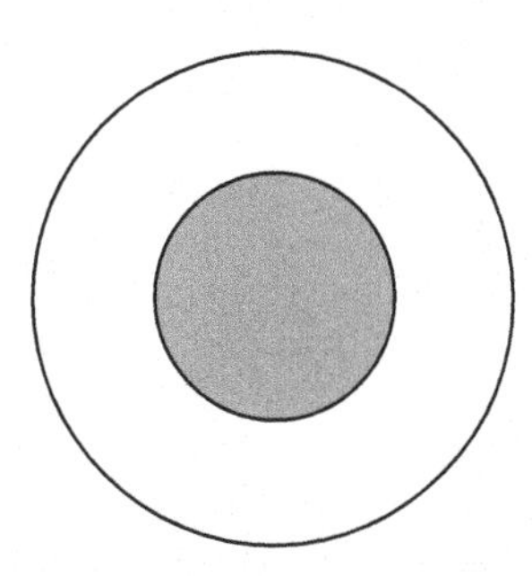

(A) 6.25%
(B) 12.5%
(C) 25%
(D) 50%

ANSWER KEYS

CHAPTER 5

QUANTITATIVE REASONING

CHAPTER 3

WORD PROBLEM STRATEGIES

EXERCISE #1: (PAGES 38-39)

1. A
2. B
3. D
4. A
5. D

EXERCISE #2: (PAGES 41-42)

1. B. In this case, all three of the other answer choices can be immediately eliminated. A is wrong because that's the probability of spinning one particular number, like 3 or 5. The probability of spinning a 3 OR a 5 must be greater than the probability of spinning just a 3 or just a 5. (Note: the probability of spinning a 3 AND a 5 is smaller than the probability of spinning a 3 OR a 5). C can be eliminated the spinner is divided into sections of 1/5 each, and it is impossible to make 1/2 with whole sections of the spinner. Remember, in spinner questions, the probability has to do with the size of the slice, but slices cannot be cut! D can also be eliminated because that corresponds to 3 slices- that's actually the probability of spinning a 1, 2, or 4.
2. The question tells you that there are four dozen chew toys and two dozen dogs. Even if you forget what a "dozen" is exactly, four is two times as many as two, so there are twice as many chew toys as dogs. If the chew toys are divided equally among the dogs, then no dog can get more than two chew toys. You can therefore eliminate all of the answers greater than 2, and your only answer left is A (2).
3. 12 is an even number, so a number divisible by 12 must also be an even number. You can therefore eliminate A, which is an odd number. 12 is also divisible by 3, so any number divisible by 12 must also be divisible by 3. Remember that you can test divisibility by 3 by adding together the digits of a number and seeing if the sum is divisible by 3. Using this method, you can determine that both B and D are not divisible by 3, so you can eliminate them. The only possible answer is C.

4. Eliminate A since Matt has to do better than his average in order to raise his average. B is a little trickier to eliminate, but you can eliminate it if you notice that the difference between 83% and 85% and between 85% and 87% is the same. Since the 85% average is from four tests and he only has two more tests to boost his average, he has to do better than an 87% on his remaining two tests in order to swing his average to an 85%. The correct answer is C.
5. A can be eliminated since that line would cross the origin, and the graph does not. B can be eliminated since the slope of the graph is positive (B might be the right answer if Jack's beanstalk were shrinking!). C is wrong since the y-intercept of that line would be 3. Also, the slope of that line would be 2. Since those values don't match the graph we see, we eliminate that answer choice. The correct answer is D.

EXERCISE #3: (PAGES 44-45)

1. 44. $9 is close to $10, so you may have guessed 40. The answer will be more than 40, however, since you can buy more books at a cheaper price. How many more? Well, 40 books cost $360, leaving the librarian with $40. She can buy 4 more books at $9 each with those extra $40. In total, the librarian can buy 44 books.
2. You might notice that the average number of legs per animal is slightly less than three, so there must be more two-legged animals (chickens) than four-legged animals (cows) in order to "swing" the average more towards 2 than 4. You could guess that there are 8 chickens and 7 cows. This yields 44 legs. That's too many; so let's try exchanging a chicken for a cow. 9 chickens and 6 cows works!
3. $2.72. Round each number to the nearest 10 cents and add back the 12 cents at the end (4×1 cent for the cans of soup and 8×1 cent for the cans of beans).
4. D
5. B

EXERCISE #4: (PAGE 47)

1. 12. Assume there were 100 people in total, so 60 people ate hamburgers and 40 people ate veggie burgers. Since 4 boxes of veggie burgers fed 40 people, there were 10 burgers per box. That means there were 5 hamburgers per box, so 12 boxes were required to feed 60 people.
2. $x + 7$. Pick any integer and add and subtract as required. She finishes 7 floors higher than where she started.

3. Pick any numbers to represent the length and width of the first rectangle, then figure out the length and width of the second rectangle. When you compare the two areas, the second rectangle is 3 times the size of the first.
4. 4.5%. Assume there were 100 fish in 2000. That means there were 110 fish in 2001 and 104.5 fish in 2002. It's kind of weird to think of half a fish, but we can still tell that percent increase was 4.5%.
5. $2(m+3)=r$. Say the maple tree started out at 5 feet. The red oak is then 16 feet tall. If you aren't able to immediately translate into algebra, try a few more values to get a feel for it and you should get $2(m+3)=r$.

EXERCISE #5: (PAGE 49)

1. B. If she splits them between herself and 5 other people, she is splitting them into 6 groups. Similarly, if she splits them between herself and 3 other people, she is splitting them between 4 people. Divide each number through by 6 and 4 and note the remainders.
2. B. Try dividing each of the numbers through.
3. A. Backsolving with C (9), she would have 57 beads in total after 5 minutes. That's too many, so try B (8). B leaves us with 52 beads in total, which is still too many, so pick A (7), the only smaller value.
4. C
5. C

WORD PROBLEM PRACTICE QUESTIONS

LOWER LEVEL QUESTIONS: (PAGES 50-59)

1. D
2. B
3. C
4. B
5. C
6. C
7. C
8. A
9. C
10. C
11. B
12. D
13. D
14. D
15. C
16. D
17. C
18. C
19. C
20. C
21. B
22. D
23. A
24. C
25. C
26. C
27. B
28. B
29. D
30. B

MIDDLE LEVEL QUESTIONS: (PAGES 60-72)

1. C
2. B
3. D
4. B
5. C
6. B
7. B
8. C
9. B
10. B
11. C
12. D
13. C
14. D
15. B
16. C
17. B
18. B
19. C
20. B
21. C
22. A
23. C
24. B
25. B
26. C
27. D
28. D
29. B
30. D
31. C
32. D
33. B
34. B
35. D
36. B
37. D
38. C
39. D
40. C
41. B
42. D
43. C
44. D
45. C
46. B
47. D
48. D

UPPER LEVEL QUESTIONS: (PAGES 73-80)

1. B
2. B
3. B
4. B
5. C
6. C
7. C
8. B
9. D
10. C
11. B
12. D
13. D
14. A
15. C
16. D
17. D
18. B
19. C
20. D
21. B
22. C
23. B
24. D
25. B

QUANTITATIVE COMPARISON STRATEGIES

EXERCISE #2: (PAGES 87-88)

1. B	2. A	3. A	4. A

EXERCISE #3: (PAGE 90)

1. D	3. B	5. C	7. C
2. A	4. A	6. B	

EXERCISE #4: (PAGES 92-93)

1. B	3. D	5. D	7. A
2. D	4. A	6. A	8. D

EXERCISE #5: (PAGES 95-96)

1. B	3. B	5. C	7. A
2. A	4. B	6. B	8. A

QUANTITATIVE COMPARISON PRACTICE QUESTIONS

MIDDLE LEVEL QUESTIONS: (PAGES 97-116)

1. A
2. A
3. D
4. A
5. B
6. B
7. C
8. A
9. A
10. A
11. D
12. B
13. A
14. C
15. C
16. D
17. C
18. A
19. C
20. A
21. C
22. A
23. A
24. D
25. C
26. B
27. C
28. B
29. C
30. A
31. A
32. A
33. C
34. D
35. A
36. B
37. B
38. D
39. A
40. B
41. B
42. D
43. C
44. B
45. C
46. A
47. C
48. B
49. B
50. D
51. A
52. C
53. B
54. A
55. D
56. C
57. B
58. B
59. B
60. C
61. A
62. C
63. B

UPPER LEVEL QUESTIONS: (PAGES 117-128)

1. C
2. A
3. D
4. B
5. C
6. A
7. B
8. B
9. A
10. C
11. B
12. C
13. B
14. B
15. B
16. B
17. A
18. A
19. B
20. A
21. B
22. B
23. A
24. D
25. B
26. C
27. D
28. B
29. B
30. A
31. A
32. A
33. C
34. D
35. A
36. A
37. C
38. B
39. B
40. B

MATH ACHIEVEMENT

CHAPTER 4

PART 1: ARITHMETIC

SECTION 1: NUMBERS AND OPERATIONS (PAGES 145-150)

ADDITION DRILLS ANSWER KEY						
27 +3 **30**	13 +9 **22**	39 +2 **41**	10 +7 **17**	42 +8 **50**	75 +6 **81**	98 +7 **105**
67 +23 **90**	72 +35 **107**	18 +49 **67**	37 +14 **51**	68 +41 **109**	99 +27 **126**	32 +85 **117**
55 +12 **67**	82 +44 **126**	32 +16 **48**	63 +14 **77**	18 +99 **117**	75 +75 **150**	69 +64 **133**
78+98=**176**	39+42=**81**	18+54=**72**	37+84=**121**	28+18=**46**	90+40=**130**	22+53=**75**
125 + 5 **130**	534 + 9 **543**	639 + 1 **640**	832 + 7 **839**	422 + 9 **431**	799 + 1 **800**	502 + 3 **505**
648 +22 **670**	331 +86 **417**	510 +27 **537**	396 +19 **415**	421 +90 **511**	307 +21 **328**	517 +17 **534**
392 +184 **576**	739 +717 **1456**	402 +184 **586**	492 +391 **883**	246 +184 **430**	582 +909 **1491**	521 +486 **1007**
329 428 +186 **943**	42 593 +204 **839**	821 12 +947 **1780**	82 194 + 53 **329**	529 438 +167 **1134**	625 14 + 39 **678**	527 941 +368 **1836**

SUBTRACTION DRILLS ANSWER KEY						
13 -2 **11**	62 - 5 **57**	41 - 9 **32**	73 - 1 **72**	64 - 4 **60**	94 - 7 **87**	40 - 3 **37**
72 -52 **20**	81 -59 **22**	54 -37 **17**	90 -31 **59**	84 -73 **11**	29 -17 **12**	40 -27 **13**
99 -42 **57**	58 -39 **19**	56 -38 **18**	84 -27 **57**	91 -57 **34**	30 -22 **8**	73 -15 **58**
86-42=**44**	72-65=**7**	62-43=**19**	95-78=**17**	48-43=**5**	81-72=**9**	57-31=**26**
613 - 5 **608**	749 - 7 **742**	397 - 9 **388**	942 - 3 **939**	264 - 4 **260**	481 - 9 **472**	285 - 7 **278**
849 - 31 **818**	762 - 40 **722**	492 - 32 **460**	781 - 39 **742**	267 - 69 **198**	843 - 85 **758**	328 - 57 **271**
752 -321 **431**	481 -278 **203**	473 -327 **146**	849 -212 **637**	747 -381 **366**	604 -518 **86**	582 -175 **407**
391 286 - 73 **32**	847 41 -316 **490**	904 269 - 79 **556**	798 280 -142 **376**	359 90 - 21 **248**	740 380 -242 **118**	867 329 -415 **123**

ADDITION AND SUBTRACTION DRILLS ANSWER KEY

76 +15 **91**	34 +76 **110**	54 -14 **40**	90 -32 **58**	86 +55 **141**	86 -55 **31**	99 -33 **66**
67 -31 **36**	89 +41 **130**	76 -66 **10**	54 -31 **23**	22 +16 **38**	87 -59 **28**	33 +99 **132**
66+42=**108**	31-27=**4**	54-29=**25**	49+96=**145**	38+57=**95**	27+64=**91**	75-35=**40**
52-36=**16**	96-43=**53**	21+68=**89**	53+94=**147**	92-61=**31**	42+53=**95**	49+77=**126**
67 +15 82	72 -59 13	32 +32 64	32 +67 99	88 -76 12	32 - 11 21	34 +21 55
74 -38 36	64 +22 86	77 +31 108	70 -23 47	39 +32 71	72 -64 8	54 +23 77
341 -142 **199**	529 +671 **1200**	904 -731 **173**	641 -232 **409**	804 +321 **1125**	922 -344 **578**	798 +421 **1219**
525 -321 204	145 +923 1068	259 -247 12	934 +817 1751	224 +378 602	717 -439 278	156 +341 497
32 +64 - 25 **71**	78 - 29 +93 **142**	65 +31 - 19 **77**	90 +22 - 78 **34**	320 - 245 +980 **1055**	975 - 629 +528 **874**	802 - 492 +375 **685**

MULTIPLICATION DRILLS ANSWER KEY						
6×8=**48**	9×6=**54**	3×4=**12**	2×12=**24**	5×9=**45**	3×6=**18**	7×12=**84**
3×7=**21**	6×3=**18**	2×7=**14**	6×0=**0**	8×2=**16**	7×9=**63**	5×4=**20**
9×5=**45**	8×4=**32**	4×7=**28**	12×8=**96**	10×5=**50**	11×3=**33**	6×4=**24**
12×11=**132**	3×9=**27**	4×9=**36**	5×3=**15**	11×9=**99**	2×8=**16**	7×7=**49**
6×2=**12**	12×9=**108**	8×8=**64**	8×7=**56**	12×4=**48**	9×9=**81**	10×6=**60**
19 ×4 **76**	22 ×9 **198**	35 ×7 **245**	76 ×3 **228**	38 ×8 **304**	24 ×6 **144**	65 ×2 **130**
53 ×97 **5141**	86 ×51 **4386**	63 ×54 **3402**	11 ×22 **242**	59 ×77 **4543**	20 ×65 **1300**	95 ×38 **3610**
477 × 7 **3339**	904 × 3 **2712**	285 × 8 **2280**	876 × 9 **7884**	337 × 5 **1685**	273 × 4 **1092**	489 × 6 **2934**
395 ×44 **17380**	411 ×97 **39867**	530 ×64 **33920**	214 ×55 **11770**	503 ×84 **42252**	375 ×70 **26250**	339 ×83 **28137**
783 ×904 **707832**	899 ×974 **875626**	318 ×814 **258852**	657 ×165 **108405**	847 ×322 **272734**	555 ×396 **219780**	286 ×862 **246532**

DIVISION DRILLS ANSWER KEY

8÷4=**2**	12÷6=**2**	12÷4=**3**	12÷3=**4**	10÷2=**5**	4÷2=**2**	18÷3=**6**
18÷6=**3**	20÷10=**2**	15÷3=**5**	21÷7=**3**	20÷5=**4**	16÷2=**8**	25÷5=**5**
21÷3=**7**	30÷5=**6**	18÷2=**9**	15÷5=**3**	24÷4=**6**	20÷4=**5**	18÷9=**2**
35÷5=**7**	24÷6=**4**	32÷4=**8**	42÷6=**7**	26÷2=**13**	40÷4=**10**	24÷8=**3**
54÷9=**6**	48÷8=**6**	42÷7=**6**	55÷5=**11**	64÷8=**8**	36÷6=**6**	48÷6=**8**
1 R=1 5)6	**2** R=1 3)7	**2** R=1 4)9	**2** R=2 4)10	**2** R=2 3)8	**4** R=1 2)9	**1** R=3 7)10
4 R=2 5)22	**6** R=2 3)20	**4** R=1 6)25	**6** R=3 6)39	**8** R=3 8)67	**8** R=2 4)34	**8** R=3 5)43
87 5)435	**254** 3)762	**65** 7)455	**49** 8)392	**126** 6)756	**374** 2)748	**79** 9)711
68 11)748	**54** 8)432	**99** 3)297	**65** 4)260	**65** 7)455	**157** 5)785	**76** 9)684

MULTIPLICATION AND DIVISION DRILLS ANSWER KEY						
6÷3=**2**	6×3=**18**	8÷2=**4**	8×2=**16**	36÷6=**6**	6×6=**36**	64÷8=**8**
10÷5=**2**	10×5=**50**	9÷3=**3**	9×3=**27**	81÷9=**9**	9×9=**81**	7×7=**49**
56 ×4 **224**	98 ×6 **588**	37 ×2 **74**	86 ×8 **688**	30 ×3 **90**	82 ×6 **492**	39 ×7 **273**
157 5)785	**304** 3)912	**66** 7)462	**50** 8)400	**102** 6)612	**426** 2)852	**112** 9)1008
6 R=**4** 5)34	**17** R=**1** 3)52	**2** R=**5** 6)17	**7** R=**3** 6)45	**8** R=**0** 8)64	**6** R=**1** 4)25	**10** R=**2** 5)52
8×**5=**40	**9**×7=63	**1**×7=7	**0**×9=0	3×**9=**27	6×**8=**48	9×**4=**36
42÷7=6	60÷**12=**5	**96**÷4=24	**144**÷6=24	12÷**3=**4	**54**÷9=6	12÷**2=**6
81÷**9=**9	7×**8=**56	**9**×4=36	**3**×12=36	42÷**7=**6	6×**3=**18	**40**÷5=8
744 ×72 **53568**	843 ×21 **17703**	904 ×50 **45200**	371 ×52 **19292**	987 ×47 **46389**	382 ×82 **31324**	426 ×18 **7668**

SECTION 2: PROPERTIES OF OPERATIONS (PAGES 159-160)

1. CORRECT, property of commutation
2. CORRECT, property of association
3. INCORRECT, property of commutation
4. CORRECT, property of distribution
5. INCORRECT, property of association
6. CORRECT, property of distribution
7. INCORRECT, property of distribution
8. CORRECT, property association
9. INCORRECT, property of association
10. CORRECT, property of commutation
11. 4
12. 33
13. 7
14. 4
15. 16
16. 61
17. even
18. odd
19. even
20. even
21. odd
22. even
23. odd
24. even

SECTION 3: FACTORS AND MULTIPLES (PAGES 166-167)

1. 2, 4, 6, 8
2. 7, 14, 21, 28, 35
3. 1, 2, 5, 10
4. 1, 2, 3, 4, 6, 8, 12, 16, 24, 48
5. 11, 13, 17, 19
6. Yes
7. Yes
8. No
9. No
10. 1
11. 2
12. 0
13. 2, 3, 3
14. 2, 17
15. 2, 2, 3, 7
16. 9
17. 1
18. 30
19. 15
20. 3

SECTION 4: FRACTIONS (PAGES 174-176)

1. $\frac{3}{6}$
2. $\frac{5}{8}$
3. $\frac{1}{3}$
4. $\frac{3}{8}$
5. $\frac{9}{12}$
6. $\frac{15}{25}$
7. $\frac{12}{7}, \frac{9}{7}, \frac{4}{7}, \frac{1}{7}$
8. $\frac{5}{2}, \frac{5}{3}, \frac{5}{6}, \frac{5}{8}$
9. $\frac{12}{8}, \frac{10}{8}, \frac{4}{8}, \frac{1}{8}$
10. $\frac{3}{2}, \frac{3}{3}, \frac{3}{7}, \frac{3}{8}$
11. $\frac{7}{10}$
12. $\frac{3}{5}$
13. $\frac{22}{15}$ or $1\frac{7}{15}$
14. $\frac{26}{15}$ or $1\frac{11}{15}$
15. $\frac{3}{10}$
16. $\frac{5}{36}$
17. $\frac{23}{12}$ or $1\frac{11}{12}$
18. $\frac{5}{3}$
19. $\frac{22}{7}$
20. $3\frac{1}{3}$
21. $1\frac{4}{5}$
22. $\frac{3}{32}$
23. $\frac{15}{16}$
24. $\frac{4}{5}$
25. $\frac{17}{7}$ or $2\frac{3}{7}$

SECTION 5: RATIOS (PAGES 180-181)

1. $\frac{2}{3}$
2. $\frac{1}{9}$
3. $\frac{3}{20}$
4. $\frac{1}{4}$
5. $\frac{5}{8}$
6. 330 students
7. 9 cups
8. $\frac{1}{2}$
9. $\frac{4}{9}$
10. 18 marbles
11. 54 marbles
12. 91.44 cm
13. $8
14. 12 cm
15. 2.4 packets
16. $26\frac{2}{3}$ pages
17. 2 kg
18. $50,000

SECTION 6: DECIMALS (PAGES 187-188)

1. 8.75
2. 18.18
3. 6
4. 8.35
5. 6.38
6. 16.095
7. 1.28
8. 5.355
9. 26.8
10. 46.2
11. 5
12. 0.05
13. 28.644
14. 6
15. 4.2
16. 29.1
17. 3189.5
18. 41.0
19. 58000
20. 75000
21. 1000
22. 0.875
23. 0.18
24. 0.12
25. 0.475
26. $\frac{1}{4}$
27. $\frac{3}{5}$
28. $\frac{7}{20}$

SECTION 7: WORD PROBLEMS (PAGES 197-199)

1. 12:07PM
2. 1 hour 39 minutes
3. 7:45AM
4. 150 miles
5. 12:35PM
6. $5.03
7. $11.22
8. $2.13
9. $28.55
10. Possible solution: 1 quarter, 2 dimes
11. Possible solution: 2 dollars, 6 dimes, 4 pennies
12. Possible solution: 1 dollar, 3 pennies
13. Possible solution: 3 dollars, 2 quarters, 7 pennies
14. $18.00
15. 4
16. $24
17. 37
18. 25,000 g
19. 0.478 l
20. 94
21. 57
22. 8
23. 81
24. 18
25. Approximately 450 marbles each

SECTION 8: PERCENTS (PAGES 205-206)

1. $\frac{3}{5}$
2. 0.37
3. $\frac{17}{20}$
4. 0.29
5. 73%
6. 32.6%
7. 60%
8. 44%
9. 62.5%
10. 36
11. 63
12. 111
13. 75
14. 45%
15. 30%
16. 18 students
17. $12.30
18. 90 jelly beans
19. 50 questions
20. $200

SECTION 9: NEGATIVE NUMBERS (PAGES 210-211)

1. –2
2. –10
3. –11
4. 12
5. –7
6. –70
7. 18
8. –6
9. 0
10. 8000
11. –18
12. 35
13. –6
14. –40
15. –9
16. 8
17. –24
18. 15
19. –6
20. 100

SECTION 10: EXPONENTS AND ROOTS (PAGES 219-221)

1. 49
2. 16
3. 125
4. 1
5. $\frac{8}{27}$
6. $\frac{1}{16}$
7. -1000
8. 81

9. 10
10. 6
11. 2
12. 4
13. $\frac{2}{3}$
14. $\frac{1}{7}$
15. $\sqrt{12} \approx 3.46$ (close to 3.5)
16. $\sqrt[3]{60} \approx 3.91$ (close to 4)
17. 13
18. 76
19. 43
20. 0
21. 34
22. 1
23. 9
24. 0
25. 5
26. 1
27. 2^7, or 128
28. 5^2, or 25
29. $\left(\frac{1}{3}\right)^5$, or $\frac{1}{243}$
30. 4^4, or 256
31. 2^{12}, or 4096
32. $5\sqrt{5}$
33. $\sqrt{2}$
34. $\sqrt{9}$, or 3
35. $4\sqrt{36}$, or 24
36. 9
37. $\frac{1}{8}$
38. 1
39. $\frac{a^3}{bc^2}$
40. x
41. 2.6235×10^1
42. 2.6235×10^2
43. 2.6235×10^{-1}
44. 2.6235×10^{-3}
45. 2.6235×10^6

SECTION 11: IMAGINARY NUMBERS (PAGE 225)

1. $4i$
2. $7i$
3. $8i$
4. $10i$
5. $-i$
6. 1
7. -1
8. $-i$
9. 3i
10. -3
11. $10i$
12. 2
13. $3 + 8i$
14. $-6i$

PART 1 REVIEW

LOWER LEVEL QUESTIONS (PAGES 226-229)

1. C
2. C
3. C
4. B
5. B
6. A
7. A
8. D
9. C
10. C
11. B
12. D
13. B
14. D
15. A

MIDDLE LEVEL QUESTIONS (PAGES 230-233)

1. A
2. C
3. C
4. D
5. C
6. C
7. B
8. B
9. D
10. B
11. C
12. C
13. B
14. C
15. B

UPPER LEVEL QUESTIONS (PAGES 234-236)

1. C
2. B
3. C
4. D
5. C
6. B
7. B
8. D
9. A
10. A

PART 2: ALGEBRA

SECTION 1: BASIC ALGEBRA (PAGES 245-248)

1. 10
2. 13
3. 27
4. 0
5. 8
6. 12
7. 5
8. 6
9. 20
10. 4
11. 8
12. 10
13. 2
14. 2
15. 18
16. 12
17. 6
18. 9
19. 3
20. 14
21. 4
22. 5
23. 5
24. 8
25. 14 marbles
26. C
27. 14
28. D
29. 17 years old
30. 5 pencils
31. 18
32. 7
33. 6
34. 15
35. $3 \times \bigcirc + 6 = \square$

SECTION 2: EXPRESSIONS (PAGES 258-260)

1. 11
2. −4
3. 22
4. 18
5. $5N$
6. $9x$
7. $2a^2$
8. $h + 7$
9. $3N + M$
10. $x^2 + 3y^2$
11. $3x^2 + 36$
12. $2a^2 - 4a + 6b^2$
13. $2x^3 + 8x^2$
14. $15y^3 - 10y^2 + 50y$
15. $g + 3$
16. $4x + 6$
17. $4(4y + z)$
18. $3(x^2 - 3x + 4)$
19. a^9
20. x^5y^3

21. x^3
22. $\frac{a^2}{bc^2}$
23. $x^2 + 7x + 10$
24. $y^2 + 6y - 40$
25. $3a^2 + 25a + 8$
26. $4x^2 - 7xy - 2y^2$
27. $(x - 7)(x + 4)$
28. $3(x + 1)(x - 5)$
29. $-2(x - 1)(x - 1)$
30. $(2x + 11)(x + 2)$
31. $(x + 1)(x - 1)$
32. $(x + 6)(x - 6)$
33. $5(x + 4)(x - 4)$
34. $(p^2 + 4)(p + 2)(p - 2)$
35. $(x + 2y)(x + 3y)$

SECTION 3: EQUATIONS (PAGES 266-268)

1. $x = 36$
2. $x = 8$
3. $x = -7$
4. $x = -9$
5. $x = 12$
6. $x = 2$
7. $x = 10$
8. $x = 3$
9. $x = 5$
10. $x = -6$
11. $x = 11$
12. $x = -14$
13. $x = 9$
14. $x = 3$
15. $x = -30$
16. $x = 10$
17. $x = 24$
18. $x = 8$
19. $x = 7$
20. $x = 4$
21. $x = 7, y = 2$
22. $m = 1, n = 3$
23. $p = -1, q = 1$
24. $x = 9, y = 3$
25. 10 cents
26. 5 cents
27. $10
28. $5

SECTION 4: INEQUALITIES (PAGES 273-274)

1. Yes
2. No
3. Yes
4. Yes
5. Any answer greater than or equal to 10
6. Any answer less than 14
7. Any answer between 3 and 13, not including 3 or 13
8. Any answer less than or equal to 4
9. Any answer greater than or equal to 7
10. Any answer greater than 9

11. $x \geq 3$
12. $x > 12$
13. $x \leq -1$
14. $x > -15$
15. $x > 2$
16. $x \geq 7$
17. $x > 5$
18. $x \leq -3$
19. $4 < x < 6$
20. $3 \leq x \leq 5$
21. $x > -1$
22. $x \leq -1$
23. $-1 \leq x < 4$

SECTION 5: STRANGE SYMBOLS (PAGES 277-278)

1. 37
2. 39
3. 31
4. 20
5. 12
6. -12
7. 4
8. 60
9. 5
10. 8
11. 14
12. -2
13. 101
14. 2
15. 4
16. 45
17. $\frac{3}{2}$

SECTION 6: ABSOLUTE VALUE (PAGES 283-284)

1. 3
2. 100
3. 1
4. 0
5. 5
6. 3
7. $x = 1, x = 5$
8. $x = 1, x = 5$
9. $x = 3, x = 7$
10. $x < -2, x > 8$
11. $1 < x < 11$
12. $x < -23, x > 17$
13. $-27 \leq x \leq 19$
14. $x \leq 4$ or $x \geq 18$
15. $x = -7$ or $x = 11$
16. $-11 < x < -3$
17. $x < 3$ or $x > 6$
18. $|x - 1.6| \leq 0.2$
19. $|x - 49| = 46$
20. $|x - 72| > 5$

SECTION 7: MATRICES (PAGES 290-291)

1. Yes
2. No
3. No
4. Undefined
5. $\begin{bmatrix} -4 & -1 & -2 \\ 1 & 0 & 0 \end{bmatrix}$
6. Undefined
7. $\begin{bmatrix} 3 & 9 \\ 1 & -2 \end{bmatrix}$
8. $\begin{bmatrix} 2 \\ 2 \\ 2 \end{bmatrix}$
9. $\begin{bmatrix} -3 & 1 \\ 1 & 0 \end{bmatrix}$
10. $\begin{bmatrix} 0 & -5 \\ 3 & 5 \end{bmatrix}$
11. Undefined
12. $\begin{bmatrix} 0 & 3 & 2 \\ -2 & -2 & -2 \end{bmatrix}$
13. Undefined

PART 2 REVIEW

LOWER LEVEL QUESTIONS (PAGES 292-296)

1. A
2. B
3. C
4. C
5. B
6. B
7. B
8. D
9. D
10. C
11. B
12. C
13. A
14. B
15. A

MIDDLE LEVEL QUESTIONS (PAGES 297-300)

1. C
2. D
3. D
4. B
5. C
6. A
7. C
8. C
9. A
10. C
11. C
12. D
13. D
14. A
15. C

UPPER LEVEL QUESTIONS (PAGES 301-303)

1. C
2. C
3. D
4. B
5. C
6. C
7. A
8. C
9. A
10. B

PART 3: GEOMETRY

SECTION 1: LINES AND ANGLES (PAGES 313-318)

1. 2
2. 8
3. 6
4. 90°
5. Acute
6. Obtuse
7. 180°
8. Parallel lines
9. Perpendicular lines
10. Congruent angles
11. 70°
12. 20°
13. 120°
14. 55°
15. 60°
16. 60°
17. 130°
18. 30°
19. 70°
20. 60°
21. 50°
22. 50°
23. 360°
24. 35°
25. 30°

SECTION 2: INTRODUCTION TO POLYGONS (PAGES 325-330)

1. Quadrilateral
2. Hexagon
3. Octagon
4. Equilateral
5. Scalene
6. Parallelogram
7. Square
8. Trapezoid
9. Rhombus
10. Kite
11. 9.5
12. 20
13. 36 cm
14. 26
15. 6
16. $12y$
17. 20
18. 25
19. 6
20. 30
21. 40 square inches
22. 49 square feet
23. 36 square cm
24. 1 square meter
25. 10
26. 8 in
27. 18 square meters
28. 10 square inches
29. 40 cm
30. 24 square inches

SECTION 3: ADVANCED TRIANGLES (PAGES 339-344)

1. 60°
2. 50°
3. 30°
4. 130°
5. 60°
6. 35°
7. 45°
8. 4 in^2
9. 8
10. 3
11. 8
12. 6
13. 13
14. 8
15. $\sqrt{39}$
16. 36
17. 10
18. $\frac{3}{5}$
19. $\frac{3}{5}$
20. $\frac{3}{4}$
21. $\frac{4}{3}$
22. $\sin(70°) \times 8, \cos(20°) \times 8$
23. $\cos(65°) \times 4, \sin(25°) \times 4$
24. $\frac{6}{\tan(40°)}, \tan(50°) \times 6$

SECTION 4: ADVANCED QUADRILATERALS (PAGES 348-352)

1. 110°
2. 180°
3. 50°
4. 45
5. 42 ft^2
6. 48
7. 12
8. 30
9. 56
10. 27 in^2
11. 34 m^2
12. 12
13. 68 ft^2
14. 18 cm^2
15. 10 in
16. 75°

SECTION 5: CIRCLES (PAGES 356-359)

1. 6 inches
2. 10 centimeters
3. 13
4. 24
5. 8
6. 30
7. 36
8. 8
9. 16π m^2
10. 10π inches

11. 64π
12. 14
13. 18π
14. 36
15. 20π
16. 18π square feet
17. 14π inches
18. $100 - 25\pi$

SECTION 6: SOLID GEOMETRY (PAGES 372-377)

1. 8
2. 8
3. 16
4. 64
5. B
6. 3 cm^3
7. 30 cm^3
8. 64 ft^3
9. 3 ft
10. 1 to 8
11. 3 m
12. 216 in^2
13. 15
14. 5
15. 166 mm^2
16. 396 ft^2
17. 30
18. 3
19. 144 m^2
20. 300 boxes
21. 64 cm^3
22. 125 cm^3
23. 24π cm^3
24. 130π cm^2
25. 100π cm^2
26. 1080 in^3
27. 8π in^3
28. 9.5π in^2
29. 36π in^3
30. 24 in^2

SECTION 7: COORDINATE GEOMETRY (PAGES 389-394)

1. E
2. B and C
3. D
4. $(-2, 3)$
5. $(1, 3)$
6. B
7. B
8. P
9. 5
10. $(4, 0)$
11. 4th
12. 5
13. $(-5, 4)$
14. 6
15. 4
16. 12
17. 3
18. $(1, -5)$
19. 10
20. 20
21. 12

SECTION 8: GRAPHS OF FUNCTIONS (PAGES 402-405)

1. 1
2. $\frac{3}{2}$
3. 1
4. $-\frac{1}{5}$
5. $-\frac{1}{2}$
6. $\frac{3}{5}$
7. $-\frac{1}{2}$
8. 0
9. $\frac{4}{3}$
10. $y = \frac{4}{3}x$
11. 2
12. 1
13. $y = x + 2$
14. $y = 1$
15. -1
16. $\frac{1}{2}$
17. 3
18. -5
19. $y = \frac{6}{5}x - 1.5$
20. $-\frac{5}{6}$

PART 3 REVIEW

LOWER LEVEL QUESTIONS (PAGES 407-413)

1. D
2. A
3. C
4. D
5. C
6. C
7. D
8. B
9. A
10. C
11. C
12. D
13. C
14. A
15. C
16. B
17. A
18. D

MIDDLE LEVEL QUESTIONS (PAGES 414-421)

1. A
2. C
3. B
4. A
5. A
6. B
7. D
8. B
9. C
10. B
11. C
12. D
13. D
14. C
15. A
16. C
17. C
18. C
19. B
20. B
21. D
22. B

UPPER LEVEL QUESTIONS (PAGES 422-425)

1. A
2. C
3. A
4. B
5. B
6. B
7. A
8. D
9. C
10. C

PART 4: DATA INTERPRETATION

SECTION 1: CHARTS AND GRAPHS (PAGES 434-441)

1. 32 apples
2. 44 apples
3. 20 apples
4. Basketball and hockey
5. 150 students
6. 32 boxes
7. $19.20
8. $4.00
9. Chocolate chip and oatmeal raisin
10. $\frac{1}{4}$
11. $180
12. Posters and Music
13. $30
14. February
15. City C
16. March
17. About 4.5 inches
18. 60,000 people
19. 250,000 people
20. 10,000 people
21. About 15 newspapers
22. 7:00 – 7:15am
23. 100 newspapers
24. During the second half
25. Glendale County
26. $6,000
27. People who are at work between 12-2pm, a large segment of the population, would be underrepresented in the survey.
28. Certain birds may prefer certain trees. As a result, birds who prefer oak trees will be overrepresented in Jessica's count.
29. Those who do not have access to the Internet will not be able to participate in the survey.

SECTION 2: RANGE, MEAN, MEDIAN, AND MODE (PAGES 452-458)

1. $2.80
2. $2.50
3. $2.40
4. $1.20
5. 3.5 min
6. 51 min
7. 50.5 min
8. 50 min
9. 12 boys
10. 25 students
11. 4 students
12. 1 girl
13. 48
14. 1 book
15. 99
16. 6
17. $740
18. 31

19. 11 years old
20. 61.5 degrees Fahrenheit
21. 60 degrees Fahrenheit
22. 10 degrees Fahrenheit
23. 21 centimeters
24. 12 centimeters
25. It is above average
26. 20
27. 11
28. 10.4
29. 11
30. 4.9 lbs
31. Greater
32. Between 2lb and 2.9lbs
33. 100 miles per hour
34. Between 70 and 80 miles per hour
35. Between the 2nd and 3rd quartile

SECTION 3: ORGANIZED COUNTING (PAGES 468-470)

1. 26 children
2. 6 children
3. 40 children
4. 20 children
5. 55 students
6. 35 students
7. 10 students
8. 8
9. 12
10. 6
11. 120
12. 900
13. 45
14. 132
15. 210
16. 56
17. 66
18. 1000

SECTION 4: PROBABILITY (PAGES 479-482)

1. $\frac{6}{13}$
2. $\frac{1}{4}$
3. 1
4. $\frac{3}{5}$
5. 12 donuts
6. 9 students
7. $\frac{2}{3}$
8. $\frac{4}{5}$
9. 64 students
10. $\frac{1}{4}$
11. $\frac{3}{4}$
12. 0
13. $\frac{1}{30}$
14. $\frac{3}{13}$
15. $\frac{1}{36}$
16. 16%

17. 3/95

18. $\frac{1}{81}$

19. $\frac{4}{17}$

20. $\frac{1}{10}$

21. $\frac{1}{16}$

22. $\frac{1}{15}$

23. $\frac{1}{720}$

PART 4 REVIEW

LOWER LEVEL QUESTIONS (PAGES 483-489)

1. C
2. B
3. C
4. D
5. A
6. B
7. D
8. A
9. C
10. A
11. B
12. B
13. C
14. B
15. A
16. D
17. B
18. A

MIDDLE LEVEL QUESTIONS (PAGES 490-497)

1. D
2. C
3. C
4. D
5. C
6. C
7. A
8. C
9. B
10. C
11. B
12. C
13. C
14. D
15. A
16. B
17. C
18. A
19. B
20. D

UPPER LEVEL QUESTIONS (PAGES 498-503)

1. C
2. C
3. C
4. D
5. C
6. C
7. C
8. D
9. B
10. B
11. A
12. C

Made in the USA
Columbia, SC
07 December 2017